STATISTICS

AMERICA

Sources for Social, Economic and Market Research

(North, Central & South America)

Joan M. Harvey, MA, FLA

Edition 2
Revised and enlarged

Distributed by
GALE RESEARCH COMPANY
Book Tower
Detroit, Michigan 48226

A Research Publication

C B D Research Ltd
Beckenham · Kent · England

Gale Research Co
Detroit · Michigan · USA

First published   1973.

Second edition, revised and enlarged   1980.

Copyright   ©   Joan M Harvey.

I S B N   900246 33 2.

Library of Congress Catalog Number : (on application to Gale Research Company)

Published by   C.B.D. Research Ltd,
                                154 High Street, Beckenham, Kent, BR3 1EA, England.
                                Telephone 01-650 7745.

            and   Gale Research Company,
                                Book Tower, Detroit, Michigan 48226 U S A.

Printed in Great Britain by
McCorquodale (Newton) Limited
Newton-le-Willows

CONTENTS

v

essential information for all concerned with business in Europe

Directory
of EUROPEAN
ASSOCIATIONS

Part 1: National industrial, trade & professional associations
over 9,000 trade associations, professional institutes, employers' associations, etc, classified by subject interest and subdivided by countries

---

Part 2: National learned, scientific & technical societies
over 5,000 academies, learned, scientific & technical societies, research associations and institutes, classified by subject interest and subdivided by countries

---

Entries in each Part contain:
name & authorised translations of name
acronym or abbreviated name
date of formation
address, telephone & telex number
membership data
activities—especially conferences, information
services, collection of statistics, etc
publications

Each Part has the following indexes:
complete alphabetical index of names and of
authorised translations of names
index of acronyms and abbreviated names
subject indexes in English, French & German
Coverage:
all European countries except Great Britain and
the Republic of Ireland

CBD Research Ltd
Beckenham · Kent · England

Gale Research Co
Detroit · Michigan · USA

1. The second edition of "Statistics America" follows the precedent set by the third edition of "Statistics Europe" and the second edition of "Statistics Africa" in that it has been given wider coverage than the first edition in order to make the work more useful not only to market researchers and others who used the first editions, but also to those engaged in broader fields of economic and social research.

Most statistical information is still collected and published by governments, although an increasing amount is being issued by the central banks.   Fluctuating political and economic conditions in some American countries tend to be reflected in the erratic publication programmes for statistical data and one of the major difficulties faced when compiling this guide has been the problem of ascertaining whether later issues, editions or parts of a particular title do, in fact, exist when the compiler has been unable to locate copies in the many libraries visited.

Not all the statistical information collected is published, either because of the problems mentioned above or because it is considered that there would be insufficient general interest for publication, and in such cases it may be possible for the enquirer to obtain the required data from the organisation responsible for collecting it; some information, however, will not be published because it has been supplied on the understanding that it will be treated as confidential.   There is also a trend, nowadays, in the publishing programmes of the more industrialised countries and of the international organisations to publish in microfiche, either solely in that form or in advance of the 'hard copy' version; these alternative forms of publication have not been mentioned in the following pages but researchers are warned that they may be offered some publications on microfiche when visiting libraries or ordering from publishers.

2. ARRANGEMENT

The main body of this guide is arranged by countries in alphabetical order, and each entry, whether for the description of an organisation or of a publication, has been allocated a unique reference number.   The list of countries (page xiii) indicates the first page number for each country. A section on America as a whole (North, Central and South America, and adjacent islands) precedes the individual countries.   Each section contains:

(1)   the name, address and telephone number (if available) of the central statistical office of the country and of other important organisations that collect and publish statistical material; this is followed by some information on the organisation and work of each agency, the facilities it provides, etc.

(2)   the principal libraries in the country where collections of statistical material may be consulted by the public.

(3)   libraries and information services in other countries (particularly English-speaking countries) where the country's publications may be consulted.

(4)   the principal bibliographies of statistics; only reasonably current bibliographies have been included, and sales lists are mentioned because of the general dearth of special bibliographies in the field; national bibliographies are not included, but should not be overlooked as a means of tracing statistical titles.

(5)   the major statistical publications, arranged in the following standard groups:

¶   A   General
¶   B   Production
        i.   Mines and mining
       ii.   Agriculture, fisheries, forestry, etc.
      iii.   Industry
       iv.   Construction
        v.   Energy

2. (5) continued

¶ C External trade

¶ D Internal distribution and service trades

¶ E Population

¶ F Social
 i.   Standard of living
 ii. Health and welfare
 iii. Education and leisure
 iv. Justice

¶ G Finance
 i.   Banking
 ii. Public finance
 iii. Company finance
 iv. Investment
 v.   Insurance

¶ H Transport and communication
 i.   Ships and shipping
 ii. Road
 iii. Rail
 iv. Air
 v.   Telecommunications and postal services

3. NOTES ON THE GROUPS

¶ A Titles listed in group A are useful only for general indications of overall patterns, and are not usually sufficiently detailed for research into a particular or specific subject.

¶ B Group B includes all production statistics. It includes reports of censuses, which are usually devoted more to the structure (finance, labour, machinery, power, etc) of the industry, etc, than to the quantity and value of the goods produced.

¶ C The classification schemes used for the tabulation of foreign trade statistics follow closely similar patterns, as they are mainly based on the Brussels Tariff Nomenclature (BTN) or on the United Nations Standard International Trade Classification (SITC), which are now correlated. Many countries classify their imports and exports in more detail then the BTN or SITC, and a useful key to the detailed classification of each country can be the International Customs Journal (Bulletin International des Douanes), which is available from the International Customs Tariff Bureau, rue de l'Association 38, Bruxelles, Belgium or from sales agents. It comprises about 200 volumes, each available separately and each containing the customs tariff of a single country; it is kept up to date by supplements and new editions as required.

¶ D Group D includes statistics of wholesale and retail trade and of service trades, including tourism.

¶ E Censuses of population and housing, demographic surveys, population projections, vital statistics and labour statistics are included in Group E.

¶ F This group in general comprises social statistics. Cost of living indices, wages and salaries, household budget surveys, etc, are included in F.i. F.ii includes statistics on national health services, hospitals, national insurance schemes social security, social insurance and social welfare. F.iii includes all aspects of education from primary schools to universities and leisure activities such as entertainment, sport, libraries, etc. F.iv includes both judicial and criminal statistics.

¶ G Group G includes all statistics of a financial nature. G.i lists publications with statistics of all types of banking, but does not specifically include publications which are solely devoted to the accounts of a particular bank. G.ii includes both national and local government financial statistics. G.iii includes statistics of all types of companies and corporations, but does

3. continued

not include publications devoted to the accounts of one particular company or corporation.   G.iv is concerned mainly with industrial investment.   G.v is concerned with statistics of the business of insurance companies, but not the accounts of individual insurance companies.

¶ H   Group H covers transport and communications statistics generally.   H.i includes statistics of ships and shipping, sea-borne transport, inland waterway transport, traffic at ports, and passenger and cargo traffic in ships.   H.ii includes statistics of roads, road traffic, road accidents, and passengers and goods conveyed by road.   H.iii includes statistics of railways, rolling stock, passenger and goods traffic.   H.iv includes statistics of airports, aircraft, passenger and goods traffic by air.   H.v includes statistics of telephones, telephone and telegraph services, post offices and postal services.

4.   FORM OF ENTRY

The entry for each publication comprises:

(1)   serial number;

(2)   title, English translation of title if the original is not in English, and name of responsible organisation;

(3)   name and address of publisher or of other agency or sales office from which the publication can be obtained;

(4)   date when first published (omitted in cases where it is difficult to determine because of changes in title, responsible organisation, etc), date of latest issue seen by compiler (not necessarily the latest published) if published annually or less frequently, price (if ascertainable, and generally given in local currency), number of pages or volumes of the issue seen of an annual or less frequent publication;

(5)   description of contents;

(6)   indication of the lapse of time between the latest data included and the date of publication (as the actual date is seldom cited in the publication and seldom coincides with the normal date of an issue, part or edition, this information has been obtained mainly by observation of dates of receipt in libraries, and should be treated with caution);

(7)   language(s) of the text, indicated by the symbol § followed by international symbols (BS 3862).

5.   REFERENCES

References have been made to relevant publications in other groups within each country section, but NOT from individual countries to the general section on America as a whole.   It will, therefore, often be worthwhile to consult the appropriate group in the general section if no suitable material is found in a particular section.

6.   CHANGES OF TITLE

Only the latest title of each publication is given, except in cases where confusion might arise or where the change is very recent.   Many statistical publications have a long history of title variations, and it would be impossible to list all the changes.   The librarian, sales agent, or publisher will be able to advise prospective users and purchasers of earlier issues if titles have changed.

7.   INDEXES

In addition to the index to titles and the index to organisations, this edition includes a subject index.   Although the grouping of entries under each country provides a ready means of

INTRODUCTION

7.   continued

identifying publications in broad classes, it was felt that a subject index was needed to enable the user to locate specialised source material more readily.   It must be emphasised, however, that the subject index is NOT a complete analytical index to all subjects covered by all statistical sources listed in the book.

8.   ACKNOWLEDGEMENTS

The compiler would, once again, like to thank everyone who has helped in the preparation of this volume.   She has had the utmost co-operation from most of the statistical offices, libraries and other organisations she has approached, and has appreciated the easy access she has been afforded to the many libraries she has used, particularly the Library of the Institute of Development Studies at the University of Sussex, the Statistics and Market Intelligence Library of the Department of Trade and Industry, and the Official Publications Library of the British Library, where much of the material has been examined.   She would also like to express her thanks to Gillian and David Wiltshire for the help they have given her in translating correspondence into and from Latin-American Spanish and Portuguese.

DISEWORTH, Derbyshire.

July   1980.

STATISTICS:

Sources for Social, Economic and Market Research

Joan M. Harvey

A series of four separate works:

Statistics—Europe
   (covering both Western & Eastern Europe)

Statistics—Africa
   (covering the whole continent & adjacent islands)

Statistics—America
   (covering North, Central & South America)

Statistics—Asia & Australasia

giving, for each country:

   central statistical office: address, description of work,
      facilities offered

   other important organisations that collect & publish
      statistics

   principal libraries of statistical material

   information services provided in other countries
      particularly the UK, the USA, Canada & Australia

   bibliographies of statistics

   description of major publishing sources, arranged
      in the standard grouping: General — Production —
      External trade — Internal distribution — Population —
      Social — Finance — Transport & communications

CBD Research Ltd,

154 High Street, Beckenham, Kent, England
01-650 7745

ABBREVIATIONS AND SYMBOLS

§	Language(s)
c	circa
De	German
ed	edition
En	English
Es	Spanish
Fr	French
Nl	Dutch
p	pages
Pt	Portuguese
Ru	Russian
t	telephone number
tg	telegraphic address
tx	telex number
vol	volume
yr	per annum (annual subscription)

LIST OF COUNTRIES - TABLE DES PAYS - LÄNDERVERZEICHNIS

Some international organisations publishing statistics

001   United Nations,
New York, NY 10017.
t   754 1234.

The Statistical Office of the United Nations collects and publishes data from as many countries as possible in periodic as well as ad hoc publications. On the basis of these statistics, the Statistical Office computes a large number of economic indicators in the form of global and regional aggregates and index numbers. It also publishes methodological studies, guides, manuals, and assists governments in implementing statistical practice recommended by the Statistical Commission. The Statistical Office is part of the United Nations Department of Economic and Social Affairs.

002   United Nations Economic Commission for Latin America (CEPAL)
United Nations Building,
Avenida Dag Hammarskjold 3030, PO Box 179-D,
Santiago, Chile.
t   48 50 51 to 48 50 61.   Cables: Unations.   tx 3520054.

Established in 1948 to promote and facilitate action for the economic and social development of Latin America; to maintain and strengthen the economic relations of Latin American Countries between themselves and throughout the world; to undertake and sponsor research, studies and investigations on economic and technical problems of development. The Commission collects, evaluates and disseminates economic, technological and statistical information.

003   Food & Agriculture Organisation of the United Nations,
via delle Terme di Caracalla,
00100 Roma, Italy.
t   (06) 5797 Ex 61181.

Created to raise the levels of nutrition and standard of living, to secure improvements in the efficiency of production and distribution of all agricultural products, and to better the conditions of rural populations. To help achieve these aims, the FAO provides an intelligence service of facts and figures relating to nutrition, agriculture, forestry and fisheries, and also appraisals and forecasts of production, distribution and consumption in these industries.

004   UNESCO (United Nations Educational, Scientific and Cultural Organisation)
75700, Paris, France.
t   577 1610.

Established in 1946 'to contribute to peace and security by promoting collaboration among nations through education, science and culture, in order to further universal respect for justice, for the rule of law, and for the human rights and fundamental freedoms for all'. The organisation is concerned with education, natural science, social science, culture, mass communications, international exchanges, and technical assistance; it collects many statistics, some of which are included in its statistical yearbook and in other, mainly textual, publications.

005   Organisation of American States, (OAS)
1725 Eye Street N.W.,
Washington DC 20006, USA.
t   (202) 331-1010.   Cables: PAN-WASH-DC.   tx 89-503.

The Organisation of American States is a regional agency within the United Nations which aims to strengthen the peace and security of the continent; to prevent possible causes of difficulties and to ensure the

[continued next page]

1

005, continued

pacific settlement of disputes among member states; to provide common action in the event of aggression; to seek the solution of political, judicial and economic problems that may arise among the member states; and to promote, by co-operative action, their economic, social and cultural development.

An outgrowth of the International Union of American Republics, created in 1890, the Organisation nowadays operates through a large number of agencies and institutions throughout the Western Hemisphere. The Pan American Union, with headquarters in Washington, is the permanent organ and general secretariat of the Organisation of American States. Member countries are Argentina, Barbados, Bolivia, Brazil, Canada, Chile, Colombia, Costa Rica, Cuba, Dominican Republic, Ecuador, El Salvador, Grenada, Guatemala, Haiti, Honduras, Jamaica, Mexico, Nicaragua, Panama, Paraguay, Peru, Surinam, Trinidad and Tobago, United States of America, Uruguay and Venezuela.

006   Inter-American Statistical Institute,   Instituto Interamericano de Estadística,
1725 Eye Street, N.W.,
Washington DC 20006, USA.
t   (202) 331-1010.

Established in 1940, mainly because the International Statistical Institute was unable to function adequately during the 1939-1945 war, it is a professional organisation affiliated to the Organisation of American States and its Secretariat, the Pan American Union, whereby it is able to assist in the economic and social development of the Americas. The Institute seeks to stimulate improved methodology in the collection, tabulation, analysis and publication of both official and unofficial statistics, to encourage measures designed to improve the comparability and availability of economic and social statistics among the nations of the Western Hemisphere, to provide a medium for professional collaboration among statisticians, and to co-operate with national and international organisations in advancing the science and administration of statistics. Many of the Institute's publications are issued jointly with the Organisation of American States and the Pan American Union.

007   Asociación Latinoamericana de Libre Comercio (ALALC)   [Latin American Free Trade Association]
Cebollati 1461, Casilla de Correo 577, Montevideo, Uruguay.
t   40-11-21 & 40-33-63.   Cables & tx: ALALC.

The Association was established in 1960, and evolved between 1962 and 1966, 'to establish a continent-wide institutional basis for economic co-operation among countries that share a common political history and cultural values and have similar productive structures'. Member countries of ALALC are Argentina, Bolivia, Brazil, Chile, Colombia, Ecuador, Mexico, Paraguay, Peru, Uruguay and Venezuela. Apart from the publications described in the following pages the Association publishes a bi-monthly 'Synthesis' ($15 a year), which includes lists of documents published by ALALC and a free 'Newsletter'.

008   Secretaria Permanente del Tratado General de Integración Económica Centroamericana (SIECA)
        [Permanent Secretariat of the General Treaty on Central American Economic Integration]
4a avenida 10-25, Zona 14, Guatemala, C.A.

Established in December 1960 in Managua on the signing of the treaty by representatives of the governments of Guatemala, El Salvador, Honduras, Nicaragua and Costa Rica. Aims are to promote integration of Central American economies and co-ordinate economic policies. It is also concerned with efforts to develop a Central American Common Market, as originally planned by the United Nations Economic Commission for Latin America.

009   Caribbean Community (CARICOM)
PO Box 607,
Georgetown, Guyana.
t   69280-9.   Cables: CARIBSEC.   tx GY 263.

Established in 1973, CARICOM has three areas of activity: the Caribbean Common Market, which

[continued next page]

009, continued

replaces the Caribbean Free Trade Area (CARIFTA) which was established in 1968 after the West Indies Federation was dissolved in 1962; co-operation in non-economic areas and co-operation of certain common services; and co-ordination of foreign policies of independent member states.   Members are Antigua, Barbados, Belize, Dominica, Grenada, Guyana, Jamaica, Montserrat, St Kitts-Nevis-Anguilla, St Lucia, St Vincent, Trinidad and Tobago.

010   Organisation for Economic Co-operation and Development (OECD)
           2 rue André-Pascal, 75775 Paris Cedex 16, France.
           t   524 82 00.   tg DEVELOPECONOMIE.

Twenty-four countries make up the OECD, a permanent co-operation designed to harmonise national policies.   They include Canada and the United States of America on the American continent.   In the course of its work OECD collects and publishes a considerable amount of information, supplied by member countries, taking care to make the figures as comparable as possible by adjusting, converting and reclassifying basic data.

011   European Communities.   Communautés Européennes,   and   Centre Européen,
           Bâtiment Berlaymont,   Kirchberg, (B.P. 1907)
           200 rue de la Loi, 1049 Bruxelles, Belgium.   Luxembourg.
           t   735 80 40.   t   47 941.   tx Comeur LU3423

The nine countries of the European Communities have bound themselves by three treaties (coal and steel, economic, and atomic energy) under which their future activities are to become more and more closely woven. American countries associated with the European Communities were originally those which were connected colonially or economically with the original six members of the Communities, but 49 states signed the Lomé Convention on 1.4.76 (including Bahamas, Barbados, Grenada, Guyana, Jamaica and Trinidad and Tobago), more signed later including Surinam which signed in 1976.   The Statistical Office of the Communities compiles, analyses and publishes statistics of the member countries and occasionally from some other countries for comparison, and also general and foreign trade statistics for the associated countries.

012   East Caribbean Common Market,
           c/o Secretariat of the West Indies (Associated States),
           Council of Ministers,
           Bridge Street,
           Castries, St Lucia.

Established in 1968 the member states are Antigua, Barbados, Dominica, Grenada, Montserrat, St Kitts-Nevis-Anguilla, St Lucia and St Vincent.

Libraries and information services

Many national, university and public libraries throughout the world are deposit libraries for United Nations publications (a "List of depository libraries receiving United Nations material" is published as a separate booklet at intervals and it is also included annually in the Cumulative Index to UNDEX, the United Nations Documents Index); such libraries should have unrestricted documents and publications available for reference.   United Nations Information Centres usually have the more recent UN publications available.

It is usual for the official statistical offices of countries to exchange their publications with other national statistical offices and these publications are often, but not always, stored in the libraries of the statistical offices.   These libraries are often accessible to those who wish to consult this type of material, even when generally closed to the public.

Libraries and information services,   continued

United Kingdom

The most accessible large collection of the publications referred to in this guide is at the Department of Industry's Statistics and Market Intelligence Library, Export House, 50 Ludgate Hill, London EC4M 7HU (t 01-248 5757, Ex 368).   A most comprehensive collection of statistical publications of the developing countries, including those on the American continent and adjacent islands, is in the Library of the Institute of Development Studies at the University of Sussex, Andrew Cohen Building, Falmer, Brighton BN1 9RE (t 0273 66261).   Other large but somewhat more limited collections are in the Official Publications Library of the British Library, Great Russell Street, London EC1B 3DG (t 01-636 1544, Ex 487), Warwick University Library, Coventry (t 0203 24011), and the British Library of Political and Economic Science, 10 Portugal Street, London WC2A 2HD (t 01-405 7686).   Many of the larger public libraries are deposit libraries for United Nations publications, and one or two have collections of statistical yearbooks of overseas countries, but none take the more detailed statistical publications of individual countries listed in the following pages.

Australia

The two largest collections of statistical publications, including those of international organisations and of individual overseas countries, are in the National Library of Australia, Camberra A.C.T. 2600 (t (062) 621111) and the Australian Bureau of Statistics, Cameron Offices, Belconnen ACT 2617 (t (062) 527011).   There are also collections of this type of material in the State libraries, situated in each capital city, and in some university libraries, particularly the University of Sydney.   The Australian National University library at Canberra has a collection of statistical material to support its research in demography.

The United Nations Information Centre at 77 Kings Street, Sydney, NSW 2000 (t (02) 292151) has a collection of United Nations publications available for reference, and the Library of the Department of Foreign Affairs, Administrative Building, Parkes ACT 2600 (t (062) 61911) holds a comprehensive collection of UN publications to which the public could be allowed access, also for reference only.

Canada

The Library of Statistics Canada, Ottawa K1A 0T6 (t (613) 992 2959) has an extensive collection of statistical material, including the historical collection of Canadian statistics, publications of international organisations and of individual countries.   The library is open to the public and materials can be borrowed via interlibrary loan.

Many of the larger university, government department and provincial libraries in Canada are deposit libraries for United Nations publications but do not collect statistical publications of individual countries outside North America to any extent.

New Zealand

Both the Library of the Department of Statistics, Aorangi House, Molesworth Street, Wellington (Postal address: Private Bag, Wellington; t 729 119) and the National Library of New Zealand, 44 The Terrace, Wellington (Postal address: Private Bag, Wellington; t 722-101) have large collections of statistical material, including publications of international organisations and of individual overseas countries.   Some material is also held in the university libraries, in the public libraries of main and secondary cities and in the libraries of certain other government departments such as the Department of Trade and Industry.   Much of the material available in New Zealand is accessible for loan through the country's library interloan system.

USA

The Bureau of the Census Library of the US Department of Commerce, Room 2451, Federal Office Building 3, Suitland, Maryland (mailing address: Washington DC 20233; t 301-763-5042) maintains a collection of final US census publications from 1790 to date as well as foreign censuses and statistical publications which may be consulted from 08.00 to 17.00, Monday through Friday.

The Library of Congress in Washington, the Joint International Monetary Fund and International Bank for Reconstruction and Development Library in Washington, and the United Nations Library in New York have extensive collections.

Libraries and information services,   continued

USA,   continued

The United Nations Information Center, 2101 L Street NW, Washington DC 20037 († 202-296-5370) has a collection of United Nations publication.   A large number of university and public libraries throughout the US are deposit libraries for United Nations publications and also have some publications of other international organisations.

Bibliographies

013   UNDEX: United Nations documents index (United Nations)
Publishing Service, United Nations, New York, NY 10017; or from sales agents.
1950-   monthly   £52 or US$80 yr.
Lists all unrestricted documents and publications of the United Nations arranged by issuing departments
of the UN.   Series A is the subject index; series B the country index; and series C the list of
documents issued.   An annual cumulative checklist and cumulative subject index are included in
the subscription and are issued some time after the end of the year covered.

014   United Nations Publications: a reference catalogue   (United Nations)
Publishing Service, United Nations, New York, NY 10017; or from sales agents.
A comprehensive list of the publications of the UN issued for sale since 1945.   The issue for 1945-1963,
published in 1964, has been followed by annual volumes.

015   Directory of international statistics   (United Nations Statistical Office)
Publishing Service, United Nations, New York, NY 10017; or from sales agents.
Published in 1975.   £6.50 or US$12.50.   296 p.
Issued as Statistical papers, series M, no 56, the directory is in four parts.   Part 1 lists international
statistical services; part 2 lists international statistical series by subject, organisation, publication
and series frequency; part 3 is devoted to international statistical standards; and part 4 deals with
computerised international statistics, including an inventory of data bases of economic and social
statistics, computer installations, and inter-organisational computer arrangements.   Reference is
only to United Nations and related bodies.

016   Bibliography of industrial and distributive-trade statistics (United Nations Statistical Office)
Publishing Service, United Nations, New York, NY 10017; or from sales agents.
£4.16   or   US$8.   177 p.
Issued as "Statistical papers, series M, no 36, rev 4" (1975) it lists the data being collected by each
reporting country, mentioning the publications in which the data is published, if it is published.

017   Catalogue of statistical materials of developing countries (Institute of the Developing Economies, Tokyo)
Asian Economic Press, 42 Hommura-cho, Ichigaya, Shinjuku-ku, Tokyo 162, Japan.
6th ed 1974.   not priced.   250 p.
A catalogue of statistical materials collected by the Statistics Division of the Institute.

018   Catalogue of publications (OECD)
Organisation for Economic Co-operation and Development, 2 rue André-Pascal, 75775 Paris Cedex 16,
France.
A sales list which is published annually.

Bibliographies,   continued

019   World index of economic forecasts (George Cyriax, ed)
          Gower Press, Teakfield Ltd, Westmead, Farnborough, Hants.
                    £60.   397p.
          A guide to sources of economic forecasts, divided into four sections – forecast access tables, forecasts
                on principal OECD countries, forecasts/development plans for other countries, and a directory of
                forecasting organisations.   Published in 1978.

020   Actividades estadísticas de las naciones americanas [Statistical activities of American nations]
          (Instituto Interamericana de Estadística)
          Organisation of American States, 1725 Eye Street NW, Washington DC 2006.
          A second edition of a series describing the official statistical activities of each country in all fields of
                economic and social activity, including vehicles of publication.   Volumes for Panama, Chile
                and the Dominican Republic have been issued so far (US$3 each volume) in 1977.
          §   Es.

Statistical publications

¶ A - General

021   Statistical yearbook   (United Nations Statistical Office).
          Publishing Service, United Nations, New York, NY 10017; or from sales agents.
          1947-   1977.   £30; $45 (paper $37).   977p.
          Main sections:

World summary	Communications
Population	Consumption
Manpower	Balance of payments
Agriculture	Wages and prices
Forestry	National accounts
Fishing	Finance
Industrial production (index numbers)	Public finance
Mining and quarrying	Development assistance
Manufacturing	Housing
Construction	Health
Energy	Education
Internal trade	Science and technology
External trade	Culture
Transport	

          An annex contains a country nomenclature and information on conversion coefficients and factors.
          Time factor: the 1977 edition, published late 1978, contains tables with figures for many years up to
                1976 (provisional).
          §   En, Es, Fr.

022   Monthly bulletin of statistics (United Nations Statistical Office).
          Publishing Service, United Nations, New York, NY 10017; or from sales agents.
          1947- $7 or $70 yr; £4.55 or £45.50 yr.
          Provides monthly statistics on a range of 73 subjects from over 200 countries and territories, similar to
                those covered by 021 above, together with special tables illustrating important economic
                developments, and "Retail price comparisons to determine salary differentials of United Nations
                officials" which indicates the cost of living in various capitals of the world.
          Time factor: most tables include data for about 7 years, and at least the last 12 months to two or three
                months prior to the date of the issue.
          §   En, Fr.

¶   A,   continued

023   World statistics in brief (United Nations Statistical Office)
         Publishing Service, United Nations, New York, NY 10017; or from sales agents.
         1976-   2nd ed 1977.   £2.60; $3.95.   261 p.
         Contains comparable statistics for several years for trade, industries, communications and social growth
             for about 140 countries of the world.   Part 1 is arranged on a country basis and part 2 on a subject
             basis, including data on population, national accounts agriculture, forestry and fishing, mining
             and quarrying, manufacturing, consumption, transport and communications, international tourist
             travel, external trade, education, and culture (radio and television).
         Time factor: the 1977 edition has data for 1960, 1965, 1970 and 1975, and was published in 1977 as
             'Statistical papers, Series 5, no 2'.
         §   En.

024   UNESCO statistical yearbook: reference tables...   (UNESCO)
         UNESCO, 7 place de Fontenoy, 75700 Paris, France; or from sales agents.
         1963-   1976.   £29.25.   938 p.
         Includes data on population, education, science and technology, culture and communications (including
             newspapers and other periodicals), book production, cultural paper, films and cinema, radio,
             broadcasting and television for more than 200 territories.
         Time factor: the 1976 edition, published in 1977, has data for several years to 1974 or 1975 or latest
             available.
         §   En,   Es,   Fr.

025   World economic survey (United Nations Department of Economic and Social Affairs)
         Publishing Service, United Nations, New York, NY 10017; or from sales agents.
         1964-   1976.   £7.15; $8.   111 p.
         Contains a mid-term review and appraisal of progress in the implementation of the international
             development strategy, and data on current economic developments, including production and trade
             in the developed market economies, in the developing countries, and in the centrally planned
             economies.
         Time factor: the 1976 survey, published in 1977, has data for 1976 (sometimes only provisional) and
             some earlier years.
         §   En.

026   La zone franc [The franc area] (Comité Monétaire de la Zone Franc)
         Comité Monétaire de la Zone Franc, 39 rue Croix-des-Petits-Champs, 75049 Paris Cedex 01, France.
         1967-   1976.   not priced.   377 p.
         Contains data on trends in production, and on foreign trade, finance and investment, money and credit,
             balance of payments, currency reserves, etc, in the French-speaking and franc CFA countries,
             including Guadeloupe, Martinique, St Pierre et Miquelon, and Guyane Française.   Tables are
             included in the text.
         Time factor: the 1976 edition, published early 1978, contains data for two or three years to 1976.
         §   Fr.

027   World tables... from the data files of the World Bank (World Bank)
         Johns Hopkins University Press, Baltimore and London.
         1971-   2nd ed 1976.   £6.75; $22.50.   558 p.
         Time series data for most developing and many industrialised countries of the world (covers over 140
             countries).   Includes (1) national accounts and prices, by country for 1950, 1955, 1960-73,
             (2) balance of payments and central government finance, by country for 1967 to 1973,
             (3) comparative economic data for various years to 1973, and (4) social indicators from 1960 to 1970.
         Time factor: the second edition was published in 1976.
         §   En.

¶   A,   continued

028   World Bank atlas: population, per capita product and growth rates   (World Bank)
      World Bank, 1818 H Street NW, Washington DC 20433, USA.
      1966-   1977.   not priced.   32 p.
      Contains tables, graphs, maps, etc, of data on the subjects covered in above, by country.
      Time factor: the 1977 edition, published in 1977, has data to mid-1975.
      §   En.

029   Trends in developing countries   (World Bank Group)
      World Bank, 1818 H Street NW, Washington DC 20433, USA.
      1968-   1973.   not priced.   no pagination.
      Contains global indicators, data on population and economic growth, social indicators, data on
          international capital flow and external debt, and data on international trade.
      Time factor: the 1973 issue has data to 1970.
      §   En.

030   World development report   (World Bank)
      World Bank, 1818 H Street NW, Washington DC 20433, USA.
      1978-   1978.   free.   121 p.
      Includes an annex on world development indicators, arranged by subject and subdivided by countries,
          and includes basic indicators, growth and structure of production, growth of selected demand
          aggregates, structure of demand, growth and structure of merchandise trade, destination of
          merchandise exports, balance of payments, flows of external capital, external public debt,
          population and labour force growth, structure of population, demographic indicators, population
          projections, health-related indicators, and education.
      Time factor: the 1978 edition, published in May 1978, has data for 1976 and also either 1960 or 1970.
      §   En.

031   Current economic and industrial relations indicators   (Industrial Relations Centre, Queen's University at
          Kingston).
      Industrial Relations Centre, Queen's University at Kingston, Ontario K7L 3N6, Canada.
      1978-   semi-annual.   not priced.
      Contains data for USA and Canada on output and income, labour market, prices, profits, wages, earnings
          and compensation, productivity and labour costs, and collective bargaining and industrial relations.
      Time factor: each issue has data for two or three quarters to about three months prior to the date of
          publication.
      §   En.

032   World in figures (Economist Newspapers Ltd)
      The Economist, 25 St James's Street, London W1.
      1976-   2nd 1978.   not priced.   294 p.
      Contains data for the world and for individual countries on population, gross domestic product, area,
          standard of living, world cities [population], world population ages, education, labour force, health,
          commodities equipment [radios, television, motor cars, commercial vehicles owned], production,
          transport, finance, economic aid, external service trades [tourism, banking, transport, invisible
          trade, etc], and foreign trade.
      Time factor: the 1978 edition contains the latest data available for either 1976 or 1977, and also data for
          1960 and 1970 or percentage growth from 1960.
      §   En.

¶   A,   continued

033   Handbook of economic statistics: a research aid (Central Intelligence Agency: US Office of Economic
              Research)
          DOCEX Project, Exchange and Gift Division, Library of Congress, Washington DC 20540, USA.
          1975-   1977.   not priced.   174 p.
          Contains graphs and tables of economic information for selected non-Communist and all Communist
              countries, including subjects such as gross national income, gross national product, production,
              prices, employment, and energy.   The USA and Canada are the only two American countries
              included.
          Time factor: the 1977 issue, published in 1977, has data for 1960, 1965 and 1970-1976.
          §   En.

034   Annuaire de statistique internationale des grandes villes.   International statistical yearbook of large towns
              (Institut Internationale de Statistique)
          Office Permanent de l'Institut Internationale de Statistique, 2 Oostduinlaan, Den Haag, Netherlands.
          1927-   vol 6, 1972.   Fl 50.   516 p.
          Main sections:

Population by sex, and excess of births over deaths	Urban transport
	Civil airport transport
Births	Telephones, radio and television licences
Deaths (including still births)	Theatres
Newly constructed dwellings classified by number of rooms	Libraries
	Sports grounds and covered sports courts
Railways, sea-borne shipping and inland waterway transport	Area and its utilisation; real estate owned by the municipality; areal change by incorporation

          Time factor: the 1972 edition, published in 1976, shows the latest information available at that time.
          §   Fr,   En.

          Note: A series "International statistics of large towns" is also issued, each volume dealing with a
              particular subject, such as population and vital statistics, housing and building statistics, economic
              data, public utilities and transport, and cultural and sports statistics.

035   World military expenditures and arms transfers   (US Arms Control and Disarmament Industry)
          Government Printing Office, Washington DC 20402, USA.
          1964-   1965/74. $1.50.
          Contains data on military expenditures for about 120 countries, and the number of armed forces, as well
              as general economic information such as population, gross national product, foreign economic aid,
              and public expenditures on education and health.
          Time factor: the 1965/74 issue, published in 1977, has data for the years 1965 to 1974.
          §   En.

036   The Commonwealth and sterling area statistical abstract (Board of Trade)
          HM Stationery Office, PO Box 569, London SE1.
          1850/63-   1967.   84 p.
          Includes statistics of values of imports and exports of each of the Commonwealth and sterling area
              countries, production and consumption of selected commodities, population estimates, and balance
              of payments statistics.
          Time factor: ceased publication with the 1967 edition.
          §   En.

037   Overseas business reports (US Department of Commerce: Industry and Trade Administration)
          Publication Sales Branch, Room 1617, US Department of Commerce, Washington DC 20230, USA.
          1962-   irregular. $0.50 or $36.50 yr; $0.65 or $45.65 yr abroad.
          An international marketing information service with reports issued on a variety of subjects, including
              a sub-series titled 'Marketing in...' which includes key economic indicators, principal imports and

[continued next page]

¶   A,   continued

037,   continued

exports, etc.   Recent relevant examples are 'Marketing in Ecuador' (OBR 79-1), 'Marketing in Honduras' (OBR 77-29), 'Marketing in Chile' (OBR 77-25), and 'Marketing in Venezuela' (OBR 77-34).   Other examples include 'US trade with major world areas, 1970-1976' (OBR 77-31), 'World trade outlook for Latin America' (OBR 77-09), and 'US foreign trade by quarters' (OBR 78-14).
§   En.

038   Allgemeine Auslandsstatistik: Länderberichte   [General foreign statistics: reports on foreign countries] (Statistisches Bundesamt, W Germany).
W Kohlhammer GmbH, Postfach 42 11 20, 6500 Mainz 42, Federal Republic of Germany.
A series of reports, each on a particular country, containing statistics on the climate, population, health, education, labour, agriculture, forestry, fisheries, production, foreign trade, transport, tourism, finance, prices and wages, etc.   The reports are supported by a series of briefer reports: "Allgemeine Auslandsstatistik: Länderkurzberichte".   There are reports, mainly the brief versions, for many countries on the American continent and adjacent islands.
Time factor: the reports are published at varying intervals and contain the latest data available from each country.
§   De.

039   Internationale Monatzahlen   [International monthly figures] (Statistisches Bundesamt, W Germany).
W Kohlhammer GmbH, Postfach 42 11 20, 6500 Mainz 42, Federal Republic of Germany.
1955-   DM 6.90 or DM 64 yr.
Contains inter-country comparisons as to selected facts which are of particular importance for the foreign trade relations of the FDR.
§   De.

040   Bulletin de statistique des départements et territoires d'outre-mer   [Statistical bulletin of the overseas territories and departments] (INSEE)
Imprimerie Nationale, 2 rue Paul Hervieu, 75732 Paris Cedex 15, France.
1959-   quarterly.   FrF 6 or FrF 16 yr;   FrF 20 abroad yr.
Contains data on climate, demography, industry, transport, prices, wages, social security, money, credit, finance, savings banks, and foreign trade for each of the French overseas departments and territories, including Martinique, Guadeloupe, Guyane and St Pierre-et-Miquelon.
§   Fr.

Note: superseded 'Bulletin mensuel de statistiques d'outre-mer'.

041   Quarterly economic review of... (Economist Intelligence Unit)
Economist Intelligence Unit, Spencer House, 27 St James's Place, London SW1A 1NT.
1965-   annual subscription for each title of 4 issues and annual supplement - £30; $66, plus postage of £1.50 or $6 by airmail.
The statistical tables, using information drawn from official sources, cover economic trends and indicators of economic activity, including industrial production, construction, employment, retail trade, wages and prices, money and banking, foreign trade and payments, exchange reserves, exchange rates, exports and imports (broad commodity classification).   American countries for which there are reviews are: Argentina; Brazil; The West Indies, Belize, Bahamas, Bermuda, Guyana; Canada; Guatemala, El Salvador, Honduras; Chile; Colombia, Ecuador; Cuba, Dominican Republic, Haiti, Puerto Rico; Mexico; Peru, Bolivia; Uruguay, Paraguay; USA; Venezuela, Netherlands Antilles, Surinam.   There are also issues on 'Oil in North America' and 'Oil in Latin America and the Caribbean'.
§   En.

¶   A,   continued

042   Review   (BOLSA)
         Lloyds Bank International Ltd, 40-66 Queen Victoria Street, London EC4P 4EL.
         1967-   monthly.   not priced.
         Includes a statistical section with cost of living indexes for LAFTA countries, central America and the
               Dominican Republic, and indicators (production, gross domestic product, exchange rates,
               international reserves, foreign trade, tourism, banking and money, public finance, employment,
               wholesale prices, and cost of living) for Bolivia, Brazil, Ecuador, Mexico, Panama, Paraguay,
               Venezuela and also Spain.
         §   En.

043   Barclays country reports   (Barclays Bank Ltd)
         Barclays Bank Ltd, 54 Lombard Street, London EC3.
                   irregular.   free.
         A loose-leaf series of economic reports on individual countries, which contain a few statistical tables.
         §   En.

044   Economic report   (Lloyds Bank Ltd)
         Lloyds Bank Ltd, 6 Eastcheap, London EC3.
                   irregular.   free.
         A series of economic reports for each of the countries of the world, which contain a few statistical tables.
         §   En.

045   International marketing data and statistics   (Euromonitor Publications)
         Euromonitor Publications, PO Box 115, 41 Russell Square, London WC1B 5DC.
         1975/76-   4th, 1978/79.   £38.   320 p.
         Contains data on population, employment, production, trade, economy, standard of living, consumption,
               housing, health and education, and communications.
         Time factor: the 1978/79 edition, published early 1979, has data for 1974/75, 1976 and 1977.
         §   En.

046   Inventaire social et économique des territoires d'outre-mer, 1950-1955   [Social and economic inventory of
               France's overseas territories, 1950-1955]   (INSEE).
         INSEE, 18 boulevard Adolphe Pinard, 75675 Paris Cedex 14, France.
                   not priced.   467 p.
         Contains data on France's overseas territories during that period on political and administrative
               organisations, geography and climate, population, public health, education, scientific organisations,
               justice, agriculture, livestock, fisheries, forestry, mining, industry, electricity, transport and
               communications, foreign trade, prices and price indexes, employment, money and credit, and public
               finance.
         Time factor: published in 1957.
         §   Fr.

047   Statistical abstract to the West Indian Conference, fifth session   (Caribbean Commission).
         Caribbean Commission, Kent House, Port of Spain, Trinidad.
                   not priced.   2 vols.
         Attempted to illustrate the main features of the composition and structure of Caribbean industry, dealing
               with Caribbean agriculture and forestry and the industries that have been developed to process them.
         Time factor: published in 1952
         §   En.

¶   A,   continued

048   Caribbean statistical yearbook, 1967   (Caribbean Economic Development Corporation)
          Caribbean Economic Development Corporation, San Juan, Puerto Rico.
                          not priced.   201 p.
          Contains data on population, demography, climate and other physical characteristics, education, labour
               force, employment and payroll, national accounts and related subjects, industry, prices, distribution
               of products and services, transport and communications, passenger movement and tourism, banking,
               finance, insurance, and external trade.
          Time factor: published in 1967 and containing data for 1958 to 1965 with some projections for 1975.
          §   En.

049   Boletin estadístico de America Latina.   Statistical bulletin for Latin America   (United Nations. Economic
               Commission for Latin America).
          CEPAL, Casilla 179-D, Santiago de Chile; or from sales agents.
          1964-   2 issues a year.
          Contains regional and national statistics on population, demography, agriculture, mining, manufacturing,
               construction, electricity, prices (wholesale and consumer), foreign trade and transport.
          Time factor: ceased publication with the June 1972 issue.   Was to be replaced by a statistical yearbook.
          §   En,   Es.

050   Economic survey of Latin America   (United Nations.   Economic Commission for Latin America).
          CEPAL, Casilla 179-D, Santiago de Chile; or from sales agents.
          1948-   1976.   £13; $20.   454 p.
          Concerned with economic growth, foreign trade, inflation, and the economic trends of Latin American
               countries.   Statistical tables are included in the text.
          Time factor: the 1976 edition, was issued in 1979 and has data for several years to 1975 and 1976.
          §   En.

051   CEPAL review (United Nations.   Economic Commission for Latin America)
          CEPAL, Casilla 179-D, Santiago de Chile; or from sales agents.
          1977-   ½-yearly.   £1.95; $3 each issue.
          Contains signed articles which often have statistical tables in the text, but there are no regular statistical
               series.
          §   En and Es eds.

          Note: supersedes 'Economic Review of Latin America'.

052   Statistical abstract of Latin America   (University of California.   Latin American Center).
          UCLA Latin America Center Publications, University of California, Los Angeles, California 90024, USA.
          1955-   vol 19, 1978.   not priced.   450 p.
          Contents:
               Introduction (social indicators; production and consumption indices)
               Geographic data (area; population; weather; land use; land tenure)
               Social data (demography; vital and disease; health care, welfare and crime; housing and sanitation;
                    education; the military, politics and religion)
               Economic data (agricultural production; ranching production; energy production and consumption;
                    transport; national accounts; revenue, budgets and money supply; exchange rates; price indices)
               International statistics.
          Time factor: the 1978 edition was published in 1978 and contains the latest data available at that time.
          §   En.

¶ A,   continued

053   America en cifras [America in figures]   (Organización de los Estados Americanos).
       Organisation of American States, Washington DC 20006; or from sales agents.
       1960-   1977. $5 each volume.   3 vols.
       Contents:
           Vol   1   Economic situation
                                  1 agriculture, livestock, forestry, hunting and fisheries
                                  2 industry
                                  3 trade, transport, communications and tourism
                     11   Economic situation (continued)
                                  4 balance of payments, national product and income, and finance
                                  5 prices wages, consumption and other economic aspects
           Vol   111   Demographic situation
                              Social situation
                              Cultural situation

       Data is for the member countries of OAS.
       Time factor: the 1977 edition published in 1977 had data for 1974 and 1975.
       §   Es.
       Note: this title is to be replaced by a different kind of yearbook in future.

054   Statistical bulletin of the OAS   (Organisation of American States)
       Organisation of American States, 1725 Eye Street NW, Washington DC 20006, USA.
       1979-   quarterly. $4 or $12 yr to OAS member states; $17 yr elsewhere
       (1965- in Spanish)
       Each issue includes one or more analytical articles on particular subjects as well as regional statistical
           tables and selected indicators for individual countries.
       Time factor: each issue has figures for a number of years up to the most recent available.
       §   En and Es eds.

055   Indicadores de coyuntura [Economic indicators] (Fundación de Investigaciones Economicas Latinoamericanas)
       Fundación de Investigaciones Economicas Latinoamericanas, Esmeralda 320, 4° piso, 1343 – Capital
           Federal, Buenos Aires.
       1966-   monthly. $4.5000 or $45.000 yr.
       §   Es.

056   Boletin estadístico [Statistical bulletin] (Organización de los Estados Americanos)
       Organisation of American States, Washington DC 20006; or from sales agents.
       1965-   monthly.   not priced.
       Up-dates "America en cifras" (053).   Information varies with each issue and may be concerned with one
           member country or internationally, and one subject such as production, foreign trade, population,
           socio-economic information, etc.
       §   Es.

       Note: replaced from 1979 by 'Statistical bulletin of the OAS' (054).

057   Series estadísticas/seleccionades de Centroamerica y Panama: indicadores económicos   (SIECA)
       SIECA, 4a Avenida 10-25, zona 14, Apartado postal 1237, Guatemala, CA.
       1967-   quarterly.   CA$5 or US$5 each issue.
       Contains data on public accounts, money, balance of payments, foreign trade, agriculture, national
           accounts and other indicators for Central American countries and Panama.
       Time factor: published at irregular intervals.
       §   Es.

¶   A,   continued

058   Annual report (Inter-American Development Bank)
           Inter-American Development Bank, 808 17th Street NW, Washington DC 20577, USA.
           1960-   1977.   not priced.   137 p.
           Includes a section of selected statistical data on Latin America, including population, gross domestic
               product, balance of payments, exports, imports, monetary reserves, finance, consumer price index,
               etc.
           Time factor: the 1977 report, published early 1978, has data for several years to 1976.
           §   En.

059   Compendio estadístico centroamericano   [Statistical compendium of Central America]   (SIECA)
           SIECA, 4a avenida 10-25, zona 14, Apartado postal 1237, Guatemala, CA.
           1955-   6th 1975.   US$8 or CA$8.   508 p.
           Contents:
               Demography   Public finance
               Agriculture   Money and banking
               Industry   Prices
               Foreign trade   Public health
               Balance of payments and national   Social security
                 accounts   Education
           Time factor: the 1975 edition, published in 1975, has data for the years 1960 to 1973.
           §   Es.

060   Annual digest of statistics   (East Caribbean Common Market)
           Secretariat, East Caribbean Common Market, Dutchman Bay, Antigua.
           1973-   3rd, 1975. $10.   101p
           Contents:
               Area and climate   Employment and industrial relations
               Population and vital   Trade
               Medical and health   Transport and communications.
               Education   Banking
               Travel and migration   National accounts and finance
               Prices   Agriculture
           The data is for member countries of ECCM.
           Time factor: the 1975 edition, published in 1977, has data for 1969 or 1970 to 1975 generally, or the
               latest available.
           §   En.

061   ACP: statistical yearbook (EUROSTAT)
           Office des Publications Officielles des Communautés Européennes, CP 1003, Luxembourg; or from sales
               agents.
           1966-   1970-1976.   £4.80; $8.25; FrF 40.30.   624 p.
           Includes various analytical tables covering particular areas of demographic and economic statistics
               (e.g. national accounts, balance of payments, external debt, external aid, government finance) for
               all ACP countries, which include Bahamas, Barbados, Grenada, Guyana, Surinam, and Trinidad and
               Tobago.
           Time factor: published in 1978.
           §   En,   Fr.

           Note: earlier titles were 'Associés - mémento statistique' and 'Associates - yearbook of general
               statistics'.

¶   A,   continued

062   Main economic indicators   (Organisation for Economic Co-operation and Development)
           OECD, 2 rue André-Pascal, 75775 Paris Cedex 16, France; or from sales agents.
           1965-   monthly.   £2.20 or £21.60 yr; $4.50 or $45 yr; FrF 18 or FrF 180 yr.
           Selected indicators for member countries, including USA and Canada, on national accounts, industrial
               production, deliveries, stocks and orders, construction, retail sales, labour, wages, prices, domestic
               and foreign finance, interest rates, trade and payments.
           Time factor: most tables contain figures for the last four years and quarterly and monthly figures for the
               last year to one or two months prior to the date of the issue.
           §   En,   Fr.

063   Main economic indicators: historical statistics   (Organisation for Economic Co-operation and Development).
           OECD, 2 rue André-Pascal, 75775 Paris Cedex 16, France; or from sales agents.
           1955/64-   1960-1975.   £8.50 or $17.50 or FrF 70.   592 p.
           Similar subject coverage to 062 above.
           Time factor: the 1960-1975 edition, with data for those years, was published late 1976.
           §   En,   Fr.

064   International economic indicators   (US Department of Commerce, Domestic and International Business
               Administration)
           Government Printing Office, Washington DC 20402, USA.
           1975-   quarterly. $12.65 ($15.85 for foreign mailing) yr.
           Contains comparative tables of economic data for the US and major international trade competitors
               (including Canada) - gross national product, production, investment, exports, imports, and balance
               of trade.
           §   En.

065   Economic indicators weekly review   (US National Foreign Assessment Center).
           Document Expediting (DOCEX) Project, Exchange and Gift Division, Library of Congress, Washington
               DC 20540, USA.
           Up to date information on changes in the domestic and external economic activities of the major non-
               Communist developed countries (including USA and Canada).
           §   En.

¶   B - Production

i. Mines and mining

066   World mineral statistics   (Institute of Geological Sciences)
           HM Stationery Office, PO Box 569, London SE1 9NH.
           1913/20-   1970-74.   £6.50.   210 p.
           Contains data on quantities produced, imported and exported of the following minerals for all countries
               so far as the information is available: aluminium and bauxite, antimony, arsenic, asbestos, barium,
               cadmium, chromium, coal, cobalt, copper, diamond diatomite, feldspar, fluorspar, gold, graphite,
               gypsum, iron ore, iron, steel and ferroalloys, kaolin, lead, manganese, mercury, mica, molybdenum,
               nickel, petroleum and natural gas, phosphates, platinum, potash minerals, pyrites, rare earth and
               thorium minerals, salt, selenium, sillimanite, silver, sulphur and pyrites, talc, tantalum and niobium,
               tin, titanium, tungsten, vanadium, zinc, zirconium, and other minerals.
           Time factor: the 1970-74 edition, containing data for those years, was published in 1978.
           §   En.

           Note: prior to this edition the title was 'Statistical summary of the mineral industry'.

¶   B.i,   continued

067   Minerals yearbook: volume III - area reports, international   (US Bureau of Mines)
       Government Printing Office, Washington DC 20402, USA.
       1932- 1974. $15.   1278 p.
       Contains detailed textual and statistical data on the mineral industry in each country of the world.
       Time factor: the 1974 edition, published in 1977, has data for 1974 and earlier years.
       §   En.

068   Metal statistics   (Metallgesellschaft A.G.)
       Metallgesellschaft AG, Postfach 3724, Frankfurt (Main), Federal Republic of Germany.
       1913- 1967/77.   not priced.   390 p.
       A world survey of production and consumption of aluminium, lead, copper, zinc, tin, antimony, cadmium,
          magnesium, nickel, mercury and silver.   There are comparisons by continent, and detailed surveys
          of the situation in producing countries.
       Time factor: the 1967/77 edition, covering those years, was published in 1978.
       §   En and   De eds.

       Note: similar publications in France and Italy are "Statistiques...cuivre, plomb, zinc, étain, antimoine,
          cadmium, cobalt, nickel, aluminium, magnesium, mercure, argent, or", issued annually by Minerais
          et Métaux SA, 61 avenue Hoche, Paris 8; and "Metalli non ferrosi e ferroleghe: statistiche",issued
          by Ammi SpA, via Malise 11, Roma.

069   Metal bulletin handbook   (Metal Bulletin Ltd)
       Metal Bulletin Ltd, Park House, 3 Park Terrace, Worcester Park, Surrey KY4 7HY.
       1913- 1978.   £15.   885 p.
       Contains data on production, consumption, deliveries, exports, and prices of non-ferrous metals and of
          iron and steel.
       Time factor: the 1978 edition, published late 1978, contains data for several years to 1977.
       §   En.

070   Non-ferrous metal data   (American Bureau of Metal Statistics Inc).
       American Bureau of Metal Statistics, Inc, 420 Lexington Avenue, New York, NY 10017.
       1921- 1977. $15.   149 p.
       Includes statistics of mines production, smelter production, consumption, imports and exports, etc, on a
          world-wide basis for copper, lead, zinc, nickel, aluminium, bauxite, gold, silver, tin, antimony,
          cadmium, cobalt, magnesium, molybdenum, platinum, etc.
       Time factor: the 1977 edition, published in 1978, has data for 1977 and also earlier figures in some
          tables.

071   World metal statistics   (World Bureau of Metal Statistics).
       World Bureau of Metal Statistics, 50 Broadway, New York, NY 10004, and 41 Doughty Street,
          London WC1N 2LF.
       1948-   monthly.   £275 or $280 yr.
       Contains data on production, consumption, trade, stocks, prices, etc, of metals, aluminium, antimony,
          cadmium, copper, lead, nickel, tin and lead.   Includes data by country as well as world-wide
          totals.
       Time factor: each issue has data to about two months earlier than the month of publication.
       §   En.

072   Metal statistics: a purchasing guide of the metal industries   (American Metal Market).
       Fairchild Publications, 7 East 12th Street, New York, NY 10003.
       1908- 1978. $30.   383 p.
       Contains data for individual metals, raw and processed, on production, deliveries, stocks, output, prices,
          etc.
       Time factor: the 1978 edition, published in 1978, has data to 1977.
       §   En.

¶ B.i,   continued

073   Anuario estadístico de la siderurgia y mineria del fierro de América Latina   [Statistical yearbook on the
            mining and manufacturing of iron and steel]   (Instituto Latinoámericano del Fierro y del Acero).
            Instituto Latinámericano del Fierro y del Acero, Casilla 16065, Santiago 9, Chile.
            1967-   1975.   not priced.   193 p.
            Contains data on production, distribution, exports, imports, consumption, prices, and use of raw materials
                in the iron and steel industry.
            Time factor: the 1975 edition, published in December 1976, has data for 1971 to 1975 or 1974.
            §   Es.

074   Survey of world iron ore resources   (United Nations.   Department of Economic and Social Affairs).
            Publishing Service, United Nations, New York, NY 10017; or from sales agents.
                      $6.50;   £2.85.   488 p.
            Contains a general report, technical papers and regional appraisals, and includes some statistics in the
                text.
            Time factor: published in 1970.
            §   En.

075   The world market for iron ore   (United Nations.   Economic Commission for Europe).
            Publishing Services, United Nations, New York, NY 10017; or from sales agents.
                     £1.70; $4.50.   333 p.
            Contains data on consumption, supplies, international trade, costs, trends in transport, and iron ore
                requirements for 1970, 1975 and 1980.   Includes some statistical tables.
            Time factor: published in 1968.
            §   En.

076   Tin statistics   (International Tin Council).
            International Tin Council, Haymarket House, 1 Oxendon Street, London SW1Y 4EQ.
            1959-   1966-1976.   £8.   60 p.
            Contains data on the production, exports, imports, stocks, consumption, trade in manufactures, and
                labour for each country.
            Time factor: the 1966-1967 edition, published in 1978, has data for the years 1966 to 1976.
            §   En.

077   Monthly statistical bulletin   (International Tin Council).
            International Tin Council, Haymarket House, 1 Oxendon Street, London SW1Y 4EQ.
            1959-   monthly.   £2.50 or £30 yr.
            Updates the information in 076 above.
            §   En.

078   Tin prices   (International Tin Council)
            International Tin Council, Haymarket House, 1 Oxendon Street, London SW1Y 4EQ.
            1973-   1976.   £4.   13 p.
            Gives a concise picture of the movement of daily tin prices on the leading international tin markets for
                each quarter of the year.
            Time factor: the 1976 issue, published in 1977, has data for the four quarters of 1976.
            §   En.

            Note: there is also a retrospective volume "Tin prices, 1956-1973, London and Penang" published in
                1974, price £3.50.

¶   B.i,   continued

079   Lead and zinc statistics: monthly bulletin...   (International Lead and Zinc Study Group).
         International Lead and Zinc Study Group, Metro House, 58 St James's Street, London SW1A 1LD.
         1966-   £35; $70 yr.
         Contains statistics of mine production, refined production, foreign trade, and consumption of lead and
            zinc.
         Time factor: each issue has about six years of annual figures and more recent quarterly and monthly
            figures to about three months prior to the date of the issue.
         §   En,   Fr.

080   Statistical summary   (International Primary Aluminium Institute)
         International Primary Aluminium Institute, 9th floor, New Zealand House, Haymarket, London SW1Y 4TQ.
         1976-   1977.   not priced.   32 p.
         Contains data on primary production, primary production capacity, receipts, inventory, and aluminium
            production: metallurgical and other uses.
         Time factor: the 1977 issue, published in 1978, has data for 1973 to 1977 by months and quarters.
         §   En.

         Note: the Institute also issues a single-sheet provisional report 'Primary aluminium production'.

081   Uranium: resources, production and demand   (Organisation for Economic Co-operation and Development)
         OECD, 2 rue André-Pascal, 75775 Paris Cedex 16; or from sales agents.
         1973-   December 1977.   £4.40; $9; FrF 36.   138 p.
         Contains estimates of the world's uranium resources and probable future demand, with consequent
            requirements for increased production capacity and enrichment services.
         Time factor: the December 1977 issue was published early 1978.
         §   En.

082   Tungsten statistics: quarterly bulletin of the UNCTAD Committee on Tungsten   (United Nations Conference
            on Trade and Development)
         Publishing Service, United Nations, New York, NY 10017; or from sales agents.
         1967-   quarterly.   £2.60; $3 each issue.
         Contains statistics on prices, production, consumption, trade and stocks of tungsten for reporting
            countries.
         Time factor: each issue has data for several years and includes the most recent annual and quarterly
            statistics available.
         §   En.

083   Statistical bulletin   (CIPEC - Intergovernmental Council of Copper Exporting Countries)
         Conseil Intergouvernemental des Pays Exportateurs de Cuivre, 177 avenue de Roule, 92200 Neuilly sur
            Seine, France.
         1975-   1976.   not priced.
         Contains data relating to copper (production, consumption, trade, scrap recovery, and prices) in a concise
            form for the copper exporting countries, including Chile, Peru and USA.
         Time factor: the 1976 issue, published in 1977, has data for ten years to 1976 (provisional).
         §   En,   Es,   Fr.

084   Quarterly review   (CIPEC - Intergovernmental Council of Copper Exporting Countries)
         Conseil Intergouvernemental des Pays Exportateurs de Cuivre, 177 avenue de Roule, 92200 Neuilly sur
            Seine, France.
         1975-   not priced.
         Mainly textual, but contains a few statistics up-dating the bulletin (see above).
         §   En,   Es,   Fr.

¶   B.i,   continued

085   Handbook of world salt resources   (Stanley J Lefond)
         Plenum Press, 227 W 17th Street, New York, NY 10010.
                        $25.   407 p.
         Includes some statistics and statistical tables in the text.
         Time factor: published in 1969.
         §   En.

086   Water resources of the world: selected statistics   (Fritz van der Leeden).
         Water Information Center Inc, 44 Sintsink Drive East, Port Washington, New York, NY 11050.
                        $32.50.   568 p.
         Contains data by continent and country on rivers, lakes, reservoirs, wells, dams, rain, etc.   Also on
            hydroelectric and thermal power generating stations.
         Time factor: published in 1975, the statistics included are the latest available at the time of compilation.
         §   En.

087   Commodity data summaries   (US Bureau of Mines)
         US Bureau of Mines, 4800 Forbes Avenue, Pittsburgh, Pa 15213, USA.
         1968-   1976.   not priced.   196 p.
         Mainly USA, but does include world resources data for 95 mineral commodities.
         Time factor: the 1976 issue, published in 1976, has data for 1975.
         §   En.

   ii.   Agriculture, fisheries, forestry, etc.

088   Production yearbook   (Food and Agriculture Organisation of the United Nations)
         FAO, via delle Terme di Caracalla, 00153 Roma, Italy; or from sales agents.
         1947-   1977.   £6.50; $17.   296 p.
         Contains data on land, population, FAO index numbers of agricultural production, statistical summary
            of world and regional agricultural production, crops, livestock numbers and products, food supply,
            means of production (farm machinery, pesticides, etc), prices.
         Time factor: the 1977 edition, published late 1978, has data for several years to 1977.
         §   En,   Es,   Fr.

089   FAO monthly bulletin of statistics   (Food and Agriculture Organisation of the United Nations).
         FAO, via delle Terme di Caracalla, 00153 Roma, Italy; or from sales agents.
         1952-   £0.65 or £5.20 yr; $1 or $8 yr.
         Each issue contains special features, notes on the tables, and statistical tables on production, trade and
            prices for agricultural, fishery and forest products of reporting countries.
         Time factor: each issue has data for about four years and several months or quarters up to between two
            and six months prior to publication.
         §   En,   Es,   Fr.

         Note: Before January 1978 issue title was "Monthly bulletin of agricultural economics and statistics".

090   World census of agriculture   (Food and Agriculture Organisation of the United Nations)
         FAO, via delle Terme di Caracalla, 00153 Roma, Italy; or from sales agents.
         1950-   1960.   5 vols in 7.
         Contents:
                Vol 1   part A.   Census results by countries (including Colombia, Puerto Rico, USA and Virgin
                                     Islands)   ($45)
                         part B.   Census results by countries, (including Argentina, Costa Rica, Dominican Republic,
                                     Mexico, Nicaragua and Uruguay)   ($9.80)

[continued next page]

19

¶   B.ii,   continued

090,   continued

       Vol 1 part C.   Census results by countries (including Canada, Jamaica, Paraguay, Peru and
                 Venezuela) ($16.50)
       Vol 2 Programme, concepts and scope   ($12)
       Vol 3 Methodology ($10)
       Vol 4 Processing and tabulation ($4.50)
       Vol 5 Analysis and international comparisons of census results ($7.50)
    Time factor: published between 1967 and 1971.
    §   En.

    Note: it is planned to take another census in 1980.

091   State of food and agriculture   (Food and Agriculture Organisation of the United Nations)
       FAO, via delle Terme di Caracalla, 00153 Roma, Italy; or from sales agents.
       1957- 1976. £4.55; $7.   157 p.
       Includes a world review and a regional review on production of agriculture, fisheries, forestry; foreign
          trade; prices; policies and programmes.
       Time factor: the 1965 edition, published in 1977, has data for a number of years to 1975 and some
          preliminary figures for 1976.
       §   En.

092   Agricultural commodity projections, 1970-1980   (Food and Agriculture Organisation of the United Nations)
       FAO, via delle Terme di Caracalla, 00153 Roma, Italy; or from sales agents.
                £2; $5 each volume.   2 vols.
    Contents:
       Vol. I, part   1 General outlook
              part 11 Projections by commodities
       Vol.II, part   1 General methodology
              part 11 Statistical appendix
    Time factor: published in 1971.
    §   En.

093   World agricultural production and trade: statistical report   (US Department of Agriculture: Foreign
          Agricultural Service).
       Foreign Agricultural Service, Department of Agriculture, Washington DC, USA.
       1964- monthly.
       Contains world agricultural production and trade summaries, several subjects within the agricultural field
          being dealt with in each issue.
       Time factor: ceased publication with the December 1975 issue, later information being carried in
          circulars, which are available to US residents only.
       §   En.

094   Commodity survey (UNCTAD)
       Publishing Service, United Nations, New York, NY 10017; or from sales agents.
          3rd, 1968. $2.   123 p.
       Contains a survey of the overall commodity situation and the problems of individual commodities and
          international commodity action.   Tables are included in the text.
       Time factor: the report was published in 1968 and has data to 1967.
       §   En.

¶ B.ii, continued

095   Commodity trade and price trends... (International Bank for Reconstruction and Development)
       World Bank, 1818 H Street NW, Washington DC 20433, USA.
       1973- 1978.   not priced.   135 p.
       Contains data on trade, price and freight rate indices, and prices of agricultural and non-agricultural
            products.   Values are in US$ for comparison.
       Time factor: the 1978 issue, published in August 1978, has long runs of figures to 1977.
       §   En,   Es,   Fr.

096   FAO commodity review and outlook (Food and Agriculture Organisation of the United Nations)
       FAO, via delle Terme di Caracalla, 00153 Roma, Italy; or from sales agents.
       1964- 1976-1977.   £5.20; $8.   113 p.
       Reviews the general commodity situation and outlook, and the situation and outlook by commodities –
            basic food and feedstuffs, other food and beverage crops, non-food crops (tobacco, pepper),
            agricultural raw materials (cotton, etc, hides and skins), and fishery products.
       Time factor: data available at May 1977 is included in the 1976-1977 edition, which was published in
            1977.
       §   En.

097   Study of trends in world supply and demand of major agricultural commodities (Organisation for Economic
            Co-operation and Development)
       OECD, 2 rue André-Pascal, 75775 Paris Cedex 16, France; or from sales agents.
                 £6; $13.50; FrF 54.   349 p.
       An assessment of world trends in the grain-livestock sector over the next 10 to 15 years, in terms of
            factors affecting supply and demand, the market and trade outlook, and the major issues ahead –
            particularly the instability of the agricultural markets and the food needs of developing countries.
            A general assessment is followed by regional analyses and commodity analyses.   There are some
            statistics and a few statistical tables in the text.
       Time factor: published in 1976.
       §   En.

098   World wheat statistics (International Wheat Council)
       International Wheat Council, 28 Haymarket, London SW1Y 4SS.
       1955- 1978.   £5; $9.50.   71 p.
       Contains data on area, field and production; wheat flour production; exports and imports of wheat and
            wheat flour; supplies and stocks of wheat; prices, etc.
       Time factor: the 1978 edition, published in 1978, has long runs of figures to the 1976/77 season.
       §   En,   Es,   Fr,   Ru.

099   Review of the world wheat situation (International Wheat Council)
       International Wheat Council, 28 Haymarket, London SW1Y 4SS.
       1958/59- 1976/77.   not priced.   118 p.
       Reviews wheat production; world trade in wheat and wheat flour; wheat prices and ocean freight rates;
            developments in wheat policies; course grains and rice production, consumption, trade, stocks and
            prices, etc.
       Time factor: the 1976/77 edition, published early 1978, includes data available for the 1976/77 crop
            year.
       §   En, with tables of contents and summaries in Es,   Fr,   Ru.

       Note: the International Wheat Council also issues a press release 'Wheat market report'.

100   Grain crops: a review of production, trade, consumption and prices relating to wheat, wheat flour, maize,
            barley, oats, rye and rice (Commonwealth Secretariat)
       Commonwealth Secretariat, Marlborough House, Pall Mall, London SW1.
       1965/66- Vol 15, 1973.   £2.25.   127 p.
       Time factor: Ceased publication with the 1973 issue.
       §   En.

¶   B.ii,   continued

101   Grain bulletin   (Commonwealth Secretariat).
            Commonwealth Secretariat, Marlborough House, Pall Mall, London SW1.
                    monthly.   £1 each issue.
            Up-dated 100.
            Time factor: ceased publication with the December 1976 issue.
            §   En.

102   International grain and feed markets forecast and statistical digest   (Turret Press).
            Turret Press, 886 High Road, Finchley, London N12 9SB.
            1977- 1977.   not priced.   38 p.
            Includes statistical tables in the text, on prices and marketing, production and distribution, nutrition.
            Time factor: the 1977 edition, published in 1977, has data for several years to the 1976/77 crop year
                (estimated figures).
            §   En.

103   International milling and feed manual...   (Turret Press).
            Turret Press, 886 High Road, Finchley, London N12 9SB.
            1972- 1975.   not priced.   84 p.
            Includes 27 pages of grain and feed statistical data (production, exports, imports, consumption, etc).
            Time factor: the 1975 edition has data for several years to 1973/74 or 1974/75.
            §   En.

104   Rice bulletin   (Commonwealth Secretariat).
            Commonwealth Secretariat, Marlborough House, Pall Mall, London SW1.
                    monthly.   £0.75 each issue.
            Contained a general review, followed by information on area and production, exports, imports and prices.
            Time factor: ceased publication with the December 1976 issue.
            §   En.

105   FAO rice report   (Food and Agriculture Organisation of the United Nations).
            FAO, via delle Terme di Caracalla, 00100 Roma, Italy; or from sales agents.
            1952- 1974/75. $2; £0.80.   27 p.
            Contains data on rice crops, stocks, market and trade.
            Time factor: the 1974/75 issue, published in 1975, has data for several years to 1973 and estimates for
                1974.
            §   En.

106   Rice trade intelligence   (Food and Agriculture Organisation of the United Nations).
            FAO, via delle Terme di Caracalla, 00100, Roma, Italy; or from sales agents.
            1957- two-monthly.   not priced.
            Contains data on price index, prices, contracts, exports, imports, stocks, paddy production, etc.
            Time factor: each issue has data for several years and months to one month prior to the date of the issue,
                which is the publication date.
            §   En.

107   Fruit: a review of production and trade relating to fresh, canned, frozen and dried fruit, fruit juices and
                wine (Commonwealth Secretariat).
            Commonwealth Secretariat, Marlborough House, Pall Mall, London SW1.
            1964/65- Vol 19, 1972.   £3.   278 p.
            Time factor: ceased publication with the 1972 issue.
            §   En.

¶ B.ii, continued

108 Fruit intelligence (Commonwealth Secretariat).
Commonwealth Secretariat, Marlborough House, Pall Mall, London SW1.
monthly. £1.67 each issue.
Up-dated 107.
Time factor: ceased publication with the December 1976 issue.
§ En.

109 Dairy produce: a review of production, trade, consumption and prices relating to butter, cheese, condensed milk, milk powder, casein, eggs, egg products and margarine (Commonwealth Secretariat).
Commonwealth Secretariat, Marlborough House, Pall Mall, London SW1.
1966- Vol 20, 1972. £2. 128 p.
Time factor: ceased publication with the 1972 issue.
§ En.

110 Meat: a review of production, trade, consumption and prices relating to beef, live cattle, mutton and lamb, live sheep, bacon and hams, pork, live pigs, canned meat, offal, poultry meat (Commonwealth Secretariat).
Commonwealth Secretariat, Marlborough House, Pall Mall, London SW1.
1964/66- Vol 19, 1973. £2.50. 131 p.
Time factor: ceased publication with the 1973 issue.
§ En.

111 Meat and dairy produce bulletin (Commonwealth Secretariat).
Commonwealth Secretariat, Marlborough House, Pall Mall, London SW1.
monthly. £1.67 each issue.
Updated 109 and 110.
Time factor: ceased publication with the December 1976 issue.
§ En.

112 International market survey (Meat and Livestock Commission).
Meat and Livestock Commission, PO Box 44, Queensway House, Bletchley, MK2 2EF, England.
quarterly. not priced.
Includes some statistical tables in the text on production, slaughter, prices, etc of cattle, sheep, pigs, etc. Includes data on Argentina, Canada and USA.
§ En.

113 Estadísticas sobre la alimentación y la agricultura en Centroamérica [Statistics of food and agriculture in Central America] (SIECA).
SIECA, 4a Avenida 10-25, zona 14, Apartado postal 1237, Guatemala, CA.
not priced. 357 p.
Contains data on food balances for each country, and area harvested and the yield for each country.
Time factor: published in 1972, the report has data for 1960 to 1970.
§ Es.

114 Animal health yearbook (FAO - WHO - OIE).
FAO, via delle Terme di Caracalla, 00153 Roma, Italy; or from sales agents.
1957- 1977. £5.20. 204 p.
Contains data on diseases of mammals, birds, bees, fish, by countries. Also number of inhabitants, livestock and veterinarians.
Time factor: the 1977 edition, published in 1978, has data available at 31st December 1977.
§ En, Es, Fr.

¶   B.ii,   continued

115   Plantation crops: a review of production, trade, consumption and prices relating to coffee, cocoa, tea,
          sugar, spices, tobacco and rubber   (Commonwealth Secretariat).
          Commonwealth Secretariat, Marlborough House, Pall Mall, London SW1.
          1966-   Vol 14, 1973.   £3.95.   318 p.
          Time factor: the 1973 issue contains data to 1973.   The review ceased publication with that issue.
          §   En.

116   Tropical products quarterly   (Commonwealth Secretariat).
          Commonwealth Secretariat, Marlborough House, Pall Mall, London SW1.
          1960-   £3 or £12 yr.
          Includes data on production, crops, imports and exports, trade, stocks, prices, sales, etc, of vegetable
              oils and oilseeds, cocoa, coffee and spices.
          Time factor: up-dated 115 and 132 until December 1976 issue, with which it ceased publication.
          §   En.

117   Sugar yearbook   (International Sugar Organisation).
          International Sugar Organisation, 28 Haymarket, London SW1Y 4SP.
          1947-   1977.   £5.   383 p.
          Contains statistics of production, exports, imports, consumption, stocks, and prices of sugar.
          Time factor: the 1977 edition, published in 1978, has data for several years to 1977.
          §   En.

118   Statistical bulletin   (International Sugar Organisation)
          International Sugar Organisation, 28 Haymarket, London SW1Y 4SP.
          1947-   monthly.   £2 or £20 yr plus postage.
          Up-dates 117 above.
          §   En.

119   World sugar statistics   (F O Licht)
          F O Licht, Ratzeburg, Federal Republic of Germany.
          1938/39-   1977/78.   not priced.   56 p.
          Includes world sugar statistics, and statistics of imports, exports, prices, consumption, and molasses by
              country.
          Time factor: the 1977/78 issue, published late 1978, has data for several years to 1976/77.
          §   De,   En.

120   Sugar review   (C Czarnikow Ltd).
          C Czarnikow Ltd, 66 Mark Lane, London EC3.
                    weekly.   not priced.
          A news bulletin which includes statistical tables on foreign trade, deliveries, futures markets, etc, for
              sugar.
          §   En.

121   Cocoa statistics   (Food and Agriculture Organisation of the United Nations).
          FAO, via delle Terme di Caracalla, 00153 Roma, Italy; or from sales agents.
          1958-   quarterly with monthly supplements.   £0.40 each quarterly issue.
          Included data on production, imports and exports of beans, butter, powder, paste, chocolate and
              chocolate products, prices of beans and stocks of beans.   Both producing countries and importing
              countries are named.
          Time factor: latest issue was for January 1975.
          §   En,   Es,   Fr.

¶   B.ii,   continued

122   Cocoa statistics   (Gill & Duffus Ltd).
            Gill & Duffus Group Ltd, St Dunstan's House, 201 Borough High Street, London SE1 1HW.
            (annual)   December, 1977.   not priced.   41 p.
            Contains statistics of production and grindings of raw cocoa, imports and exports, supply and demand,
                and market prices.   There is also data for cocoa butter and cocoa powder.
            Time factor: the 1977 issue, published in December 1977, has long runs of figures to 1976.
            §   En.

            Note: Gill and Duffus Ltd also issue a "Cocoa market report" about every two months, which includes
                statistics on supply and demand, raw cocoa grindings, world production and grindings of raw cocoa,
                and world production of cocoa beans.

123   Quarterly bulletin of cocoa statistics   (International Cocoa Organisation).
            International Cocoa Organisation, 22 Berners Street, London W1P 3DB.
            1975-   £6;   £8 outside Europe.
            Contains data on the world cocoa bean position, production, grindings, exports by country of cocoa beans
                and products, imports by country, prices, etc.
            Time factor: each issue has the latest available data to six months or more before the date of the issue.
            §   En,   Fr,   Ru.

124   Cocoa price index and deflated cocoa prices   (International Cocoa Organisation).
            International Cocoa Organisation, 22 Berners Street, London W1P 3DB.
            1975-   irregular.   free.
            §   En.

            Note: also issued is the weekly 'Daily and indicator prices of cocoa beans...'

125   Annual coffee statistics   (Pan American Coffee Bureau).
            Pan American Coffee Bureau, 1350 Avenue of the Americas, New York, NY 10019.
            1934-   1975. $5.   216 p.
            The annual review of coffee statistics, including price movements, world production, world trade, as
                well as foreign exchange rates, barter and compensation agreements.   Information is given for
                individual countries as well as world-wide.
            Time factor: the 1975 issue, published in 1976, has data for 1975 and also earlier years in some tables.
            §   En.

126   General statistical document: coffee year...   (International Coffee Organisation).
            International Coffee Organisation, 22 Berners Street, London W1P 3DB.
            1968/69-   1975/76.   £1.50.   43 p.
            Contains data on imports, exports, re-exports and inventories of coffee, by country.
            Time factor: the 1975/76 issue, published in 1976, has data for the coffee year 1975/76 and about five
                earlier years in some tables.   Superseded by the 'Quarterly statistical bulletin on coffee' (see 127
                below).
            §   En.

127   Quarterly statistical bulletin on coffee   (International Coffee Organisation).
            International Coffee Organisation, 22 Berners Street, London W1P 3DB.
            1977- $5 or $20 yr.
            Contains data on exports, imports, re-exports, supplies, prices, and selected background statistics.
            Time factor: each issue has data up to about six months prior to the date of the issue.
            §   En,   Es,   Fr,   Pt.

¶   B.ii,   continued

128   Annual bulletin of statistics   (International Tea Committee)
          International Tea Committee, Sir John Lyon House, 5 High Timber Street, Upper Thames Street,
              London EC4V 3NH.
          1946-   1978.   £25 (including supplement).   67 p.
          Contains data on area and production, exports, imports and consumption, stocks, auction prices, instant
              tea, etc.
          Time factor: the 1978 edition, published mid-1978, has data for several years to 1977.   The supplement
              was published in December 1978.
          §   En.

129   Monthly statistical summary   (International Tea Committee).
          International Tea Committee, Sir John Lyon House, 5 High Timber Street, Upper Thames Street,
              London EC4V 3NH.
          1946-   £15 yr.
          Contains data on planting, production, exports, imports, re-exports, stocks, monthly price quotations,
              consumption, and import duties.
          Time factor: up-dates the above title (128).
          §   En.

130   Tea statistics   (J Thomas and Company Private Ltd).
          J Thomas and Company Private Ltd, Nilhat House, 11 RN Mukherjee Road, PO Box 69, Calcutta 700001,
              India.
          1972-   Season 1975-1976.   not priced.   74 p.
          Contains data on area under production, production, sales, exports and consumption of tea.
          Time factor: the 1975/76 issue, with data for that crop year, was published mid-1976.
          §   En.

131   Hides and skins quarterly   (Commonwealth Secretariat).
          Commonwealth Secretariat, Marlborough House, Pall Mall, London SW1.
          Contains data on trade in cattle hides, calfskins, sheepskins, goatskins and leather.
          Time factor: ceased publication with the issue for the 4th quarter 1976.
          §   En.

132   Vegetable oils and oilseeds: a review of production, trade, utilisation and prices relating to groundnuts,
              cottonseed, linseed, soya beans, coconut oil and palm oil productions, olive oil, and other oilseeds
              and oils   (Commonwealth Secretariat).
          Commonwealth Secretariat, Marlborough House, Pall Mall, London SW1.
          1965/66-   Vol 23, 1973.   £3.50.   215 p.
          Time factor: ceased publication with the 1973 issue.
          §   En.

133   Annual review of oilseeds, oils, oilcakes, and other commodities   (Frank Fehr & Co Ltd).
          Frank Fehr & Co Ltd, 64 Queen Street, London EC4R 1ER.
          (annual)   1977.   not priced.   77 p.
          Following a general review there is data for each of the commodities dealt with by the firm, including
              prices, production, imports, exports, etc.
          Time factor: the 1977 issue, published mid-1978, has data for several years to 1976 and 1977
              (preliminary).
          §   En.

¶ B.ii,   continued

134   World oils and fats statistics (Economic and Statistics Dept, Unilever Ltd, for the International Association
                o f Seed Crushers)

        Unilever Ltd, Unilever House, London EC4P 4BQ.
        1966/67- 1972/75.   £5.   14 p.
        Contains a world summary; world production of types of oils and fats, producing areas, and production of
                oilcake and meat; European vegetable oil supplies; a summary of world exports; and world exports.
        Time factor: the 1972/75 issue, with data for those years, was published mid-1976.
        §   En.

135   Producción y comercio exterior de grasias y aceites vegetales en America Latina   [Production and foreign
                trade of vegetable oils and oilseeds in Latin America] (CEPAL)
        United Nations Economic Commission for Latin America, United Nations Building, Avenida Dag
                Hammarskjold 3030, PO Box 179-D, Santiago, Chile.
                        not priced.   57 p.
        Time factor: published in 1978, the report has data for 1961 to 1976.
        §   Es.

136   Tobacco intelligence   (Commonwealth Secretariat)
        Commonwealth Secretariat, Marlborough House, Pall Mall, London SW1.
                quarterly.   £3 or £12 yr.
        Contains data for manufactured tobacco, including a general review and a country review, with
                information on area and production, foreign trade, consumption, sales, prices, etc.
        Time factor: ceased publication with the issue for the 4th quarter 1976.
        §   En.

137   Edible nut statistics   (Gill & Duffus Ltd)
        Gill & Duffus Ltd, 23 St Dunstan's Hill, London EC3R 8HR.
                quarterly.   not priced.
        Contains statistics of crops, imports, exports and edible nut kernel prices.
        Time factor: each issue has long runs of annual and monthly figures to the date of the issue or the latest
                data available, and is published in the month of the issue.
        §   En.

        Note: there is also an 'Edible nut market report'.

138   Rubber statistical bulletin   (International Rubber Study Group)
        International Rubber Study Group, Brettenham House, 5-6 Lancaster Place, London WC2E 7ET.
        1947- monthly.   £30; $55 yr.
        Contains statistics of production, consumption, stocks, exports and imports of natural, synthetic and
                reclaimed rubber, and end products.
        Time factor: each issue has data for about ten years and twelve months to three months prior to the date
                of the issue.
        §   En.

139   World rubber statistics habdbook   (International Rubber Study Group)
        International Rubber Study Group, Brettenham House, 5-6 Lancaster Place, London WC2E 7ET.
                Vol 1, 1946-1970.   £4.50; $8.   35 p.
        A historical base book to 138 above.
        Time factor: published in December 1974.
        §   En.

¶   B.ii,   continued

140   Yearbook of fishery statistics: catches and landings   (Food and Agriculture Organisation of the United
              Nations)
          FAO, via delle Terme di Caracalla, 00100 Roma, Italy; or from sales agents.
          1942-   Vol 44, 1977.   £7.80; $20.   343 p.
          Contains annual statistics on nominal catches on a world-wide basis, with detailed breakdowns by
              countries, by species, and by major fishing areas.
          Time factor: the 1977 edition, with data for several years to 1977, was published in 1978.
          §   En,   Es,   Fr.

141   Yearbook of fishery statistics: fishery commodities   (Food and Agriculture Organisation of the United
              Nations)
          FAO, via delle Terme di Caracalla, 00100 Roma, Italy; or from sales agents.
          1942-   Vol 43, 1976.   £7.80; $20.   336 p.
          Relates to production and international trade in fishery commodities.
          Time factor: the 1976 edition, published late 1977, has data for 1976 and some earlier years.
          §   En,   Es,   Fr.

142   Statistical bulletin   (International Commission for the Northwest Atlantic Fisheries)
          ICNAF, PO Box 638, Dartmouth, NS, Canada B2Y3Y9.
          1951-   1976.   Can$12   c 250 p.
          Contains data on commercial catches in the Northwest Atlantic area, including summaries of catches by
              species and country and detailed fishery statistics.
          Time factor: the 1976 issue, published late 1977, has summary data for the years 1960 to 1975 and
              detailed statistics for 1975.
          §   En.

143   Statistical yearbook   (International North Pacific Fisheries Commission)
          INPFC, 6640 Northwest Marine Drive, Vancouver, BC, Canada V6T1X2.
          1952-   1974.   not priced (limited distribution).   97 p.
          Contains summary statistics of catches, etc, in the North Pacific area.
          Time factor: the 1974 issue, published in 1977, has data for 1974.
          §   En.

144   International whaling statistics   (Norske Hvalraad [Committee for Whaling Statistics])
          Norske Hvalraad, Oslo.
          1930-   1976/77.   free on request.   19 p.
          Contains data on whaling results for various countries, including information on species, size, etc.
          Time factor: the 1977 issue, published in 1977, has data for the 1976/77 season.
          §   En.

145   Review of fisheries in OECD member countries   (Organisation for Economic Co-operation and Development)
          OECD, 2 rue André-Pascal, 75775 Paris Cedex 16, France.
          1967-   1977.   £4.90; $10; FrF 40.   246 p.
          A general survey of the more important international developments, and statistical tables for each OECD
              member country (including USA and Canada) on all aspects of the fisheries situation.
          §   En.

¶   B.ii,   continued

146   Yearbook of forest products (Food and Agriculture Organisation of the United Nations)
           FAO, via delle Terme di Caracalla, 00100 Roma, Italy; or from sales agents.
           1947- 1976   £7.80; $20.   449 p.
           Contains data on production and trade of all kinds of round-woods, sawnwoods, wood-based panels,
               wood-pulp, paper and board, and forest products.   Also includes direction of trade for the
               main classes.
           Time factor: the 1976 edition, published in 1978, has data for the years 1966 to 1976.
           §   En,   Es,   Fr.

           Note: for earlier statistics there is "World forest products statistics: a ten-year summary, 1954-1963"
               published in 1965.

147   World forest inventory   (Food and Agriculture Organisation of the United Nations)
           FAO, via delle Terme di Caracalla, 00100 Roma, Italy; or from sales agents.
           1948- 5th, 1963.   £0.65; $2.50; FrF 8.75.   113 p.
           Based on the results of censuses taken every five years, the inventory contains data on area, growing
               stock, forest per caput, including utilisation and removals.
           Time factor: the 1963 inventory was published in 1966.
           §   En,   Es,   Fr.

148   Food consumption statistics   (Organisation for Economic Co-operation and Development)
           OECD, 2 rue André-Pascal, 75775 Paris Cedex 16, France; or from sales agents.
           1954/56- 1970-1975.   £9.30; $19; FrF 76.   318 p.
           A full statistical review of the flow of each food product, including production, stocks, foreign trade,
               consumption, etc, and global food balances for each OECD member country, including USA and
               Canada.
           Time factor: the 1970-1975 edition, published mid-1978, has data for the years 1970 to 1975.
           §   En,   Fr.

149   Review of food consumption surveys (household food consumption by economic groups) (Food and Agriculture
               Organisation of the United Nations)
           FAO, via delle Terme di Caracalla, 00100 Roma, Italy; or from sales agents.
           1977- 1977.   Vol 1: $6.50.   2 vols.
                          Vol 2: in preparation
           Vol 1 covers Europe, North America and Oceania and vol 2 will cover Latin America, Africa, Far and
               Near East.   Contents are data from selected surveys in which household food consumption is
               classified by income, total expenditure or some indicators of economic status.
           Time factor: vol 1 was published in 1977.
           §   En.

     iii.   Industry

150   Yearbook of industrial statistics (United Nations Statistical Office)
           Publishing Service, United Nations, New York, NY 10017; or from sales agents.
           1938/61- 9th, 1976.   Vol 1: £19.50; $32.   2 vols.
                                  Vol 2: £19.50; $32.
           Vol 1, titled 'General industrial statistics', contains basic national data for each country and Vol 2,
               titled 'Commodity production data, 1967-1976', contains detailed information on world production
               of individual industrial commodities.
           Time factor: the 1976 edition, published in 1978, has data for several years to 1976 or the latest figures
               available in Vol 1, and for 1967-1976 in Vol 2.
           §   En.

           Note: earlier title was 'Growth of world industry'.

¶ B.iii,   continued

151   Industrial production: historical statistics   (Organisation for Economic Co-operation and Development).
          OECD, 2 rue André-Pascal, 75775 Paris Cedex 16, France; or from sales agents.
          1955/64- 1960-1975.   £4.40; $10; FrF 40.   296 p.
          Contains long-term monthly quarterly and annual indices of industrial production by sectional groups for
                OECD member countries, including USA and Canada, with similar coverage to the industrial
                production supplement to 'Main economic indicators' (062).   Up-dated from time to time by
                supplements.
          Time factor: the 1960-1975 edition, with data for those years, was published in 1976.
          §   En,   Fr.

152   Short term economic indicators for manufacturing industries   (Organisation for Economic Co-operation and
                Development).
          OECD, 2 rue André-Pascal, 75775 Paris Cedex 16, France; or from sales agents.
          1976-   11th issue, 1973-1978.   £3; $6.25; FrF 25.   120 p.
          The most recent indicators of the trends in the manufacturing industries, including indices of production,
                prices, deliveries, employment, unfilled and new orders.
          Time factor: Updated issues published every three or four months.
          §   En,   Fr.

153   Production index: ice cream and related products/United States and Canada with international section
                (International Association of Ice Cream Manufacturers).
          International Association of Ice Cream Manufacturers, 910 17th Street NW, Washington DC 20006, USA.
          1974- 1974. $2.50 to members; $5 to non-members.   28 p.
          Time factor: the 1974 issue, published in 1975, has data for 1974 and some earlier years.
          §   En.

154   International coal   (National Coal Association & Coal Exporters Association of the United States Inc).
          National Coal Association, 1130 17th Street NW, Washington DC 20036, USA.
          1976- 1977. $25; ($30 abroad).   free to members of the associations.   65 p.
          Contains data on world coal statistics (reserves, production, shipments, consumption, etc), United States
                coal in world trade, and coal statistics for selected countries.
          Time factor: the 1977 issue, published early 1978, has data for 1977 and some earlier years.
          §   En.

          Note: a successor to 'World coal trade'.

155   International coal trade   (US Bureau of Mines).
          US Bureau of Mines, 4800 Forbes Avenue, Pittsburgh, Pa 15213, USA.
          1931- monthly.   not priced.
          Contains textual summaries supported by tables and maps of the highlights of the solid fuels industry, by
                geographic areas.   Also, for selected countries, statistics of production, consumption, imports and
                exports, and ocean freight rates of coal.
          §   En.

156   The iron and steel industry   (Organisation for Economic Co-operation and Development)
          OECD, 2 rue André-Pascal, 75775 Paris Cedex 16, France; or from sales agents.
          1954- 1976.   £2.20; $4.50; FrF 18.   38 p.
          Contains data on the supply and demand, production, raw materials, supplies, manpower, prices and
                investment trends in the iron and steel industry in OECD member countries, including the USA and
                Canada.
          Time factor: the 1976 issue, published mid-1978, has data for 1976.
          §   En,   Fr.

¶ B.iii,   continued

157   International steel statistics   (British Steel Corporation)
       British Steel Corporation, 12 Addiscombe Road, Croydon CR9 3JH, England.
       1959- 1977.   not priced.
       Currently published in a number of separate booklets, some devoted to one country and some having data
           for two or three countries, containing statistical data on the production, imports and exports of the
           various types of iron and steel for every iron and steel producing country.
       Time factor: the booklets are issued as and when the information for the relevant country or countries
           becomes available.
       §   En.

158   World stainless steel statistics   (International Nickel Ltd).
       Metal Bulletin Books Ltd, 46 Wigmore Street, London W1H 0BJ.
       1974- 1976.   £28.   144 p.
       A comprehensive review of stainless steel production and international trade in the non-Communist
           countries of the world.
       Time factor: the 1976 edition, published in 1976, has data for several years to 1975.
       §   En.

159   The non-ferrous metals industry   (Organisation for Economic Co-operation and Development).
       OECD, 2 rue André-Pascal, 75775 Paris Cedex 16, France; or from sales agents.
       1954- 1976.   £1.70; $3; FrF 14.   40 p.
       Contains data on production and consumption, trade, first processing stage of the main non-ferrous metals
           for OECD member countries, including USA and Canada.
       Time factor: the 1976 issue, published late 1977, has data for 1976 and some earlier years.
       §   En, Fr.

160   Wood pulp and fibre statistics   (American Paper Institute Inc).
       American Paper Institute Inc, 260 Madison Avenue, New York, NY 10016.
       1937- 1976.   Free to API members.
                    $25 to non-members in North America for each volume; $40 for 2 vols.   2 vols.
                    $27.50 to non-members elsewhere for each volume; $45 for 2 vols.
       Book 1 deals with the USA and Canada and Book 2 with other countries.   Data on production, imports
           and exports by type are given for each country.
       Time factor: the 1976 edition, published late 1978, has long runs of figures to 1976.
       §   En.

161   Pulp and paper industry   (Organisation for Economic Co-operation and Development).
       OECD, 2 rue André-Pascal, 75775 Paris Cedex 16, France; or from sales agents.
       1954- 1976/77.   £4.90; $10; FrF 40.   132 p.
       A statistical report on the situation in the pulp and paper markets of the OECD member countries,
           including USA and Canada.
       Time factor: the 1976/77 edition, published early 1978, has data for 1976 and 1977 and trends for 1978.
       §   En, Fr.

162   Pulp and paper   (Organisation for Economic Co-operation and Development).
       OECD, 2 rue André-Pascal, 75775 Paris Cedex 16, France; or from sales agents.
       1974- quarterly.   £2 or £5.90 yr; $4 or $12 yr; FrF 16 or FrF 48 yr.
       Contains statistical tables on stocks of paper pulp and waste paper, pulp and paper production and trade,
           and shipments of market pulp.
       Time factor: each issue is published about four or five months after the end of the period covered.
       §   En, Fr.

¶   B.iii,   continued

163   Pulp and paper capacities...: survey   (Food and Agriculture Organisation of the United Nations)
         FAO, via delle Terme di Caracalla, 00100 Roma, Italy; or from sales agents.
         1976/81-   1977-1982.   not priced.   various pagings.
         One of the annexes to the report has data by countries.
         Time factor: the results of the 1977-1982 survey were published in 1977.
         §   En,   Es,   Fr.

164   Newsprint data - statistics of world demand and supply   (Canadian Pulp and Paper Association)
         Canadian Pulp and Paper Association, Sun Life Building, Montreal H3B 2X9, Quebec, Canada.
         1947-   1976.   not priced.   32 p.
         Time factor: the 1976 issue, published mid-1977, has data from 1962 to 1973 (provisional).
         §   En,   Fr.

165   Monthly newsprint statistics   (Canadian Pulp and Paper Association)
         Canadian Pulp and Paper Association, Sun Life Building, Montreal H3B 2X9, Quebec, Canada.
                          not priced.
         A 4 page booklet with data on production, shipments, etc, in Canada and USA of newsprint.
         §   En,   Fr.

166   The chemical industry   (Organisation for Economic Co-operation and Development)
         OECD, 2 rue André-Pascal, 75775 Paris Cedex 16, France; or from sales agents.
         1953-   1975.   £4.60; $9.50;   FrF 38.   122 p.
         General trends in the industry: production, demand, raw materials, employment, prices, investments,
            and foreign trade for OECD member countries, including USA and Canada.
         Time factor: the 1975 issue, published in January 1978, has data for 1975 and future trends.
         §   En,   Fr.

167   Annual fertilizer review   (Food and Agriculture Organisation of the United Nations)
         FAO, via delle Terme di Caracalla, 00153 Roma, Italy; or from sales agents.
         1951/54-   1977.   £3.25; $8.50.   115 p.
         Contains data on world production, consumption, trade, supply and prices of fertilizers (nitrogenous,
            phosphate and potash).
         Time factor: the 1977 edition, published in 1978, has long runs of figures to 1976/77.
         §   En,   notes and glossary also in Fr & Es.

168   The British Sulphur Corporation's statistical supplement...raw materials supply/demand...fertilizers
            supply/demand.
         British Sulphur Corporation, Parnell House, 25 Wilton Road, London SW1V 1NH.
         1970-   half yearly.   not priced.
         Contains data on world production of sulphur in all forms, by country; consumption, supply and demand;
            world sulphuric acid production, by country, supply and demand; world phosphate rock production
            and consumption, by country; world nitrogen fertilizer production and consumption, by country;
            world phosphate fertilizer production and consumption, by country; and world potash fertilizer
            production and consumption, by country.
         §   En.

169   The cement industry: statistics...trend   (Organisation for Economic Co-operation and Development)
         OECD, 2 rue André-Pascal, 75775 Paris Cedex 16, France; or from sales agents.
         1954-   1975-1976.   £1.50; $3;   FrF 12.   32 p.
         Includes data on employment, production capacity, consumption and prices, international trade, and
            investment programme for the industry in member countries, including USA and Canada.
         Time factor: the 1975-1976 issue, published in December 1976, has statistics for 1975 and trends for 1976.
         §   En,   Fr.

¶ B.iii, continued

170   Statistics on narcotic drugs (United Nations. International Narcotics Control Board).
           Publishing Service, United Nations, New York, NY 10017; or from sales agents.
           (annual) 1976. £5.20; $10. 100 p.
           Contains data in trends in licit movement of narcotic drugs, including raw materials (opium, poppy,
               morphine, codeine, heroin, etc), cannabis and cannabis resin, coca leaf, cocaine, and 'synthetic'
               drugs, by country.
           Time factor: the 1976 edition, published in 1978, has data for several years to 1976.

171   Estimated world requirements of narcotic drugs and estimates of world production of opium... (United Nations.
               International Narcotics Control Board).
           Publishing Service, United Nations, New York, NY 10017; or from sales agents.
           (annual) 1977. £3.25; $5. 67 p.
           Time factor: the 1977 edition, published in December 1976, is up-dated during the year by supplements
               as new information becomes available.
           § En, Es, Fr.

172   International textile review (McGraw-Hill Publications).
           McGraw-Hill, 457 National Press Building, Washington DC 20045, USA.
           1st [1978] [1978] $97 in USA; $117 elsewhere. loose-leaf.
           Outlines current statistics of the textile industry in 26 countries, including production, consumption, prices,
               employment, foreign trade, and national trade policies. Mainly textual, but includes some statistics
               and statistical tables.
           Time factor: published in 1979.
           § En.

173   Quarterly statistical review (Textile Statistics Bureau).
           Textile Statistics Bureau, 5th Floor, Royal Exchange, Manchester M2 7ER, England.
           1946- £3.50; $12 yr.
           Apart from detailed United Kingdom statistics, the review contains figures for world production of yarn and
               cloth, and world imports and exports.
           Time factor: each issue includes long runs of figures to the latest available on each subject or country.
           § En.

174   Textile industry in OECD countries (Organisation for Economic Co-operation and Development)
           OECD, 2 rue André-Pascal, 75775 Paris Cedex 16, France; or from sales agents.
           1953- 1976. £3; $6; FrF 24. 70 p.
           Contains data on production and trade for textile goods and raw materials in OECD member countries,
               including USA and Canada.
           Time factor: the 1976 issue, published mid-1978, has data for 1976 and some earlier years.
           § En, Fr.

175   Industrial fibres: a review of production, trade and consumption relating to wool, cotton and man-made fibres,
               silk, flax, jute, sisal and other hemps, mohair and kapok (Commonwealth Secretariat).
           Commonwealth Secretariat, Marlborough House, Pall Mall, London SW1.
           1966/67- vol 20, 1973. £3.25. 243 p.
           Time factor: the review ceased publication with the 1973 issue.
           § En.

¶ B.iii,   continued

176   Information sur les textiles synthétiques et cellulosiques [Information on man-made fibres] (Comité
           International de la Rayonne et des Fibres Synthétiques (CIRFS) [International Rayon and Synthetic
           Fibre Committee]).
       CIRFS, 29 rue de Courcelles, 75008 Paris, France.
       1969- 1978.   not priced.   180 p.
       Contains data on production, consumption and foreign trade in man-made fibres; production of dissolving
           pulp; national product and expenditure; labour; and population, for various countries including USA.
       Time factor: the 1978 edition, published in 1978, has data for 1977 and also one or two earlier years in
           some tables.
       §   En,   Fr,   De.

177   International man-made fibre production statistics   (International Textile Manufacturers' Federation).
       International Textile Manufacturers' Federation, Am Schanzengraben 29, CH-8039 Zürich, Switzerland.
           quarterly.   not priced.
       Contains data on production and stocks in producing areas, including USA, Mexico and Brazil.
       Time factor: each issue has data for several quarters to the quarter of the issue, and is published three or
           four months later.
       §   En.

178   Wool statistics   (Commonwealth Secretariat, International Wool Textile Organisation, and International Wool
           Study Group).
       Commonwealth Secretariat, Marlborough House, Pall Mall, London SW1.
       1947/48-   1975/76.   free to subscribers of 'Wool intelligence'.
       Contains the results of the annual wool questionnaire, and includes data on production, supplies, stocks,
           consumption, trade, etc, of raw wool, yarns, products, machinery, etc.
       Time factor: Publication ceased with the 1975/76 issue.
       §   En.

179   Wool intelligence   (Commonwealth Secretariat).
       Commonwealth Secretariat, Marlborough House, Pall Mall, London SW1.
           monthly.   £1.67 or £20 yr.
       Contained more recent data than 178 above.
       Time factor: ceased publication with the December 1976 issue.
       §   En.

180   Cotton - world statistics: quarterly bulletin of the International Cotton Advisory Committee.
       International Cotton Advisory Committee, South Agriculture Building, Washington DC 20250.
       1948- $9 yr to North American member countries; $10 to other member countries; $50 yr
                         to non-member countries.
       Contains world tables and country tables on the supply, distribution, production, consumption, imports and
           exports, stocks and prices of cotton.   Also production, imports and exports of cotton yarn, cotton
           cloth, and rayon cloth.
       Time factor: the latest figures available for each country are published.
       §   En.

       Note: 'Cotton: monthly review of the world situation' is included in the subscription.

181   International cotton industry statistics   (International Federation of Cotton and Allied Textile Industries).
       International Federation of Cotton and Allied Textile Industries, Am Schanzengraben 29, Postfach 289,
           CH-8039 Zürich, Switzerland.
       1958- 1976.   not priced.   27 p.
       Time factor: the 1976 issue, published late 1977, has data for several years to 1976.
       §   En.

¶   B.iii,   continued

182   The footwear, raw hides and skins and leather industry in OECD countries   (Organisation for Economic
                Co-operation and Development).
            OECD, 2 rue André Pascal, 75775 Paris Cedex 16, France; or from sales agents.
            1955-   1975-1976.   £2; $4;   FrF 16.   62 p.
            Contains data on trends in production, consumption, international trade, and prices.   Countries covered
                include USA and Canada.
            Time factor: the 1975-1976 issue, published in May 1977, has data for 1975 and trends for 1976.
            §   En,   Fr.

183   The engineering industries in OECD member countries: basic statistics   (Organisation for Economic
                Co-operation and Development).
            OECD, 2 rue André-Pascal, 75775 Paris Cedex 16, France; or from sales agents.
            1963/70-   1972-1975.   £2.50; $5;   FrF 20.   94 p.
            Contains basic data on the shipments of selected products; data on the principal factors of production
                (employment, added value, investments, wages and salaries, etc) of several important branches of
                the industry; and data on product groupings at current and constant prices.
            Time factor: the 1972-1975 edition, published mid-1977, has data for the years 1972 to 1975.
            §   En,   Fr.

184   Economic handbook of the machine tool industry   (National Machine Tool Builders Association).
            National Machine Tool Builders Association, 7901 Westpark Drive, McLean, Va 22101, USA.
            1969/70-   1978/79. $15.   266 p.
            Contains data on the national economy and machine tools, the world economy, the machine tool industry,
                machine tool shipments and orders, foreign trade, employment and earnings, finance, and machine
                tools in use.
            Time factor: the 1978/79 edition, published in 1978, has data to 1977.
            §   En.

185   Motor industry of Great Britain   (Society of Motor Manufacturers and Traders).
            SMMT, Forbes House, Halkin Street, London SW1X 7JF.
            1947-   1978.   £9.50 to members;   £17.50 to non-members.   289 p.
            Contains detailed statistics of production of cars, commercial vehicles, tractors, etc, in the United
                Kingdom and overseas, and foreign trade of the United Kingdom and overseas countries (including
                USA and Canada).
            Time factor: the 1978 edition, published late 1978, has data for 1977 and some earlier years.
            §   En.

186   World automotive market   (Automobile International)
            Automobile International, 386 Park Avenue South, New York, NY 10016.
            1966-   1978. $12.   48 p.
            Includes data on vehicle production (including Argentina, Brazil, Canada, Colombia, Mexico, Peru, USA
                and Venezuela), registrations of motor cars and trucks and buses by country, and import statistics of
                individual countries.
            Time factor: the 1978 edition, published in 1978, has data for several years to 1977.
            §   En.

187   World motor vehicle data   (Motor Vehicle Manufacturers' Association).
            Motor Vehicle Manufacturers' Association, 300 New Center Building, Detroit, Michigan 48202, USA.
            (annual)   1977. $20.   206 p.
            Contains data on world production, vehicle assembly, new registrations, imports, sales, etc.
            Time factor: the 1977 edition, published late 1977, has data for several years to 1976.
            §   En.

¶   B.iii,   continued

188   World motor vehicle and trailer production and registration   (US Industry and Trade Administration).
        Government Printing Office, Washington DC 20402, USA.
        1969/70-   1974/75. $0.35.
        Time factor: the 1974/75 issue, with data for the fiscal year, was published late 1978.
        §   En.

189   L'automobile dans le monde. De automobiel in de wereld   [The motor car in the world]   (Fabrimetal).
        Fabrimetal, rue des Drapiers 21, 1050 Bruxelles, Belgium.
            1977.   not priced.   139 p.
        Includes data on production, exports, registrations, people with cars, for the world, north America,
           Europe, Japan, and some other countries, including Argentina, Mexico and Peru.
        Time factor: the 1977 issue, published in 1978, has data for 1976 and 1977.
        §   Fr,   Nl.

190   World record markets   (EMI)
        Henry Melland Ltd, 23 Ridgmount Street, London WC1E 7AH.
        1968-   3rd, 1976.   £2.50.   110 p.
        Contains data on the numbers of record companies, recording studios, record labels, retail outlets, records
           manufactured, records imported, radio stations and receivers, television stations and receivers, etc.
        Time factor: the 1976 edition, published in 1976, has data for 1975.
        §   En.

     iv.   Construction

191   Yearbook of construction statistics   (United Nations Statistical Office).
        Publishing Service, United Nations, New York, NY 10017; or from sales agents.
        1963/72-   1967/76.   £14.30; $18.   296 p.
        Contains data by country, including data on all buildings, residential buildings, non-residential buildings,
           commercial buildings, other buildings, employment, wages and salaries, value of construction, costs,
           etc.
        Time factor: the 1967/76 edition, published in 1978, had data for the years 1967 to 1976.
        §   En.

     v.   Energy

192   World energy supplies   (United Nations Statistical Office).
        Publishing Service, United Nations, New York, NY 10017; or from sales agents.
        1952-   1972-1976. $14; £9.10.   261 p.
        A study on energy supplies, which includes statistics on production, trade and consumption of solid fuels,
           crude petroleum, petroleum products, gaseous fuels, electrical energy, nuclear fuels, and non-
           commercial fuels, for approximately 150 countries, with regional and global totals.
        Time factor: the 1972-1976 edition, published in 1978, has data for the years 1972 to 1976.
        §   En.

193   World energy conference: survey of energy resources...   (Oak Ridge National Laboratory, US Atomic Energy
        Commission).
        United States National Committee of the World Energy Conference, 345 East 47th Street, New York,
           NY 10017 and WEC, Central Office, 5 Bury Street, London SW1Y 6AB.
        1929-   1974.   not priced.   400 p & 7 pages of maps.
        Contains statistical data on solid fuels; crude oil, natural gas and natural gas liquids; oil shale and

[continued next page]

AMERICA,   continued

¶   B.v,   continued

193,   continued.
        bituminous sands; hydraulic resources; nuclear resources; and other renewable resources, for each
        country.
        Time factor: a survey is taken every six or seven years and the 1974 results were published in 1974.
        §   En.

194   Energy statistics   (Organisation for Economic Co-operation and Development).
        OECD, 2 rue André-Pascal, 75775 Paris Cedex 16, France; or from sales agents.
        1950/64- 1974-1976.   £5.50; $11.25; FrF 45.   192 p.
        Contains data on energy production, trade, stock changes, bunkers, transformation and consumption, as
        well as detailed analysis by end use, for OECD member countries, including USA and Canada.
        Time factor: the 1974-1976 edition, published early 1978, has data for the years 1974 to 1976.
        §   En,   Fr.

195   Energy balances of OECD member countries   (Organisation for Economic Co-operation and Development).
        OECD, 2 rue André-Pascal, 75775 Paris Cedex 16, France; or from sales agents.
        1969/74- 1974-1976.   £4.40; $9; FrF 36.   130 p.
        Includes data on energy supply, demand and transformation, and end use.
        Time factor: the 1974-1976 edition, published early 1978, has data for the years 1974 to 1976.
        §   En,   Fr.

196   Energia ed idrocarburi: sommario statistico   [Energy and hydrocarbon fuels: statistical summary]
        (ENI: Ente Nazionale Idrocarburi)
        Ente Nazionale Idrocarburi, Piazzale E Mattei 1, 00144 Roma, Italy.
        1955/74- 1976.   not priced.   315 p.
        Contains data on economic indicators, world energy consumption, fuel energy consumption, reserves and
        production of oil and gas, refining, imports and consumption of hydrocarbons, transport of
        hydrocarbons, prices of crude oil and petroleum products, nuclear energy - uranium reserves and
        production, nuclear energy - installed capacity, nuclear power production, orders for nuclear power
        generating stations, world reserves of solid fuels, and Italian national statistics.
        Time factor: the 1976 edition, published in 1977, has data for several years to 1975.
        §   It,   contains an index and glossary in English.

197   Pétrole...elements statistiques...activité de l'industrie pétrolière   [Petroleum...statistics...activities of
        the industry]   (Comité Professionnel du Pétrole).
        Comité Professionnel du Pétrole, 51 blvd de Courcelles, 75008 Paris, France.
        1974- 1976.   not priced.   381 p.
        Mainly concerned with activities in France, but also has a section on world data (production, consumption,
        activities, frozen reserves, refining, pipe-lines, etc) and total figures (not for individual countries)
        for the overseas departments and territories of France.
        Time factor: the 1976 issue was published mid-1977.
        §   Fr.

198   Annual statistical bulletin   (Organisation of the Petroleum Exporting Countries)
        OPEC, Dr Karl-Lueger-Ring 10, 1010 Wien, Austria.
        1973- 1976.   öS 100.   180 p.
        Contains data on producing wells and wells completed; production of natural gas and crude oil; refining,
        consumption of refined products; OPEC member countries exports of crude oil and refined products;
        world trade in natural gas, crude oil and refined products; tanker fleets and tanker fleet rates; major
        pipelines in OPEC member countries; posted prices; oil revenues; and the financial situation of major
        oil companies.   Countries include Venezuela and Ecuador.
        Time factor: the 1976 edition, published in 1977, has data to 1976.
        §   En.

¶ B.v, continued

199   B P statistical review of the world oil industry   (British Petroleum Co Ltd).
       British Petroleum Company Ltd, Britannic House, Moor Lane, London EC2Y 9BU.
       (annual)   1977.   not priced.   32 p.
       Contains data on reserves, production, consumption, trade, refining, tankers and energy.
       Time factor: the 1977 edition, published in 1978, has data for several years to 1977.
       § En.

200   Oil statistics: supply and disposal   (Organisation for Economic Co-operation and Development).
       OECD, 2 rue André-Pascal, 75775 Paris Cedex 16, France; or from sales agents.
       1961-   1976.   £6.70; $13; FrF 55.   280 p.
       Contains data on supply and disposal of crude oil, feedstocks, components and petroleum products;
            sources of imports; processing of crude oil, feedstocks, and natural gas; refinery output and
            consumption of main petroleum products in OECD member countries, including USA and Canada.
       Time factor: the 1976 edition, published late 1977, has data for 1976.
       § En,   Fr.

201   Quarterly oil statistics   (Organisation for Economic Co-operation and Development).
       OECD, 2 rue André-Pascal, 75775 Paris Cedex 16, France; or from sales agents.
       1964-   £4.90 or £14.60 yr; $10 or $30 yr;   FrF 40 or FrF 120 yr.
       Up-dates 200 above.
       Time factor: each issue is published about four months after the end of the quarter to which it refers.
       § En,   Fr.

202   Outlook for world oil into the 21st century   (Petroleum Industry Research Foundation Inc).
       Electric Power Research Institute, 3412 Hillview Avenue, Palo Alto, California 94304, USA.
                  not priced.   various pagings.
       Attempts to forecast oil supply and demand in the non-Communist world for 1976 to 1990 and from 1990
            to 2005.   Statistical tables are included in the text.
       Time factor: published in 1978.
       § En.

203   International petroleum annual   (US Bureau of Mines).
       Bureau of Mines, Washington DC 20241, USA.
                  1975.   free.   37 p.
       Includes data on production, refining, supply and demand of crude petroleum and refined products,
            imports and exports, etc.
       Time factor: the 1975 issue, published in 1977, has data for 1975 and some earlier years.
       § En.

204   World offshore oil and gas: a review of offshore activity and an assessment of worldwide market prospects for
                  offshore exploration/products equipment and materials   (Scottish Council (Development & Industry))
       Scottish Council, 15 Union Terrace, Aberdeen, AB1 1NJ, Scotland.
                  £21.50.   210 p.
       Time factor: published in 1975.
       § En.

205   Petroleum economist   (Petroleum Press Bureau Ltd).
       Petroleum Press Bureau Ltd, 5 Pemberton Row, Regent Street, London EC4A 3DP.
       1934-   monthly.   £26 in the UK; $60 in Europe; $56 rest of world yr.
       Some statistical tables are included in the articles, and there are regular tables on world oil production,
            prices, and oil share quotations.
       § En, Fr, and Japanese eds.

¶   B.v,   continued

206   Know more about oil: world statistics   (Institute of Petroleum).
             Institute of Petroleum, 61 New Cavendish Street, London W1M 8AR.
             (annual)   August 1976.   £0.10.   10 p.
             Contains statistics of production, refining, capacity, consumption, tanker tonnage, etc, pf po; by
                  countries.
             Time factor: the August 1976 issue, published in August 1976, has data for several years to 1975.
             §   En.

207   Twentieth century petroleum statistics   (DeGolyer and MacNaughton).
             De Golyer and MacNaughton, One Energy Square, Dallas, Texas 75206, USA.
             1945-   1978. $15.   105 p.
             Presents statistics in graphs and tables on world-wide petroleum reserves, production, prices, imports,
                  refinery capacity, consumption, drilling, etc.
             Time factor: the 1978 issue, published late 1978, has long runs of figures to 1977.
             §   En.

208   Resources for the future   (Joel Darmstadter et al).
             Johns Hopkins University Press, Baltimore and London.
                             $25.   800 p.
             Examines historical trends between 1925-1965 of trade, consumption and production of solid fuels, liquid
                  fuels, natural gas and electric energy.
             Time factor: published in 1972.
             §   En.

209   Reserves of crude oil, natural gas liquids, and natural gas in the United States and Canada, and United States
                  production capacity   (American Gas Association Inc, American Petroleum Institute, and Canadian
                  Petroleum Association).
             American Gas Association Inc, 1515 Wilson Boulevard, Arlington, Va 22209; American Petroleum Institute,
                  1801 K Street NW, Washington DC 20006, USA; or Canadian Petroleum Association, 330 Ninth
                  Avenue SW, Calgary, Alberta, Canada.
             1947-   1971. $3.50.   273 p.
             Includes data by states of the USA and by provinces of Canada.
             Time factor: the 1971 edition, published in May 1971, has data to 1969 or 1970.
             §   En.

210   The electricity supply industry in OECD countries...and prospects...   (Organisation for Economic Co-operation
                  and Development)
             OECD, 2 rue André-Pascal, 75775 Paris Cedex 16, France; or from sales agents.
             1959/66-   1974-1976.   £4.40; $9; FrF 30.   188 p.
             A general review, including data on production, consumption, production capacity, investment, and fuel
                  consumption by the power plants for OECD member countries, including USA and Canada.
             Time factor: the 1974-1976 edition, published in May 1978, has data for 1974 to 1976 and prospects for
                  1980-1985-1990.
             §   En,   Fr.

211   ...Survey of electric power equipment   (Organisation for Economic Co-operation and Development).
             OECD, 2 rue André-Pascal, 75775 Paris Cedex 16, France; or from sales agents.
             1948-   27th, 1974.   £2.90; $6.50; FrF 26.   156 p.
             Covers trends in deliveries and orders and gives a general picture of the achievements and prospects in the
                  industry.   Includes data on USA and Canada.
             Time factor: the 1974 edition, published late 1975, has data on trends for future years.
             §   En,   Fr.

¶   B.v,   continued

212   World electric power industry   (N B Goyol).
          University of California Press, Berkeley, California, USA.
                    $30.   366 p
          162-country study of the electric power industry which includes statistical presentation of uses of
                electricity by industry, electric loads, electricity used per capita, etc.
          Time factor: published in 1969, the volume includes data for the years 1958 to 1964.
          §   En.

213   World natural gas   (US Bureau of Mines: Division of Petroleum and Natural Gas).
          Bureau of Mines, Washington DC 20241, USA.
                    free.   10 p.
          Time factor: published in 1976, the report contains data for the years 1968 to 1974.
          §   En.

¶   C   -   External trade

214   Yearbook of international trade statistics   (United Nations Statistical Office)
          Publishing Services, United Nations, New York, NY 10017; or from sales agents.
          1950-   1976. $50 or £39 for two volumes.   2 vols.
          Provides the basic information for individual countries' external trade performance in terms of overall
                trends in current value as well as in volume and price, the importance of trading partners and the
                significance of individual commodities imports and exports.   Volume 1 deals with trade by country;
                volume 2 with trade by commodity, with commodity matrix tables,
          Time factor: the 1976 edition, published in 1977, has data for 1976.
          §   En.

215   Commodity trade statistics   (United Nations Statistical Office).
          Publishing Services, United Nations, New York, NY 10017; or from sales agents.
          fortnightly.   £1.95 each; $3 or $64 yr.
          Issued in fascicules of about 250 pages each as quarterly data becomes available from the reporting
                countries.   Each country's imports and exports are shown in the 625 sub-groups of the SITC, sub-
                divided by countries of origin and destination.   Values in each case are converted to US$, and
                quantities are in metric units.   In the front of each fascicule is an index showing in which issues
                appeared the latest data for each country.   American reporting countries are Argentina, Canada,
                Colombia, Costa Rica, French Guiana, Guadeloupe, Honduras, Martinique, Netherlands Antilles,
                Nicaragua, Puerto Rico, Trinidad and Tobago, USA and Venezuela, with others as trading partners.
          Time factor: varies for each country.   Data is cumulated January-March, January-June, January-
                September and January-December.   January-March is not always published.
          §   En.

216   World trade annual   (Walker & Co, by agreement with the United Nations Statistical Office).
          Walker & Company, 720 Fifth Avenue, New York, NY 10019.
          1963-   1973. $33 each volume; 5 supplementary volumes, $75.90 each.
          The main volumes contain statistics of foreign trade in each of 1312 items of the SITC as reported by 24
                principal countries, the data being arranged in commodity order and sub-divided by countries of
                origin and destination.   Vol I relates to food, beverages, crude inedible materials except fuel,
                animal and vegetable oils and fats; Vol II to mineral fuels, lubricants and related materials, and
                chemicals; Vol III to manufactured goods classified chiefly by material; Vol IV to miscellaneous
                manufactured articles; and Vol V to machinery and transport equipment, and commodities and
                transactions not classified according to kind.   Supplementary volumes are also published dealing
                with the trade of Eastern Europe and the developing countries.   Volume II of the supplementary
                volumes contains detailed foreign trade statistics for individual countries of South and Central America,

[continued next page]

216,   continued

including the Caribbean and Bermuda, as reported by the 24 principal trading countries.   The prime
purpose of the supplementary volumes is to serve those who are interested in individual countries for
which trade statistics are not easily available in internationally comparable form.   Values are given
in US$ and quantities in metric units.
Time factor: the 1973 edition contains data for 1973.
§   En.

217   Handbook of international trade and development statistics.   (UNCTAD)
Publishing Service, United Nations, New York, NY 10017; or from sales agents.
1964-   1976.   £14.40; $24.   673 p.
        1977 supplement   £12.35; $22.   400 p.
Intended to provide a complete basic collection of statistical data relevant to the analysis of problems of
world trade and development, for the use of UNCTAD, etc.   Contents are:
        Part 1   Value of world trade by regions and countries, 1950-1975
        Part 2   Volume, unit value, and terms of trade index numbers by regions; commodity prices
        Part 3   Network of world trade; summary by selected regions of origin and destination and structure
                of imports and exports by selected commodity groups.
        Part 4   Imports and exports for individual countries by commodity structure, and major exports of
                developing countries by leading exporters
        Part 5   Financial flows, aid and balance of payments for developing countries
        Part 6   Some basic indicators of development
        Part 7   Special studies
        Annex A   Network of world exports by selected commodity classes and regions of origin and
                destination, 1955-1974
            B   Ranking of countries and territories according to per capita GNP
Time factor: the 1976 edition, published in 1976, generally has data for 1974 and some earlier years;
        the 1977 supplement up-dates the information.
§   En,   Fr.

218   Review of international trade and development (UNCTAD)
Publishing Service, United Nations, New York, NY 10017; or from sales agents.
1967-   1975.   £3.60; $6.   109 p.
Part 1 of the review provides an analysis of the recent economic experiences of developing countries in
        relation to the goals and objectives of the International Development Strategy, while part 2 contains
        a review of the implementation of measures envisaged in the strategy.   Tables are included in the
        text.
§   En.

219   Trade in manufactures of developing countries and territories (UNCTAD)
Publishing Service, United Nations, New York, NY 10017; or from sales agents.
1968-   1974.   £3.60; $6.   106 p.
Part 1 is a review of recent trends in trade in manufactures of developing countries and territories.   Part
        2 deals with trade in textiles of the developing countries in the context of international arrangements
        and of the world energy situation.
Time factor: the 1974 edition, published in 1976, has data for 1972 and earlier years in some tables.
§   En.

¶   C,   continued

220   International trade   (General Agreement on Tariffs and Trade).
  GATT, Palais des Nations, 1211 Genève 10, Switzerland.
  (annual) 1977/78.   £9.45; $18;   SFr 27.   171 p.
  The report is concerned with main trends in international trade, trade in commodities, trade in industrial
    areas, trade in non-industrial areas, and trade of the eastern trading areas.   Statistical tables are
    included in the text.
  Time factor: the 1977/78 edition, published in 1978, covers the years 1973 to 1977.
  §   En.

221   Direction of trade   (International Monetary Fund & International Bank for Reconstruction and Development)
  International Monetary Fund, Washington DC 20431; or from sales agents.
  1958/62-   11 monthly issues with annual summary.   £0.97; $3;   £10.40; $10 yr.
  Contains data on the value of trade with other countries in US$, both imports and exports.
  Time factor: up to dateness varies from country to country, but each issue contains data for the two
    latest months available and comparative figures for the previous year.
  §   En.

222   World invisible trade   (Committee on Invisible Exports)
  Committee on Invisible Exports, 7th floor, Stock Exchange, London EC2N 1HP.
  1966-   1977.   £2.   32 p.
  Time factor: the 1977 issue, published in August 1977, has data for 1975 and some earlier years.
  §   En.

223   Statistiques du commerce extérieur des départements d'outre-mer: importations - exportations   [Foreign trade
    statistics of overseas departments: imports - exports] (Direction Générale des Douanes)
  Centre de Renseignements Statistiques, 182 rue Saint-Honoré, 75001 Paris, France.
  1938/45-   1971.   not priced.   949 p.
  Includes statistics of foreign trade for Martinique, Guyane and Guadeloupe.
  Time factor: the 1971 issue has data for the year 1971.
  §   Fr.

224   Statistiques du commerce extérieur: départements d'outre-mer. Résultats trimestriels   [Foreign trade statistics
    of overseas departments. Quarterly results] (Direction Générale des Douanes)
  Centre de Renseignements Statistiques, 182 rue Saint-Honoré, 75001 Paris, France.
  1968-   not priced.
  Includes statistics of foreign trade for Martinique, Guyane and Guadeloupe, showing detailed trade by
    product and by country.
  Time factor: ceased publication with 1970 issue.
  §   Fr.

225   EC trade with the ACP states and the south Mediterranean states   (Eurostat)
  Office des Publications Officielles des Communautés Européennes, B P 1003, Luxembourg; or from sales
    agents.
  1979-   quarterly.   £2 50; $4.90;   BFr 150 yr.
  Contains data on trade of the European Communities with individual countries.   Data is for the EC as a
    whole and includes developing American countries by country.
  Time factor: each issue has data for several quarters to about six months prior to the quarter of the issue
    or the latest data available.
  §   En,   Fr.

¶   C,   continued

226   The Commonwealth in world trade (Commonwealth Economic Committee)
          Commonwealth Secretariat, Marlborough House, Pall Mall, London SW1.
          1962- 1973/74. £3. 138 p.
          Includes statistical data on the total trade of Commonwealth countries, trade of Commonwealth countries
               with the UK, and trade of individual Commonwealth countries (including Canada, Grenada, Guyana,
               Jamaica, and Trinidad and Tobago).
          Time factor: the 1973/74 issue, published in 1975, covers the period 1969 to 1973.   This was the final
               issue.
          §   En.

227   Digest of external trade statistics   (East Caribbean Common Market).
          East Caribbean Common Market, Dutchman Bay, Antigua.
          1976- 1976. $5. 69 p.
          Contains summary tables and data on trade among ECCM member states, trade between ECCM member
               states and the rest of the Caribbean, direction of trade of ECCM member states, and trade by SITC
               section of ECCM member states.
          Time factor: the 1976 issue, published in 1978, refers mainly to data for the years 1970 to 1976.
          §   En.

228   Anuario estadístico centroaméricano de comercio exterior   [Annual foreign trade statistics of Central America]
          (SIECA)
          SIECA, 4a Avenida 10-25, zona 14, Apartado postal 1237, Guatemala, CA.
          1964- 1972. $CA 10. 1099 p.
          Main tables show detailed statistics of imports and exports arranged by commodity and subdivided by
               countries of origin and destination, for Guatemala, El Salvador, Honduras, Nicaragua, Costa Rica,
               Panama and totals for Central America.
          Time factor: the 1972 issue, published in 1974, has data for 1972.
          §   Es.

229   Integración en cifras   [Integration in figures] (SIECA)
          SIECA, 4a avenida 10-25, zona 14, Apartado postal 1237, Guatemala, CA.
          1972- monthly. $CA 1.25 or from $CA 7 to $CA 11 yr depending on destination.
          Brief data on inter central American trade and the trade of particular countries.
          §   Es.

230   ACP: yearbook of foreign trade statistics (Eurostat)
          Office des Publications Officielles des Communautés Européennes, BP 1003, Luxembourg; or from sales
               agents.
          1968/73- 1968-1976. £9.60; $18.60; FrB 600. 980 p.
          A summary of trade flows of the African, Caribbean and Pacific (ACP) countries, signatories of the Lomé
               convention, including Bahamas, Barbados, Grenada, Guyana, Jamaica, and Trinidad and Tobago.
               Contents include chapters on the ACP countries and world trade, ACP country tables, and the
               European Communities and the ACP.
          Time factor: the 1968-1976 issue was published late 1977 and has data for the years 1968 to 1976.
          §   En,   Fr.

231   A digest of trade statistics of Caribbean Community member states (Caribbean Community).
          Caribbean Community Secretariat, Third Floor, Bank of Guyana Building, Avenue of the Republic,
               Georgetown, Guyana.
          1976- 1978.
          Time factor: the 1978 revision was due for publication in 1978.
          §   En.

¶   C,   continued

232   Statistics of foreign trade: series A: monthly bulletin   (Organisation for Economic Co-operation and
              Development).
           OECD, 2 rue André-Pascal, 75775 Paris Cedex 16, France; or from sales agents.
           1950-   £2.20 or £21.60 yr; $4.50 or $45 yr;   FrF 18 or FrF 180 yr.
           Contains seasonally adjusted foreign trade indicators, indices of average value and volume, trade of
              member countries (including USA and Canada) by sections of the SITC, and data on the foreign trade
              of the OECD member countries.
           Time factor: each issue has annual data for the last two years, quarterly data for the last three years, and
              monthly data for the last six months to three or four months prior to the date of the issue.
           §   En,   Fr.

233   Statistics of foreign trade: series B: annual: tables by reporting countries   (Organisation for Economic
              Co-operation and Development).
           OECD, 2 rue André-Pascal, 75775 Paris Cedex 16, France; or from sales agents.
           1950-   1978.   £14.60; $30;   FrF 120 for four volumes.   4 vols.
           Contains statistics of foreign trade flows by member countries (including USA and Canada) with 40-50
              countries or geographic zones for approximately 150 products or groups of products.
           Time factor: the 1978 issue, in the new format, is to be published in 1979.
           §   En,   Fr.

234   Statistics of foreign trade: series C: annual: tables by commodities   (Organisation for Economic Co-operation
              and Development).
           OECD, 2 rue André-Pascal, 75775 Paris Cedex 16, France: or from sales agents.
           1950-   1977.   £14.60; $30;   FrF 120 for 2 volumes.   2 vols.
           Contains detailed statistics for principal products of the SITC (Standard International Trade Classification).
           Time factor: the 1977 edition, in the new format, is to be published in 1979.
           §   En,   Fr.

235   Microtables imports - exports of OECD countries   (Organisation for Economic Co-operation and Development)
           OECD, 2 rue André-Pascal, 75775 Paris Cedex 16, France; or from sales agents.
                                 Imports   £60; $125;   FrF 500   approx 120 microfiches a year.
                                 Exports   £73; $150;   FrF 600
                       complete series   £120; $250;   FrF 1000
                       (selective subscription for data for one or several countries also available)
           An express service by microfiche of annual statistics relating to the overall trade of member countries,
              including USA and Canada.
           §   En,   Fr.

236   Trade yearbook   (Food and Agriculture Organisation of the United Nations)
           FAO, via delle Terme di Caracalla, 00100 Roma, Italy; or from sales agents.
           1947-   1976.   £5.20; $13.50.   354 p.
           Contains data on imports and exports of agricultural commodities and agricultural requisites, classified by
              SITC, for each reporting country.   Data is in US$ and metric quantities.
           Time factor: the 1976 edition, published mid-1977, contains data for varying periods to 1976.
           §   En,   Es,   Fr.

237   World grain trade statistics: exports by source and destination (Food and Agriculture Organisation of the UN).
           FAO, via delle Terme di Caracalla, 00100 Roma, Italy; or from sales agents.
           1954/56-   1973/74.   £1.60; $4.   78p.
           Contains data on world trade in grain, grain exports by source and destination, trade in grains of centrally
              planned countries, trade in grains by regions and selected countries, recent international grain trade
              contracts and world trade in wheat and coarse grains.
           Time factor: the 1973/74 edition, published in 1975, has data for 1973 or for 1973/74 provisionally.
           §   En,   Es,   Fr.

¶   C,   continued

238   World whisky market   (Economic Associates).
            Economic Associates Ltd, Sceptre House, 169 Regent Street, London W1.
                    6th ed, 1965-1977.   not priced.   32 p.
            Includes a statistical section on the world whisky market, 1965-71; whisky exports by country, 1965-71;
                whisky exports by type, 1971; and principal markets by type, 1971.
            Time factor: published in 1972.
            §   En.

239   Bulletin of statistics on world trade in engineering products   (United Nations Economic Commission for Europe)
            Publishing Service, United Nations, New York, NY 10017; or from sales agents.
            1963-   1976.   £14.30; $19.   395 p.
            Shows the flow of engineering products in world trade.
            Time factor: the 1976 issue, published in 1978, has data for 1976.
            §   En,   Fr,   Ru.

240   Statistics of world trade in steel   (United Nations: Economic Commission for Europe).
            Publishing Service, United Nations, New York, NY 10017; or from sales agents.
            1913/59-   1977.   £3.25; $5.   73 p.
            Contains data on the exports of the various semi-finished and finished steel products by regions and
                countries of destination.   Exporting countries include USA but many American countries are listed
                as importers.
            §   En,   Fr,   Ru.

241   Exporters' guide to the wool textile markets of the world   (National Wool Textile Export Corporation).
            National Wool Textile Export Corporation, Lloyds Bank Chambers, 43 Hustlergate, Bradford BD1 1PE,
                England.
                    6th, 1977/78.   free.   c 100 p.
            Contains data on domestic production, imports and exports of tops, yarn and cloth for each country.
            Time factor: the 1977/78 edition, published early 1978, has data for 1976 and some earlier years.   A
                supplement is published to up-date the guide and further up-dating is accomplished by publishing the
                necessary amendments in the Corporation's bi-monthly 'Newsletter'.
            §   En.

242   Annual bulletin of trade in chemical products   (United Nations: Economic Commission for Europe).
            Publishing Service, United Nations, New York, NY 10017; or from sales agents.
            1973-   1977.   £10.40; $16.   315 p.
            Contains detailed breakdown of trade in chemical products, arranged by commodities and subdivided by
                countries of origin and destination.
            Time factor: the 1977 issue, published in December 1978, has data for 1977.
            §   En,   Fr,   Ru.

        ¶   D - Internal distribution and service trades

243   Fachserie Auslandsstatistik.   Reihe 5: Preise und Preisindizes im Ausland [Foreign statistics series.   Series 5
                prices and price indices in foreign countries]   (Statistisches Bundesamt).
            W Kohlhammer GmbH, Postfach 42 11 20, 6500 Mainz 42, Federal Republic of Germany.
                    monthly.   DM 3.50 each issue.
            Time factor: each issue has data for the period of the issue and the current year to date, and also
                averages for the past few years.
            §   De.

¶   D,   continued

244   Retail trade international   (Euromonitor Publications Ltd).
          Euromonitor Publications Ltd, PO Box 115, 41 Russell Square, London WC1B 5DL.
          1977/78-   1977/78.   £55.   260 p.
          Contains data on the number of retail outlets, retail trade by organisation and type of outlet, retail sales
              by product, distribution by commodity, and there is a directory of leading retailers for a large
              number of countries including Brazil, Canada, Mexico and USA.
          Time factor: the 1977/78 edition, published in 1978, has data for 1971 or 1972 to 1977.
          §   En.

245   Consumer markets in Latin America   (Euromonitor Publications Ltd).
          Euromonitor Publications Ltd, PO Box 115, 41 Russell Square, London WC1B 5DL.
                    £55.   297 p.
          Contains data on Argentina, Brazil, Bolivia, Chile, Colombia, Ecuador, Mexico, Panama, Paraguay,
              Peru, Uruguay, Venezuela and Central America.   The analysis for each country is (1) basic
              marketing situation (basic marketing parameters, demographic and regional development, employment
              situation, economic indicators, finance and investment, political structure, resources, industrial
              development, trade and standard of living) and (2) the division of consumer markets into main
              commodity groups (food, alcoholic beverages, tobacco, pharmaceuticals, cosmetics and toiletries,
              household chemicals, textiles, clothing and footwear, electronic equipment, electrical appliances,
              and passenger cars).
          Time factor: published in 1978, the volume generally covers the years 1970/71 to 1975/76.
          §   En.

246   Tobacco consumption in various countries   (P N Lee).
          Tobacco Research Council, Glen House, Stag Place, London SW1E 5AG.
          1963-   4th, 1975.   not priced.   86 p.
          Issued as 'Research paper no 6', the document contains statistics of consumption of cigarettes, cigars,
              cigarillos, smoking tobacco, snuff, population, and consumption per adult for each country.
          Time factor: the 1975 edition has long runs of statistics to 1972, 1973 or 1974, depending on the country
              and availability of the data.
          §   En.

247   World travel statistics   (World Tourism Organisation).
          Organisation Mundial del Turismo, Avda del Generalísimo 59, Madrid 16, Spain.
          1947-   1977.   not priced.   looseleaf.
          Arranged by country, and contains data of visitors and tourists arriving, foreign visitors arriving, cruise
              passengers, by country of residence, length of stay, rooms and hotels, receipts and expenditures.
          Time factor: the 1977 edition, published in 1978, with pages added as information becomes available)
              has data for 1977 and 1976.
          §   En,   Es,   Fr.

          Note: previously 'International travel statistics'.

248   Regional breakdown of world travel statistics   (World Tourism Organisation)
          Organizacion Mundial del Turismo, Avda del Generalísimo 59, Madrid 16, Spain.
          1972/76-   1972-1976.   not priced.   215 p.
          Contains data on arrivals, nights in hotels, etc, excursionists arrivals, cruise passengers arrivals, by mode
              of transport, length of stay, and departures of nationals and residents.   Also some socio-economic
              statistics and transport statistics.
          Time factor: published in 1978, the volume covers the years 1972 to 1976.
          §   En,   Es,   Fr.

¶ D,   continued

249   Tourism policy and international tourism in OECD member countries   (Organisation for Economic Co-operation
            and Development).
        OECD, 2 rue André-Pascal, 75775 Paris Cedex 16, France; or from sales agents.
        1970- 1978.   £7.80; $16; FrF 64.   195 p.
        Includes statistical data on government policy and action concerning tourism, international tourist flows
            in member countries (including USA and Canada), the economic importance of international tourism,
            transport (reasons for travel and mode of transport, trend in air traffic), and tourist accommodation.
        Time factor: the 1978 edition, published in 1978, has data mainly for 1976 and 1977.
        §   En and Fr eds.

250   Worldwide lodging industry (Horwath & Horwath International and Laventhol Krekstern Horwath & Horwath)
        Laventhol Krekstern Horwath & Horwath, 919 Third Avenue, New York, NY 10022.
        1971- 1977.   not priced.   55 p.
        Mainly international figures, but one or two tables are subdivided into regions or countries (i.e. Canada,
            USA, Mexico, Central America, South America, and Caribbean).
        Time factor: the 1977 issue, published in 1977, has data for 1976.
        §   En.

        Note: Title was 'Worldwide operating statistics of the hotel industry'.

251   Economic review of world tourism   (International Union of Official Travel Organisations).
        World Tourism Organisation, avenida del Generalísimo 59, Madrid 16, Spain.
        1966- 1978. $20.   116 p.
        Contains data on the development of international tourism, international tourism receipts and expenditure,
            domestic tourism, international tourism and world trade, tourism and balance of payments,
            accommodation, transport, and the tourism sector compared with other sectors.   Statistical tables
            in the text.
        Time factor: the 1978 issue, published in 1978, has data for two or three years to 1975.
        §   En.

252   Report on tourist travel to the Caribbean for 1975 (Caribbean Tourism Association).
        Caribbean Tourism Association, 20 East 46th Street, New York, NY 10017.
                            not priced.
        Contains statistics of visitors to all Caribbean islands in 1975.
        Time factor: published late 1976.
        §   En.

253   Advertising expenditures around the world: a survey   (Starch Inra Hooper and International Advertising
            Association).
        Starch Inra Hooper, 566E Boston Post Road, Maroneck, NY 10543.
                13th, 1978. $50 ($35 to members) plus postage.   53 p.
        Cover title is 'World advertising expenditures'.   Contains data on worldwide advertising by media and
            category, per capita advertising expenditure, advertising expenditure as a percentage of GNP, print
            advertising, television advertising, and radio advertising.
        Time factor: the 1978 issue, published in 1978, has data for 1976 and one or two earlier years.
        §   En.

254   Advertising expenditures: international comparisons, 1960-1975 (JWT Information Service).
        JWT Information Service, 40 Berkeley Square, London W1.
                            not priced.   48 p.
        Contains data on the USA and Europe.
        Time factor: published in 1977.
        §   En.

¶   E - Population

255   Demographic yearbook   (United Nations Statistical Office).
           Publishing Service, United Nations, New York, NY 10017; or from sales agents.
           1948- 1976.   £27.30; $42.   994 p.
           Includes population figures for about 250 geographic areas of the world, including tables by age and sex,
               the population of capital cities over 100,000 inhabitants, and totals from the latest censuses of
               population.   A different field of demographic statistics receives intensive treatment each year
               (1976 - marriage and divorce statistics).
           Time factor: the 1976 edition, published in 1977, contains the latest available data for each country.
           §   En,   Fr.

256   Population and vital statistics report   (United Nations Statistical Office).
           Publishing Service, United Nations, New York, NY 10017; or from sales agents.
                    quarterly.   £1.95 or £6.50 yr; $3 or $10 yr.
           Contains data from the latest census returns and demographic statistics for all reporting countries.
           §   En.

257   Datos básicos de población en América Latina, 1970   [Basic data of the population of Latin America, 1970]
               (Organisation of American States).
           Organisation of American States, 1725 Eye Street NW, Washington DC 20006.
           Time factor: published in 1971.
           §   Es.

258   Population census of the Commonwealth Caribbean   (Census Research Programme. University of the West
               Indies).
           University of the West Indies, Kingston, Jamaica.
                    1970.
           Contents: Final reports:
               Vol 1   Administration
               Vol 2   Enumeration district tabulations
               Vol 3   Age tabulations
               Vol 4   Economic activity
                           Part 1   Jamaica
                                  2   Trinidad & Tobago
                                  3   Guyana
                                  4   Barbados
                                  5   Belize
                                  6   St Lucia
                                  7   Grenada
                                  8   St Vincent
                                 12   Montserrat
                                 13   Cayman Islands
                                 14   British Virgin Islands
                                 15   Turks and Caicos Islands
                                 16   Occupation and industry
               Vol 5   Internal migration
               Vol 6   Education (3 vols)
               Vol 7   Race and religion
               Vol 8   Fertility, union states, and marriage
               Vol 9   Housing and households (4 vols)
               Vol 10   Miscellaneous - income (4 vols)

¶   E,   continued

258,   continued

Bulletins:
1   Population by parish, sex, age groups, urban/rural areas: provisional totals
2   Dwellings: provisional totals
3   Education
4   Internal migrants
5   Economic activity
Time factor: the reports were published between 1973 and 1976.   Vol 4, parts 9, 10 and 11,
presumably allocated to Dominica, Bermuda and St Kitts-Nevis-Anguilla, have not yet been issued.
§   En.

259   Recensement général de la population...départements d'outre-mer   [General census of population...overseas
departments] (INSEE)
INSEE, 18 boulevard Adolphe Pinard, 75675 Paris Cedex 14, France.
1954- 1974.   FrF 4.
Time factor: reported to be published in 1976.
§   Fr.

260   Recensement des agents de l'état et des collectivités locales des départements d'outre-mer, 1 mai 1969
[Census of civil servants and local authority personnel in overseas departments]   (INSEE)
not priced.   27 p.
Includes Martinique, Guadeloupe, Guyane Française, etc.
§   Fr.

261   Tendances démographiques dans les départements insulaires d'outre-mer: Martinique, Guadeloupe et Réunion
[Demographic tendencies in the French departments overseas: Martinique, Guadeloupe and Réunion)
(INSEE)
INSEE, 18 boulevard Adolphe Pinard, 75675 Paris Cedex 14, France.
not priced.   261 p.
Time factor: published in 1972 with data to 1970-1971.
§   Fr.

262   Statistiques du mouvement de la population dans les départements d'outre-mer   [Vital statistics for the overseas
departments] (INSEE)
INSEE, 18 boulevard Adolphe Pinard, 75675 Paris Cedex 14, France.
1951/56- 1965-1970.   not priced.   187 p.
Includes data for Martinique, Guyane, and Guadeloupe.
Time factor: the issue covering 1965-1970 was published in 1973.
§   Fr.

263   Les causes de décès dans les départements d'outre-mer   [Causes of death in the overseas departments] (INSEE)
INSEE, 18 boulevard Adolphe Pinard, 75675 Paris Cedex 14, France.
1960- 1971.   not priced.   86 p.
Includes data for Martinique, Guyane and Guadeloupe.
Time factor: the 1971 issue has data for 1970 and 1971.
§   Fr.

264   Boletín demográfico   [Demographic bulletin] (Centro Latinoámericano de Demográfia).
CELADE, Edificio Naciones Unidas, Avenida Dag Hammerskjold, Casilla 91, Santiago, Chile.
1968- 2 a year. $50 yr.
Contents vary, each issue having particular demographic statistics for Latin American countries.
§   Es.

¶   E,   continued

265   World population prospects   (United Nations Department of Economic and Social Affairs).
        Publishing Service, United Nations, New York, NY 10017; or from sales agents.
        1963-   2nd, 1968.   £1.76; $4.   174 p.
        Assesses the prospects for major areas and regions for 1965 to 2000 and for individual countries for 1965 to
            1985.
        Time factor: the 1968 assessment was published in 1973, as Population Studies no 53.
        §   En.

266   Compendium of housing statistics   (United Nations Statistical Office).
        Publishing Service, United Nations, New York, NY 10017; or from sales agents.
        1971-   2nd, 1972-1974.   £10.80; $18.   312 p.
        Contains information derived from national housing censuses or from national sample surveys.   Includes
            data on population growth, dwelling construction, the cost of housing, and capital formation in
            housing for 176 countries.   Issued as document ST/ESA/STAT/SER.N/2.
        Time factor: the 2nd edition was published in 1976 and contains data received by the UN during the
            period 1972 to 1974.
        §   En,   Fr.

267   World housing survey, 1974   (United Nations: Department of Economic and Social Affairs).
        Publishing Service, United Nations, New York, NY 10017; or from sales agents.
                            £5.40; $9.   200 p.
        An overview of the state of housing, building and planning within human settlements.   Includes a
            statistical annex (p 142-190).   Topics dealt with are urbanisation trends, slums and squatters
            settlements, housing conditions and housing requirements, land use and development, housing
            finance, house building industry and materials, human resources, housing and development policy.
        Time factor: published in 1976.
        §   En.

268   Yearbook of labour statistics   (International Labour Office).
        Bureau International du Travail, rue de Lausanne 154, CH-1211 Genève 22, Switzerland.
        1935/36-   1977.   SFr 95.   936 p.
        Contains data on the total and economically active population, employment, unemployment, hours of
            work, labour productivity, wages, consumer prices, industrial accidents, and industrial disputes.
            Indices of consumer prices include general indices, food indices, fuel and light indices, clothing
            indices, and rent indices.
        Time factor: the 1977 edition, published late 1977, contains data for several years to 1974 or 1975 or
            the latest available.
        §   En,   Es,   Fr.

269   Bulletin of labour statistics   (International Labour Office).
        Bureau International du Travail, rue de Lausanne 154, CH-1211 Genève 22, Switzerland.
        1965-   quarterly, with 8 supplements.   SFr 15 or SFr 45 yr.
        Contains monthly and quarterly series of indices of the general level of employment and of unemployment
            in non-agricultural sectors, indices of numbers employed and total hours worked in manufacturing,
            numbers and percentages employed, average number of hours worked in non-agricultural sectors and
            in manufacturing, average earnings or wage-rates in non-agricultural sectors and in manufacturing,
            general indices and food indices of consumer prices.   In addition, the results of the ILO October
            enquiry on hourly wages of adult wage-earners in 41 occupations, monthly salaries and normal hours
            of work per week in selected occupations, and on retail prices of selected consumer goods, are
            included in the second quarterly issue each year.
        Time factor: varies with each country.   Tables contain monthly, quarterly and half-yearly data for the
            last three years.
        §   En,   Es,   Fr.

¶   E,   continued

270   Labour force estimates and projections   (International Labour Office).
          Bureau International du Travail, rue de Lausanne 154, CH-1211 Genève 22, Switzerland.
          1971-   2nd, 1977.   SFr 80 for 6 volumes.   6 vols.
          Prepared as a joint international effort of the United Nations and specialised agencies, and designed to
               produce a co-ordinated series of comprehensive demographic and related projections.   The volumes
               are:
                    I   Asia (SFr 15)
                    II Africa (SFr 15)
                    III Latin America (SFr 12.50)
                    IV North America, Europe, Oceania and USSR (SFr 15)
                    V   World summary (SFr 12.50)
                    VI Methodological supplement (SFr 17.50)
          Time factor: the second edition, published in 1977, has data for the period 1950 to 2000.
          §   Vol I - V are in En,   Es,   Fr,   vol VI has separate editions in each of those languages.

271   Labour force statistics   (Organisation for Economic Co-operation and Development).
          OECD, 2 rue André-Pascal, 75775 Paris Cedex 16, France; or from sales agents.
          1956/66-   14th, 1965-1976.   £9.80; $20; FrF 80.   440 p.
          Includes statistics of population, employment, labour force, and unemployment for member countries,
               including USA and Canada.
          Time factor: the 1965-1976 issue, covering those years, was published in June 1978.
          §   En,   Fr.

          Note: there is also a quarterly supplement (£5.40 or $11 or FrF 44 yr)

272   Fachserie Auslandsstatistik: Reihe 4: Löhne und Gehälter im Ausland   [Wages and salaries abroad]
               (Statistisches Bundesamt).
          W Kohlhammer GmbH, Postfach 42 11 20, 6500 Mainz 42, Federal Republic of Germany.
               1977.   Reihe 4.1 DM 8.60; 4.2 DM 5.40.   2 vols.
          Content:
               Reihe 4.1:   Arbeitnehmerverdienste im Ausland
               Reihe 4.2:   Tariflöhne und -gehälter im Ausland
          Reihe 4.1 contains data on employment, hours of work, strikes and lockouts; Reihe 4.2 contains data on
               basic wage rates and index numbers of earnings.
          §   De.

273   La population active et sa structure.   The working population and its structure (P Bairoch)
          Université Libre de Bruxelles, Institut de Sociologie, Bruxelles, Belgium.
               FB 360.   236 p.
          Issued as 'Statistiques Internationales Rétrospectives. International historical statistics' vol 1, the work
               includes statistics of the economically active population by sex and by percentages of occupation,
               and structure by branch of activity of the active population, all arranged by continent and by
               country.
          Time factor: published in 1968, the periods covered vary.
          §   En,   Fr.

¶   F   -   Social

274   Compendium of social statistics   (United Nations Statistical Office).
        Publishing Service, United Nations, New York, NY 10017; or from sales agents.
        1963-   2nd 1967.   £3.83; $8.75.   662 p.
        An international compendium presenting basic national statistical indicators required for describing the
            major aspects of the social situation in the world, as well as changes and trends in levels of living.
            It is organised in eight sections as follows: population and vital statistics, health conditions, food
            consumption and nutrition, housing, education and cultural activities, labour force and conditions
            of employment, income and expenditure, consumer prices.
        Time factor: the 1967 edition was published in 1968 and there have been no later ones.
        §   En,   Fr.

275   Report on the world social situation   (United Nations: Department of Economic and Social Affairs).
        Publishing Service, United Nations, New York, NY 10017, USA; or from sales agents.
        1952-   8th, 1974.   £5.72; $11.   279 p.
        Contents:
            Part 1   Regional developments
            Part 2   Sectoral developments (population; employment, wage and price trends; social security;
                    food and agriculture; health; education; housing; women, youth and social welfare;
                    crime prevention and criminal justice; children and adolescents; and environment).
        Tables are included in the text.
        Time factor: the 1974 edition, published in November 1975, has data for various periods to 1973.   The
            report is now published every four years.
        §   En.

276   Estadísticas sociales   [Social statistics]   (SIECA)
        SIECA, 4a Avenida 10-25, zona 14, Apartado postal 1237, Guatemala, CA.
                $CA 3.   93 p.
        Includes data on population, vital statistics, education, public health, social security and housing.
        Time factor: published in 1973, the volume has data for various dates between 1960 and 1972.
        §   Es.

    i.   Standard of living

277   Fachserie 17. Preise. Reihe 10: Internationaler Vergleich der Preise für die Lebenshaltung   [Prices. Series 10:
            International comparison of consumer prices]   (Statistisches Bundesamt).
        W Kohlhammer GmbH, Postfach 42 11 20, 6500 Mainz 42, Federal Republic of Germany.
                monthly.   DM 2.30 each issue.
        §   De.

278   Income distribution in Latin America   (United Nations Economic Commission for Latin America).
        Publishing Service, United Nations, New York, NY 10017; or from sales agents.
                £1.05; $2.50.   148 p.
        Contains data on the general aspects of the income distribution structure; a comparison of Latin America
            with the Western industrial countries; variations within regions - Argentina, Venezuela, Mexico,
            Brazil and El Salvador; and more specific aspects of income distribution studies.   Tables are
            included in the text.
        Time factor: published in 1971.
        §   En.

¶   F.i,   continued

279   Household income and expenditure statistics   (International Labour Office).
        Bureau International du Travail, rue de Lausanne 154, CH-1211 Genève 22, Switzerland.
        1950/54-   no 2, 1960-1972.   2 vols.
        Contains data on level, components and size distribution of household income and expenditure.   The
            data is presented for urban and rural sectors, social and occupational groups, and households of
            different sizes.   One volume is devoted to Africa, Asia and Latin America (SFr 17.50), and the
            other to North America, Europe, USSR and Oceania (SFr 22.50).
        Time factor: the second edition covers the years 1960 to 1972 and the volumes were published in 1974
            and 1976 respectively.
        §   En.

280   Retail price comparisons for international salary determination   (United Nations Statistical Office).
        Publishing Services, United Nations, New York, NY 10017; or from sales agents.
                        £1.95; $3.   171 p.
        Published as 'Statistical papers, series M, no 14, rev 1', this is the UN system for equalising purchasing
            power of salaries of employees abroad.   Basically retail price comparisons as indicated by the
            price levels of a 'basket' of goods and services of the kind purchased by international officials, it
            gives the retail prices (November 1969) of foods, beverages and drinks, housing, transport, house
            furnishings, medicines and toilet articles, and cleaning and paper supplies in New York and capital
            cities throughout the world.
        Time factor: published in 1971.
        §   En.

        Note: 'Retail price indexes relating to living expenditures of United Nations officials' is published in
            the United Nations' 'Monthly bulletin of statistics' in March and September each year.

281   Prices and earnings around the globe: a comparison of purchasing power in 41 cities   (Union Bank of
            Switzerland).
        Union Bank of Switzerland, Zürich, Switzerland.
        1971-   4th ed, October 1978.   not priced.   50 p.
        Time factor: published in October 1978.   The next edition is due in 1980.
        §   De,   Es,   En,   Fr,   It, eds.

282   Living costs overseas: a guide for businessmen   (Financial Times Ltd)
        Financial Times Ltd, Minster House, Arthur Street, London EC4R 9AX.
        1976-   January 1979.   not priced.   141 p.
        Time factor: published annually.
        §   En.

283   Executive living costs in major cities worldwide   (Business International SA).
        Business International SA, 1 Dag Hammarskjold Plaza, Genève, Switzerland.
        1978-   1979.   not priced.   2 looseleaf volumes.
        Time factor: published in March 1979.
        §   En.

284   Boletín de precios internacionales de productos basicos/Bulletin of international prices of basic commodities
            (Organisation of American States).
        Organisation of American States, 1725 Eye Street NW, Washington DC 20006.
        1974-   monthly. $1 or $12 yr.
        Time factor: each issue has runs of data to about three months prior to publication.
        §   Es.

¶ F.ii, Health and welfare

285 World health statistics annual (World Health Organisation).
World Health Organisation, CH-1211 Genève 27, Switzerland; or from sales agents.
1939/46- Vol I 1978. £33.60; SFr 96
Vol II 1978. £11.20; SFr 32 3 vols
Vol III 1977. £11.20; SFr 40
Volume I contains data on vital statistics and causes of death, volume II on infectious diseases: cases and deaths, and volume III on health personnel and hospital establishments.
Time factor: Vol I has data for 1975 and Vols II and III have data for 1976. Vols I and II were published in 1978 and Vol III in 1977.
§ En, Fr.

286 World health statistics report (World Health Organisation).
World Health Organisation, CH-1211 Genève 27, Switzerland; or from sales agents.
1948- quarterly. £7.20 or £19.60 yr; SFr 12 or SFr 48 yr.
Up-dates 285 above.
§ En, Fr.

287 The cost of social security (International Labour Office).
Bureau International du Travail, route des Morillons 4, CH-1202 Genève, Switzerland.
1949- 8th, 1967-1971. SFr 60. 198 p.
The results of an enquiry aimed at establishing a consolidated statement of the financial operations of social security schemes existing in various countries, etc. Includes comparative tables of receipts and expenditures, benefits, etc. Also national accounts data, population data, and consumer price indices.
Time factor: the 8th edition has data for the years 1960 to 1971 or the latest available at time of publication.
§ En, Es, Fr.

288 Health conditions in the Americas (Pan American Health Organisation, a regional office of the World Health Organisation).
World Health Organisation, 525 23rd Street NW, Washington DC 20037.
1954- 6th, 1969-1972. $2. 233 p.
Contains data on vital statistics, communicable diseases, health services, hospital services, environmental health, and health manpower (doctors, nurses, etc) for each American country.
Time factor: the 6th edition, with data for 1969 to 1972, was published in 1974.
§ En.

iii. Education and leisure

289 Educational statistics yearbook (Organisation for Economic Co-operation and Development).
OECD, 2 rue André-Pascal, 75775 Paris Cedex 16, France; or from sales agents.
Vol 1 International tables (£1 50; $3 75; FrF 15)
Vol II Country tables (£5; $12.50; FrF 50)
Includes data on numbers of establishments, pupils, teachers, awards, etc, relating to pre-primary schools, primary schools, secondary schools, and higher (university and college) education.
Time factor: only one issue has been issued at time of going to press. Vol I was published in 1974 and Vol II in 1975; data included is the latest available at the time, usually to 1970, 1971 or 1972.
§ En and Fr eds.

¶ F.iii,   continued

290   Statistics of educational attainment and illiteracy, 1945-1974   (UNESCO)
          UNESCO, 7 place de Fontenoy, 75700 Paris, France; or from sales agents.
                           £3.90; $8.50.   233 p.
          Derived from censuses and surveys plus some estimates, the volume includes population classified by age,
               by population sub-groups, and by level of educational attainment.   It also includes tables of basic
               data, such as educational attainment by age and sex, illiteracy by age and sex, etc.
          Time factor: published in 1977, the volume has data for the years 1945 to 1974.
          §   En,   Es,   Fr.

291   Statistics of students abroad   (UNESCO)
          UNESCO, 7 place de Fontenoy, 75700 Paris, France; or from sales agents.
          1962/68-   1969-1973.   £4.80; FrF 26.   345 p.
          Arranged in two parts, Part 1 is an analysis of general trends, including an appendix on numbers of foreign
               students in countries of study, and Part 2 contains country tables showing for each country the number
               of students enrolled abroad by country of study.
          Time factor: the 1969-1973 edition, published in 1976, has data for the years 1969 to 1973.
          §   En,   Fr.

292   Higher education; international trends, 1960-1970   (UNESCO)
          UNESCO, 7 place de Fontenoy, 75700 Paris, France; or from sales agents.
                           £2.80; FrF 26.   254 p.
          Analyses the main trends in the quantitative development of higher education.   Includes statistical data,
               by continent and country, of teachers and students by type of institution, distribution of students by
               field of study, distribution of graduates by field of study, distribution of graduates by level of degree
               or diploma, and distribution of graduates by level of degree or diploma and level of study.
          Time factor: the report was published in 1975.
          §   En   and   Fr eds.

293   L'enseignement dans les départements d'outre-mer   [Education in the overseas departments]   (INSEE)
          INSEE, 18 boulevard Adolphe Pinard, 75675 Paris Cedex 14, France.
          1968/69-   1973/74.   not priced.   35 p.
          Contains data on number of schools, classes, etc, in first, second, technical and professional education;
               bursaries, diplomas, etc, for each of the French overseas departments including Martinique,
               Guadeloupe and Guyane.
          Time factor: the 1973/74 issue, with data for the academic year 1973/74, was published in 1977.
          §   Fr.

294   Statistics of newspapers and other periodicals   (UNESCO)
          UNESCO, 7 place de Fontenoy, Paris 75700, France; or from sales agents.
                           $1; £0.25; FrF 350.   70 p.
          Contains statistics by country and by frequency of numbers of newspapers and other periodicals.
          Time factor: published in 1959, the report has data for 1956 and 1957.
          §   En.

295   International statistics of city libraries   (J Eyssen, for the International Association of Metropolitan City
               Libraries).
          1969-   1976. published in "International library review", vol 10, no 1, January 1978.
          The results of a survey, the report includes for each town the number of inhabitants, book stock,
               periodicals, audio-visual media, loans, budget, staff, libraries and branch libraries.
          §   En.

AMERICA,   continued

¶   G   -   Finance

296   International financial statistics   (International Monetary Fund)
              International Monetary Fund, Washington DC 20431, USA; or from sales agents.
              1948-   monthly.   £1.30 or £8.50 yr; $3.50 or $35 yr.
              Contains general data on par values and central rates, exchange rates, exchange transactions, inter-
                    national reserves, use of Fund credit, deposit money bank's foreign assets, interest rates, major
                    world trade commodities, prices, changes in consumer prices, and world trade.   For each country
                    data is given on exchange rates, international liquidity, banks, monetary survey, finance, inter-
                    national transactions, interest, prices and production, government finance, national accounts, etc.
              Time factor: varies with the country, but generally the last eight quarters and the last seven months are
                    given up to about three months prior to the date of the issue.
              §   En.

297   OECD financial statistics   (Organisation for Economic Co-operation and Development).
              OECD, 2 rue André-Pascal, 75775 Paris Cedex 16, France; or from sales agents.
              1969-   No.11, 1977/78.   £20; $42; FrF 168 for two basic volumes.   2 basic volumes and 5 two-
                                        £40; $84; FrF 336 for two basic volumes   monthly supplements a year.
                                        and five supplements.
              Provides a unique collection of statistical and descriptive data on the international financial market and
                    on the domestic markets of OECD member countries, including USA and Canada.
              Time factor: the two basic volumes of the 1977/78 issue were published in December 1977 and April 1978.
              §   En,   Fr.

298   Boletín estadístico   [Statistical bulletin]   (Consejo Monetario Centroaméricano).
              Consejo Monetario Centroaméricano, San José, Costa Rica, CA.
              1964-   1977.   not priced.   189 p.
              Contains data on money and banking, public finance, balance of payments and foreign trade, and other
                    economic indicators, including price indicators, for Central America, Guatemala, El Salvador,
                    Honduras, Nicaragua and Costa Rica.
              Time factor: the 1977 issue, published late 1978, has long runs of annual and monthly figures to December
                    1977.
              §   Es.

299   Economic and financial review   (East Caribbean Currency Authority).
              East Caribbean Currency Authority, PO Box 89, Basseterre, St Kitts, WI.
              1970-   3 a year.   not priced.
              Contains an economic survey, currency and banking statistics, banking statistics for the Leeward Islands,
                    banking statistics for the Windward Islands, interest rates, and statistics on treasury bills.
              Time factor: each issue has annual and monthly runs of statistics to the month of issue, and is published
                    some three or four months later.
              §   En.

              Note: the ECCA also issues an annual report with money and banking statistics for the East Caribbean
                    countries (Antigua, Dominica, Grenada, Montserrat, St Kitts-Anguilla-Nevis, St Lucia and
                    St Vincent).

¶   G,   continued

300   International comparisons of real product and purchasing power   (United Nations Statistical Office and the
             World Bank).
         Johns Hopkins University Press, Baltimore and London.
                        £5.25.   264 p.
         Time factor: published in 1978.
         §   En.

301   World financial markets   (Morgan Guaranty Trust Company of New York).
         Morgan Guaranty Trust Company of New York, 23 Wall Street, New York, NY 10015.
         1974-   monthly.   not priced.
         Includes a statistical appendix with data on exchange rates, bond yields and issues, central bank discount
             rates, day to day money rate, etc.
         Time factor: each issue has data for four years to the month prior to the date of the issue.
         §   En.

302   Boletín estadístico   [Statistical bulletin]   (Bancos Centrales de los Paises del Acuerdo de Cartagena).
         1974- 1976.   not priced.   241 p.
         Contains financial accounts of banks and other banking statistics for Bolivia, Colombia, Chile, Ecuador,
             Peru and Venezuela.
         Time factor: the 1976 issue, published in 1976, has data generally for 1970 to 1975.
         §   Es.

      ii.   Public finance

303   Yearbook of national accounts statistics   (United Nations Statistical Office).
         Publishing Service, United Nations, New York, NY 10017; or from sales agents.
         1957-   1976.   £32.50; $50 for 2 vols.   2 vols.
         The detailed statistical data and tables provide comparisons between the situation in the countries and
             regions covered.   Vol 1 has individual country data on gross product by type of expenditure and
             industrial origin, national income by distribution shares, finance and composition of gross domestic
             capital formation, composition of private consumption expenditure, etc.   Vol 2 has international
             tables, including estimates of total and per capita national income, gross domestic product and gross
             national product in US$ for comparison.
         Time factor: the 1976 edition, published in 1977, has data for 1960 to 1974.
         §   En.

304   Government financial statistics yearbook   (International Monetary Fund).
         International Monetary Fund, Washington DC 20431, USA; or from sales agents.
         1977-   1978.   £6.50; $10.   317 p.
         Contains data on revenue and grants, expenditure by function, lending minus repayments by function,
             outstanding debts, etc, for each country.
         Time factor: the 1978 edition, published in 1978, has data for 1972 to 1975 or 1976 or the latest
             available.
         §   En,   Es,   Fr.

305   National accounts of OECD countries   (Organisation for Economic Co-operation and Development).
         OECD, 2 rue André-Pascal, 75775 Paris Cedex 16, France; or from sales agents.
         1950/61-   1976.   Vol I £3.40; $7;   FrF 28   2 vols.
                             Vol II £7.30; $15;   FrF 60.
         Includes statistics of national accounts for USA and Canada.
         Time factor: the 1976 issue, published mid-1978, has data for 1976.
         §   En,   Fr.

¶   G.ii,   continued

306   Quarterly national accounts bulletin   (Organisation for Economic Co-operation and Development).
         OECD, 2 rue André-Pascal, 75775 Paris Cedex 16, France; or from sales agents.
         1976-   £5.40; $11;   FrF 44 yr.
         Contains the latest national accounts statistics for OECD member countries, including USA and Canada.
         §   En,   Fr.

         Note: there is also "Quarterly national accounts: historical statistics, 1960-1971" (£3; $6; FrF 24)

307   Revenue statistics of OECD member countries   (Organisation for Economic Co-operation and Development)
         OECD, 2 rue André-Pascal, 75775 Paris Cedex 16, France; or from sales agents.
         1965/74-   1965-1976.   £7.60; $15.50;   FrF 62.   291 p.
         Contains comparable data on the tax revenues and social security contributions, and an analysis of the
             data.   Covers member countries including the USA and Canada.
         Time factor: the 1965-1976 edition, with data for those years, was published late 1978.
         §   En,   Fr.

308   World debt tables: external public debt of developing countries   (World Bank)
         World Bank, 1818 H Street NW, Washington DC 20433, USA.
         1976-   1978.   not priced.   2 vols plus up-dating supplements.
         A compilation of data on the external public and publicly guaranteed debt of 96 developing countries.
             Vol I is a general volume; Vol II has data country by country.
         Time factor: the 1978 report, published late 1978, has data for 1970 to 1976.
         §   En.

309   Geographical distribution of financial flows to developing countries...data on disbursements...   (Organisation
            for Economic Co-operation and Development).
         OECD, 2 rue André-Pascal, 75775 Paris Cedex 16, France; or from sales agents.
         1960/64-   1971-1977.   £10; $21;   FrF 84.   285 p.
         Section A has two tables showing total net receipts of each developing country; Section B has tables for
             each individual developing country showing its resource receipts by type and by donor; and Section
             C has similar data to Section B but is concerned with selected groups of recipients.
         Time factor: the 1971-1977 issue, published in 1978, has data for the years 1971 to 1977.
         §   En,   Fr.

310   Balance of payments yearbook   (International Monetary Fund)
         International Monetary Fund, Washington DC 20431, USA; or from sales agents.
         1948-   monthly.   £13; $20 yr, including annual supplement.
         Includes, for over 100 countries, value of goods, services and transfers; capital (excluding reserves) and
             related items; allocation of special drawing rights; and reserves and related items.
         §   En.

         Note: until recently the yearbook was a looseleaf volume.

311   **Centroamérica balanza de pagos**   [Central American balance of payments]   (Consejo Monetario
            Centroaméricano).
         Consejo Monetario Centroaméricano, San José, Costa Rica.
         1973-   1975.   not priced.   117 p.
         Time factor: the 1975 issue, published in 1976, has data for 1975.
         §   Es.

¶ H - Transport and communications

312   World transport data   (International Road Transport Union).
             Union Internationale des Transports Routiers, Centre Internationale, CH-1202 Genève, Switzerland.
                        not priced.   259 p.
             Published as a recognition of 25 years of the Union's existence, the volume covers railway, sea and inland
                   waterway transport as well as road transport.
             Time factor: published in 1973, the volume includes runs of several years' statistics to about 1970.
             §   En,   Fr.

313   International statistical handbook of urban public transport   (International Union of Public Transport).
             Union Internationale des Transports Publics, Avenue de l'Uruguay 19, B-1050 Bruxelles, Belgium.
                        not priced.   2 vols.
             The report of a study concerned with metropolitan railway/rapid transit, multi-mode surface transport,
                   uni-mode (bus only) surface transport.   Includes data for more than 250 cities throughout the world.
             Time factor: the report was published in 1975.
             §   De,   En,   Fr.

      i.   Ships and shipping

314   Shipping statistics. Statistik der Schiffahrt   (Institut für Seeverkehrswirtschaft)   [Institute of Shipping
                   Economics]
             Institut für Seeverkehrswirtschaft, Werderstrasse 73, 2800 Bremen 1, Germany.
             1956- 1977.   DM 62.   c 320 p.
             Contains facts and figures about shipping, shipbuilding, seaports and sea-borne trade.
             Time factor: the 1977 edition, published in 1977, has data for several years to 1976.
             §   De,   En.

315   Shipping statistics. Statistik der Schiffahrt   (Institut für Seeverkehrswirtschaft).
             Institut für Seeverkehrswirtschaft, Werderstrasse 73, 2800 Bremen, Germany.
             1956-   monthly.   DM 10;   DM 90 yr, plus postage.
             Contains monthly figures of shipping, shipbuilding, ports and sea trade, including data on the world
                   merchant fleet, shipping and sea-borne trade, shipbuilding and ports and sea canals.
             Time factor: each issue has data for several years and months up to one or two months prior to the date of
                   the issue.
             §   De,   En.

316   Statistical tables   (Lloyds Register of Shipping)
             Lloyds Register of Shipping, 71 Fenchurch Street, London EC3M 4BS.
             1955- 1978.   not priced.   77 p.
             Contains statistical data on ships registered at Lloyds, including country of registration, size and age,
                   type, propulsion.   Also numbers and tonnage of ships registered, launched, and lost.
             Time factor: the 1978 edition, published late 1978, has data for several years to 1978.
             §   En.

317   Annual summary of merchant ships completed in the world during...   (Lloyds Register of Shipping).
             Lloyds Register of Shipping, 71 Fenchurch Street, London EC3M 4BS.
             1922- 1978.   not priced.   14 p.
             Also includes the annual summary of merchant ships launched in the world during the year under review.
                   Data includes type of ship, gross tonnage, countries of registration, when built, and where launched.
             Time factor: the 1978 edition, published early 1979, has data for 1978 and some earlier years in some
                   tables.
             §   En.
             Note: Lloyds also publish other titles, including the annual 'Statistical summary of merchant ships
                   totally lost, broken up, etc' and the quarterly 'Merchant shipbuilding return' and 'Casualty return'.

¶   H.i,   continued

318   Large crude carriers in excess of 175000 DWT at...   (E A Gibson Shipbrokers Ltd)
         E A Gibson Shipbrokers Ltd, PO Box 278, Remington House, 61/65 Holborn Viaduct, London EC1P 1HP.
         1966-   1st January 1977.   not priced.   74 p.
         Includes a statistical appendix on vessels, shipyards, fixtures, and owners.
         Time factor: the 1st January 1977 issue has data as at that date, and was published early 1977.
         §   En.

319   World shipping statistics   (H P Drewry (Shipping Consultants) Ltd)
         H P Drewry (Shipping Consultants) Ltd, 34 Brook Street, London W1Y 2LL.
         1975-   1978.   £25; $60 yr to SSE subscribers (see below)   c 75 p.
                          £30; $75 yr to others.
         Contains data on tankers (market, fleets, charters, rates, etc), dry cargo, world shipping, and gas (LPG)
             carriers.
         Time factor: the 1978 edition, published early 1979, has data for 1978 and some earlier years.
         §   En.

320   Shipping statistics and economics   (H P Drewry (Shipping Consultants) Ltd)
         H P Drewry (Shipping Consultants) Ltd, 34 Brook Street, London W1Y 2LL.
         1970-   monthly.   £85 or $205 yr.
         Contains data on the tanker market, combined carrier market, dry cargo market, and reported fixtures.
         Time factor: each issue has data for the previous month.
         §   En.

321   Review of maritime transport   (UNCTAD)
         Publishing Service, United Nations, New York, NY 10017; or from sales agents.
         1969-   1975.   £3.12; $8.   c 120 p.
         A review of current and long-term aspects of maritime transport.   Includes data on the development of
             seaborne trade, world seaborne trade, distribution of world tonnage, cargoes, fleets, etc.
         Time factor: the 1975 review, published in 1977, has data for 1972 to 1974 or 1975.
         §   En.

322   Maritime transport   (Organisation for Economic Co-operation and Development)
         OECD, 2 rue André-Pascal, 75775 Paris Cedex 16, France; or from sales agents.
         1961-   1977.   £4.20; $8.50; FrF 34.   156 p.
         Contains data on world shipping developments, national and international shipping policies, shipping
             demand and supply, and the freight markets, for OECD member countries, including USA and
             Canada.
         Time factor: the 1977 edition, published mid-1978, has data for 1977.
         §   En.

323   Merchant fleets of the world...   (US Maritime Administration)
         Government Printing Office, Washington DC 20402, USA.
         1956-   1976. $2.20.
         Contains data on ocean-going steam and motor ships of 1000 gross tons and over.   Number of ships,
             gross tons, deadweight tons, etc.
         Time factor: the 1976 issue, with data for 1976, was published in 1978.
         §   En.

¶   H.i,   continued

324   Analysis of world tanker tonnage   (Davies & Newman Ltd)
            Davies & Newman Ltd, Bilbao House, 36-38 New Broad Street, London EC2M 1NH.
            1971-   twice a year, in January and July.   not priced.
            Time factor: data is for the situation as at the date of the issue, and is published a month or two later.
            §   En.

325   World bulk fleet: tankers, combined carriers, bulk carriers   (Fearnley & Egers Chartering Co Ltd).
            Fearnley & Egers Chartering Co Ltd, Rådhusgt 27, Oslo 1, Norway.
            1972-   January 1979.   not priced.
            Contains data on flag, size, age, draft, speed, countries registered, etc, of existing fleet, bulk tonnage
                on order, active bulk fleet, etc.   Tables are included in the text.
            Time factor: the January 1979 issue gives data as at that date, and was published in March 1979.
                Previously annual, there are now two issues a year.
            §   En.

326   World bulk trades   (Fearnley & Egers Chartering Co Ltd)
            Fearnley & Egers Chartering Co Ltd, Rådhusgt 27, Oslo 1, Norway.
            1971-   1977.   not priced.   47 p.
            A statistical review of international sea-borne trade in liquid and dry bulk commodities and the employ-
                ment of tankers, combined carriers and bulk carriers in these shipments.
            Time factor: the 1977 edition, published late 1978 has data for 1977.
            §   En.

    ii.   Road

327   World road statistics   (International Road Federation).
            International Road Federation, 1023 Washington Building, Washington DC, USA and Fédération
                Routière Internationale, 63 rue de Lausanne, CH-1202 Genève, Switzerland.
            1951-   1973-1977.   SFr 125.   211 p.
            Contains data on road networks, production and export of motor vehicles, first registration and import of
                motor vehicles, vehicles in use, road traffic, motor fuels, road accidents, rates and basis of assess-
                ment of road user taxes, examples of average annual taxation, annual receipts from road user
                taxation, and road expenditure.
            Time factor: the 1973-1977 edition, published in September 1978, has data for the years 1973 to 1977.
            §   En,   Fr,   De.

328   Parc des véhicules automobiles des départements d'outre-mer   [Registration of motor vehicles in overseas
                departments] (INSEE)
            INSEE, 18 boulevard Adolphe Pinard, 75675 Paris Cedex 14, France.
            1959-   1972.   not priced.   52 p.
            Includes data for Martinique, Guadeloupe and Guyane.
            Time factor: the 1972 issue, with data as at 1st January 1972, was published in 1976.
            §   Fr.

    iii.   Rail

329   International railway statistics: statistics of individual railways   (International Union of Railways)
            Union Internationale des Chemins de Fer, 14-16 rue Jean Rey, 75015 Paris, France.
            1925-   1976.   not priced.   213 p.
            Contains data on the composition and means of the railway system, technical operating results, financial
                results, and miscellaneous information (fuels, electricity used, accidents, taxes, etc), for each
                railway.
            Time factor: the 1976 issue, published in 1978, has data mainly for 1976.
            §   En, De, and Fr eds.

¶   H,   continued

iv.   Air

330   World air transport statistics   (International Air Transport Association)
        IATA, PO Box 160, CH-1216 Cointrin, Genève, Switzerland and 1155 Mansfield Street, Montreal 113,
            Quebec, Canada.
        1957-   1977. $15.   78 p.
        Contains summary statistics, data on the development of world air transport, IATA members summary
            statistics, IATA members individual statistics, and international regional statistics.
        Time factor: the 1977 edition, published mid-1978, has data for 1977 and some earlier years.
        §   En.

331   Digest of statistics   (International Civil Aviation Organisation).
        ICAO, PO Box 400, Succursale, Montreal, Quebec, Canada; Civil Aviation Authority, Greville House,
            37 Gratton Road, Cheltenham, Glos GL50 2BN, England; or from sales agents.
                irreg.   various prices.
        Each issue of the digest is devoted to a particular topic, some titles being published regularly.   Subjects
            covered include traffic flow, airport traffic, fleet personnel, aircraft on register, financial data,
            non-scheduled air transport, etc.
        §   En.

332   Civil aviation statistics of the world   (International Civil Aviation Organisation).
        ICAO, PO Box 400, Succursale, Montreal, Quebec, Canada; Civil Aviation Authority, Greville House,
            37 Gratton Road, Cheltenham, Glos GL50 2BN, England; or other sales agents.
        1976-   1977. $5.50.   147 p.
        Contains world data on aircraft, safety, fleets, traffic, and financial data; aircraft and airline statistics
            by region and state; commercial air transport operations; and airports.   Mainly summarised and
            selected data from statistics provided to ICAO by contracting states.
        Time factor: the 1977 issue, published in 1978, has data for the years 1975 and 1976.
        §   En,   Es,   Fr,   and Ru eds.

v.   Communications

333   Yearbook of common carrier telecommunication statistics...and radio communications statistics   (Union
            Internationale des Télécommunications).
        Union Internationale des Télécommunications, Genève, Switzerland.
        1964/73-   5th, 1967-1976.   not priced.   356 p.
        In two parts, Part 1 deals with common carrier telecommunications statistics and contains a chronological
            series of statistics from 1967 to 1976 arranged by country, and including data on population,
            telephone statistics, households, residential telephone stations, telephone calls, telegrams, telex
            connections, telex calls, modems, revenue, investment, maintenance and repairs, and exchange
            rates.   Part 2 deals with radio communications statistics by country for the year 1976 with data on
            numbers of stations (coast, ship and amateur) and traffic at coast stations.
        Time factor: the 1967-1976 edition was published in 1978.
        §   En,   Es,   Fr.

334   The world's telephones   (American Telephone and Telegraph Company)
        American Telephone and Telegraph Company, Bedminster, New Jersey 07921, USA.
        1912-   1 January 1977.   not priced.   34 p.
        Contains, for the principal cities of the world, numbers of telephones in use, numbers in each city as a
            percentage of the number in the world, number in each city as a percentage of the population, and
            the number that are automatic.
        Time factor: the 1977 issue was published in December 1977.
        §   En.

335   A Statistics Unit is being established in the Financial Department of the Secretariat, The Valley, Anguilla,
        (t 451-5.   tg ANGGOVT.   tx 301 ADMIN AXA LA).

Statistical publications

Refer to St Kitts-Nevis-Anguilla for statistical publications.

ANTIGUA

Antigua, one of the Leeward Islands, now has self-government in association with Britain, which retains powers and responsibilities for defence and external affairs.   There is no central statistical office but enquiries about statistical data can be made to the Ministry of Trade, Production and Labour at St John's, or to the Antigua Chamber of Commerce, St Mary's Street, St John's.

Statistical publications

¶ A - General

336   Statistical yearbook   (Statistics Division, Ministry of Finance).
         Government Printing Office, St John's.
         1975- 1976. $6.   106 p.
         Main sections:
        Physical features   Manufacturing
        Demography   Public utilities
        Housing   Construction
        Migration   Distribution
        Education   Foreign trade
        Health   Tourism
        Labour   Transport and communications
        Wages and prices   Finance and banking
        Social security   Public finance & national accounts
        Agriculture   Justice and crime
         Time factor: the 1976 edition, published late 1976, has data for 1975 and also for some earlier years in
            some tables.
         §   En.

337   Antigua: report for the year...   (Foreign and Commonwealth Office).
         HM Stationery Office, PO Box 569, London SE1 9NH.
         1955/56- 1963/64. £0.32½.   61 p.
         Mainly textual, but includes some statistics of population, employment, commerce, tourism, production,
            etc.
         Time factor: the 1963/64 report was published in 1966.
         §   En.

¶   B - Production

         Refer to 336, 337

¶   C - External trade

338   Annual trade report   (Statistics Division, Ministry of Finance).
         Government Printing Office, St John's.
         1958- 1975. $6.   201 p.
         Main tables show detailed statistics of imports and exports and re-exports arranged by commodity and
            subdivided by countries of origin and destination.
         Time factor: the 1975 issue, with data for 1975, was published in 1977.
         §   En.

         Refer also to 336.

¶   D - Internal distribution and service trades

         Refer to 336, 337.

¶   E - Population

339   Census of population   (Statistics Division, Ministry of Planning, Development and External Affairs).
          Government Printing Office, St John's.
          1946-   1970. $3 each volume.   3 vols.
          Contents:
                Vol I   Housing characteristics
                Vol II   Social and demographic characteristics
                Vol III Economic characteristics
          Time factor: the results of the census of 1970 were published in 1975 and 1976.
          §   En.

340   Annual report of the Labour Department   (Ministry of Home Affairs).
          Government Printing Office, St John's.
          1968-   1974. $5.   85 p.
          Includes statistics tables on the numbers of unemployed by industry, sex, occupation, nationality, public
                and private sector; employment; training courses; immigration; work permits; etc.
          Time factor: the 1974 report, with data for 1974, was published in 1976.
          §   En.

          Refer also to 336, 337.

¶   F - Social

i.   Standard of living

341   Cost of living index   (Statistics Division, Ministry of Planning, Development and External Affairs).
          Government Printing Office, St John's.
          1969/73-   Vol III, 1969-1975. $2.   16 p.
          Time factor: the 1969-1975 issue, with data for those years, was published in 1975.
          §   En.

342   Cost of living index   (Statistics Division, Ministry of Finance).
          Government Printing Office, St John's.
          1976-   quarterly. $2 each issue.
          Time factor: each issue has data for that quarter and is published about one month later.
          §   En.

          Refer also to 336.

ii.   Health and welfare

          Refer to 336.

iii.   Education and leisure

343   Educational statistics   (Educational Statistics Unit, Ministry of Education, Health and Culture).
          Government Printing Office, St John's.
          1974/75-   1975-1976.   not priced.   30 p.
          Contains data on school enrolment estimates, teachers and enrolment of pupils, intake and loss of
                students and teachers, attendance, examination results, and finance.
          Time factor: the 1975-1976 issue, published mid-1978, has data for the academic year 1975/76.
          §   En.

¶   F.iii,   continued

344   Report on the Education Division   (Ministry of Education, Health and Culture).
           Government Printing Office, St John's.
           1971/73-   1974 & 1975. $3.   47 p.
           Includes a statistical appendix with tables on the establishment (in primary and secondary education),
                schools library service, examination results, and summaries of numbers of schools, teachers, pupils,
                etc.
           Time factor: the 1974 & 1975 report, published in 1976, has data for the two years 1974 and 1975.
                A report is not published every year.

           Refer also to 336

    iv.   Justice

           Refer to 336.

¶   G   -   Finance

           Refer to 336

¶   H   -   Transport and communications

           Refer to 336

Central statistical office

345   Instituto Nacional de Estadística y Censos   [National Institute of Statistics and Censuses],
Hipolito Yrigoyen 250, piso 12, oficina 210,
Buenos Aires.
† 33-7872.   tx 012 1952 (answerback AR MINEC)

The Institute, which is a part of the Ministry of Economy, is responsible for the collection, analysis and publication of official economic statistics of Argentina.   Unpublished statistical information can be provided if available, for which a fee is charged based on the amount of work to be done.   A photocopying service is also available.

Libraries

There are three libraries in the building which houses the Ministry of Economy at Hipolito Yrigoyen 250, Buenos Aires, which have collections of statistical publications.   They are Biblioteca y Sector Divulgación [Information Section Library] on the twelfth floor, office 1213 and 1210, which is open from 13.30 to 18.15 hours; Biblioteca del Ministerio de Económia [Ministry of Economy Library] on the 19th floor, office 941, which is open from 12.30 to 19.00 hours; and Biblioteca del Instituto Nacional de Planificación Económica [Library of the National Institute for Economic Planning] on the 8th floor, office 851, which is open from 13.30 to 19.00 hours.   The Biblioteca Nacional [National Library], México 564, Buenos Aires, also has a collection of statistical materials; as has the Banco Central de la República Argentina, reconquista 266, Buenos Aires († 40-0181).

Libraries and information services abroad

Argentina embassies abroad receive copies of statistical publications for reference, including:
United Kingdom   Argentina Embassy, 9 Wilton Crescent, London SW1.   † 01-235 3717.
USA   Argentina Embassy, 1600 New Hampshire Avenue NW, Washington DC.
      † (202) 387 0705.
Canada   Argentina Embassy, 620-56 Sparks Street, Ottawa.   († 236-9431)

Bibliographies

The Instituto Nacional de Estadística y Censos issues a sales list of its publications from time to time.

Statistical publications

¶   A   -   General

346   Anuario estadístico   [Statistical yearbook]   (Instituto Nacional de Estadística y Censos).
Instituto Nacional de Estadística y Censos, Hipolito Yrigoyen 250, Buenos Aires.
1948- 1973.   not priced.   423 p.
Main sections:

Geography	Social (education, culture, health, justice, religion,
Climate	tourism and recreation, housing, water and sewage,
Provinces (mainly demography)	social security)
Population	Economic (natural resources, agriculture, livestock,
Employment	manufacturing industry, construction, energy, fuels,
Cooperatives	transport, communications, internal trade and
National accounts	consumption, money and credit and finance, public
	finance, foreign trade. and international tables)

Time factor: the 1973 edition, published in 1974, has data for several years to 1973.
§   Es.

Note: a new edition is to be published during 1979.

¶   A,   continued

347   Boletin estadística trimestral   [Quarterly statistical bulletin]   (Instituto Nacional de Estadística y Censos)
        Instituto Nacional de Estadística y Censos, Hipolito Yrigoyen 250, Buenos Aires.
        1956- $700 or $2800 yr;   US$9 or US$30 yr.
        Contains data on demography, social, agriculture, industry, construction, internal trade, stocks, foreign
              trade, transport, communications, finance, leisure activities, gambling.
        Time factor: each issue has data for the last two years and six quarters to about six months prior to the
              date of the issue and publication.
        §   Es.

348   Informe económico   [Economic report]   (Ministerio de Económia y Trabajo).
        Ministerio de Económia y Trabajo, Balcarce 136 - 6° piso, oficina 621, Buenos Aires.
        1968-   quarterly.   not priced.
        Contains data on supply and demand (gross national product, mining, manufacturing industry, construction,
              services, imports), prices, wages, balance of payments and foreign trade, public finance, money and
              credit.   Statistical data is included in the text.
        Time factor: each issue has the latest data available.
        §   Es.

349   Economic report: summary   (Ministerio de Económia y Trabajo).
        Ministerio de Económia y Trabajo, Balcarce 136 - 6° piso, oficina 621, Buenos Aires.
        1968-   quarterly.   not priced.
        An English summary of 'Informe económico' above (348).
        §   En.

350   Economic survey: boletín económico semanal (Rodolfo Katz)
        Economic Survey SA, 456 ler piso, oficinas 11 y 12, Buenos Aires.
        1942-   weekly.   not priced.
        Includes some statistics in the text, but no regular tables.
        §   En,   Es.

351   Censo nacional económico   [National economic census]   (Instituto Nacional de Estadística y Censos).
        Instituto Nacional de Estadística y Censos, Hipolito Yrigoyen 250, Buenos Aires.
        1950-   1974.
        The census covered the fields of industry, employment, commerce (wholesale and retail), food and
              restaurants, and service trades.   Provisional results by region are being published (US$3 each
              volume or US$25 the set).
        §   Es.

352   Review of the River Plate: revista de Rio de la Plata
        SA The Review of the River Plate, Casilla de Correo 294 (suc 13-B), 1413 Buenos Aires.
        1891-   3 issues a month. $1200 ($1800 abroad) or $40,000 ($57,600 abroad) yr.
        Deals with the financial, economic, agricultural and shipping affairs in Argentina, and also developments
              in other South American countries.   Some statistics are included in the text, such as rates of
              exchange, livestock prices and movement, stock exchange quotations, but there are no regular
              statistical tables.
        §   En,   with commentaries in Es.

¶   A,   continued

353   Business trends: a concise and systematic weekly report to management on the Argentine economy   (Consejo
               Técnico de Inversiones SA).
        Consejo Técnico de Inversiones SA, Esmeralda 320 - 6°, Buenos Aires.
        1965-   not priced.
        Includes price indices, select economic indicators, financial statistics, etc.
        §   En.

354   Business conditions in Argentina   (Ernesto Tornquist & Cia Ltda)
        Ernesto Tornquist & Cia Ltda, Bartolome Mitre 559, Buenos Aires.
        1884-   quarterly.   not priced.
        Contains data on Argentine economic conditions and a few statistics, including banking, building,
               agricultural products, hides and meat, cost of living indices, foreign affairs and foreign trade,
               domestic affairs and finance, shipping, stock exchange, transport and communications.
        §   En   and   Es   eds.

¶   B   -   Production

i.   Mines and mining

355   Estadística minera de la República Argentina   [Mineral statistics of Argentina]   (Dirección Nacional de
               Económia Minera).
        Dirección Nacional de Económia Minera, Ministerio de Económia, Buenos Aires.
        1960/65-   1975.   not priced.   309 p.
        Contains data on total production of minerals, production by types, production by provinces, exports and
               uses.
        Time factor: the 1975 issue, published in 1977, has data for 1975.
        §   Es.

        Refer also to 346, 348.

ii.   Agriculture, fisheries, forestry, etc.

356   Censo nacional de agropecuario   [National census of agriculture and livestock]   (Instituto Nacional de
               Estadística y Censos).
        Instituto Nacional de Estadística y Censos, Hipolito Yrigoyen 250, Buenos Aires.
        1952-   1969.   not priced.
        Provisional figures are included in 'Censo nacional agropecuario, 1969: datos comparativos, 1969-1960'
               which was published in 1970.
        §   Es.

357   Estadística forestal   [Forestry statistics]   (Servicio Nacional Forestal, Ministerio de Económica y Trabajo).
        Servicio Forestal, Ministerio de Económica y Trabajo, Buenos Aires.
        1961-   1969.   not priced.   119 p.
        Contains data on consumption of forest products, their manufacture, use as fuel, pulp and its products,
               foreign trade, etc.
        §   Es.

        Refer also to 346, 347, 384.

¶   B,   continued

iii.   Industry

358   Estadística industrial: principales datos de algunas ramas y productos   [Industrial statistics: principal data on
            general sectors of industry and products]   (Instituto Nacional de Estadística y Censos).
            Instituto Nacional de Estadística y Censos, Hipolito Yrigoyen 250, Buenos Aires.
            1965/69-   1972.   not priced.
            Contains data on production, employment and wages.
            Time factor: ceased publication with the 1972 issue.
            §   Es.

359   Indicadores industriales   [Industrial indicators]   (Instituto Nacional de Estadística y Censos).
            Instituto Nacional de Estadística y Censos, Hipolito Yrigoyen, 250, Buenos Aires.
            1974-   half-yearly. $500; US$16.
            Contains data on the physical volume of production, and employment, income from production, wages,
            and taxation.
            Time factor: each issue has data for four years and several quarters to the date of the issue and is
            published about 12 months later.
            §   Es.

360   La siderurgia argentina   [The Argentine iron and steel industry]   (Centro de Industriales Siderurgicos).
            Centro de Industriales Siderurgicos, Cangallo 525 - 6° piso - 1038, Buenos Aires.
            1974/75-   1974-75.   not priced.   not paged.
            Includes statistics in the text and a statistical section on production and trade, raw materials, foreign
            trade, etc.
            Time factor: the 1974-75 issue was published in 1976.
            §   Es.

            Refer also to 346, 347, 348, 351.

iv.   Construction

361   Edificación   [Construction]   (Dirección General de Estadística y Censos).
            Instituto Nacional de Estadística y Censos, Hipolito Yrigoyen 250, Buenos Aires.
            1966-   quarterly. $33 each issue.
            Contains data on permissions granted etc.
            Time factor: ceased publication in 1971.
            §   Es.

362   Estadística mensual: fascicolo CC - indice del costa de la construcción en el capital federal   [Monthly
            statistics: fascicule CC - indices of the cost of construction in the federal capital]   (Instituto
            Nacional de Estadística y Censos).
            Instituto Nacional de Estadistica y Censos, Hipolito Yrigoyen 250, Buenos Aires.
            1969- $300 or $3500 yr;   US$3 or US$7 yr.
            Time factor: each issue has data for that month and some earlier comparative figures and is published the
            following month.
            §   Es.

363   Indicadores regionales   [Regional indicators]   (Instituto Nacional de Estadística y Censos).
            Instituto Nacional de Estadística y Censos, Hipolito Yrigoyen 250, Buenos Aires.
            An irregular series for which one publication has appeared, which is 'Sectores viviendas y construcciones
            privadas. Valor agregado por provincias, 1960/1973' ($20 or US$2) concerning the housing sector
            and private construction.
            §   Es.

ARGENTINA,   continued

¶   B.iv,   continued

Refer also to 346, 347, 348.

v.   Energy

364   Energia electrica: boletín mensual: cifras provisionales   [Electric energy: monthly bulletin: provisional
                figures]   (Secretaria de Estado de Energia).
        Secretaria de Estado de Energia, Buenos Aires.
        1960-   not priced.   118 p.
        Contains data on production, consumption, etc, of electric energy.
        Time factor: each issue has data to the month of the issue and is published shortly afterwards.

365   Combustibles   [Fuels]   (Secretaria de Estado de Energia).
        Secretaria de Estado de Energia, Buenos Aires.
        1964-   1972.   not priced.   51 p.
        Contains data on production, imports and exports, sales, consumption and transport of oil, natural gas,
                distilled gas, carbon minerals, etc.
        Time factor: the 1972 issue, with data for 1972, was published in 1975.
        §   Es.

366   Gas del Estado: boletín estadístico anual   [State Gas: annual statistical bulletin]
        Gas del Estado, Buenos Aires.
        1960/61-   1973.   not priced.   90 p.
        Contains commercial statistics on production, sales and use of gas, exploitation statistics on natural and
                liquid gas, economic statistics and data on personnel.
        Time factor: the 1973 issue, published in 1974, has data for 1973 and some earlier years.
        §   Es.

        Refer also to 346.

¶   C   -   External trade

367   Comercio exterior (edición anual)   [Foreign trade (annual edition)]   (Instituto Nacional de Estadística y
                Censos).
        Instituto Nacional de Estadística y Censos, Hipolito Yrigoyen 250, Buenos Aires.
        1887-   1976. $5000;   US$30 for 3 vols.   3 vols in 4.
        Contents:
                Vol I   General summary
                Vol II   Exports
                Vol III   (2 parts) Imports.
        Vols 2 and 3 include detailed statistics of trade by commodity subdivided by countries of origin and
                destination.
        Time factor: the 1976 issue, published late 1977, has data for 1976.
        §   Es.

368   Comercio exterior   [Foreign trade]   (Instituto Nacional de Estadística y Censos).
        Instituto Nacional de Estadística y Censos, Hipolito Yrigoyen 250, Buenos Aires.
        1915-   quarterly.   not priced.
        Contains data on foreign trade by country or origin and destination and foreign trade by commodity section
                by months.
        Time factor: ceased publication with the 1972 issues.
        §   Es.

¶   C,   continued

369   Fasciculo ICA - intercambio comercial argentino   [Fascicule ICA - foreign trade of Argentina]   (Instituto
           Nacional de Estadística y Censos).
           Instituto Nacional de Estadística y Censos, Hipolito Yrigoyen 250, Buenos Aires.
           1973-   monthly. $50 or $600 yr;   US$2 or US$20 yr.
           Contains brief tables of imports and exports by broad commodity groups and by countries.
           §   Es.

370   Intercambio comercial argentino segun CUCI   [Foreign trade of Argentina by SITC]   (Instituto Nacional de
           Estadística y Censos).
           Instituto Nacional de Estadística y Censos, Hipolito Yrigoyen 250, Buenos Aires.
           1960-   1976. $100;   US$3.   16 p.
           §   Es.

371   Intercambio comercial argentino segun NAB   [Foreign trade of Argentina by the Brussels Nomenclature]
           (Instituto Nacional de Estadística y Censos)
           Instituto Nacional de Estadística y Censos, Hipolito Yrigoyen 250, Buenos Aires.
           1967-   1976. $200;   US$3.   29 p.
           §   Es.

372   Informe serie ZLC - intercambio comercial argentino con los paises de la ALALC   [Foreign trade of Argentina
           with the countries of the Latin American Free Trade Association]   (Instituto Nacional de Estadística
           y Censos).
           Instituto Nacional de Estadística y Censos, Hipolito Yrigoyen 250, Buenos Aires.
           1962-   monthly. $50 or $600 yr plus $1000 postage;   US$2 or US$20 yr.
           Contains brief statistics of foreign trade of Argentina with the other countries of ALALC arranged by
               commodities and subdivided by countries of origin and destination.
           §   Es.

       Refer also to 346, 347, 348.

   ¶   D   -   Internal distribution and service trades

373   Comercio interior   [Internal trade]   (Instituto Nacional de Estadística y Censos).
           Instituto Nacional de Estadística y Censos, Hipolito Yrigoyen 250, Buenos Aires.
           1963-   quarterly.   not priced.
           Contains data on wholesale prices, retail trade (index numbers of sales), and service trades (index
               numbers).
           Time factor: ceased publication with the issues for 1972.
           §   Es.

374   Indice de precios al por mayor   [Index of wholesale prices]   (Instituto Nacional de Estadística y Censos).
           Instituto Nacional de Estadística y Censos, Hipolito Yrigoyen 250, Buenos Aires.
           1956/72-   monthly. $300 or $3500 yr plus $1000 postage.   US$3 or US$7 yr.
           §   Es.

375   Encuesta de turismo nacional: informe preliminar   [Survey of national tourism: preliminary report]   (Instituto
           Nacional de Estadística y Censos).
           Instituto Nacional de Estadística y Censos, Hipolito Yrigoyen 250, Buenos Aires.
                           $30;   US$10.   85 p.
           Time factor: the report refers to 1971 and was published in 1971.
           §   Es.

       Refer also to 346, 347, 348, 351.

ARGENTINA,   continued

¶   E - Population

376   Censo nacional de población, familias y viviendas   [Census of population, families and housing]   (Instituto
            Nacional de Estadística y Censos).
            Instituto Nacional de Estadística y Censos, Hipolito Yrigoyen 250, Buenos Aires.
            1869-   10th, 1970.   not priced.
            Volumes published are 'Resultados obtenidos por muestra' [Sample results] in 26 regional volumes and one
                for the country as a whole, and several booklets of provisional statistics.
            Time factor: the results were published in 1971.

377   Hechos demograficos en la République Argentina   [Demographic data for Argentina]   (Instituto Nacional de
            Estadística y Censos).
            Instituto Nacional de Estadística y Censos, Hipolito Yrigoyen 250, Buenos Aires.
            1954/60-   1961-1966.   not priced.   2 vols.
            Contains data on births, deaths and marriages.
            Time factor: published quinquennially.
            §   Es.

            Note: an earlier volume of a similar nature was 'Informe demografico de la République Argentina,
                1944-1954'.

378   La migración interna en la Argentina, 1960/1970   [Internal migration in Argentina, 1960/1970]   (Instituto
            Nacional de Estadística y Censos).
            Instituto Nacional de Estadística y Censos, Hipolito Yrigoyen 250, Buenos Aires.
                            $150;   US$10.
            Time factor: published in 1972.
            §   Es.

379   Evolución de la población argentina, 1950-2000   [Evolution of the population of Argentina, 1950-2000]
            (Instituto Nacional de Estadística y Censos).
            Instituto Nacional de Estadística y Censos, Hipolito Yrigoyen 250, Buenos Aires.
                            not priced.   43 p.
            Time factor: published in 1974.
            §   Es.

380   Encuesta de empleo y desempleo   [Survey of employment and unemployment]   (Instituto Nacional de
            Estadística y Censos).
            Instituto Nacional de Estadística y Censos, Hipolito Yrigoyen 250, Buenos Aires.
                            not priced.   6 vols.
            The volumes contains data for Rosario, Gran Mendoza, Tucuman, Cordoba, Gran Buenos Aires, and a
                general volume for the whole country.
            Time factor: the survey was carried out between 1966 and 1969 and the results published in 1970.
            §   Es.

            Refer also to 346, 347, 351.

¶   F - Social

i.   Standard of living

381   Costa de vida   [Cost of living]   (Instituto Nacional de Estadística y Censos).
            Instituto Nacional de Estadística y Censos, Hipolito Yrigoyen 250, Buenos Aires.
            1963-   monthly. $119 yr.
            Time factor: ceased publication with the 1972 issues.
            §   Es.

ARGENTINA,   continued

¶   F.i,   continued

382   Indice de precios al consumidor: base 1960 100   [Consumer price index: base 1960 100]   (Instituto Nacional
            de Estadística y Censos).
        Instituto Nacional de Estadística y Censos, Hipolito Yrigoyen 250, Buenos Aires.
        1960/65-   3rd, 1971/75. $400; US$30.
        Time factor: the 3rd issue was published in 1976.
        §   Es.

383   Indice de precios al consumidor y salarios industriales: base 1974 100   [Index of consumer prices and industrial
            wages: base 1974 100]   (Instituto Nacional de Estadística y Censos).
        Instituto Nacional de Estadística y Censos, Hipolito Yrigoyen 250, Buenos Aires.
        1973-   monthly. $300 or $3500 yr plus $1000 postage;   US$3 or US$7 yr.
        Time factor: each issue has the latest data available.
        §   Es.

384   Remuneraciones sector agropecuario: perioda 1950-1969   [Wages in the agricultural sector, period 1950-1969]
            (Secretaria de Estado de Trabajo).
        Secretaria de Estado de Trabajo, Buenos Aires.
                            $100.   34 p.
        Contains data by province.
        Time factor: published in 1969.
        §   Es.

        Refer also to 346.

    ii.   Health and welfare

        Refer to 346.

    iii.   Education and leisure

385   Estadísticas de la educación   [Statistics of education]   (Ministerio de Cultura y Educación).
        Ministerio de Cultura y Educación, Avda E Madero 235, Buenos Aires.
        1965-   1974.   not priced.   403 p.
        Contains, for each geographical area, data on establishments, teachers, pupils, classes, etc, in pre-
            primary, primary, secondary and university education.
        Time factor: the 1974 issue, with data for that year, was published in 1975.
        §   Es.

        Note: also issued by the Ministry is 'Estadística educativa: sintesis 1966-1970', published in 1971.

386   Argentina: la educación en cifras   [Argentina: education in figures]   (Ministerio de Cultura y Educación).
        Ministerio de Cultura y Educación, Avda E Madero 235, Buenos Aires.
        1961/70-   1963-1972.   not priced.   2 vols.
        Similar content, but not so detailed, to 385 above.
        Time factor: the 1963-1972 issue, with data for those years, was published in 1973.
        §   Es.

        Refer also to 346.

    iv.   Justice

        Refer to 346.

¶ G - Finance

387   Boletín estadístico [Statistical bulletin] (Banco Central de la República Argentina).
          Banco Central de la República Argentina, Reconquista 266, Buenos Aires.
          1937- monthly.   not priced.
          Contains data on banking and money, exchanges, market values, the state of the banks, public debt,
              and national product and income.
          Time factor: each issue has data for three or four years and 12 months to about two months prior to the
              date of publication.
          §   Es.

          Note: the bank also issues an annual 'Memoria' [report] which includes a very few statistics other than
              those related to the activities of the bank.

          Refer also to 346, 347, 348.

¶   H   - Transport and communications

          Refer also to 346, 347.

i.   Ships and shipping

388   Navegación comercial argentina   [Argentine commercial shipping] (Instituto Nacional de Estadística y
              Censos).
          Instituto Nacional de Estadística y Censos, Hipolito Yrigoyen 250, Buenos Aires.
          1967- 1975. $200; US$15.   154 p.
          Contains data on the movement of ships, their passengers and cargoes, including movements abroad, by
              river, coastal traffic, and port traffic.
          Time factor: the 1975 issue, was published in 1977, has data for 1975.
          §   Es.

iii.   Rail

389   Ferrocarriles Argentinos: memoria y balance   [Argentine Railways: report and accounts]
          Ferrocarriles Argentinos, Buenos Aires.
          1968- 1971.   not priced.
          Includes some traffic statistics as well as the financial accounts of the railway.
          §   Es.

iv.   Air

390   Aeronavegación comercial argentina   [Argentine commercial air traffic] (Instituto Nacional de Estadística
              y Censos).
          Instituto Nacional de Estadística y Censos, Hipolito Yrigoyen 250, Buenos Aires.
          1960/69- 1976. $300; US$7.   79 p.
          Contains data on the activities of airlines, traffic, international traffic, servicing of aircraft, etc.
          Time factor: the 1976 issue, published early 1978, has data for 1976 and some earlier years.
          §   Es.

v.   Telecommunications and postal services

391   Estadística telefonica [Telephone statistics] (Instituto Nacional de Estadística y Censos).
          Instituto Nacional de Estadística y Censos, Hipolito Yrigoyen 250, Buenos Aires.
          1960/69- 1970-1974. $100; US$8.   35 p.
          Contains data on installations, traffic, employees, wages, and a summary of income and expenditure.
          Time factor: the 1970-1974 issue, with information for those years, was published in 1976.
          §   Es.

Central statistical office

392   Department of Statistics,
           Cabinet Office,
           PO Box 3904,
           Nassau.
           t 56511 - 20.

       The Department collects statistical information, directly or through other government departments,
analyses and publishes it.   Unpublished statistical information may be supplied on request, and usually there
is no fee.

Libraries

       The Department of Statistics has a library but it is not open to the general public.   Libraries where
statistical publications of the Bahamas may be consulted are Nassau Public Library, PO Box N-3210, Nassau
(t 24907) which is open Monday to Wednesday, 10.00 to 21.00 hours, Thursday, 10.00 to 14.00 hours, and
Friday and Saturday, 10.00 to 17.00 hours; Southern Public Library, PO Box 2437 GT, Nassau (t 21056)
which is open Monday to Friday 9.00 to 20.00 hours and Saturday, 9.00 to 17.00 hours; and Eastern Public
Library, PO Box 5602, Nassau (t 21096) which is open Monday to Friday from 10.00 to 21.00 hours and
Saturday, 10.00 to 13.00 hours.

Libraries and information services abroad

       Publications of the Department of Statistics are available for consultation in the High Commissioner's
Office, 39 Pall Mall, London SW1.

Bibliographies

393   Quarterly newsletter   (Department of Statistics).
           1971-   B$1.50 or B$5 yr
           An information bulletin, which also lists new Department of Statistics' publications.

Statistical publications

¶   A - General

394   Commonwealth of the Bahamas statistical abstract   (Department of Statistics).
           Department of Statistics, Cabinet Office, PO Box N-3904, Nassau.
           1969- 1976.   B$5.   214 p.
           Main sections:
               Climate   Health
               Vital statistics   Crime, court cases and police
               Population and migration   Education
               Tourism   Agriculture, forestry and fishing
               External trade   Banking, finance and insurance
               Building and construction   Politics
               Public utilities   Labour
               Transportation (land, air and sea)   Retail price index
               Communications - telecommunications &
                   post office.
           Time factor: the 1976 edition, published late 1977, has data for the years 1967 to 1976.
           §   En.

¶ A, continued

395   Commonwealth of the Bahamas quarterly statistical summary   (Department of Statistics).
            Department of Statistics, Cabinet Office, PO Box N-3904, Nassau.
            1971-   B$2 each issue.
            Contains social and economic indicators, and data on meteorology, population and vital statistics,
                external trade, tourism, traffic, aviation, agriculture, forestry, fishing, building, construction,
                public utilities, retail prices, crime and legal, health, banking, finance, and immigration.
            Time factor: each issue has data for several years, quarters and months to the date of the issue and is
                published about 6 months later.
            §   En.

396   Quarterly review   (Central Bank of the Bahamas).
            Central Bank of the Bahamas, PO Box N-4868, Nassau.
            1975-   not priced.
            Includes statistical tables on money and banking, government finance, balance of payments, foreign
                trade, prices, retail price index, tourism, construction, electricity, and general economic
                indicators.
            Time factor: each issue has some long and some short runs of statistical tables to the month of the issue,
                and is published about three months later.
            §   En.

            Note: the bank also issues an 'Annual report and statement of accounts' which includes some monetary
                and economic statistics as well as the report on the activities of the bank.

¶ B - Production

ii. Agriculture, fisheries, forestry etc.

397   Agricultural and fishing statistics report   (Department of Statistics)
            Department of Statistics, Cabinet Office, PO Box N-3904, Nassau.
            1974- quarterly.   B$1.50 each issue.
            Contains data on ecology, labour force, household personal income, finance, agricultural production
                marketed by the government owned and operated produce exchange, and landings of marine products.
            Time factor: data refers to the quarter of the issue plus cumulations to date and is published four months
                later.
            §   En.

            Refer also to 394, 395.

iii. Industry

            Refer to 394, 395.

iv. Construction

398   Quarterly bulletin of construction statistics   (Department of Statistics).
            Department of Statistics, Cabinet Office, PO Box N-3904, Nassau.
            1975-   B$1 each issue.
            Contains quarterly data on building permits approved, building starts and building completions, classified
                by economic sector and by value group.
            Time factor: each issue covers the quarter of the issue and is published about four months later.
            §   En.

            Refer also to 394, 395.

¶ B,   continued

v.   Energy

399   Annual report and accounts   (Bahamas Electricity Corporation).
           Bahamas Electricity Corporation, Nassau.
           1958/59-   1975/76.   not priced.   44 p.
           Contains data on the operations and finances.
           Time factor: the 1975/76 report, published early 1978, has data for the fiscal year 1975/76.
           § En.

           Refer also to 396.

¶ C - External trade

400   External trade report   (Department of Statistics).
           Department of Statistics, Cabinet Office, PO Box N-3904, Nassau.
           1918- 1976.   B$6.   740 p.
           Main tables show statistics of imports and exports arranged by commodity and subdivided by countries of
                origin and destination, and arranged by country of origin and destination subdivided by commodities.
           Time factor: the 1976 issue, published Autumn, 1977, has data for 1976.
           § En.

401   Summary report of external trade statistics   (Department of Statistics).
           Department of Statistics, Cabinet Office, PO Box N-3904, Nassau.
           1970-   quarterly.   B$3 or B$15 yr.
           Main tables show imports and exports arranged by sections of commodity classification.
           Time factor: each issue has data for that quarter and three previous ones and is published about six months
                later.
           § En.

           Refer also to 394, 395, 396.

¶ D - Internal distribution and service trades

402   Annual report of tourism   (Ministry of Tourism)
           Ministry of Tourism, PO Box N-3701, Nassau.
           1968-   1976.   not priced.   17 p.
           The report includes some statistical tables on tourism.
           Time factor: the 1976 report was published in 1977.
           § En.

           Note: the Ministry also published 'Bahamas Islands: visitors statistics' for 1968 and 1969.

           Refer also to 394, 395, 396.

¶ E - Population

403   Report of the census of population   (Department of Statistics).
           Department of Statistics, Cabinet Office, PO Box 3904, Nassau.
           1838- 1970.   B$10.   480 p.
           The main tables have data on the number of households, members and visitors by enumeration district and
                island; the local population by sex, age, relationship to the head of the household, religion, marital
                status as well as other characteristics.   The report also contains data on internal migration, the
                labour force and household income.
           Time factor: the report of the 1970 census was published in 1972.
           § En.

¶   E,   continued

404   Manpower and income   (Department of Statistics).
             Department of Statistics, Cabinet Office, PO Box 3904, Nassau.
                          out of print.
             Issued as 'Census monograph No 1'.
             Time factor: published in 1974.
             §   En.

405   Report on the Bahamas life tables, 1962–1974 & 1969–1971   (Department of Statistics).
             Department of Statistics, Cabinet Office, PO Box 3904, Nassau.
                          B$3.   36 p.
             Time factor: published in 1973.
             §   En.

406   Demographic aspects of Bahamian population, 1901–1974   (Department of Statistics).
             Department of Statistics, Cabinet Office, PO Box 3904, Nassau.
                          B$5.   53 p.
             Issued as 'Census monograph No 2'.
             Time factor: published in 1975.
             §   En.

407   Vital statistics   (Department of Statistics).
             Department of Statistics, Cabinet Office, PO Box 3904, Nassau.
             1968–   1976. B$2.50.   85 p.
             Births, deaths, marriages and divorces by age group, sex, permanent residence in the Bahamas, occupation
                  group, etc.
             Time factor: the 1976 issue, published in late 1977, has data for 1976.
             §   En.

408   Immigration statistics report   (Department of Statistics).
             Department of Statistics, Cabinet Office, PO Box 3904, Nassau.
             1975–   1976. B$2.   36 p.
             Contains statistics of approved permits classified by age, nationality, economic sector, and occupation.
             Time factor: the 1976 report, with data for 1976, was published late 1977.
             §   En.

409   Annual report of the Ministry of Labour.
             Ministry of Labour, Nassau.
             1965–   1968. B$3.50.   88 p.
             Includes an appendix with statistical data on the hourly wage scale, persons registered by occupation,
                  vacancies filled and vacancies notified.
             Time factor: the 1968 report, published in 1969, has data for 1968.
             §   En.

410   Labour force and income distribution, 1973   (Department of Statistics).
             Department of Statistics, Cabinet Office, PO Box 3904, Nassau.
                          not priced.   168 p.
             Time factor: the report was published in 1974.
             §   En.

¶   E,   continued

411   The labour force report   (Department of Statistics).
          Department of Statistics, Cabinet Office, PO Box 3904, Nassau.
          1974-   1975.   B$3.   65 p.
          Includes estimates of the potentially economically active population, the employed and the unemployed,
             classification by sex, age group, occupational groups, type of industry, and nationality and by
             island in the Bahamas.
          Time factor: the 1975 report, with data for 1975, was published in 1976.
          §   En.

¶   F   -   Social

i.   Standard of living

412   Household expenditure in the Bahamas, 1973   (Department of Statistics).
          Department of Statistics, Cabinet Office, PO Box 3904, Nassau.
                      B$3.   97 p.
          Includes estimates of household expenditure by size of household, income group, type of dwelling,
             occupational division, economic activity, nationality, sex and age group.
          Time factor: the report was published mid-1975. .
          §   En.

413   Household income in the Bahamas, 1975   (Department of Statistics)
          Department of Statistics, Cabinet Office, PO Box 3904, Nassau.
                      B$5.   30 p.
          Contains statistics of households and household income by sex, age group, occupation and economic
             activity of the heads of households, by income group and marital status.
          Time factor: the report was published in 1977.
          §   En.

414   Retail price index   (Department of Statistics).
          Department of Statistics, Cabinet Office, PO Box 3904, Nassau.
                monthly   B$3 yr.
                annual issue   B$0.25
          Two separate indexes are published, one for New Providence and one for Freeport, Grand Bahama Island.
          Time factor: generally available two or three months following the period covered.
          §   En.

415   Annual review of prices report   (Department of Statistics)
          Department of Statistics, Cabinet Office, PO Box 3904, Nassau.
          1974-   1976.   B$2.   57 p.
          Contains a general analysis of retail price movements for the year in New Providence and Grand Bahama.
          Time factor: the 1976 review was published mid-1977.
          §   En.

416   Household budgetary survey   (Department of Statistics).
          Department of Statistics, Cabinet Office, PO Box 3904, Nassau.
          1970-
          Published so far are:
                1970 household budget survey report: New Providence (B$3)
                1973/4 household budget survey report: Grand Bahama (B$2)
          §   En.

          Refer also to 394, 395, 396.

¶   F,   continued

ii.   Health and welfare

417   Annual report of the Chief Medical Officer   (Ministry of Health).
         Ministry of Health, Nassau.
              1974.   not priced.   37 p.
         Some statistical tables in the text, which is devoted to the health situation, health services, environmental
              health services, supporting services, health infrastructure, etc.
         Time factor: the report for 1974, published in 1975, has data for 1974 and some earlier years.
         §   En.

         Refer also to 394, 395.

iii.   Education and leisure

418   Annual report   (Ministry of Education and Culture).
         Ministry of Education and Culture, Nassau.
         1948- 1970/71.   not priced.   c 50 p.
         Includes a statistical appendix with data on numbers of schools, teachers, enrolments, classes, etc.
         §   En.

         Refer also to 394.

iv.   Justice

         Refer to 394, 395.

¶   G   -   Finance

i.   Banking

         Refer to 394, 395, 396.

ii.   Public finance

419   Government revenue and expenditure report   (Department of Statistics).
         Department of Statistics, Cabinet Office, PO Box N-3904, Nassau.
         1970/73- 1970-1975.   B$1.   23 p.
         Time factor: the 1970-1975 issue, with data for those years, was published early 1978.
         §   En.

         Refer also to 394, 395, 396.

iii.   Company finance

420   Company statistics report   (Department of Statistics).
         Department of Statistics, Cabinet Office, PO Box 3904, Nassau.
         1970- 1971.   B$2.   23 p.
         Contains data on the number of registered companies, their authorised capital classified by economic
              activity and subdivided by town or geographical area.
         Time factor: the 1971 issue, published in 1972, has data for 1971.
         §   En.

BAHAMAS,   continued

¶   G,   continued

v.   Insurance

Refer to 394.

¶   H   -   Transport and communications

Refer also to 394, 395.

i.   Ships and shipping

421   Annual shipping statistics report   (Department of Statistics).
Department of Statistics, Cabinet Office, PO Box 3904, Nassau.
1969-   1976.   B$2.   69 p.
Contains data on the number of vessels entering and being cleared by port, and the net tonnage of such
vessels.
Time factor: the 1976 issue, published in 1977, has data for 1976.
§   En.

ii.   Road

422   Annual report   (Road Traffic Department).
Road Traffic Department, PO Box N 1615, Nassau.
1966-   1973.   not priced.   12 p.
Includes statistical data on revenue collection, expenditures, and numbers of motor vehicles, trucks,
motor cycles, cars, buses and taxicabs licensed.
Time factor: the report for 1973 was published in 1974 and has data from 1968 to 1973.
§   En.

iv.   Air

423   Annual report   (Department of Civil Aviation).
Department of Civil Aviation, Nassau.
1964-   1976.   not priced.   12 p.
Includes statistical appendices on movements at Nassau International Airport, passenger arrivals and
departures, domestic and international flights, aircraft operations, and a summary of revenue and
expenditure.
Time factor: the 1976 report, published in 1977, has data for 1976.
§   En.

v.   Telecommunications and postal services

424   Annual report   (Post Office Department).
Post Office Department, Nassau.
1966-   1976.   not priced.   14 p.
Includes appendices on the number of articles handled, revenue and expenditure, etc.
Time factor: the 1976 report, published mid-1977, has data for 1976.
§   En.

Central statistical office

425   Barbados Statistical Service,
           3rd Floor, National Insurance Building,
           Fairchild Street,
           St Michael.
           t 77 841.

           The Statistical Service is responsible for the collection, analysis and publication of statistics for
           Barbados.

Statistical publications

¶   A   -   General

426   Abstract of statistics   (Barbados Statistical Service).
       Barbados Statistical Service, 3rd Floor, National Insurance Building, Fairchild Street, St Michael.
       1956-   No 6, 1969.   B$1.50.   129 p.
       Main sections:
           Climate   Savings and investments
           Population and vital statistics   Households
           Social conditions and services   Government
           Sugar industry   Trade
           Other industry   Internal transport
       Time factor: the 1969 edition, published in 1971, has long runs of figures to 1969.
       §   En.

427   Monthly digest of statistics   (Barbados Statistical Service).
       Barbados Statistical Service, 3rd Floor, National Insurance Building, Fairchild Street, St Michael.
       1956-   B$0.50 each issue.
       Contains data on population, tourism, transport, industrial production, overseas trade, finance, prices
           (retail price index and retail prices of selected food items), and short-term interest rates.
       Time factor: each issue has annual figures for the last four years and 24 months to the month of the issue,
           and is published about two months later.
       §   En.

428   Economic survey   (Economic Planning Unit).
       Economic Planning Unit, Office of the Prime Minister, Bridgetown.
       1962-   1972.   not priced.   69 p.
       Contains data on foreign trade, population and migration, gross domestic product, industry, agriculture
           and fisheries, tourism, construction, public utilities, external communications, banking and finance,
           public finance, and retail price index.
       Time factor: the 1972 edition, published in 1973, has data for 1972 and some earlier years in some
           tables.
       §   En.

429   Annual statistical digest   (Central Bank of Barbados).
       Central Bank of Barbados, PO Box 1016, Bridgetown.
       1975-   1977.   not priced.   155 p.
       Supplements the Bank's monthly 'Economic and financial statistics' (430) and includes data on the assets
           and liabilities of the Central Bank and commercial banks, the banking system (monetary supply,
           monetary survey), other financial institutions and statutory boards, interest rates, securities, public
           finance, foreign trade, and general statistics (retail price index; production of sugar, etc; output of
           crude oil, electricity generation and consumption).
       Time factor: the 1977 issue, with long runs of figures to 1977, was published in 1978.
       §   En.

¶   A,   continued

430   Economic and financial statistics   (Central Bank of Barbados).
            Central Bank of Barbados, PO Box 1016, Bridgetown.
            1973-   monthly.   not priced.
            Contains data on the monetary authority (Central Bank), commercial banks, banking system (money),
                other financial institutions, interest rates, securities, public finance, foreign trade - international
                payments, and general statistics (retail price index, index of industrial production).
            Time factor: each issue has runs of four years and 18 months to about three months before the date of the
                issue and publication.
            §   En.

431   Quarterly report   (Central Bank of Barbados).
            Central Bank of Barbados, PO Box 1016, Bridgetown.
            1974-   not priced.
            Mainly textual, but includes an economic review, monetary survey, and statistics of public finance,
                production and prices, foreign trade and payments, regional developments, index of agricultural
                production, sugar export prices, etc.
            §   Es.

            Note: the Bank also issues an annual report which includes an economic report, as well as data on the
                operations of the bank, administration, financial statement, etc.

¶   B   -   Production

432   Barbados sugar industry review   (Barbados Sugar Producers' Association (Inc)).
            Barbados Sugar Producers' Association (Inc), Warrens, St Michael.
                    quarterly.   not priced.
            Mainly text, but has statistics on production and prices.
            §   En.

            Refer also to 426, 427, 428, 429.

¶   C   -   External trade

433   Annual overseas trade   (Barbados Statistical Service).
            Barbados Statistical Service, 3rd Floor, National Insurance Building, Fairchild Street, St Michael.
            1896-   1976.   B$5.   381 p.
            Main tables show imports and exports arranged by commodity and subdivided by countries of origin and
                destination.
            Time factor: the 1976 issue, published in 1977, has data for 1976.
            §   En.

434   Statistics of monthly overseas trade   (Barbados Statistical Service).
            Barbados Statistical Service, 3rd Floor, National Insurance Building, Fairchild Street, St Michael.
            1957-   B$1 each issue
            Main tables show imports and exports arranged by commodity and subdivided by countries of origin and
                destination.
            Time factor: each issue is published about four months after the end of the period covered.
            §   En.

            Refer also to 426, 427, 429.

¶ D - Internal distribution and service trades

435 Digest of tourist statistics (Barbados Statistical Service).
Barbados Statistical Service, 3rd Floor, National Insurance Building, Fairchild Street, St Michael.
1964- 3rd, 1976. B$1. 48 p.
Contains tourist statistics generally, including bednights by country of residence and by type of accommo-
dation, occupancy by type of accommodation, and length of stay.
Time factor: the 1976 edition, published mid-1977, has data for 1976, including monthly statistics.
§ En.

436 A bednight's survey of hotels and guest houses (Barbados Statistical Service).
Barbados Statistical Service, 3rd Floor, National Insurance Building, Fairchild Street, St Michael.
1965- 7th, 1971. not priced. 21 p.
Time factor: the 1971 issue, published in 1972, has data for 1971.
§ En.

437 Annual report (Barbados Tourist Board).
Barbados Tourist Board, Bridgetown.
1959/60- 1973-1974. not priced. 28 p.
Includes statistical data on numbers of visitors, arrivals, accommodation, and visitors' expenditures.
Time factor: the 1973-1974 report, published in 1974, has data for several years to 1973.
§ En.

Note: the financial statement of the Board is published separately.

Refer also to 426, 427.

¶ E - Population

438 Census of population (Barbados Statistical Service).
Barbados Statistical Service, 3rd Floor, National Insurance Building, Fairchild Street, St Michael.
1851- 1970.
Refer to 258 for details of the final reports of the 1970 Commonwealth Caribbean population census, which
includes Barbados. Preliminary bulletins on education, population, housing, and the working
population were issued by the Barbados Statistical Service in 1974, 1973, 1972 and 1972 respectively.
§ En.

439 Report on vital statistics and registrations (Registration Office).
Registration Office, Law Courts, Bridgetown.
1938- 1975. not priced. 25 p.
Time factor: the 1975 issue, published in 1977, has data for 1975 and some earlier years.
§ En.

440 Annual report of the Department of Labour.
Department of Labour, Bridgetown.
1962- 1975. not priced. 89 p.
Contains statistical data on employment, vacancies, migrants, wage rates in main industries, labour
disputes, trade unions, accidents, and index of retail prices.
Time factor: the 1975 report, published in 1977, has data for 1975 and for earlier years in some tables.
§ En.

Refer also to 426, 427, 428.

BARBADOS,   continued

¶   F - Social

i.   Standard of living

Refer to 426, 427, 430.

ii.   Health and welfare

441   Annual report of the Chief Medical Officer   (Ministry of Health and Welfare).
Ministry of Health and Welfare, Bridgetown.
1961/62-   1976.   not priced.   58 p.
Includes tables on population, causes of death, hospitalisation, and causes of hospitalisation, etc.
Time factor: the 1976 report, published in 1977, has data for 1976.
§   En.

¶   G - Finance

442   Financial statistics   (Barbados Statistical Service).
Barbados Statistical Service, 3rd Floor, National Insurance Building, Fairchild Street, St Michael.
1959/68-   1966-1976.   B$0.25.   24 p.
Includes data on the money supply, commercial banking, savings and loan association, life insurance
companies, public finances, and interest rates.
Time factor: the 1966-1976 issue, published in 1977, has data for ten years to the fiscal year 1975/76.
§   En.

Refer also to 426, 427, 428, 429, 430.

ii.   Public finance

443   Balance of payments   (Central Bank of Barbados).
Central Bank of Barbados, PO Box 1016, Bridgetown.
1967-   1976.   not priced.   55 p.
Time factor: the 1976 issue, published in 1976, has data for the years 1970 to 1976.
§   En.

Note: the first seven issues, from 1967 to 1973, were produced by the Barbados Statistical Service with
the title 'Balance of payments of Barbados'.

444   Annual report of the Commissioner of Inland Revenue
Commissioner of Inland Revenue, Bridgetown.
1973/74.   not priced.   not paged.
Includes statistics of individual and company income tax.
Time factor: the 1973/74 report, with data for that fiscal year, was published in 1975.
§   En.

¶   H - Transport and communications

Refer to 426, 427.

BELIZE

Central statistical office

445   Central Planning Unit,
          Ministry of Finance and Economic Planning,
          Belmopan,
          Cayo District.

          The Unit's responsibilities include the preparation of the annual abstract, the development plan, the
trade report, and the economic survey.   Unpublished statistical information will be supplied on request if
available.

Libraries

          The Ministry of Finance and Economic Planning has a departmental library, which is open to the public
during working hours, Monday to Friday, from 8.00 to 12.00 and 13.00 to 17.00 hours.   The library has
statistical publications relating to Belize and also a limited collection of publications from other countries
and of international organisations.

          The National Library, Bliss Institute, Belize City (t 3367) has a collection of statistical publications
which may be consulted.   The library is open Mondays to Fridays from 9.00 to 12.00 and 15.00 to 20.00
hours.

Statistical publications

¶   A - General

446   Annual abstract of statistics   (Central Planning Unit: Ministry of Finance and Economic Planning).
          Government Printer, 1 Church Street, Belize City.
          1961-   1973-74.   B$2.50.   168 p.
                    Supplement 1975. B$2.50.   130 p.
          Main sections:
                    Population   Agriculture
                    Vital statistics   Education
                    Area and climate   Medical
                    Overseas trade   Miscellaneous (arrivals and departures   postal services,
                    Public finance   licensing and registration of motor vehicles and
                    National accounts   bicycles, traffic, traffic accidents, juvenile
                    Banking and finance   delinquency, registration of aliens, and shipping)
                    Forestry
          Time factor: the 1973-74 edition, published late 1976, has data for 1974 and many earlier years; the
                    supplement 1975 was published in 1977.
          §   En.

447   British Honduras report for the years...   (Foreign and Commonwealth Office).
          HM Stationery Office, PO Box 569, London SE1.
                    1966 & 1967.   £0.85.   134 p.
          Some statistical tables in the text, including employment, wages and hours of work, consumer price index,
                    retail prices, revenue and expenditure, public finance, income tax, land, agriculture and husbandry,
                    currency and banking, production, social services, justice and crime.
          Time factor: the report for the years 1966 and 1967 was published in 1974.
          §   En.

¶   A,   continued

448   Annual economic survey   (Central Planning Unit: Ministry of Finance and Economic Planning).
            Government Printer, 1 Church Street, Belize City.
            1971- 1975. $2.   65 p.
            The survey has chapters on the economy, regional and international developments, balance of payments,
                foreign trade, banking and finance, population and migration, agriculture including livestock,
                manufacturing and processing, construction, forestry, fisheries, public utilities, transport and
                communications.   Statistical tables are included in the text.
            Time factor: the 1975 edition, published in 1977, has data for 1975 and some earlier years.
            §   En.

¶   B -   Production

ii.   Agriculture, fisheries, forestry, etc.

449   Annual report of the Department of Agriculture
            Government Printer, 1 Church Street, Belize City.
            1953- 1974.   not priced.   35 p.
            Part 1 is a general review of agriculture including weather, export crops, food crops, other crops, pests
                and diseases, and the livestock industry; part II is concerned with the work of the Department.
                Some statistics and statistical tables are included.
            Time factor: the 1974 report, published in 1977, has data for 1974.
            §   En.

            Refer also to 446.

iii.   Industry

            Refer to 448.

¶   C -   External trade

450   Trade report
            Government Printer, 1 Church Street, Belize City.
            1920- 1975.   B$3.50.   221 p.
            Main tables show detailed imports and exports arranged by commodities and subdivided by countries of
                origin and destination.
            Time factor: the 1975 issue, published in 1977, has data for 1975.   The 1976 issue was in preparation
                in July 1978.
            §   En.

            Refer also to 446, 448.

¶   E -   Population

451   Census of population
            1901- 1970.
            See 258 for details of the 1970 Commonwealth Caribbean Census of population, which includes Belize.

            Refer also to 446, 448.

¶   F -   Social

            Refer to 446.

BELIZE, continued

    ¶ G - Finance

    i. Banking

        Refer to 446, 448.

    ii. Public finance

452   National accounts   (Central Planning Unit)
          Government Printer, 1 Church Street, Belize City.
          1973- 1975. B$2.   c 60 p.
          Time factor: the 1975 issue, with data for 1975, was published in 1976.
          §   En.

          Note: 'National accounts sources and methods' has been published ($2).

453   Accounts of the public sector   (Central Planning Unit)
          Government Printer, 1 Church Street, Belize City.
          1973- 1973. B$2.   c 60 p.
          Time factor: the 1975 issue, with data for that year, was published in 1976.
          §   En.

          Refer to 446, 448.

    ¶ H - Transport and communications

        Refer to 446, 448.

There is no central statistical office in Bermuda, but enquiries about statistical information could be made to the Department of Tourism and Trade Development, or to the Bermuda Chamber of Commerce, both in Hamilton.

Statistical publications

¶ A - General

454   Bermuda digest of statistica   (Statistical Office, Finance Department)
         Statistical Office, Finance Department, Lightbourne Building, Cedar Avenue, Hamilton, 5-31.
         1973-   1973.   not priced.   82 p.
         Main sections:
                   Population and vital statistics   Passenger movement
                   Crime and justice   Home finance
                   Education   Home finance mortgage registrations
                   Labour   Agriculture and fisheries
                   Wages and prices   Weather
                   External trade   Miscellaneous (electricity, land, building, etc)
                   Transport
         Time factor: the 1973 edition, published in 1974, has long runs of data to 1970 or 1971.   It was
                   intended to be issued annually.

455   Bermuda: report for the year...   (Foreign and Commonwealth Office)
         HM Stationery Office, PO Box 569, London SE1 9NH.
         1920-   1971.   £1.30.   83 p.
         Statistical tables are included in the text which reports on the geography and climate, justice and
                   defence, population and employment, labour administration and social security, finance and
                   taxation, tourism, education, health and welfare, power and communications, transport, public
                   works, agriculture and fisheries.
         Time factor: the 1971 report, published in 1975, has data for 1970 and 1971.
         §   En.

¶ B - Production

ii.   Agriculture, fisheries, forestry, etc.

456   Report of the Department of Agriculture and Fisheries.
         Department of Agriculture and Fisheries, Hamilton.
         1946-   1974.   not priced.   25 p.
         Includes a statistical appendix with data on land usage, agricultural production (vegetables, fruits),
                   livestock, and fisheries (catches).
         Time factor: the report for 1974, published 1976, has data for 1974.
         §   En.

         Refer also to 454.

iii.   Industry

457   Report on Bermuda's first economic census (census of establishments, 1971) (Statistical Office, Finance Dept).
         Statistical Office, Finance Department, Lightbourne Building, Cedar Avenue, Hamilton 5-31.
                              B$4 each volume.   2 vols.
         Vol I contains general results; Vol II data on local industries; international companies; government,
                   local authorities and non-profitmaking organisations.   Data includes number of establishments,
                   employees, receipts, purchases, stocks, etc, for each industry.
         Time factor: the report was published in 1973.
         §   En.

BERMUDA,   continued

¶   C   -   External trade

458   Report of the Customs imports and exports   (HM Customs).
            HM Customs, Hamilton.
            1952-   1976.   not priced.   143 p.
            Main tables show imports and exports arranged by commodity and subdivided by countries of origin and
                destination.
            Time factor: the 1976 issue, published in 1977, has data for 1976.
            §   En.

            Refer also to 454.

¶   D   -   Internal distribution and service trades

            Refer to 455.

¶   E   -   Population

459   Report of the population census   (Bermuda Government).
            Bermuda Government, Hamilton.
            1861-   1970.   not priced.   271 p.
            Contains data on the total de facto population; households and families; characteristics of age, race,
                religion, and marital status; migration; education and specialised training; fertility; economic
                activity; housing; etc.
            Time factor: the report of the 1970 census was published in 1973.
            §   En.

            Note: Also published in the reports of the population census of the Commonwealth Caribbean (see 258)

            Refer also to 454, 455.

¶   G   -   Finance

460   Annual report   (Bank of Bermuda Ltd)
            Bank of Bermuda Ltd, Front Street, Hamilton 5-31.
            1857-   1976.   not priced.   21 p.
            Contains statistical information on the activities of the bank.
            Time factor: the 1976 report was published late 1976.
            §   En.

461   Final accounts and annual report   (Bermuda Monetary Authority).
            Bermuda Monetary Authority, Hamilton.
                    1977.   not priced.   23 p.
            §   En.

            Refer also to 454, 455.

¶   H   -   Transport and communications

            Refer to 454, 455.

BOLIVIA - BOLIVIE - BOLIVIEN

Central statistical office

462   Instituto Nacional de Estadística   [National Institute of Statistics],
        Plaza Murillo,
        Palacio Legislativo,
        Plant Baja,
        (casilla 6129),
        La Paz.
        † 29384 & 25085.   Cables: INE

        The Institute is a part of the Ministerio de Planeamiento y Coordinación [Ministry of Planning and
Co-ordination], and is responsible for the collection, analysis and publication of official economic statistics
for Bolivia.

Libraries

        The Instituto Nacional de Estadística (see above) has a library which is open to the public for reference
and has a collection of statistical publications.   The staff speak Spanish.   The Library of the Ministerio
de Planeamiento y Coordinación (casilla no 3116) also has a collection of statistical publications.

Bibliographies

        The Instituto Nacional de Estadística issues a sales list of new publications from time to time.

Statistical publications

¶   A - General

463   Bolivia en cifras [Bolivia in figures] (Instituto Nacional de Estadística).
        Instituto Nacional de Estadística, casilla no 6129, La Paz.
                1972.   not priced.   261 p.
        Main sections:
            General   Foreign trade
            Agriculture   Finance
            Industry, minerals, petroleum and electric   Social
              energy.   Prices indices
            Consumption of selected articles.   National accounts
            Transport and communications
        Time factor: the 1972 edition, published in 1973, has data for 1972 and some earlier years in some tables.
        §   Es.

464   Boletin estadistico [Statistical bulletin] (Instituto Nacional de Estadística).
        Instituto Nacional de Estadística, casilla no 6129, La Paz.
        1901-   monthly.   not priced.
        A 4-page bulletin which includes new statistical data on a variety of subjects, depending on what
            information has been issued during the month.
        §   Es.

465   Estadisticas regionales departamento...   [Statistics of regional departments...] (Instituto Nacional de
            Estadística).
        Instituto Nacional de Estadística, casilla no 6129, La Paz.
                $b39 each vol.   5 vols.
        The volumes are for the regions of Chuquisaca, Oruro, Cochabamba, Beni and Tarija.   Contents include
            data on demography, economy, health, education, and culture.
        §   Es.

¶   A,   continued

466   Memoria   [Report]   (Camara Nacional de Industrias).
        Camara Nacional de Industrias, La Paz.
        (annual)   1973-1974.   not priced.
        Contains data on gross domestic product, industry, banking, foreign trade, production, etc.
        Time factor: the 1973-1974 issue has data for seven or eight years to 1971 or 1973.
        §   Es.

467   Boletín estadístico   [Statistical bulletin]   (Banco Central de Bolivia).
        Banco Central de Bolivia, La Paz.
        1922-   quarterly.   not priced.
        Contains data on money, credit, banking, exchange, public finance, external trade, and general
            economic indicators, including the consumer price index.
        Time factor: each issue has data for about 10 years and 18 months up to the month of the issue, and is
            published about three months later.
        §   Es.

        Note: the bank also publishes 'Memoria anual' [Annual report] with a section of economic statistics
            covering the same subjects as in the statistical bulletin.

¶   B   -   Production

    i.   Mines and mining

468   Boletín estadístico   [Statistical bulletin]   (Ministerio de Mineria y Metalurgia).
        Ministerio de Mineria y Metalurgia, La Paz.
                monthly.   not priced.
        Contains data on exports and production of minerals and metals.
        §   Es.

469   Revista minera   [Mineral review]   (Banco Minera de Bolivia).
        Banco Minera de Bolivia, La Paz.
        1965-   monthly.   not priced.
        Mainly textual, but includes statistics of mining, refining, exports, etc, of minerals.
        §   Es.

        Refer also to 463.

    ii.   Agriculture, fisheries, forestry, etc.

470   Estadísticas agropecuarias, 1961-75   [Agricultural statistics, 1961-75]   (Ministerio de Asuntos Campesinos y
            Agropecuarios)
        Ministerio de Asuntos Campesinos y Agropecuarios, La Paz.
                        not priced.
        Contains data on cereals, root crops, horticulture, fruit, etc.
        Time factor: published in 1977.
        §   Es.

471   Diagnostico del sector agropecuario, 1974   [Diagnosis of the agricultural sector]   (Ministerio de Asuntos
            Campesinos y Agropecuarios).
        Ministerio de Asuntos Campesinos y Agropecuarios, La Paz.
                        not priced.   2 vols.
        Contains data on labour resources, agricultural and livestock production, forest production, foreign
            trade, etc.
        Time factor: Contains data for 1974, and was published in 1976.
        §   Es.

¶   B.ii,   continued

472   Boletín de noticias de mercado agropecuario   [Bulletin of information on the agricultural trade]   (Ministerio
de Asuntos Campesinos Agropecuarios).
Ministerio de Asuntos Campesinos y Agropecuarios, La Paz.
quarterly.   not priced.
Contains average, top and bottom prices; cost of transport, etc.
§   Es.

Refer also to 463.

iii.   Industry

473   Anuario industriales   [Industrial yearbook]   (Instituto Nacional de Estadística).
Instituto Nacional de Estadística, casilla 6129, La Paz.
1965-   1975. $b23.50.   278 p.
Contains data on production and sales, primary materials, employment and wages, personnel in production
and wages, electric energy used, fuels and lubricants used, fixed capital and depreciations, and
aggregated values.
Time factor: the 1975 issue, published in 1976, has data for 1975.
§   Es.

Refer also to 463, 466.

v.   Energy

474   Boletin estadístico semestral   [Half-yearly statistical bulletin]   (Yacimientos Petroliferos Fiscales Bolivianos)
Yacimientos Petroliferos Fiscales Bolivianos, La Paz.
not priced.
Contains data on the production of petroleum, oil and gas; industrialisation; transport; etc.
§   Es.

475   Memoria anual   [Annual report]   (Yacimientos Petroliferos Fiscales Bolivianos).
Yacimientos Petroliferos Fiscales Bolivianos, La Paz.
1977.   not priced.
Includes data on exploration, drilling, production, sales, etc, of petroleum, oil and gas.
§   Es.

Refer also to 463.

¶   C   -   External trade

476   **Anuario de comercio exterior** [Foreign trade yearbook]   (Instituto Nacional de Estadística)
Instituto Nacional de Estadística, casilla 6129, La Paz.
1912-   1972. $b440.50.   665 p.
Main tables show imports and exports arranged by commodity and subdivided by countries of origin and
destination.
Time factor: the 1972 issue, with data for 1972, was published in 1976.
§   Es.

Refer also to 463, 466, 467.

¶ D - Internal distribution and service trades

Refer to 463.

¶ E - Population

477 Censo de población y vivienda [Census of population and housing] (Instituto Nacional de Estadística).
Instituto Nacional de Estadística, Casilla 6129, La Paz.
1845- 1976.
Publications include:
'Resultados antisipados por muestreo' [Sample results], containing total population by sex and age group, economically active population, educational attainments, housing, etc, ($b74; $84.50 in USA; $92 in Europe).
'Resultados provisionales' [Provisional results], one volume for each department of the country ($b16.50 each issue; $24 in USA; $29.50 in Europe).
Time factor: the results listed above were published in 1976 and 1977.
§ Es.

478 Encuesta demográfica nacional de Bolivia, 1976 [National demographic survey of Bolivia] (Instituto Nacional de Estadística).
Instituto Nacional de Estadística, Casilla 6129, La Paz.
Published reports include:
Principales resultados [Principal results] ($b49; $85 in USA; $113 in Europe).
Informe sobre aspectos demográficos [Report on demographic aspects] ($b49; $85 in USA; $113 in Europe.)
Time factor: published in 1977.
§ Es.

479 Encuesta de empleo La Paz, Cochabamba, Santa Cruz, 1977 [Survey of employment in La Paz, Cochabamba, Santa Cruz, 1977] (Instituto Nacional de Estadística).
Instituto Nacional de Estadística, Casilla 6129, La Paz.
Contains data on employment, unemployment, disguised employment, etc, in the three cities.
Time factor: published in 1978.
§ Es.

Refer also to 463, 465.

¶ F - Social

i. Standard of living

480 Indice de precios al consumidor: cuidad de La Paz [Consumer price index: La Paz] (Instituto Nacional de Estadística).
1974- 1977. $b49; $85 in USA; $113 in Europe. 36 p.
Time factor: the 1977 issue, published in 1978, has data for 1977 and some earlier figures.
§ Es.

Refer also to 463, 467.

ii. Health and welfare

Refer to 465.

iii. Education and leisure

¶   F.iii,   continued

481   El desarrollo reciente de la educación en Bolivia: algunas de sus caracteristicas   [Recent developments in
            education in Bolivia: some characteristics]   (S R Pittari).
            Instituto Nacional de Estadística, Casilla 6129, La Paz.
                            $b49; $85 in USA; $113 in Europe.
            Time factor: published in 1977.
            §   Es.

482   Estadísticas educativas   [Education statistics]   (Ministerio de Educación y Cultura).
            Ministerio de Educación y Cultura, La Paz.
            (annual)   1976.   not priced.
            Contains data on number of pupils/students, illiteracy, teaching, educational establishments, etc.
            Time factor: the 1976 issue was published in 1977 and has data for 1976.
            §   Es.

            Refer also to 465.

¶   G - Finance

            Refer to 463, 466, 467.

¶   H - Transport and communications

            Refer to 463.

iv.   Air

483   Boletín estadístico: transporte aereo   [Statistical Bulletin: air transport]   (Ministerio de Transportes,
            Comunicaciones y Aeronautica Civil).
            Ministerio de Transportes, Comunicaciones y Aeronautica Civil, La Paz.
            1970- 1976.   not priced.   214 p.
            Contains data on numbers of passengers and amounts of cargo flown, number of aircraft, etc.
            Time factor: the 1976 issue, published in 1977, has data from 1971 to 1976.
            §   Es.

484   Boletín estadístico   [Statistical bulletin]   (Administración de Aeropuertos y Servicios Auxiliares a la
            Navigación Aérea).
            Administración de Aeropuertos y Servicios a la Navigación Aérea, La Paz.
            (annual)   1976.   not priced.
            Contains data on the aeronautical infrastructure, statistics of air traffic, etc.
            Time factor: the 1976 issue was published in 1977.
            §   Es.

485   Boletín de comunicaciones   [Communications bulletin]   (Ministerio de Transportes, Comunicaciones y
            Aeronautica Civil).
            Ministerio de Transportes, Comunicaciones y Aeronautica Civil, La Paz.
            (annual)   1977.   not priced.
            Contains statistics of posts, telecommunications, etc.
            Time factor: the 1977 issue was published in 1978.
            §   Es.

BRAZIL - BRESIL - BRASILIEN - BRASIL

Central statistical office

486   Fundação Instituto Brasileiro de Geografia e Estatística   [Brazilian Institute of Geography and Statistics
           Foundation],
       Av Franklin Roosevelt 166,
       20021 - Rio de Janeiro, RJ.

       The Institute is in charge of statistical, geographical, cartographic, geodetic, demographic, socio-
       economic, natural resources and environmental information.   'Revista Brasileira de Estatistica' is the
       institute's professional journal.

Libraries

       The Instituto Brasileiro de Geografia e Estatística (see above) has a library, formed by merging the
       Biblioteca "Waldemar Lopez" and the Bibliografia de Geografia, which has a collection of publications of
       the Institute and of foreign statistical publications.   The library is open to the public, as are the libraries
       in each of the Institute's branches throughout Brazil.

       Note: Brazil has 5 grand regions (north, north-east, south-east, south and central-west; 9 units of
              federation (Minos Gerais, Pernambuco, etc); and 24 ordinary regions.

Statistical publications

¶   A - General

487   Anuário estatístico do Brasil   [Statistical yearbook of Brazil]   (Fundação Instituto Brasileiro de Geografia e
           Estatística).
       IBGE, Av Franklin Roosevelt 166, 20021 - Rio de Janeiro, RJ.
       1908- 1977.   Cr$200.   816 p.
       Main sections:
           Area and climate
           Demography
           Economic resources (forestry, fisheries, agriculture and livestock, industry, commerce, insurance,
             services, transport, communications, money market and finance, corporations, consumption,
             national accounts).
           Social situation (housing, urban public services, employment, health, social security and assistance,
             associations and co-operatives, religion, suicides and accidents)
           Culture (education, cultural associations, libraries, theatres and cinemas, radio and television,
             publishing)
           Administration and the political situation (administrative divisions, public finance, justice and
             public security, elections)
       Time factor: the 1977 edition, published late 1978, has data for the years 1974 to 1977.
       §   Pt.

       Note: there are also statistical yearbooks for individual regions, etc, issued by the local governments.

488   Boletim estatístico   [Statistical bulletin]   (Fundação Instituto Brasileiro de Geografia e Estatística)
       IBGE, Av Franklin Roosevelt 166, 20021 - Rio de Janeiro, RJ.
       1943-   quarterly.   Cr$25 or Cr$90 yr;   US$3 or US$12 yr.
       Up-dates the statistical yearbook (487) including data on industrial production, foreign trade, coastal
           trade, prices, transport, finance, banking, consumption, on a national, regional, municipal and
           international basis.
       Time factor: contains long runs of annual and monthly figures to the date of the issue and is published
           two or three months later.
       §   Pt.

¶   A,   continued

489   Conjunctura econômica   [Economic situation]   (Fundação Getulio Vargas).
        Fundação Getulio Vargas, Praia de Botafogo 188, Caixa postal 9062 ZC-02, Rio de Janeiro.
        1947-   monthly.   Cr$40 (special numbers Cr$60) or Cr$43 yr.
        Contains economic and business articles which include some statistical tables, and also national and
            regional economic indices of prices, foreign trade, building permits, transport, and wholesale
            prices of domestic products, etc.
        Time factor: has indices for three years and months up to one or two months prior to the date of the issue.
        §   Pt.

        Note: a brief international edition "Economics and business in Brazil" is also available.

490   Sinopse estatística do Brasil   [Statistical abstract of Brazil]   (Fundação Instituto Brasileiro de Geografia e
            Estatística).
        IBGE, Av Franklin Roosevelt 166, 20021 - Rio de Janeiro, RJ.
        1968-   Vol 5, 1977.   Cr$120.   628 p.
        Contains data on the physical, demographic, economic, social, cultural, administrative and political
            situations, similar to the content of the statistical yearbook (487).
        Time factor: the 1977 edition, published early 1978, contains the latest data available at the time of
            compilation, usually for 1975 and 1976 and some earlier figures.
        §   Pt.   An English version is published for some years, the latest being for 1975 (Cr$100).

        Note: there is also a 'Sinopse estatística...' for each of the 24 regions of Brazil.

491   Brasil, séries estatísticas retrospectivas, 1970   [Brazil, retrospective statistical series, 1970]   (Fundação
            Instituto Brasileiro de Geografia e Estatística).
        IBGE, Av Franklin Roosevelt 166, 20021 - Rio de Janeiro, RJ.
                        US$3.   280 p.
        A chronological series for the decade 1959 to 1968, intended to portray the changes in the behaviour of
            social and economic phenomena, as well as cultural, demographic, administrative, economic and
            financial aspects.
        Time factor: published in 1970.
        §   Pt.

492   Indice do Brasil, 1977/78.   [Brazilian index yearbook]   (Banco Denasa de Investimento SA).
        Banco Denasa de Investimento SA, rue da Alfândega 28, Rio de Janeiro.
                        not priced.   c 400 p.
        Contains major indicators and indicators of agriculture, industry, foreign trade, internal trade, power
            sources, transport and communications, financial and money market, stock market, government
            finance, demography and social, and regional.
        Time factor: published early 1978, the volume has data for the years 1957 to 1976.
        §   En,   Pt.

493   APEC: análise e perspectiva econômica   [APEC: economic analysis and perspective]   (APEC)
        APEC, rua Sorocaba 316, Rio de Janeiro.
        1960-   fortnightly.   not priced.
        An economic letter which includes statistics of industrial production, foreign trade, finance, government
            expenditure, banking, price indices, etc.
        §   En and Pt eds.

BRAZIL, continued

¶ B - Production

494   Censo industrial [Census of industry] (Fundação Instituto Brasileiro de Geografia e Estatística.).
       IBGE, Av Franklin Roosevelt 166, 20021 – Rio de Janeiro, RJ.
       1920-   5th, 1970.
       Deals with the activities of the mining, processing and manufacturing industries, including number of
           establishments, employees, wages, expenditures, value of production, value of industrial manu-
           facture, energy and raw materials used, etc.   One volume covers the territories of Rondônia,
           Roraima and Amapá, the others are for each of the ordinary regions, one is for Brazil and one for
           Brazil – physical production, 24 volumes in all (Cr$70 or Cr$80; US$10 or US$12 each volume).
       Time factor: the reports were published in 1974, as Volume IV of the Economic Census.
       §   Pt.

       Refer also to 487, 488.

       i.   Mines and mining

495   Anuario mineral brasileiro [Brazilian mineral yearbook] (Ministerio das Minas e Energia, Departamento
           Nacional de Produção Mineral).
       Ministerio das Minas e Energia, Brasília, DF.
       1947- 1978. Cr$140.   320 p.
       Contains statistics of mineral production by substance and global mineral statistics.
       Time factor: the 1978 issue, published in 1978, has data from 1966 to 1977.
       §   Pt.

       ii. Agriculture, fisheries, forestry, etc.

496   Anuário estatístico [Statistical yearbook] (Comissão de Financiamento da Produção, Ministerio da
           Agricultura).
       Ministerio da Agricultura, W.3Norte – 0.514 – Bl. "B", Brasília DF.
       1939- 1977. not priced.   486 p.
       Contains data on production, prices, etc, for each crop, giving data by regions.
       Time factor: the 1977 edition, published in 1977, has data from 1969 to 1976 or latest available, both
           annual and monthly.
       §   Pt.

       Note: from 1939 to 1972 title was 'Produção agricola'.

497   Censo agropecuario [Agricultural census] (Fundação Instituto Brasileiro de Geografia e Estatística).
       IBGE, Av Franklin Roosevelt 166, 20021 – Rio de Janeiro, RJ.
              8th, 1970.
       Volumes published are:
           Sinopse preliminar do censo agropecuário: Brasil e Unidas de Federação [Preliminary synopsis of the
               agriculture and livestock census: Brazil and the federated units]
           Dados preliminares gerais do censo agropecuário [Preliminary results for each of the five regions]
           Serie regional [regional volumes, one for each of the ordinary regions and one for Brazil as a whole]
       The census covered agriculture, livestock, aviculture, apiculture, sericulture, horticulture, forestry,
           and extraction of vegetable products, and included data on establishments, total area, employees,
           herds, agricultural production, economic activity, agricultural tools and machines, fertilisation,
           irrigation, etc.
       Time factor: the reports were published between 1971 and 1973.
       §   Pt.

       Note: preliminary results ('Sinopse preliminar do censo agropecuário') of the 1975 census have been
           published in 14 volumes.   The reports are being published as Volume III of the 1975 economic
           censuses.

¶   B.ii,   continued

498   Produção extrativa vegetal   [Extraction of vegetable products]   (Fundação Instituto Brasileiro de Geografia
           e Estatística)
       IBGE, Av Franklin Roosevelt 166, 20021 - Rio de Janeiro, DF.
       1938/42-   1974.   Cr$15;   US$2.   84 p.
       Contains data on the extraction of 37 vegetable products.
       Time factor: the 1974 issue has data for 1974.
       §   Pt.

499   Produção agricola municipal - culturas temporárias e permanentes   [Municipal agricultural production -
           temporary and permanent crops]   (Fundação Instituto Brasileiro de Geografia e Estatística)
       IBGE, Av Franklin Roosevelt 166, 20021 - Rio de Janeiro, DF.
       1974-   1974.   Cr$30;   US$3 each volume.   5 vols.
       Contains data on the area under agriculture, quantity of crops produced, average income and value of the
           production of agricultural products of a temporary and permanent nature.   The volumes are for the
           North Region; Pernambuco, Alagoas, Sergipe and Bahia; Minas Gerais; Rio Grande do Sul.
       Time factor: the 1974 issue, with data for 1974, was published in 1976.
       §   Pt.

500   Produção da pecuária municipal   [Municipal livestock production]   (Fundação Instituto Brasileiro de Geografia
           e Estatística)
       IBGE, Av Franklin Roosevelt 166, 20021 - Rio de Janeiro, DF.
       1974-   1974.   Cr$30;   US$2 each volume.   5 vols.
       Contains data on the quantity and value of oxen, asses, buffaloes, mules, horses, pigs, goats and poultry;
           production and value of milk, eggs, wool, honey, wax and cocoon.   The volumes are for the North
           Region, Northeast Region, South and Centre-west Regions, Southeast Region, and Brazil as a whole.
       Time factor: the 1974 issue, with data for 1974, was published in 1976.
       §   Pt.

501   Anuário estatistico   [Statistical yearbook]   (Comissão de Financiamento da Produção: Ministerio da
           Agricultura)
       Comissão de Financiamento da Produção, Ministerio da Agricultura, Rio de Janeiro.
       1973-   1977.   not priced.   486 p.
       Contains data on production, prices, etc, for each crop.
       Time factor: the 1977 issue, published in 1977, has data for each month for the years 1969 to 1976, or the
           latest available.
       §   Pt.

502   Anuário estatistico do arroz   [Statistical yearbook of rice]   (Instituto Rio Grandense do Arroz).
       Instituto Rio Grandense do Arroz, Av Júlio de Castilhos 585 - 1° andar, 90,000 Pôrto Alegre, RS.
       1944-   1978.   free.   128 p.
       Contains data on employment, water and irrigation, machinery and agricultural implements, production,
           trade (prices, exports), cost of production, and socio-economic aspects.
       Time factor: the 1978 edition, published in 1978, has data for the crop year 1976/77.
       §   Pt.

503   Anuário estatístico do café   [Statistical yearbook of coffee]   (Instituto Brasileiro do Café).
       Instituto Brasileiro do Café, Rodrigues Alves 129, Rio de Janeiro, RJ.
       1939/40-   1975.   not priced.   136 p.
       Contains data on Brazilian and world production of coffee, consumption in Brazil, Brazilian and world
           exports, imports of green coffee, internal and external prices.
       Time factor: the 1975 edition, published in 1976, has data for several years to 1975.
       §   Pt.

¶   B.ii,   continued

504   Anuário estatístico mercada nacional   [Statistical yearbook of national trade]   (Ministerio da Industria e do
            Comercio. Superintendencia da Borracha).
            Superintendencia da Borracha, Rio de Janeiro.
            1967-   1977.   not priced.   53 p.
            Contains data on production, sales, and consumption of rubber.
            Time factor: the 1977 edition, published in 1978, has data for several years and months to December
            1977.
            §   Pt.

505   Mercado da borracha no Brasil: **boletim mensal**   [Trade in rubber in Brazil: monthly bulletin]
            (Superintendencia da Borracha).
            Superintendencia da Borracha, Rio de Janeiro.
            1967-   not priced.
            Up-dates the above (504).
            Time factor: each issue has data for the month of the issue and is published a month or two later.
            §   Pt.

506   Produção florestal   [Forestry]   (Ministerio da Agricultura).
            Ministerio da Agricultura, W.3 Norte - 0.514 - Bl. "B", Brasília DF.
            1941-   1969.   not priced.   30 p.
            Contains data on forestry and forestry products.
            Time factor: the 1969 issue, published in 1971, has data for 1969.
            §   Pt.

iii.   Industry

507   Pesquisa industrial - Brasil - aspectos gerais das atividades industriais   [Industrial survey - Brazil - general
            aspects of industrial activities]   (Fundação Instituto Brasileiro de Geografia e Estatística).
            IBGE, Av Franklin Roosevelt 166, 20021 - Rio de Janeiro, RJ.
            1972-   1974.   Cr$80;   US$10 each volume.   5 vols.
            General and regional aspects of industrial activity, such as investment of capital, employed people,
            fluctuations of employment, expenditures on industrial operations, value of production, distribution
            of population, value of industrial manufacture, etc.   There is one volume for each of the grand
            regions and a sixth volume : Pesquisa industrial - Brasil - produção fisica [Industrial survey - Brazil
            - physical production] published in 1973 complements the 1972 edition of the above title (Cr$60 or
            US$9).
            Time factor: the results of the 1974 survey were published in 1976.
            §   Pt

508   Indústria de transformação - pesquisa trimestral   [Manufacturing industry - quarterly survey]   (Fundação
            Instituto Brasileiro de Geografia e Estatística).
            IBGE, Av Franklin Roosevelt 166, 20021 - Rio de Janeiro, RJ.
            1968-   1972.   US$2.   61 p.
            Presents monthly and quarterly results relating to the survey - number of establishments, production,
            stocks, employees, etc.
            Time factor: ceased publication with the 1972 issue.
            §   Pt.

¶   B.iii,   continued

509   Indústria de transformação - pesquisa mensal   [Manufacturing industry - monthly survey]   (Fundação Instituto
          Brasileiro de Geografia e Estatística).
          IBGE, Av Franklin Roosevelt 166, 20021 - Rio de Janeiro, RJ.
          1967-   monthly.   US$2 each issue.
          Surveys the most representative establishments of the main industrial sectors, showing general aspects,
             production and stocks of 15 industrial products including 2060 establishments.
          Time factor: each issue has data for that month and is published about six months later.
          §   Pt.

510   IBS yearbook. Anuario estatístico da industria siderúrgica brasileira   [IBS yearbook. Statistical yearbook of
          the Brazilian iron and steel industry]   (Instituto Brasileiro de Siderúrgia).
          Instituto Brasileiro de Siderúrgia, rua Araújo, Pôrto Alegre, 36 7° andar, Rio de Janeiro.
          1974- 1978.   not priced.   141 p.
          Contains data on production, sales for the domestic market, exports, imports, market, raw materials,
             ferroalloys, and general data.
          Time factor: the 1978 edition, published in 1978, has data from 1968 to 1977.
          §   En,   Pt.

511   IBS statistics   (Brazilian Iron and Steel Institute).
          Instituto Brasileiro de Siderúrgia, rua Araújo , Pôrto Alegre, 36 7° andar, Rio de Janeiro
          1970-   monthly.   not priced.
          Contains similar data to 510 above, but on a monthly basis.
          §   En,   Pt.

512   Noticias da ANFAVEA   [Associação Nacional dos Fabricantes de Veiculos Automotores]
          ANFAVEA, Av Indianópolis 496, Saõ Paulo.
          1955-   monthly.   not priced.
          A 2-page bulletin which includes statistics of production in the Brazilian automobile industry.
          §   Pt.

513   Anuário da indústria electro-eletrônica do Brasil   [Yearbook of the electrical and electronic industry of
          Brazil]   (Associação Brasileira da Indústria Elétrica e Eletrônica).
          ABINEE, Rio de Janeiro.
          1973/74- 1978.   not priced.   154 p.
          Includes a number of charts and tables on all aspects of the industry - production, sales, foreign trade,
             etc.
          §   Pt.

      iv. Construction

514   Censo predial   [Building census]   (Fundação Instituto Brasileiro de Geografia e Estatística).
          IBGE, Av Franklin Roosevelt 166, 20021 - Rio de Janeiro, RJ.
          1970-   1970.   Cr$50 to $80 or US$8 to $12 each volume.   6 vols.
          Contains data about the characteristics of the buildings, including the situation (urban and rural), number
             of floors, aspects of the buildings (materials for walls, floors, roofs, etc).   There are five regional
             volumes for north, northeast, southeast, south, and centre-west of Brazil and one national volume
             covering all Brazil.
          Time factor: the reports were published in 1974 as Volume II of the Economic Census.
          §   Pt.

¶ B.iv, continued

515 Indústria da construção - preços de material de construção no comércio atacadista - salários na indústria da
construção [The construction industry - wholesale prices of materials - wages in the construction
industry] (Fundação Instituto Brasileiro de Geografia e Estatística).
IBGE, Av Franklin Roosevelt 166, 20021 - Rio de Janeiro, RJ.
1969- quarterly. Cr$15; US$2 each issue.
The results of a monthly survey in towns and cities with a population of 50,000 or more.
Time factor: each issue has data for the three monthly surveys taken in that quarter.
§ Pt.

516 Indústria da construção [Construction industry] (Fundação Instituto Brasileiro de Geografia e Estatística).
IBGE, Av Franklin Roosevelt 166, 20021 - Rio de Janeiro, RJ.
1970- monthly. Cr$15; US$2 each issue.
Contains data on licences issued for construction, characteristics and purposes of construction, area, its
value and distribution. Covers towns and cities of 50,000 population and more.
Time factor: each issue has data for the month and cumulative figures for the year to date, and is
published about three months later.
§ Pt.

v. Energy

Refer to 492.

¶ C - External trade

517 Comércio exterior do Brasil: importação [Foreign trade of Brazil: imports] (Ministério da Fazenda).
Ministério da Fazenda, Esplanada dos Ministérios, Bloco 5 - 9° andar, 70.000 Brasília, DF.
1900- 1977. free. 3 vols.
Contains comprehensive statistical data on imports by commodities, by countries, by method of transport,
etc.
Time factor: the 1977 issue, published in 1978, has data for 1977.
§ Pt.

518 Comércio exterior do Brasil: exportação [Foreign trade of Brazil: exports] (Ministério da Fazenda).
Ministério da Fazenda, Esplanada dos Ministérios, Bloco 5 - 9° andar, 70.000 Brasília, DF.
1900- 1977. free. 2 vols.
Contains comprehensive statistical data on exports by commodites, by countries, by method of transport,
etc.
Time factor: the 1977 issue, published in 1978, has data for 1977.
§ Pt.

519 Boletim do comércio exterior [Bulletin of foreign trade] (Ministério da Fazenda).
Ministério da Fazenda, Esplanada dos Ministérios, Bloco 5 - 9° andar, 70.000 Brasília, DF.
1970- quarterly. not priced.
Contains statistical tables showing details of imports by commodities, imports by countries, and exports
by principal commodities subdivided by countries of origin and destination.
Time factor: each issue has cumulated data for the year to the date of the issue.
§ Pt.

¶   C,   continued

520   Foreign trade of Brazil   (Ministério da Fazenda).
        Ministério da Fazenda, Esplanada dos Ministérios, Bloco 5 - 9° andar, 70.000 Brasília, DF.
        1955/56-   1977.   not priced.   529 p.
        Contains statistical tables showing imports and exports, according to SITC, arranged by countries of origin
            and destination and arranged by groups of the SITC subdivided by countries of origin and destination.
        Time factor: the 1977 issue, published in 1978, has data for 1977.
        §   Pt.

521   Comércio interstadual: exportação por vias internas   [Interstate trade: exports by mode of transport]
            (Fundação Instituto Brasileiro de Geografia e Estatística)
        IBGE, Av Franklin Roosevelt, 166, 20021 - Rio de Janeiro, DF.
        1969-   1976.   Cr$16; US$2 each volume.
        Each volume contains a collection of tables on the interstate export of a Brazilian state, including
            quantity, value, mode of transport and destination of the goods.
        Time factor: the 1976 issue, published in 1977, has data for 1976.
        §   Pt.

522   Brasil - comércio exterior   [Brazil - foreign trade]   (Banco do Brasil SA).
        Banco do Brasil SA, Rio de Janeiro.
        1969-   1976.   not priced.   2 vols.
        Contains data on exports from Brazil arranged by country subdivided by commodities.
        Time factor: the 1976 issue, published late 1977, has data for 1976.
        §   Pt.

523   Brasil exportação   [Brazilian exports]   (Banco do Brasil).
        Banco do Brasil, Rio de Janeiro.
                quarterly.   not priced.
        Contains data on exports, month by month, by product, means of transport, by countries, by ports of
            clearance, etc.
        Time factor: each issue has cumulated data for the year to date as well as monthly data, and is published
            some three or four months later.
        §   Pt.

524   Intercambio comercial - 1953-1976   [Commercial trade - 1953-1976]   (Banco do Brasil).
        Banco do Brasil, Rio de Janeiro.
                        not priced.   3 vols.
        Vol 1 deals with balance of payments, and Vols 2 & 3 with foreign trade arranged by country and sub-
            divided by commodities (NBM).
        Time factor: published late 1977, the publication has data for each year from 1953 to 1976.
        §   Pt.

        Refer also to 487, 488.

    ¶   D   -   Internal distribution and service trades

525   Censo comercial   [Census of trade]   (Fundação Instituto Brasileiro de Geografia e Estatística).
        IBGE, Av Franklin Roosevelt 166, 20021 - Rio de Janeiro, RJ.
        1963-   1970   US$8; Cr$64 each volume.   5 federal volumes, 24 regional volumes.
        Deals with trade in goods and administration of real estate, including estates owned by private
            organisations, mixed economy corporations, and government enterprises dealing with purchase, sale
            and exchange of goods.   Data is given on the structure of establishments, persons engaged, salaries,
            expenditures, and receipts of wholesale and retail trade.
        Time factor: published as Vol VI of the national census, the reports were issued in 1974.
        §   Pt.

¶ D,   continued

526   Movimento da comercialização de café, segundo estados, municipios e micro-regiões homogêneas   [The
            coffee trade]   (Instituto Brasiliero do Café).
        Instituto Brasileiro do Café, Rodrigues Alves 129, Rio de Janeiro, RJ.
                    not priced.   73 p.
        Time factor: published in 1977, the report covers the crop years 1971/72 to 1975/76.
        §   Pt.

527   Censo dos serviços   [Census of service trades]   (Fundação Instituto Brasileiro de Geografia e Estatística).
        IBGE, Av Franklin Roosevelt 166, 20021 - Rio de Janeiro, RJ.
        1963-   1970.   Cr$64; US$8 each volume.   5 federal volumes, 24 regional volumes.
        Covers the activities related to the services rendered to persons or to collective groups, including
            lodgings and food, repair and maintenance services, personal hygiene services, commercial services,
            amusements and recreation, radio broadcasting and television services.   Includes the characteristics
            of the establishments, persons engaged, salaries, value of receipts, etc, by classes and kinds of
            services.
        Time factor: published as volume VIII of the national census, the reports were issued in 1974.
        §   Pt.

528   Anuário estatístico Embratur   [Statistical yearbook of the Brazilian Tourist Office]   (Ministerio de Industria
            e do Comércio).
        Ministerio de Industria e do Comércio, Rio de Janeiro.
        1970-   1977.   not priced.   187 p.
        Contains data by geographical area of arrivals, departures, and financial expenditures of tourists.
        Time factor: the 1977 issue, published in 1978, has data for 1977.
        §   Pt.

529   Meios de hospedagem   [Accommodation]   (Fundação Instituto Brasileiro de Geografia e Estatística).
        IBGE, Av Franklin Roosevelt 166, 20021 - Rio de Janeiro, RJ.
        1969-   1972/74.   Cr$24; US$3.   190 p.
        Contains the results of an annual enquiry into the main characteristics and activities of approximately
            17,500 hotels and similar establishments, including numbers of establishments, by city; services
            offered; staff; movement of people; finances; etc.
        Time factor: the 1972/74 issue, published late 1976, has data for 1974 or 1972/73.
        §   Pt.

        Refer also to 487, 488.

¶   E - Population

530   Censo demografico   [Demographic census]   (Fundação Instituto Brasileiro de Geografia e Estatística).
        IBGE, Av Franklin Roosevelt 166, 20021 - Rio de Janeiro, RJ.
        1872-   8th, 1970.   Cr$60 to Cr$120 each volume.
        Publications of the results of the census include 5 federal volumes and 24 regional volumes, as well as a
            number of preliminary and advance reports.
        Time factor: published as Volume 1 of the national census, the reports were issued in 1974 and 1975.
        §   Pt.

        Note: IBGE also issue a 'Boletin demográfico' [Demographic bulletin] annually, which contains a few
            statistics as well as study reports.

¶   E,   continued

531   Brasil - estimativa da população - julho de 1975   [Brazil - population estimates - July 1975]   (Fundação
              Instituto Brasileiro de Geografia y Estatística).
              IBGE, Av Franklin Roosevelt 166, 20021 - Rio de Janeiro, RJ.
                          Cr$24;   US$3.   80 p.
              Contains data on population by municipalities, estimated population of the great regions, states,
                  homogeneous microregions, and metropolitan areas.
              Time factor: published in 1975.
              §   Pt.

532   Pesquisa nacional por amostra de domicilios - PNAD   [National household sample survey]   (Fundação
              Instituto Brasileiro de Geografia y Estatística).
              IBGE, Av Franklin Roosevelt 166, 20021 - Rio de Janeiro, RJ.
                      1972.   Cr$40.
              Time factor: published in 1976.
              §   Pt.

              Refer also to 487, 488, 490.

        ¶   F   -   Social

533   Indicadores sociais - para áreas urbanas   [Social indexes for urban areas]   (Fundação Instituto Brasileiro de
              Geografia y Estatística).
              IBGE, Av Franklin Roosevelt 166, 20021 - Rio de Janeiro, RJ.
                          Cr$50;   US$8.   162 p.
              Time factor: published in 1977.
              §   Pt.

534   Anuario estatístico   [Statistical yearbook]   (Serviço Social do Comercio).
              Serviço Social do Comercio, Rio de Janeiro.
              1962-   1976-   not priced.   208 p.
              Contains a general summary, information on the activities of the Serviço Social do Comercio by regions
                  and activities, including education, libraries, arts and crafts, recreation, etc.
              Time factor: the 1976 issue, published in 1977, has data for 1976.
              §   Pt.

    i.   Standard of living

535   Estudo nacional da despesa familiar - ENDEF   [National survey of family expenditure]   (Fundação Instituto
              Brasileiro de Geografia y Estatística).
              IBGE, Av Franklin Roosevelt 166, 20021 - Rio de Janeiro, RJ.
                          Cr$40   to Cr$80 each volume.   5 vols.
              Time factor: published in 1976 as part of the 1972 household survey.
              §   Pt.

536   Inquérito nacional de preços - gêneros alimenticios e artigos do vestuário: comércio atacadista e varejista nas
              unidades da federação   [National survey on prices - foodstuffs and clothing: wholesale and retail
              trade in the states]   (Fundação Instituto Brasileiro de Geografia e Estatística).
              IBGE, Av Franklin Roosevelt 166, 20021 - Rio de Janeiro, RJ.
              1971-   monthly.   Cr$15;   US$2 each issue.
              The results of a monthly survey carried out in 87 towns, on the prices of 54 main foodstuffs and 18 articles
                  of clothing.
              §   Pt.

F.i,   continued

537   Inquérito nacional de preços - gêneros alimenticios e artigos do vestuário: comércio atacadista e varejista
            nas capitais   [National survey on prices; foodstuffs and clothing: wholesale and retail trade in the
            capitals]   (Fundação Instituto Brasileiro de Geografia e Estatística).
        IBGE, Av Franklin Roosevelt 166, 20021 - Rio de Janeiro, RJ.
        1971-   monthly.   Cr$15;   US$2 each issue.
        The results of a monthly survey carried out in the state capitals of Brazil, on the prices of 54 main food-
            stuffs and 18 articles of clothing.
        §   Pt.

    ii.   Health and welfare

        Refer to 487, 490.

    iii.   Education and leisure

538   Educação especial: dados estatísticos, 1974   [Special education: some statistics]   (Ministerio da Educação
            e Cultura).
        Ministerio de Educação e Cultura, Rio de Janeiro, RJ.
                            not priced.   198 p.
        Contains data on establishments, teachers, types of education, students, etc.
        Time factor: published in 1975, the report has data for 1974.
        §   Pt.

        Refer also to 487, 490.

    iv.   Justice

        Refer to 487, 490.

    ¶   G - Finance

539   Boletim do Banco Central do Brasil   [Bulletin of the Central Bank of Brazil]
        Banco Central do Brasil, 5BN-Ed Palácio da Agricultura, Sala 1805, Caixa postal 04-0170-70.000,
            Brasília, DF.
        1965-   monthly.   Cr$39 or Cr$390 yr;   (abroad US$3.30 or US$33 yr)
        Includes data on the national financial system, the Brazilian economy, public finance, domestic public
            debt, the stock market, and international economy.
        Time factor: each issue contains long runs of 10 years and about 36 months to three months prior to the
            date of the issue.
        §   En,   Pt.

        Refer also to 487, 488.

    i.   Banking

540   Movimento bancário do Brasil   [Banking in Brazil]   (Ministerio de Fazenda).
        Ministerio de Fazenda, Centro de Informações Econômico-Fiscaia, Esplanada dos Ministérios, Bloco
            5, 9° andar, Brasília, DF.
        1968/69-   1974/75.   free.   256 p.
        Contains banking statistics by area.
        Time factor: the 1974/75 issue, published in 1977, has data for 1974 and 1975.
        §   Pt.

BRAZIL, continued

¶ G, continued

ii. Public finance

541 Anuário econômico-fiscal [Economic-financial yearbook] (Ministerio de Fazenda).
Ministerio de Fazenda, Centro de Informações Econômico-Fiscaia, Esplanada dos Ministérios, Bloco
5, 9° andar, Brasília, DF.
1970- 1976. not priced. 667 p.
Contains detailed information on public finance for the federation and for the states, and some foreign
trade statistics.
Time factor: the 1976 issue, published in 1978, has data for 1976.
§ Pt.

542 Estatísticas tributárias básicas [Taxation statistics] (Ministerio de Fazenda).
Ministerio de Fazenda, Centro de Informações Econômico-Fiscaia, Esplanada dos Ministérios, Bloco
5, 9° andar, Brasilia, DF.
1973- monthly. free.
Contains detailed statistics of taxation collected in Brazil.
Time factor: each issue has data for that month and is published three or four months later.
§ Pt.

¶ H - Transport and communications

543 Anuário estatístico dos transportes [Statistical yearbook of transport] (Ministerio dos Transportes).
Ministerio dos Transportes, Rio de Janeiro, RJ.
1970- 1975 e 1976. not priced. 459 p.
Contains some general statistics and data on road, rail, water and air transport.
Time factor: the 1975 & 1976 issue, published in 1977, has data from 1971 or 1973 to 1975.
§ Pt.

Refer also to 487, 488.

i. Ships and shipping

544 Estatística portuária [Port statistics] Ministerio dos Transportes).
Ministerio dos Transportes, Rio de Janeiro, RJ.
1973- 1975. not priced. 57 p.
Contains statistical information for each Brazilian port, including cargoes, equipment, manpower, hours
worked, ship details (tonnage, etc), utilisation, finance, etc.
Time factor: the 1975 issue, published in 1977, has data for several years to 1975.
§ Pt.

ii. Road

545 Empresas de transporte rodoviário [Highway transport companies] (Fundação Instituto Brasileiro de
Geografia e Estatística).
IBGE, Av Franklin Roosevelt 166, 20021 - Rio de Janeiro, RJ.
1968/70- 1971/1972/1973. Cr$40; US$7. 224 p.
The results of an annual survey covering about 5,000 companies and indicating the general characteristics,
employed people, number of vehicles, fuel and lubricant consumption, investments of capital, etc.
Time factor: the 1971/1972/1973 issue, published late 1976, has data for the years 1971, 1972 and 1973.
§ Pt.

¶ H,   continued

iii. Rail

546   Estatísticas das estradas de ferro de Brasil   [Statistics of railways in Brazil]   (Departamento Nacional de
           Estradas de Ferro).
           Departamento Nacional de Estradas de Ferro, rua do Mercado 34, Rio de Janeiro, RJ.
           1970- `1972.   not priced.   254 p.
           Contains detailed statistics of Brazilian railways, including passengers, freight, mileage, lines, finances,
               employment, etc.
           Time factor: the 1972 issue, published in 1973, has data for 1971 and 1972.
           §   Pt.

547   Anuario das estradas de ferro   [Railway yearbook]   (Revista Ferroviaria).
           Revista Ferroviaria, rua México 41 - 9° andar - Rio de Janeiro, RJ.
           1914-   1977.   not priced.   200 p.
           Issued as a supplement to the journal 'Revista Ferroviaria', the yearbook includes a few statistics in the
               text.
           Time factor: the 1977 issue was published early 1978.
           §   Pt.

   iv. Air

           Refer to 543.

   v. Communications

548   Empresas telefônicas   [Telephone companies]   (Fundação Instituto Brasileiro de Geografia e Estatística).
           IBGE, Av Franklin Roosevelt 166, 20021 - Rio de Janeiro, RJ.
           1971-   1974.   Cr$60; US$6.   270 p.
           The results of an annual survey on 750 telephone companies, including general activities, structure,
               employment, receipts, expenditures, investment of capital, and equipment of urban and interurban
               telephones.
           Time factor: the 1974 issue, published in 1976, has data for 1974.
           §   Pt.

The islands are now governed by an Administrator who is responsible for defence and internal security, external affairs, the public service, and courts and finance.   There is no central statistical office but enquiries on statistical matters concerning the islands could be made to the Administrator at Tortola, or to the Ministry of Finance, also at Tortola.

Statistical publications

¶   A   -   General

549   Statistical abstract   (Statistics Office: Ministry of Finance).
        Statistics Office, Ministry of Finance, Tortola.
        1974-   1974.   US$6.   169 p.
        Main sections:

Demography	External trade
Passenger movement	Public finance
Tourism	Banking
Education	Agriculture
Medicine and health	Transport and communications
Crime and justice	Public utilities
Labour and employment	Miscellaneous (rainfall, land areas, building permits,
Earnings	etc)
Prices	

        Time factor: the 1974 edition, published in 1975, contains the latest data available and some earlier
            figures.
        §   En.

550   British Virgin Islands: report for...   (Foreign and Commonwealth Office).
        HM Stationery Office, PO Box 569, London SE1 9NH.
        1955/56-   1975.   £1.15   77 p.
        Mainly textual, but includes some statistics on population, migration, public finance, taxation, currency
            and banking, commerce, production, education, health and medicine, justice, registration of
            vehicles, and road accidents.
        Time factor: the 1975 report was published in 1976.
        §   En.

    ¶   B   -   Production

        Refer to 549, 550.

    ¶   C   -   External trade

551   Trade report   (Ministry of Finance).
        Statistics Office, Ministry of Finance, Tortola.
        1970-   1974.   US$4.   142 p.
        Main tables show imports and exports arranged by commodity and subdivided by countries of origin and
            destination.
        Time factor: the 1974 issue, published late 1975, has data for 1974.
        §   En.

¶   C,   continued

552   Summary of trade statistics for the quarter... (Ministry of Finance).
        Statistics Office, Ministry of Finance, Tortola.
        1967-   US$1. each issue.
        Main tables show imports and exports arranged by commodity and subdivided by countries of origin and
            destination.
        Time factor: each issue has data for the quarter
        §   En.

        Refer also to 549.

¶   D   -   Internal distribution and service trades

553   Tourism in the British Virgin Islands...a statistical analysis   (Statistics Office, Finance Department).
        Statistics Office, Finance Department, Road Town, Tortola.
        1973- 1975.   US$3.   77 p.
        Contains data on numbers of visitors, passengers, aircraft, tourists, length of stay, and expenditure by
            visitors, etc.
        Time factor: the 1975 issue, published mid-1976, has data for 1975 or 1974 and 1975.
        §   En.

554   Visitors expenditure survey, February to August 1975   (Statistics Office, Finance Department).
        Statistics Office, Finance Department, Road Town, Tortola.
                        US$1.50.   18 p.
        Time factor: the report was published in October 1975.
        §   En.

        Refer also to 549.

¶   E   -   Population

555   Census of population
        1891-   1970.
        Refer to 258 for the 1970 census of population of the Commonwealth Caribbean which includes data for
            the British Virgin Islands.

556   Employment in the British Virgin Islands   (Labour Department)
        Labour Department, Road Town, Tortola.
        1970/73-   1975.   US$2.   36 p.
        Contains data on the number of establishments, the number employed, and average earnings.
        Time factor: the 1975 issue, published in 1976, has data for 1975.
        §   En.

        Refer also to 549, 550.

¶   F   -   Social

i.   Standard of living

        Refer to 549.

¶   F.ii,   Health and welfare

557   Annual report   (Medical and Health Department).
           Medical and Health Department, Tortola.
           1935-   1974.   not priced.   34 p.
           Contains data on population and vital statistics, hospitals, diseases, finances, etc.
           Time factor: the 1974 report, published in 1976, has data for 1974.
           §   En.

           Refer also to 549, 550.

    iii.   Education and leisure

558   Report of the Education Department
           Education Department, Tortola.
           1956-   1976.   not priced.   21 p.
           Includes statistics of pupils in primary and secondary education, examinations, qualifications of staff,
                finances, etc.
           Time factor: the 1976 report, published early 1977, has data for 1976.
           §   En.

           Refer also to 549, 550.

    iv.   Justice

559   Annual report of the British Virgin Islands Prison Service
           Office of the Keeper of the Prison, Road Town, Tortola.
           1956-   1974.   not priced.   5 p.
           Includes statistical tables on staff, prisoners, expenditure, sentences, and offences.
           Time factor: the 1974 report, published in 1976, has data for 1974.
           §   En.

560   Annual report of the Royal Virgin Islands Police Force
           Police Headquarters, Tortola.
           1972-   1976.   not priced.   29 p.
           Some statistics are included in the text on the strength of the force, criminal and traffic offences, etc.
           Time factor: the 1976 report, published late 1977, has data for 1976 and some earlier years.
           §   En.

           Refer also to 549, 550.

¶   G - Finance

    i.   Banking

561   Banking statistics   (Statistics Office: Ministry of Finance)
           Statistics Office, Ministry of Finance, Tortola.
           1975-   1975.   US$1.50.   8 p.
           Time factor: the 1975 issue, published late 1976, has data for 1975 and some earlier years.
           §   En.

           Refer also to 549, 550.

¶   G,   continued

ii.   Public finance

562   National income and expenditure, 1969-1974   (Statistics Office: Ministry of Finance).
            Statistics Office, Ministry of Finance, Tortola.
                        US$3.50.   85 p.
            Time factor: published in 1976.
            §   En.

563   Balance of payments, 1969-1974   (Statistics Office, Ministry of Finance)
            Statistics Office, Ministry of Finance, Tortola.
                        US$2.   36 p.
            Time factor: published in 1976.
            §   En.

            Refer also to 549, 550.

¶   H   -   Transport and communications

        Refer to 549, 550.

Central statistical office

564   Statistics Canada. Statistiques Canada,
          Ottawa K1A 0T6,
          Ontario.
          t (613) 992 2959.   tx 013-424

The Dominion Bureau of Statistics became Statistics Canada in May 1971, and its duties are to collect, compile, analyse, abstract and publish statistical information relating to the commercial, industrial, financial, social, economic and general activities and conditions of the people; to collaborate with Canadian government departments in the collection, compilation and publication of statistical information, including statistics derived from the activities of those departments; to take the censuses of population and agriculture of Canada; to endeavour to avoid duplication of collection of information; and generally to promote and develop integrated social and economic statistics pertaining to the whole of Canada and each province.

It is possible to request certain unpublished statistical information from Statistics Canada which may require a special tabulation.   Depending on the nature of the request, the availability of the information, and the time taken to prepare it, there may be a charge based on the time and costs involved.

An annual 'Report of Statistics Canada' is issued which contains the report of the Chief Statistician and a detailed review of work done.

Libraries

Statistics Canada (referred to above) has a large reference library at headquarters in Ottawa as well as smaller libraries in each of the eight regional offices located in St John's, Halifax, Montreal, Toronto, Regina, Winnipeg, Edmonton and Vancouver.   The headquarters library has a complete collection of all reports published by Statistics Canada from 1918 to the present day, and also an extensive collection of publications of foreign governments and agencies.   The libraries are open to the public during normal working hours.

Canadian university libraries maintain extensive holdings of the publications of Statistics Canada for reference and research work, and most large public libraries in the major Canadian cities maintain a large assortment of such publications.

Libraries and information services abroad

Canadian embassies abroad stock only those publications which they feel are necessary for local reference, and the number at each embassy varies considerably.

Bibliographies

565   Catalogue (Statistics Canada)
          Issued every two or three years and up-dated by supplements, the catalogue is in two parts: part I
              containing data on publications and part II on data files and unpublished information.   This is a
              sales list and is available free from Statistics Canada.
          §   En and Fr eds.

566   Federal services for business   (Department of Industry, Trade and Commerce).
          Summarises the range of services and information available from Federal government departments and
              agencies.   The revised edition was published in 1970.

567   Statistics Canada daily (Statistics Canada)
          A four page daily bulletin which includes lists of titles of new publications released, as well as news
              summaries and announcements of reports, reference papers, etc. $25 yr.
          §   En and Fr eds.

Bibliographies,   continued

568   Informat (Statistics Canada)
            A weekly digest with similar information to 'Statistics Canada daily'.
                                free.
            §   En   and   Fr   eds.

569   New surveys (Statistics Canada)
            A quarterly published from 1975, which reports on new surveys and major revisions.
                                free.
            §   En,   Fr.

Statistical publications

¶   A - General

570   Canada year book   (Ministry of Industry, Trade and Customs).
            Publications Distribution, Statistics Canada, Ottawa K1A 0T6.
            1905-   1976-77.   Can$12.50;   Can$15 in other countries.   1157 p..
            An annual review of economic, social and political developments in Canada, with statistical tables in
                the text.
                Main sections are:
                    Physiography   Agriculture
                    Constitution and legal system   Mines and minerals
                    Government   Energy
                    Demography   Housing and construction
                    Health   Transportation
                    Incomes and social security   Communications
                    Education, training and cultural activities   Manufacturing
                    Labour   Merchandising and trade
                    Scientific research and development   Banking, finance and insurance
                    Renewable resources   Government finance
                                                              Selected economic indicators
            Time factor: the 1976-77 edition, published early 1978, has data for several years to 1975.
            §   En   and   Fr   eds.

            Note: also available are statistical yearbooks for provinces, issued by the governments of the provinces.

571   Canada handbook   (Statistics Canada)
            Publications Distribution, Statistics Canada, Ottawa K1A 0T6.
            1932-   47th ed, 1978.   Can$3.75.   376 p.
            An annual handbook of present conditions and recent progress in Canada, describing the country's physical
                environment, people, economy, etc.   Includes a few statistical tables.
            §   En   and   Fr   eds.

572   Historical statistics of Canada   (M C Urquhart & K A H Buckley)
            Macmillan Company of Canada, Toronto, and Cambridge University Press, Cambridge, GB.
                            not priced.   687 p.
            Contains data on population and migration, vital statistics, health and welfare, labour force, wages and
                working conditions, national income and the capital stock, balance of international payments,
                international indebtedness, foreign trade, government finance, banking and finance, price indexes,
                lands and forests, agriculture, fisheries, minerals and fuel, electric power, manufactures, construction
                and housing, transport and communications, internal trade and services, education, politics and
                government, and justice.
            Time factor: published in 1965, the volume has a wide range of statistical time series covering, where
                possible, the years from 1867 to 1960.
            §   En.

CANADA,   continued

A,   continued

573   Canadian statistical review.   Revue statistique du Canada   (Statistics Canada)
         Publications Distribution, Statistics Canada, Ottawa K1A 0T6.
         1926-   monthly, with weekly and annual supplements.   Can$0.70; $7 yr.
         Contains economic articles and a summary of current economic indicators, including population, national
              accounts, labour, prices (including cost of living index), manufacturing, fuel, power, mining,
              construction, food and agriculture, domestic trade, external trade, transport and finance.
         Time factor: each issue has data for a period up to about three months prior to the date of the issue.
         §   En & Fr eds except for annual supplements which are bilingual.

574   Canadian statistical review - historical summary   (Statistics Canada)
         Publications Distribution, Statistics Canada, Ottawa K1A 0T6.
         1963-   2nd, 1970.   free to subscribers to above; otherwise Can$1.50.   148 p.
         Contains annual data for the statistical series published monthly in 573 above, extending back to 1926
              or as far back as available.
         §   En.

575   Bank of Canada review.   Revue de la Banque du Canada   (Bank of Canada)
         Bank of Canada, Ottawa K1A 0G9.
                  monthly.   Can$1 or $10 yr; ($12 abroad)
         Contains charts and statistical tables on banking, capital markets and interest rates, financial institutions,
              general economic statistics (population, national accounts, gross national expenditure, real domestic
              product, employment, construction, mortgages, consumer price index, etc), external trade, etc.
         Time factor: each issue has data for a period up to the month previous to the data of the issue.
         §   En,   Fr.

576   Report on Canada   (Maclean-Hunter Research Bureau)
         Maclean-Hunter Research Bureau, 481 University Ave, Toronto, Ontario M5W.
         1964-   14th, 1977.   Can$12.   55 p.
         Contains data on population, households and families, construction, retail trade, motor vehicles,
              economic indicators, manufacturing, miscellaneous (employment, consumer price indices, mineral
              production, foreign trade, growth of capital expenditure), etc.
         Time factor: the 1977 edition, published late 1977, has data to 1977 and some projections to 1986-2000.
         §   En.

577   OECD economic surveys - Canada   (Organisation for Economic Co-operation and Development)
         OECD, 2 rue André-Pascal, 75775 Paris Cedex 16, France.
         1962-   1978.   £1.50;   US$3;   F12.   60 p.
         An analysis of the economic policy of the country which includes statistics showing recent developments
              in demand, production, wages and prices, conditions in the money and capital markets, and
              developments in the balance of payments.
         Time factor: the 1978 issue was published mid-1978.

578   Annual report of the Economic Council of Canada
         Information Canada, Publishing Division, Ottawa.
         1964-   1975.   Can$4.50.   110 p.
         Each annual issue has a different title, the title of the 1975 edition being 'Options for growth'. Dealing
              mainly with the economic situation of the country, it usually includes a statistical section on the
              main topic of the edition.
         Time factor: the 1975 report was published in 1975.
         §   En,   Fr.

¶ A, continued

579 Annual review of science statistics (Statistics Canada)
 Publications Distribution, Statistics Canada, Ottawa K1A 0T6.
 1977- 1977. Can$2.10. 176 p.
 Contains chapters on science statistics, total expenditure on research and development in Canada,
  Canadian industry, the federal government, the provincial governments, the universities, and the
  social sciences and humanities. The aim of the publication is to provide historical data, to
  provide sector and reconciled national statistics, to give national projections for one or two years,
  and to reproduce questionnaires used during the year.
 Time factor: the 1977 issue, published in 1978, has data for 1975.
 § En, Fr.

 Note: there is also a 'Service bulletin: science statistics' (Can$1.40 yr; Can$1.70 yr abroad).

 Note: the 'Annual review...' supersedes 'Federal government activities in the natural sciences',
  'Federal government activities in the human sciences', 'Industrial research and development
  expenditures in Canada', 'Expenditures of provincial non-profit industrial research institutes',
  'Research and development expenditure in Canada', and 'Expenditures on scientific activities by
  private non-profit organisations'.

580 Culture statistics (Statistics Canada)
 Publications Distribution, Statistics Canada, Ottawa K1A 0T6.
 1978- irregular. Can$1.40 yr.
 A series of service bulletins issued on a variety of subjects, including book publishing, the recording
  industry, leisure time activities, travel price index, etc.
 § En, Fr.

¶ B - Production

i. Mines and mining

581 Canadian minerals yearbook (Department of Energy, Mines and Resources: Mineral Resources Division).
 Printing and Publishing, Ottawa K1A 0S9.
 (annual) 1972. Can$7.50. 527 p.
 Contains chapters on individual minerals showing production, imports, exports, consumption, and
  descriptions of developments and operations in the industry.
 Time factor: the 1972 edition, with data for 1972 was published in 1976. However, advance preprints of later volumes (1976 were published in mid-1978) are available only from the Department
  of Energy, Mines and Resources at Ottawa, Can$0.25 each or Can$5 the set; combined price of
  yearbook and preprints is Can$10.
 § En, & Fr eds.

582 General review of the mineral industries (mines, quarries and oil wells): annual census of mines (Statistics
  Canada).
 Publications Distribution, Statistics Canada, K1A 0T6.
 (annual) 1975. Can$1.40. 70 p.
 Contains final statistics of the mining industry, including production and value of minerals by kinds and
  by provinces, average prices of leading minerals, etc.
 Time factor: the 1975 issue, published in 1978, has data for 1975 and some earlier years.
 § En, Fr.

583 Mineral industries: principal statistics (Statistics Canada)
 Publications Distribution, Statistics Canada, K1A 0T6.
 (annual) 1975. Can$0.35. 2 p.
 Contains data on number of mines, wells, quarries, employees, salaries and wages, cost of process supplies

[continued next page]

¶   B.i,   continued

583,   continued

       and fuel, and net value added by processing, by main groups, and by provinces.
       Time factor: the 1975 issue, published early 1978, has data for 1975.
       §   En,   Fr.

       Note: also published are the annual 'Canada's mineral production, preliminary estimate' (Can$0.70),
          monthly periodicals on particular minerals, and annual reports on individual industries.

584   Statistical review of coal in Canada, 1977   (Ministry of Supply and Services).
       Ministry of Supply and Services, 123 Slater Street, Ottawa K1A 0S5.
                 not priced.   19 p.
       Contains data on supply by types, production, imports, disposition of domestic coal production, demand
          - by type of consumers, demand - by type of coal, stocks, and export demand.
       Time factor: the 1977 issue, published in 1978, has data for 1977 and also earlier years in some tables.
       §   En.

       Refer also to 570, 572, 573.

    ii.   Agriculture, fisheries, forestry, etc

585   Census of Canada: agriculture (Statistics Canada)
       Publications Distribution, Statistics Canada, Ottawa K1A 0T6.
       1911- 1971.   Can$32 the set.   3 parts.
       Part 1 (Can$12) contains the general summary tables for Canada, showing numbers of farms, areas, tenure,
          crops, livestock, machinery, etc, and more detailed data for Newfoundland, Prince Edward Island,
          Nova Scotia and New Brunswick; part 2 (Can$10) has detailed results for Quebec and Ontario; and
          part 3 (Can$10) has detailed results for the Western provinces of Manitoba, Saskatchewan, Alberta
          and British Columbia.   The three volumes are issued as Vol IV of the Census of Canada.
       Time factor: the results of the 1971 census were published in 1973.
       §   En,   Fr.

       Note: a later census was taken in 1976.

586   Handbook of agricultural statistics   (Statistics Canada)
       Publications Distribution, Statistics Canada, Ottawa K1A 0T6.
       This handbook, each part of which is updated at intervals, consolidates the data already published monthly
          and annually for Canada and for the provinces.   It is issued in 7 parts:
          Part   I Field crops, 1921-1974 (Can$2.80)
          Part   II Farm income, including operating expenses (latest issue covers 1926 to 1965) (Can$1)
          Part   III Trends in Canadian agriculture (latest issue covers 1926 to 1954)
          Part   IV Food consumption (latest issue covers 1926 to 1955)
          Part   V Vegetables and fruits: acreage, production and value of vegetables, 1940-1966; production
              and value of fruits, 1926-1967.
          Part   VI Livestock and animal products, 1871-1973 (Can$2.10)
          Part   VII Dairy statistics, 1920-1973 (Can$1.05)
       §   En.

587   Quarterly bulletin of agricultural statistics   (Statistics Canada)
       Publications Distribution, Statistics Canada, Ottawa K1A 0T6.
       1918-   Can$1.40 or Can$5.60 yr.
       Contains statistical data on farm finance; field crops; livestock, poultry and dairying; special crops and
          enterprises; meteorological records; and prices of agricultural products.
       Time factor: each issue has data mainly for the period of the issue and is published some three months
          later.
       §   En,   Fr.

¶   B.ii,   continued

588   Canadian farm economics   (Department of Agriculture: Economic Branch)
            Department of Agriculture, Ottawa.
                      quarterly.   free.
            Contains articles and statistical tables on current economic problems and developments of Canadian
                  agriculture.   A statistical appendix has average prices of selected farm commodities for various
                  markets and grades, and some price and production indexes of concern to agriculture.   An annual
                  outlook issue supplements the quarterly information.
            §   En,   Fr.

589   Grain and oilseeds review   (Statistics Canada)
            Publications Distribution, Statistics Canada, Ottawa K1A 0T6.
            1978-   quarterly.   Can$0.70 or Can$2.80 yr.
            Contains data on the supply disposition, processed products, exports, prices, etc, of grain and oilseeds.
            §   En,   Fr.

            Note: replaces 'Wheat review', 'Course grains review' and 'Oilseeds review'.

590   Grain trade of Canada   (Statistics Canada)
            Publications Distribution, Statistics Canada, Ottawa K1A 0T6.
            (annual)   1976/77.   Can$1.40.   91 p.
            Summary of acreage, production of grains, marketing, inspection, receipts and shipments, movement in
                  Canada, exports, and flour-milling statistics.
            Time factor: the 1976/77 issue, published in 1979, has data for the 1976/77 crop year.
            §   En,   Fr.

591   Livestock and animal products statistics   (Statistics Canada)
            Publications Distribution, Statistics Canada, Ottawa K1A 0T6.
            1909/19-   1977.   Can$1.40.   84 p.
            Detailed statistical coverage of livestock population, marketings, meat stocks, wool and hides, and
                  other animal products.
            Time factor: the 1977 issue, published mid-1978, has data for 1977 and long earlier runs of figures for
                  some tables.
            §   En,   Fr.

592   Fisheries statistics of Canada   (Statistics Canada)
            Publications Distribution, Statistics Canada, Ottawa K1A 0T6.
            1947-   1976.   Can$0.70 each, except for Quebec which is Can$1.05.   8 reports.
            Contains data on landings, quantity, value of species; value of fishery products and byproducts; sales
                  of freshwater fish; number and value of craft employed in fishing; employment; and value of imports
                  and exports of fish and fishery products.   The volumes cover Canada summary; Newfoundland;
                  Prince Edward Island; New Brunswick; Nova Scotia; Quebec; Ontario, Manitoba, Saskatchewan;
                  Alberta and Northwest Territories; British Columbia and Yukon.
            Time factor: the 1976 issues, published early 1978, have data for 1976 and 1975.
            §   En,   Fr.

593   Monthly review of Canadian fishery statistics   (Statistics Canada)
            Publications Distribution, Statistics Canada, Ottawa K1A 0T6.
            1947-   Can$0.40 or Can$4 yr.
            Up-dates the information in the annual (592 above).
            §   En,   Fr.

¶ B.ii,   continued

594   Fish freezings and stocks   (Statistics Canada)
          Publications Distribution, Statistics Canada, Ottawa K1A 0T6.
                    monthly.   Can$0.40 or Can$4 yr.
          Contains data on stocks of fish in cold storage by provinces, and fish frozen during the month.
          § En,   Fr.

595   Canadian forestry statistics   (Statistics Canada)
          Publications Distribution, Statistics Canada, Ottawa K1A 0T6.
          (annual) 1976.   Can$1.05.   47 p.
          Contains the principal statistics of logging, wood industries, paper and allied industries, production,
               shipments and exports of principal commodities, imports of roundwood, capital and repair expendi-
               tures of forest industries, data on National Forest Inventory.
          Time factor: the 1976 issue, published late 1978, has data for 1976.
          § En,   Fr.

          Note: there is also a historical issue 'Canadian forestry statistics revised, 1974' with statistics from the
               earliest years to 1974 (Can$1.05).

596   Logging (Statistics Canada)
          Publications Distribution, Statistics Canada, Ottawa K1A 0T6.
          (annual) 1976.   Can$0.70.   29 p.
          Contains the principal statistics of the logging industry, including number of establishments, etc.
               Includes results of a census of logging.
          Time factor: the 1976 issue, published mid-1978, has data for 1976 and 1975.
          § En,   Fr.

597   Pulpwood and wood residue statistics   (Statistics Canada)
          Publications Distribution, Statistics Canada, Ottawa K1A 0T6.
          1958-   monthly.   Can$0.15 or Can$1.50 yr.
          Contains data on production, consumption and inventories of pulpwood for Canada and the provinces.
          Time factor: each issue has data for the month and cumulative figures for the year to date, being
               published two or three months later.
          § En,   Fr.

          Refer also to 570, 572, 573.

    iii.   Industry

598   General review of the manufacturing industries of Canada: national and provincial areas   (Statistics Canada)
          Publications Distribution, Statistics Canada, Ottawa K1A 0T6.
          1968- 1972.   Can$2.80.   215 p.
          Contains the principal statistics for Canada and the provinces by industries and industry groups.
          Time factor: the 1972 issue, published in 1976, has data for 1972.
          § En,   Fr.

599   Manufacturing industries of Canada: sub-provincial areas   (Statistics Canada)
          Publications Distribution, Statistics Canada, Ottawa K1A 0T6.
          1968- 1975.   Can$6.   349 p.
          Contains data similar to the above (598) for smaller areas.
          Time factor: the 1975 issue, published early 1979, has data for 1975.
          § En,   Fr.

¶   B.iii,   continued

600   Manufacturing industries of Canada: type of organisation and size of establishment   (Statistics Canada)
        Publications Distribution, Statistics Canada, Ottawa K1A 0T6.
        1968- 1975. Can$2.10.   119 p.
        Contains principal statistics by type of organisation and by size of establishments according to numbers
            employed and value of production.
        Time factor: the 1975 issue, published early 1978, has data for 1975.
        §   En,   Fr.

601   [Reports for individual industries]   (Statistics Canada)
        Publications Distribution, Statistics Canada, Ottawa K1A 0T6.
        These are the separate monthly, quarterly or annual publications not issued within a series.   The
            contents of each report are similar in character and include such principal statistics as number of
            establishments, number and type of employees and their salaries and wages, cost of fuel and
            electricity, value of shipments of goods of own manufacture, and value added.   The reports
            currently issued are listed below in broad subject groupings:
          Food, Beverage and tobacco industries:
            Biscuit manufacturers   (a) $0.70.   c 8 p.
            Bakeries   (a) $0.70.   c 10 p.
            Breweries   (a) $0.70.   c 10 p.
            Distilleries   (a) $0.70.   c 9 p.
            Wineries   (a) $0.70.   c 8 p.
            Soft drink manufacturers   (a) $0.70.   c 10 p.
            Dairy products industry   (a) $0.70.   c 12 p.
            Canned and frozen processed foods   (a) $0.35.   c 7 p.
            Confectionery manufacturers   (a) $0.70.   c 9 p.
            Feed industry   (a) $0.70.   c 14 p.
            Flour and breakfast cereal products industry   (a) $0.70.   c 13 p.
            Fish products industry   (a) $0.70.   c 8 p.
            Fruit and vegetable processing industries   (a) $0.70.   c 14 p.
            Slaughtering and meat processors   (a) $0.70.   c 11 p.
            Cane and beet sugar processors...   (a) $0.70.   c 10 p.
            Vegetable oil mills   (a) $0.70.   c 8 p.
            Miscellaneous food processors   (a) $0.70.   c 14 p.
            Tobacco products industries   (a) $0.70.   c 14 p.
            Monthly production of soft drinks   (m) $0.15. or $1.50 yr.
            Dairy factory production   (m) $0.15 or $1.50 yr.
            Grain milling statistics   (m) $0.30 or $3 yr.
            Oils and fats   (m) $0.30 or $3 yr.
            Stocks of dairy and poultry products   (m) $0.30 or $3 yr.
            Stocks of fruit and vegetables   (m) $0.30 or $3 yr.
            Pack, shipments and stocks of selected canned fruits and vegetables   (m) $0.30 or $3 yr.
            Stocks of frozen meat products   (m) $0.30 or $3 yr.
            Sugar situation   (m) $0.15 or $1.50 yr.
            Tobacco and tobacco products statistics   (q) $0.70 or $2.80 yr.
            Bread and other bakery products   (q) $0.35 or $1.40 yr.
            Biscuits and confectionery   (q) $0.35 or $1.40 yr.
            Fruit and vegetable preparations   (q) $0.35 or $1.40 yr.
            Miscellaneous food preparations   (q) $0.35 or $1.40 yr.
            Breweries   (m) $0.15 or $1.50 yr.
            Selected meat and meat preparations   (m) $0.15 or $1.50 yr.
            Distilled beverage spirits and industrial ethyl alcohol   (m) $0.15 or $1.50 yr.

          Leather and rubber products:
            Leather tanneries   (a) $0.70.   c 8 p.
            Shoe factories and boot & shoe findings manufacturers   (a) $0.70.   c 14 p.
            Leather glove factories   (a) $0.70.   c 8 p.
            Miscellaneous leather products manufacturers   (a) $0.70.   c 8 p.

[continued next page]

Rubber products industries   (a) $0.70.   c 14 p.
Raw hides, skins and finished leather   (m) $0.30 or $3 yr.
Footwear statistics   (m) $0.30 or $3 yr.
Consumption, production and inventories of rubber   (m) $0.15 or $1.50 yr.
Textiles and apparel:
Canvas products and cotton and jute bags industries   (a) $0.70   c 14 p.
Cordage and twine industry   (a) $0.70.   c 8 p.
Cotton yarn and cloth mills   (a) $0.70.   c 11 p.
Man-made fibre yarn and cloth mills   (a) $0.70.   c 16 p.
Wool yarn and cloth mills   (a) $0.70.   c 12 p.
Miscellaneous textile industries   (a) $1.05.   c 33 p.
Foundation garment industry   (a) $0.70.   c 8 p.
Fur goods industry   (a) $0.70.   c 8 p.
Knitting mills   (a) $0.70.   c 28 p.
Men's clothing industries   (a) $0.70.   c 22 p.
Women's and children's clothing industries   (a) $0.70.   c 25 p.
Miscellaneous clothing industries (including fabric glove manufacturers, hat and cap industry,
    and miscellaneous clothing industries). (a) $0.70.   c 19 p.
Felt and fibre processing mills   (a) $0.70.   c 14 p.
Carpet, mat and rug industry   (a) $0.70   c 14 p.

Wood products:
Sawmills and planing mills and shingle mills   (a) $0.70.   c 24 p.
Sash, door and other millwork plants   (a) $1.05.   c 42 p.
Veneer and plywood mills   (a) $0.70.   c 10 p.
Miscellaneous wood industries   (a) $0.70.   c 10 p.
Wooden box factories   (a) $0.70.   c 8 p.
Coffin and casket industry   (a) $0.70   c 8 p.
Household furniture manufacturers   (a) $1.05   c 40 p.
Office furniture manufacturers   (a) $0.70.   c 8 p.
Miscellaneous furniture and fixtures manufacturers   (a) $0.70.   c 10 p.
Electric lamp and shade manufacturers   (a) $0.70.   c 8 p.
Peeler logs, veneers and plywoods   (m) $0.30 or $3 yr.
Production, shipments and stocks on hand of sawmills east of the Rockies   (m) $0.30 or $3 yr.
Production, shipments and stocks on hand of sawmills in British Columbia   (m) $0.30 or
    $3 yr.
Quarterly shipments of flush type doors (wood) by Canadian manufacturers   (q) $0.35 or
    $1.40 yr.
Quarterly shipments of office furniture products   (q) $0.35 or $1.40 yr.

Paper products and printing:
Printing, publishing and allied industries   (a) $1.40.   c 30 p.
Pulp and paper mills   (a) $0.70.   c 16 p.
Asphalt roofing manufacturers   (a) $0.70.   c 8 p.
Miscellaneous paper converters   (a) $0.70.   c 12 p.
Paper and plastic bag manufacturers   (a) $0.70.   c 9 p.
Corrugated box manufacturers   (a) $0.70.   c 8 p.
Folding carton and set-up box manufacturers   (a) $0.70.   c 8 p.
Hardboard   (m) $0.15 or $1.50 yr.
Rigid insulating board   (m) $0.15 or $1.50 yr.
Particle board   (m) $0.15 or $1.50 yr.
Monthly shipments of corrugated boxes and wrappers   (m) $0.15 or $1.50 yr.

Metal (manufactures):
Iron and steel mills   (a) $0.70.   c 18 p.
Aluminium rolling, casting and extruding   (a) $0.70.   c 8 p.
Fabricated structural metal industry   (a) $0.70.   c 8 p.

[continued next page]

Hardware, tool and cutlery manufacturers   (a) $0.70   c 8 p.
Scrap iron and steel   (a) $0.35   c 5 p.
Smelting and refining   (a) $0.70   c 12 p.
Metal rolling, casting and extruding   (a) $0.70   c 8 p.
Wire and wire products manufacturers   (a) $0.70   c 10 p.
Steel pipe and tube mills   (a) $0.70   c 8 p.
Ornamental and architectural metal industry   (a) $1.05   c 30 p.
Boiler and plate works   (a) $0.70   c 8 p.
Copper and alloy rolling, casting and extruding   (a) $0.70   c 8 p.
Heating equipment manufacturers   (a) $0.70   c 10 p.
Iron foundries   (a) $0.70   c 8 p.
Metal stamping, pressing and coating industry   (a) $0.70   c 17 p.
Miscellaneous metal fabricating industries   (a) $0.70   c 8 p.
Primary iron and steel   (m) $0.40 or $4 yr.
Steel ingots and pig iron   (m) $0.15 or $1.50 yr.
Iron castings and cast iron pipes and fittings   (m) $0.15 or $1.50 yr.
Stoves and furnaces   (m) $0.30 or $3 yr.
Steel wire and specified wire products   (m) $0.15 or $1.50 yr.
Oil burners and oil-fired water heaters   (m) $0.15 or $1.50 yr.
Fabricated metal products service bulletin   (w) $2.80 yr.
Metals and minerals service bulletin   (m) $2.80 yr.

Machinery and transport equipment:
Agricultural implement industry   (a) $0.70   c 10 p.
Aircraft and parts manufacturers   (a) $0.70   c 8 p.
Boatbuilding and repair   (a) $0.70   c 8 p.
Shipbuilding and repair   (a) $0.70   c 8 p.
Machine shops   (a) $0.70   c 8 p.
Motor vehicle manufacturers   (a) $0.70   c 11 p.
Motor vehicle parts and accessories manufacturers   (a) $0.70   c 8 p.
Railroad rolling stock industry   (a) $0.70   c 9 p.
Miscellaneous vehicle manufacturers   (a) $0.70   c 8 p.
Miscellaneous machinery and equipment manufacturers   (a) $0.70   c 11 p.
Commercial refrigeration and air conditioning equipment manufacturers   (a) $0.70   c 8 p.
Office and store machinery manufacturers   (a) $0.70   c 8 p.
Truck body and trailer manufacturers   (a) $0.70   c 22 p.
Motor vehicle shipments   (m) $0.15 or $1.50 yr.

Electrical equipment:
Manufacturers of small electrical appliances   (a) $0.70   c 10 p.
Manufacturers of major appliances (electric and non-electric)   (a) $0.70   c 10 p.
Manufacturers of household radio and television receivers   (a) $0.70   c 9 p.
Communications equipment manufacturers   (a) $0.70   c 10 p.
Manufacturers of electrical industrial equipment   (a) $0.70   c 14 p.
Manufacturers of electric wire and cable   (a) $0.70   c 8 p.
Manufacturers of miscellaneous electrical products   (a) $0.70   c 9 p.
Manufacturers of lighting fixtures   (a) $0.70   c 8 p.
Domestic refrigerators and freezers   (m) $0.15 or $1.50 yr.
Domestic washing machines and clothes dryers   (m) $0.15 or $1.50 yr.
Specified domestic electrical appliances   (m) $0.15 or $1.50 yr.
Radios and television sets, including record players   (m) $0.30 or $3 yr.
Factory sales of electric storage batteries   (m) $0.15 or $1.50 yr.
Electrical products service bulletin   (m) $1.40 yr.

Non-metallic mineral products:
Abrasive manufacturers   (a) $0.70   c 8 p.
Cement manufacturers   (a) $0.70   c 8 p.

[continued next page]

¶　B.iii,　continued

601,　continued

        Concrete products manufacturers　(a)　$0.70　c 14 p.
        Glass and glass products manufacturers　(a)　$0.70　c 8 p.
        Lime manufacturers　(a)　$0.70　c 8 p.
        Miscellaneous non-metallic mineral products industries　(a)　$0.70　c 12 p.
        Ready-mix concrete manufacturers　(a)　$0.70 c 8 p.
        Stone products manufacturers　(a)　$0.70　c 8 p.
        Refractories manufacturers　(a)　$0.70　c 8 p.
        Clay products manufacturers (from domestic clays)　(a)　$0.70　c 8 p.
        Clay products manufacturers (from imported clays)　(a)　$0.70　c 8 p.
        Cement　(m)　$0.15 or $1.50 yr.
        Concrete products　(m)　$0.15 or $1.50 yr.
        Gypsum products　(m)　$0.15 or $1.50 yr.
        Mineral wool　(m)　$0.15 or $1.50 yr.
        Products made from Canadian clays　(m)　$0.15 or $1.50 yr.

     Petroleum and coal products:
        Petroleum refineries　(a)　$0.70　c 17 p.
        Miscellaneous petroleum and coal products industries　(a)　$0.70　c 8 p.
        Asphalt roofing　(m)　$0.15 or $1.50 yr.
        Coal and coke statistics　(m)　$0.40 or $4 yr.
        Refined petroleum products　(m)　$0.40 or $4 yr.

     Chemicals:
        Fertilizer trade　(a)　$0.70　c 28 p.
        Manufacturers of pharmaceuticals and medicines　(a)　$0.70　c 9 p.
        Paint and varnish manufacturers　(a)　$0.70　c 14 p.
        Manufacturers of plastics and synthetic resins　(a)　$0.70　c 8 p.
        Sales of pest control products by Canadian registrants　(a)　$0.70　c 15 p.
        Manufacturers of soap and cleaning compounds　(a)　$0.70　c 10 p.
        Manufacturers of toilet preparations　(a)　$0.70　c 10 p.
        Miscellaneous chemical industries n.e.s.　(a)　$0.70　c 14 p.
        Manufacturers of industrial chemicals　(a)　$0.70　c 14 p.
        Manufacturers of mixed fertilizers　(a)　$0.70　c 8 p.
        Sales of toilet preparations in Canada　(a)　$0.35　c 8 p.
        Sales of paints, varnishes and lacquers　(m)　$0.15 or $1.50 yr.
        Specified chemicals　(m)　$0.15 or $1.50 yr.
        Soaps and synthetic detergents　(m)　$0.15 or $1.50 yr.
        Chemicals service bulletin　(m)　$2.80 yr.

     Miscellaneous manufacturers:
        Sporting goods and toy industries　(a)　$0.70　c 9 p.
        Miscellaneous manufacturing industries　(a)　$1.40　c 72 p.
        Scientific and professional equipment manufacturers　(a)　$0.70　c 29 p.
        Plastics fabricating industry　(a)　$0.70　c 10 p.
        Signs and display industry　(a)　$0.70　c 8 p.
        Jewellery and silverware industry　(a)　$0.70　c 8 p.
        Vinyl-asbestos floor tile service bulletin　(m)　$1.40 yr.
        Rubber and plastics industries service bulletin　(m)　$1.40 yr.
        Miscellaneous industries service bulletin　(m)　$1.40 yr.
        Phonograph records and pre-recorded tapes service bulletin　(m)　$1.40 yr.

  Time factor: varies with each publication, but the data is issued as soon as it is available.　Figures for earlier years or for the previous year are included for comparison.
   §　En,　Fr.

¶ B.iii, continued

602 Inventories, shipments and orders in manufacturing industries (Statistics Canada)
 Publications Distribution, Statistics Canada, Ottawa K1A 0T6.
  monthly. Can$0.55 or Can$5.50 yr.
 A summary of trends, and data for individual industries.
 Time factor: each issue has long runs of figures to the date of the issue and is published some three months
  later.
 § En, Fr.

 Note: also available are 'Inventories, shipments and orders in manufacturing industries. Historical
  supplement, 1970-1973' and a similar volume for 1972-1974, both free to subscribers to the above
  publication.

603 Indexes of real domestic product by industry (including the index of industrial production) (Statistics Canada)
 Publications Distribution, Statistics Canada, Ottawa K1A 0T6.
 1971- monthly. Can$0.40 or Can$4 yr.
 Issued in the general series 'System of national accounts'.
 § En, Fr.

604 Industrial prices newsletter (Statistics Canada)
 Publications Distribution, Statistics Canada, Ottawa K1A 0T6.
 1978- monthly. not priced.
 Notes changes in price indexes.
 § En.

605 Production and disposition of tobacco products (Statistics Canada)
 Publications Distribution, Statistics Canada, Ottawa K1A 0T6.
 1972- monthly. Can$0.15 or Can$1.50 yr.
 Time factor: each issue has data for that month and is published two months later.
 § En, Fr.

606 Facts and figures of the automotive industry (Motor Vehicle Manufacturers' Association).
 Motor Vehicle Manufacturers' Association, 25 Adelaide Street East, Toronto M5C 1Y7
 1969- 1974. not priced. 47 p.
 Includes statistical tables of the industry (production and shipments, employees, earnings of motor vehicle
  and allied industries), exports and imports, retail trade, registration, revenue and tax rates, motor
  fuel sales, etc.
 Time factor: the 1974 edition, published in 1974, has data for 1971, 1972 and 1973.
 § En.

 Note: a monthly with the same title has been published since 1970 and contains figures up-dating the
  annual issues.

607 Heavy engineering contracting industry (Statistics Canada)
 Publications Distribution, Statistics Canada, Ottawa K1A 0T6.
 1975- 1976. Can$1.05. 39 p.
 Contains statistical data on selected financial and operational characteristics of general contracting
  establishments primarily engaged in the construction, reconstruction and repair of heavy engineering
  structures. Data is national and by provinces.
 Time factor: the 1976 issue, published in 1978, has national data for 1973 to 1978 and provincial data
  for 1976.
 § En, Fr.

¶   B.iii,   continued

608   The publishing industry in Canada: a report...   (Bureau of Management Consulting)
            Printing and Publishing Services of Canada, Ottawa K1A 0S9.
                            Can$10.   418 p.
            Contains chapters on statistics and the structure of the book publishing industry, financial affairs,
                marketing and distribution channels, and policy analysis.   Tables are included in the text.
            Time factor: published in 1977, the report includes data for several years to 1974.
            ⧽ En.

            Refer also to 570, 573, 580.

    iv.   Construction

609   Construction in Canada   (Statistics Canada)
            Publications Distribution, Statistics Canada, Ottawa K1A 0T6.
                    1976-1978.   Can$1.40.   81 p.
            Contains the principal statistics on construction, including new and repair work performed by type of
                structure for each province, labour content and costs of materials used in Canada and the provinces,
                by contractors, governments, utilities and others.
            Time factor: the 1976-1978 edition, published mid-1978, has data for 1976 and 1977.
            §   En,   Fr.

            Note: a monthly 'Service bulletin: construction statistics' commenced publication in 1978.

610   Construction price statistics   (Statistics Canada)
            Publications Distribution, Statistics Canada, Ottawa K1A 0T6.
            1974-   monthly and   Can$0.40 or Can$4 yr.
                     quarterly   Can$1.40 or Can$5.60 yr.
            Includes data on inputs into construction, structure - plant indexes, contractors selling price indexes,
                highway construction price indexes, fabricated structural steel indexes, and precast concrete indexes.
            Time factor: the issues have long runs of figures to about three months prior to the date of the issue or the
                latest figures available.
            §   En,   Fr.

611   Special trades contracting industry   (Statistics Canada)
            Publications Distribution, Statistics Canada, Ottawa K1A 0T6.
            1975-   1976.   Can$2.10.   105 p.
            Contains statistical data on selected organisational and operational characteristics of building construction
                establishments generally (known as special trades contractors).
            Time factor: the 1976 issue, published in 1978, has data for 1976.
            §   En,   Fr.

            Refer to 572, 573.

    v.   Energy

612   Detailed energy supply and demand in Canada   (Statistics Canada)
            Publications Distribution, Statistics Canada, Ottawa K1A 0T6.
            1958/69-   1976.   Can$1.05.   41 p.
            Contains data on the supply and demand of coal, coke, coke oven gas, liquified petroleum gas, crude
                oil, still gas, motor gasoline, kerosene, diesel fuel oil.
            Time factor: the 1976 issue, published mid-1978, has data for 1976.
            §   En,   Fr.

            Note: an advance information release 'Service bulletin: energy statistics' has been published since
                1966 (Can$4.20).

¶   B.v,   continued

613   Quarterly report on energy supply-demand in Canada   (Statistics Canada)
        Publications Distribution, Statistics Canada, Ottawa K1A 0T6.
        1976-   Can$1.05 or Can$4.20 yr.
        Time factor: the first two issues, for 1976 and 1977, are annual and are intended to provide a base for
            subsequent quarterly issues.
        §   En,   Fr.

614   Annual report   (National Energy Board)
        National Energy Board, Ottawa.
        1970- 1977.   not priced.   80 p.
        Includes statistical data on consumption of selected energies, imports and exports of natural gas and
            electricity, production of natural gas and electricity.
        Time factor: the 1977 report, published mid-1978, has data for 1977.
        §   En.

615   Electric power statistics   (Statistics Canada)
        Publications Distribution, Statistics Canada, Ottawa K1A 0T6.
        (annual)   1976.   3 vols.
        Contents:
            Vol 1   24th annual electric power survey of capability and load (Can$1.05)
              II   Annual statistics (Can$1.40)
              III   Inventory of prime mover and electric generating equipment (Can$2.10)
        Volume I includes current and projected data of capability and load of major producers of electric energy
            by province; volume II has summary and detailed analyses of generation and use of electric energy,
            power plant equipment, customers, employees, salaries and wages, financial statistics, and supply
            and disposal of electric energy by province; and volume III has a list of generating plants in Canada
            by ownership, showing the location, year of installation, nameplate rating and other details.
        Time factor: the volumes for 1976 were published in 1978.
        §   En,   Fr.

616   Electric power statistics   (Statistics Canada)
        Publications Distribution, Statistics Canada, Ottawa K1A 0T6.
        1933-   monthly.   Can$0.30 or Can$3 yr.
        Contains data on electric power by province, supply and disposal, demand and generation.
        Time factor: each issue has data for the month of issue and is published about three months later.
        §   En,   Fr.

617   Electric power in Canada   (Department of Energy, Mines and Resources)
        Department of Energy, Mines and Resources, Ottawa.
        (annual) 1975.   free.   77 p.
        Includes a very few statistical tables in the text.
        Time factor: the 1975 issue was published mid-1978.
        §   En,   Fr.

618   Consumption of purchased fuel and electricity by the manufacturing, mining and electric power industries
        (Statistics Canada)
        Publications Distribution, Statistics Canada, Ottawa K1A 0T6.
        1962/74- 1975.   Can$1.05.   56 p.
        Time factor: the 1975 issue, published early 1978, has data for 1975.
        §   En,   Fr.

CANADA,   continued

¶   B.v,   continued

619   Gas utilities (transport and distribution systems)   (Statistics Canada)
         Publications Distribution, Statistics Canada, Ottawa K1A 0T6.
         1959-   1977.   Can$1.40.   81 p.
         Time factor: the 1977 issue, published early 1979, has data for 1977.
         §   En,   Fr.

620   Gas utilities   (Statistics Canada)
         Publications Distribution, Statistics Canada, Ottawa K1A 0T6.
         1959-   monthly.   Can$0.30 or Can$3 yr.
         Contains data on receipts, dispositions, sales, etc, of natural gas for the whole of Canada and by province.
         Time factor: each issue has data for that month and is published about three months later.
         §   En,   Fr.

         Refer also to 570, 572, 573.

¶   C   -   External trade

621   Exports - merchandise trade   (Statistics Canada)
         Publications Distribution, Statistics Canada, Ottawa K1A 0T6.
         1930/31-   1975-1977.   Can$16.50.   1063 p.
         Includes detailed foreign trade statistics arranged by commodity and sub-divided by countries of destination
             as well as summary tables.
         Time factor: the 1975-1977 issue, published mid-1978, has data for the years 1975, 1976 and 1977.
         §   En,   Fr.

         Note: early title was 'Trade of Canada, vol II'.

622   Imports - merchandise trade   (Statistics Canada)
         Publications Distribution, Statistics Canada, Ottawa K1A 0T6.
         1930/31-   1975-1977.   Can$16.   1007 p.
         Includes detailed foreign trade statistics arranged by commodity and sub-divided by countries of origin as
             well as summary tables.
         Time factor: the 1975-1977 issue, published mid-1978, has data for 1976, 1977 and 1978.
         §   En,   Fr.

         Note: early title was 'Trade of Canada, vol III'.

623   Summary of external trade   (Statistics Canada)
         Publications Distribution, Statistics Canada, Ottawa K1A 0T6.
         1931-   monthly.   Can$0.40 or Can$4 yr.
         A summarized presentation of monthly imports and exports, and 3-year cumulative totals by country and
             commodity categories.
         §   En,   Fr.

624   Exports by commodities   (Statistics Canada)
         Publications Distribution, Statistics Canada, Ottawa K1A 0T6.
         1944-   monthly.   Can$0.80 or Can$8 yr.
         Contains detailed statistics of exports from Canada arranged by commodities and sub-divided by countries
             of destination.
         Time factor: each issue has data for the date of the issue and cumulated totals for the year to date, and is
             issued between one and two months later.
         §   En,   Fr.

¶   C,   continued

625   Imports by commodities   (Statistics Canada)
          Publications Distribution, Statistics Canada, Ottawa K1A 0T6.
          1944-   monthly.   Can$0.80 or Can$8 yr.
          Contains detailed statistics of imports into Canada arranged by commodities and sub-divided by countries
               of origin.
          Time factor: each issue has data for the date of the issue and cumulated totals for the year to date, and
               is issued between one and two months later.
          §   En,   Fr.

626   Exports by countries   (Statistics Canada)
          Publications Distribution, Statistics Canada, Ottawa K1A 0T6.
          1944-   quarterly.   Can$2.10 or Can$8.40 yr.
          Contains detailed statistics of exports arranged by country of destination and sub-divided by commodities.
          Time factor: each issue has cumulated statistics for the year to date and comparative information for the
               preceding year.   Publication is two or three months after the end of the period covered.
          §   En,   Fr.

627   Imports by countries   (Statistics Canada)
          Publications Distribution, Statistics Canada, Ottawa K1A 0T6.
          1944-   quarterly.   Can$2.10 or Can$8.40 yr.
          Contains detailed statistics of imports arranged by country of origin and sub-divided by commodities.
          Time factor: each issue has cumulated statistics for the year to date and comparative information for the
               preceding year.   Publication is two or three months after the end of the period covered.
          §   En,   Fr.

          Refer also to 570, 572, 573.

¶   D   -   Internal distribution and service trades

628   Retail trade   (Statistics Canada)
          Publications Distribution, Statistics Canada, Ottawa K1A 0T6.
                    monthly.   Can$0.55 or Can$5.50 yr.
          Contains data on 17 kinds of business: grocery and combination stores, other food stores, department
               stores, general merchandise stores, general stores, variety stores, motor vehicle dealers, service
               stations, men's clothing stores, women's clothing stores, family clothing stores, shoe stores, hardware
               stores, furniture, TV, radio and appliance stores, fuel dealers, drug stores, jewellery stores, all
               other stores.
          §   En,   Fr.

629   Retail commodity survey   (Statistics Canada)
          Publications Distribution, Statistics Canada, Ottawa K1A 0T6.
          1968-   1974.   Can$2.80.   171 p.
          An enquiry into sales of approximately 150 major commodity lines in retail stores, by province and by
               kind of business.
          Time factor: the survey is conducted at five-yearly intervals, and the 1974 survey results were published
               late 1976.
          §   En,   Fr.

630   Shopping centres in Canada   (retail and service trade)   (Statistics Canada)
          Publications Distribution, Statistics Canada, Ottawa K1A 0T6.
          1956-   1951-1973.   Can$1.40.   91 p.
          The results of an annual survey of shopping centres and their retail and service outlets.
          Time factor: the 1951-1973 issue, published in 1976, has data for the years 1951 to 1973.
          §   En,   Fr.

¶   D,   continued

631   Wholesale trade   (Statistics Canada)
           Publications Distribution, Statistics Canada, Ottawa K1A 0T6.
                   monthly.   Can$0.15 or Can$1.50 yr.
           Contains data on the trade of wholesale merchants only, and includes trade in consumer goods and
               industrial goods.   Also preliminary estimates of wholesale sales inventories.
           Time factor: each issue has data for the month of the issue and cumulated figures for the year to date,
               and is published about one month later.
           §   En,   Fr.

632   Market research handbook   (Statistics Canada)
           Publications Distribution, Statistics Canada, Ottawa K1A 0T6.
           1931-   1977-78.   Can$9.75.   674 p.
           Contains data on selected economic indicators, merchandising, advertising and media, population
               characteristics, personal income and expenditure, housing, motor vehicles, household facilities
               and equipment, and small area market data.
           Time factor: the 1977-78 edition, published mid-1978, has data for several years to 1976 or 1975 in
               some tables.
           §   En,   Fr.

633   Survey of markets   (The Financial Post)
           Maclean-Hunter Ltd, 481 University Avenue, Toronto, Ontario M5W 1A7.
           1925-   1975/76.   Can$15.   348 p.
           An annual market survey of Canada's provinces, cities and towns, plus special reviews of the major
               economic and business indicators of the nation.
           Time factor: the 1975/76 edition was published in 1975 and contains the most recent actual figures as
               well as forecasts for the future.
           §   En.

634   Merchandising businesses survey: wholesale merchants   (Statistics Canada)
           Publications Distribution, Statistics Canada, Ottawa K1A 0T6.
           1973-   1975.   Can$1.05.   70 p.
           Includes data on number of establishments, kind of business, in Canada and regions; number of locations,
               volume of trade, kind of business, in Canada and regions; sources of revenue in Canada and
               provinces; and sources of revenue by standard industrial classification in Canada, the data being
               collected as part of a biennial survey of the wholesale sector of the distribution industry.
           Time factor: the results of the 1975 survey were published early 1978.
           §   En,   Fr.

635   Merchandising businesses survey: agents and brokers   (Statistics Canada)
           Publications Distribution, Statistics Canada, Ottawa K1A 0T6.
           1973-   1974.   Can$1.05.   42 p.
           Contains data of a similar nature to the above (634), but for agents and brokers.
           Time factor: the results of the 1974 survey were published in 1977.
           §   En,   Fr.

636   Motion picture theatres and film distributors   (Statistics Canada)
           Publications Distribution, Statistics Canada, Ottawa K1A 0T6.
           (annual)   1977.   Can$0.70.   22 p.
           Contains the results of regular surveys on regular motion picture theatres, drive-in theatres, and film
               distributors.
           Time factor: the results of the 1977 survey were published early 1979.
           §   En,   Fr.

¶   D,   continued

637   Consulting engineering services   (Statistics Canada)
       Publications Distribution, Statistics Canada, Ottawa KIA 0T6.
       1974-   1974.   Can$0.70.   42 p.
       Data on income and expenditure of firms mainly concerned with the provision of consulting engineering
           services, including numbers of projects by sector, location and source of finance.
       Time factor: the 1974 issue, published in 1977, has data for 1974.
       §   En,   Fr.

638   Travel, tourism and outdoor recreation: a statistical digest   (Statistics Canada)
       Publications Distribution, Statistics Canada, Ottawa KIA 0T6.
       1972-   1976 & 1977.   Can$3.50.   253 p.
       Contains statistical data on recreation participation: parks, camping, hunting, and fishing; travel to
           work; domestic travel by residents of Canada; travel between Canada and the USA; travel between
           Canada and other countries; balance of payments and international travel; locations, etc, (business
           of travel - hotels, etc); and employment.
       Time factor: the 1976 & 1977 edition, published in 1979, has data for 1976 and also some earlier years
           in some tables.
       §   En,   Fr.

639   Travel between Canada and other countries   (Statistics Canada)
       Publications Distribution, Statistics Canada, Ottawa KIA 0T6.
       1906-   quarterly and annual.   Can$1.75 or Can$7 yr.   (Annual issue: $1.40)
       Contains totals for Canada and for the provinces and detailed statistics by port of entry.
       Time factor: each issue has data for each of the three months of the quarter and long runs of earlier
           annual and monthly figures; published about three months later.
       §   En,   Fr.

       Note: a monthly 'International travel - advance information' is also published (Can$0.15 or
           Can$1.50 yr).

       Refer also to 570, 572, 573, 580.

¶   E - Population

640   Census of Canada   (Statistics Canada)
       Publications Distribution, Statistics Canada, Ottawa KIA 0T6.
       1851/52-.   1976.
       Contents:
           Vol   I   Population: geographic distributions (complete set of 12 reports and binder Can$35.75)
           Vol   II   Population: demographic characteristics (complete set of 9 reports and binder Can$38.50)
           Vol   III   Dwellings and households (complete set of 11 reports and binder (Can$30.25)
           Vol   IV   Families (complete set of 6 reports and binder Can$17)
           Vol   V   Labour force activity (complete set of 9 reports and binder Can$21)
           Vol   VI   Census tracts (complete set of tracts and binder Can$66)
           Vol   VII   Provincial census tracts (complete set of tracts and binder Can$24)
           Vol   VIII Supplementary bulletins to Vols I & II: geographic and demographic (complete set of 6
                       bulletins and binder Can$20.25)
           Vol   IX   Supplementary bulletins to Vols III & IV: housing and families (complete set of 6 bulletins
                       and binder Can$23.75)
           Vol   X   Supplementary bulletins: economic characteristics (complete set of 8 bulletins Can$21.25)
       Time factor: the reports were published between 1972 and 1978.
       §   En,   Fr.

¶   E,   continued

641   Vital statistics   (Statistics Canada)
        Publications Distribution, Statistics Canada, Ottawa K1A 0T6.
        1971-   1976.   3 vols.
        Contents:
            Vol I   Births, 1975 & 1976 (Can$1.40)
            Vol II   Marriages and divorces, 1976 (Can$1.05)
            Vol III   Deaths, 1976 (Can$2.80)
        Time factor: the above volumes were published in 1978, and Vol I contains data for 1975 and 1976,
            whilst Vols II & III have long runs of figures to 1976.
        §   En,   Fr.

642   Vital statistics   (Statistics Canada)
        Publications Distribution, Statistics Canada, Ottawa K1A 0T6.
        1973-   quarterly.   Can$0.35 or Can$1.40 yr.
        Updates the above (641).
        §   En,   Fr.

643   Immigration quarterly statistics   (Employment and Immigration Canada)
        Employment and Immigration Canada, Ottawa.
                            free.
        Contains data on immigration by country of last permanent residence, by country of citizenship, by
            intended occupation groups and provinces of destination, by age group and sex, and by area of
            former residence.   Also language capabilities of immigrants, and number and percentage of
            distribution by province.
        Time factor: each issue has data for that quarter and is published about six months later.
        §   En,   Fr.

644   The labour force   (Statistics Canada)
        Publications Distribution, Statistics Canada, Ottawa K1A 0T6.
        1945-   monthly.   Can$0.55 or Can$5.50 yr.
        Contains seasonally adjusted data, and unadjusted data for all characteristics (sex, age, marital status,
            etc, by province), labour force (sex, age, marital status, etc, by province), employment by industry
            and occupation, unemployment, family data, numbers not in labour, the labour force, and sub-
            provincial data.
        Time factor: each issue has data for that month and is published about one month later.
        §   En,   Fr.

645   Historical labour force statistics, actual data, seasonal factors, seasonally adjusted data   (Statistics Canada)
        Publications Distribution, Statistics Canada, Ottawa K1A 0T6.
        1978-   Can$2.10.   168 p.
        Time factor: the 1978 issue, published early 1979, has data for the years 1966 to 1978.
        §   En,   Fr.

        Note: formerly 'Seasonally adjusted labour force statistics'.

646   Employment, earnings and hours   (Statistics Canada)
        Publications Distribution, Statistics Canada, Ottawa K1A 0T6.
        1923-   monthly.   Can$0.70 or Can$7 yr.
        Contains data by provinces and towns.
        Time factor: each issue has data for the month prior to the date of publication.
        §   En,   Fr.

¶   E,   continued

647   Canadian housing statistics   (Central Mortgage and Housing Corporation)
        Statistical Services Division, Central Mortgage and Housing Corporation, Ottawa.
        1955-   1976.   free.   110 p.
        Brings together data relating to house building and mortgage lending activity in Canada, and includes
            data on house building activity, mortgage lending activity, financing under National Housing Act,
            characteristics of dwellings and loans under National Housing Act, characteristics of participants
            under N H A, price and cost indexes, population change and housing demand, etc.
        Time factor: the 1976 issue, published early 1977, has long runs of statistics to 1976.   Updated by
            monthly supplements titled 'Monthly housing statistics'.
        §   En,   Fr.

        Note: replaced 'Housing in Canada' in 1955.

        Refer also to 570, 572, 573.

¶   F   -   Social

648   Perspective Canada: a compendium of social statistics   (Statistics Canada)
        Publications Distribution, Statistics Canada, Ottawa K1A 0T6
        1976-   2nd, 1977.   Can$9.25.   335 p.
        Contains information on basic social issues, including population, changing family, older Canadians,
            health, education, work, leisure, income, consumption, urban profiles of Montreal, Toronto and
            Vancouver, environment, housing, bilingualism, native peoples, crime and justice.
        Time factor: the 1977 issue, published early 1977, has data for several years to the latest available,
            usually 1974.
        §   En   &   Fr   eds.

649   Canadian social structure: a statistical profile   (John Porter)
        McClelland and Stewart Ltd, Toronto.
                        Can$2.95.   159 p.
        Includes data on the demographic structure, marriage and family, immigration, language, ethnicity and
            religion, the economy, government, education, leisure, deviant behaviour, illness and mortality.
        Time factor: published in 1967.
        §   En.

        Refer also to 570, 572.

    i.   Standard of living

650   Income distribution by size in Canada   (Statistics Canada)
        Publications Distribution, Statistics Canada, Ottawa K1A 0T6.
        1965-   4th, 1976.   Can$1.05.   59 p.
        The results of a survey, showing estimates of family and individual income by size of income and by major
            source, region, age, sex, and other characteristics.
        Time factor: the report for 1976 was published in 1979.
        §   En,   Fr.

        Note: Prior to the publication of the final reports, preliminary information is given in 'Income
            distribution by size in Canada, preliminary estimates' (Can$0.70).

651   Family expenditure in Canada, 1969   (Statistics Canada)
        Publications Distribution, Statistics Canada, Ottawa K1A 0T6.
        Contents: 3 vols.
            Vol   I   All Canada, urban and rural (Can$2.80)
            Vol II   Regions (Can$2.50)
            Vol III   Major urban cities (Can$1.50)
        §   En   &   Fr   eds.

CANADA, continued

¶ F.i, continued

652 Urban family expenditure (Statistics Canada)
Publications Distribution, Statistics Canada, Ottawa K1A 0T6.
1953- 1974. Can$3.50. 246 p.
A small sample survey of family expenditure in fourteen major urban cities, including detailed expenditure
for families and unattached individuals, classified by city, income level, family type, etc.
Time factor: an enquiry is carried out at two or three-yearly intervals, and the results of the 1974 survey
were published in 1977.
§ En, Fr.

653 Family food expenditure in Canada (Statistics Canada)
Publications Distribution, Statistics Canada, Ottawa K1A 0T6.
1969- 2nd, 1974. Can$3.50. 272 p.
Contains detailed information on family food purchases recorded by a sample survey of just over 7,500
Canadian households.
Time factor: the results of the 1974 survey were published in 1977.
§ En, Fr.

654 Consumer prices and price indexes (Statistics Canada)
Publications Distribution, Statistics Canada, Ottawa K1A 0T6.
1975- quarterly. Can$1.40 or Can$5.60 yr.
A compendium of consumer prices and price index related information, including place-to-place price
comparisons and selected retail price averages.
§ En, Fr.

Note: advance information is given in the monthly 'Consumer price index' (Can$0.30 or Can$3 yr),
'Consumer price indexes for regional cities' (Can$0.30 or Can$3 yr), and 'Retail prices and living
costs service bulletin' (Can$2.80 yr).

655 Household facilities by income and other characteristics (Statistics Canada)
Publications Distribution, Statistics Canada, Ottawa K1A 0T6.
1969- 2nd, 1974. Can$2.10. 165 p.
Contains data on the interrelationships of household incomes and household facilities and equipment.
Time factor: the results of the 1974 survey were published in 1978.
§ En, Fr.

ii. Health and welfare

656 Hospital statistics (Statistics Canada)
Publications Distribution, Statistics Canada, Ottawa K1A 0T6.
(annual) 1975. 3 vols.
Contents:
Vol I Beds, services and personnel (Can$3.50)
Vol II Expenditures, revenues and balance sheets (Can$2.10)
Vol III Indicators [of other hospital activity] (Can$1.40)
Time factor: each of the 1975 volumes has data for 1975 and was published in 1978.
§ En, Fr.

Note: 'Hospital statistics: preliminary annual report' (Can$1.05) is issued about 8 months prior to the
above title.

¶   F.ii,   continued

657   Hospital indicators   (Statistics Canada)
          Publications Distribution, Statistics Canada, Ottawa K1A 0T6.
          1969-   quarterly.   Can$1.75 or Can$7 yr.
          Time factor: each issue has data for that quarter and cumulated figures for the year to date, and is
             published ten or eleven months later.
          §   En,   Fr.

658   Mental health statistics   (Statistics Canada)
          Publications Distribution, Statistics Canada, Ottawa K1A 0T6.
          1932-   1976.   3 vols.
          Contents:
             Vol I   Institutional admissions and separations (Can$3.50)
             Vol II   Patients in institutions (Can$2.10)
             Vol III   Institutional facilities, services and finances (Can$1.40)
          Time factor: the 1976 volumes have data for 1976.
          §   En,   Fr.

659   Tuberculosis statistics   (Statistics Canada)
          Publications Distribution, Statistics Canada, Ottawa K1A 0T6.
          1937-   1975.   Can$1.40.   82 p.
          Time factor: the 1975 issue, published early 1978, has data for 1975.
          §   En,   Fr.

660   Nursing in Canada: Canadian nursing statistics   (Statistics Canada)
          Publications Distribution, Statistics Canada, Ottawa K1A 0T6.
          1975-   1975.   Can$2.10.   143 p.
          A statistical compendium on the nursing profession in Canada, including data on distribution of nurses,
             salaries, education, hospital facilities, etc.
          Time factor: the 1975 issue, published in 1976, has data for 1975.
          §   En,   Fr.

       iii.   Education and leisure

661   Education in Canada: a statistical review... (Statistics Canada)
          Publications Distribution, Statistics Canada, Ottawa K1A 0T6.
          1973-   1977.   Can$1.40.   137 p.
          Contains retrospective statistical summaries, summary tables, and data on educational institutions,
             enrolment, graduates, teachers, and expenditures.
          Time factor: the 1977 edition, published mid-1978, has data for the academic years 1976/77, 1975/76
             and 1974/75.
          §   En,   Fr.

          Note: the 1973 edition covered the years 1960/61 to 1970/71.

662   Advance statistics of education   (Statistics Canada)
          Publications Distribution, Statistics Canada, Ottawa K1A 0T6.
          1967/68-   1976-77.   Can$1.05.   54 p.
          Contains estimates of key educational variables for the beginning of the school year, provincial forecasts
             for the following year, and national forecasts for a year later.
          Time factor: the 1976-77 issue, published mid-1976, has data for 1974/75, 1975/76 (preliminary) and
             forecasts for the following three years.
          §   En,   Fr.

¶   F.iii,   continued

663   Financial statistics of education   (Statistics Canada)
           Publications Distribution, Statistics Canada, Ottawa K1A 0T6.
           1971/72-1973/74-   1974-75.   Can$2.10.   124 p.
           Includes data at all levels, elementary and secondary, post-secondary, and vocational training.
           Time factor: the 1974-75 issue, published late 1977, has data for the academic year 1974-75 and
                 historical tables back to 1950-51.
           §   En,   Fr.

664   Universities: financial statistics   (Statistics Canada)
           Publications Distribution, Statistics Canada, Ottawa K1A 0T6.
           1967/67-   1976-77.   Can$1.05.   65 p.
           Financial data for universities and colleges.
           Time factor: the 1976-77 issue, published late 1978, has data for the academic year 1976-77 and some
                 earlier years.
           §   En,   Fr.

665   Elementary-secondary education; financial statistics   (Statistics Canada)
           Publications Distribution, Statistics Canada, Ottawa K1A 0T6.
           1970/71-   1975-76.   Can$2.10.   129 p.
           Contains consolidated financial statistics, school board financial statistics, and private school financial
                 statistics.
           Time factor: the 1975-76 issue, published mid-1978, has data for the academic year 1975-76 and some
                 earlier years.
           §   En,   Fr.

666   Public libraries in Canada   (Statistics Canada)
           Publications Distribution, Statistics Canada, Ottawa K1A 0T6.
           1929/30-   1974.   Can$1.05.   56 p.
           Contains data on public library systems in centres of 10,000 population and over, and regional and
                 provincial library services.   Also summary data on smaller centres.
           Time factor: the 1974 issue, published in 1977, has data for 1974.
           §   En,   Fr.

           Note: continues 'Survey of libraries, part 1'.

667   University and college libraries in Canada   (Statistics Canada)
           Publications Distribution, Statistics Canada, Ottawa K1A 0T6.
           1929/30-   1969/70.   Can$2.10.   136 p.
           As well as college and university libraries, the publication includes technical institutes, trade school and
                 teachers' college libraries, centralised school libraries, and library school graduates.
           Time factor: publication ceased with the 1969/70 issue.
           §   En,   Fr.

           Refer also to 580.

¶   G   -   Finance

668   Financial institutions: financial statistics   (Statistics Canada)
           Publications Distribution, Statistics Canada, Ottawa K1A 0T6.
           1963-   quarterly.   Can$1.40 or Can$5.60 yr.
           Contains financial statistics for financial institutions and financial intermediaries operating in Canada,
                 including balance sheets, income statements, retained earnings statements, etc.
           Time factor: each issue has data for seven or eight quarters to the quarter of the issue and is published
                 three or four months later.
           §   En,   Fr.

           Refer also to 570, 572, 573.

CANADA,   continued

¶   G,   continued

i.   Banks and banking

        Refer to 570, 572.

ii.   Public finance

669   System of national accounts - national income and expenditure accounts, 1963-1977 (Statistics Canada)
            Publications Distribution, Statistics Canada, Ottawa K1A 0T6.
                        Can$2.10.   110 p.
            Contains summary tables of income and expenditure, sector accounts, industrial distribution of gross
                domestic product, geographical distribution of personal income, etc.
            Time factor: published late 1978.
            §   En,   Fr.

670   National income and expenditure accounts, 1926-1974 (Statistics Canada)
            Publications Distribution, Statistics Canada, Ottawa K1A 0T6.
            Contents:
                    Vol I   The annual estimates, 1926-1974 (Can$5.25)
                    Vol II   The quarterly estimates, 1947-1974 (Can$3.50)
                    Vol III   A guide to the national income and expenditure accounts: definitions - concepts -
                                sources - methods (Can$6.75)
            Time factor: Vols I & II were published in 1976, Vol III in 1975.
            §   En,   Fr.

671   National income and expenditure accounts. System of national accounts (Statistics Canada)
            Publications Distribution, Statistics Canada, Ottawa K1A 0T6.
            1953-   quarterly.   Can$1.05 or Can$5.60 yr.
            Contains data on gross national product, personal income and gross saving, government revenue and
                expenditure, etc.
            Time factor: each issue has data for each quarter of the past three years and of the current year to date,
                and is published about six months later.
            §   En,   Fr.

672   Financial flow accounts. System of national accounts (Statistics Canada)
            Publications Distribution, Statistics Canada, Ottawa K1A 0T6.
            1967-   quarterly.   Can$1.75 or Can$7 yr.
            Contains matrices, economic sector and financial category tables, as well as a review of the Canadian
                financial and monetary developments.
            Time factor: each issue has data for each quarter of the past three years and of the current year to date,
                and is published about six months later.
            §   En,   Fr.

673   Gross national product: advance information (Statistics Canada)
            Publications Distribution, Statistics Canada, Ottawa K1A 0T6.
            1978-   quarterly.   not priced.
            Contains seasonally adjusted data.
            Time factor: includes data for several quarters to about three months prior to the date of the publication.
            §   En,   Fr.

¶   G.ii,   continued

674   The Canadian balance of international payments   (Statistics Canada)
          Publications Distribution, Statistics Canada, Ottawa K1A 0T6.
          1965-   1973-1974.   Can$2.80.   237 p.
          Time factor: the 1973-1974 issue was published late 1977.
          §   En,   Fr.

          Note: also published is 'The Canadian balance of international payments - a compendium of statistics
              from 1946 to 1965' (Can$2.50).

675   Quarterly estimates of the Canadian balance of international payments. System of national accounts
              (Statistics Canada)
          Publications Distribution, Statistics Canada, Ottawa K1A 0T6.
          1953-   Can$1.05 or Can$4.20 yr.
          Time factor: each issue has annual and quarterly figures for the past three years up to the quarter of the
              issue, and is published about four months later.
          §   En,   Fr.

676   Government finance: in accordance with the system of national accounts   (Statistics Canada)
          Publications Distribution, Statistics Canada, Ottawa K1A 0T6.
          1974-   quarterly.   Can$1.05 or Can$4.20 yr.
          Contains details of aggregates published quarterly in 'National income and expenditure accounts' (see
              671).
          Time factor: each issue has data for the last eight quarters, including the quarter of the issue, and is
              published about three months later.
          §   En,   Fr.

677   Federal government finance   (Statistics Canada)
          Publications Distribution, Statistics Canada, Ottawa K1A 0T6.
          1962-   1977.   Can$1.05.   c 50 p.
          An analysis of federal government revenue and expenditure, assets, liabilities, etc.
          Time factor: the 1977 issue, published in 1978, has data for 1977.
          §   En,   Fr.

          Note: this publication is complemented by 'Federal government enterprise finance' (Can$1.05).

678   Provincial government finance   (Statistics Canada)
          Publications Distribution, Statistics Canada, Ottawa K1A 0T6.
          1962-   1977.   Can$1.40 each.   2 vols.
          One volume is sub-titled 'revenue and expenditure' and the other 'assets, liabilities and sources and uses
              of funds'.
          Time factor: the 1977 issues, published in 1978 have data for 1977.
          §   En,   Fr.

679   Taxation statistics   (Taxation Division, Department of National Revenue)
          Information Canada, Publishing Division, Ottawa.
          1944-   1972.   Can$2.50.   214 p.
          Contains statistics of tax returns filed by individual taxpayers for income classes, occupation, age and
              sex, and for provinces, cities, etc.
          Time factor: the 1972 issue, published in 1972, has data for 1970.
          §   En,   Fr.

¶   G.ii,   continued

680   Corporation taxation statistics   (Statistics Canada)
           Publications Distribution, Statistics Canada, Ottawa K1A 0T6.
           1965- 1976.   Can$2.10.   123 p.
           Contains data on taxation of corporation income, indicating industries earning the income on which tax
               is based, province in which it was earned, and reconciliation of corporation profit and taxable
               income.
           Time factor: the 1976 issue, published early 1979, has data for 1976 and 1975.
           §   En,   Fr.

       iii.   Company finance

681   Fixed capital flows and stocks   (Statistics Canada)
           Publications Distribution, Statistics Canada, Ottawa K1A 0T6.
           1925/60- 1926-1978.   Can$5.25.   348 p.
           Contains data on fixed capital flows and stocks in manufacturing and non-manufacturing industries,
               1926-1978; price indices for capital expenditure on plant and equipment by industry in manufacturing
               and non-manufacturing industries, 1871-1978; and non-residential investment expenditure by
               industry in manufacturing and non-manufacturing industries, 1871-1978.
           Time factor: the 1926-1978 issue was published late 1978.
           §   En,   Fr.

682   Corporation financial statistics   (Statistics Canada)
           Publications Distribution, Statistics Canada, Ottawa K1A 0T6.
           1965- 1975.   Can$2.80.   209 p.
           Contains data on the financial operations and position of corporations in Canada as shown by audited
               financial statements of corporations.
           Time factor: the 1975 issue, published in 1978, has data for 1974 and 1975.
           §   En,   Fr.

       iv.   Investment

683   Canada's international investment position   (Statistics Canada)
           Publications Distribution, Statistics Canada, Ottawa K1A 0T6.
               1974.   Can$2.10.   127 p.
           A detailed analysis of foreign investments in Canada and Canadian investments abroad.   Includes
               analytical information on the relative position of foreign capital in the ownership and control of
               Canadian industry, the financing of investment and the distribution of income.
           Time factor: the 1974 issue, published early 1979, has data for 1974 and some earlier years.
           §   En,   Fr.

684   Private and public investment in Canada: outlook   (Statistics Canada)
           Publications Distribution, Statistics Canada, Ottawa K1A 0T6.
               1979.   Can$1.05.   50 p.
           Describes the capital spending intentions for all sectors of the economy for the coming year.
           Time factor: the 1979 issue, published in April, 1979, has information for 1979.
           §   En,   Fr.

       Note: there is also a 'Mid-year review' (Can$1.05) published in August which gives revised information.

CANADA,   continued

¶   G.v.   Insurance

685   Annual report of the Superintendent of Insurance for Canada.
            Insurance Department, Ottawa, or Information Canada, Ottawa.
                              not priced.   3 vols.
            Vol I, entitled 'Abstracts of statements of insurance companies in Canada', includes general statistics on
                fire and casualty companies, life insurance and fraternal benefit societies, Vol II deals with fire
                and casualty insurance, and Vol III with life insurance.
            §   En,   Fr.

686   Pension plans in Canada   (Statistics Canada)
            Publications Distribution, Statistics Canada, Ottawa K1A 0T6.
            1970- 1976.   Can$1.40.   89 p.
            Includes data on numbers of plans, number of people covered, contributions and benefit rates, vesting
                and total contributions, etc.
            Time factor: published every two years, the 1976 edition, was published in 1978 and has data for 1976.
            §   En & Fr eds.

687   Trusteed pension plans: financial statistics   (Statistics Canada)
            Publications Distribution, Statistics Canada, Ottawa K1A 0T6.
            1958- 1976.   Can$1.05.   68 p.
            Time factor: the 1976 issue, published in 1978, has data for 1975 and 1976.
            §   En,   Fr.

            Note: also published is 'Quarterly estimates of trusteed pension funds' (Can$0.35 or Can$1.40 yr)

688   Statistical report on the operation of the Unemployment Insurance Act   (Statistics Canada)
            Publications Distribution, Statistics Canada, Ottawa K1A 0T6.
            1942- quarterly.   Can$1.05 or Can$4.20 yr.
            Time factor: each issue has data for each separate month of the period of the issue and is published
                about five months later.
            §   En,   Fr.

¶   H - Transport and communications

689   Oil pipe line transport   (Statistics Canada)
            Publications Distribution, Statistics Canada, Ottawa K1A 0T6.
            1964- 1976.   Can$1.05.   41 p.
            Includes statistical data on receipts and dispositions of crude oil, pipe line movements, pipe line mileage,
                pumping stations, finances, payroll, employment and man-hours in the industry.
            Time factor: the 1976 issue, published in 1978, has data for 1976.
            §   En,   Fr.

690   Oil pipe line transport   (Statistics Canada)
            Publications Distribution, Statistics Canada, Ottawa K1A 0T6.
            1951- monthly.   Can$0.30 or Can$3 yr.
            Up-dates the above (689).
            Time factor: each issue has data for that month and corresponding month in the previous year, and is
                published three months later.
            §   En,   Fr.

            Refer also to 570, 572, 573.

¶ H, continued

i. Ships and shipping

691 Shipping report (Statistics Canada)
Publications Distribution, Statistics Canada, Ottawa K1A 0T6.
(annual) 1977. 5 vols.
Contents:
Part I International seaborne shipping (by country) (Can$2.80)
Part II International seaborne shipping (by port) (Can$1.05)
Part III Coastwise shipping (Can$2.10)
Part IV Origin and destination for selected ports (Can$2.10)
Part V Origin and destination for selected commodities (Can$1.05)
Time factor: the reports for 1977 were published between late 1978 and early 1979, and have data for 1977.
§ En, Fr.

692 Shipping statistics (Statistics Canada)
Publications Distribution, Statistics Canada, Ottawa K1A 0T6.
1957- monthly. Can$0.30 or Can$3 yr.
Contains preliminary statistics on commodity and vessel traffic at Canadian ports for both international and domestic shipping.
Time factor: each issue has data for that month and is published three or four months later.
§ En, Fr.

693 Water transportation (Statistics Canada)
Publications Distribution, Statistics Canada, Ottawa K1A 0T6.
(annual) 1977. Can$1.05. 77 p.
Contains the results of a census of Canadian domiciled water carriers, revenues, vessel crew and wages, numbers of vessels, property and equipment, for-hire carriers, private carriers, government carriers, and sightseeing.
Time factor: the 1977 issue, published early 1979, has data for 1977.
§ En, Fr.

Note: the annual is up-dated by a service bulletin 'Water transport'.

ii. Road

694 The motor vehicle (Statistics Canada)
Publications Distribution, Statistics Canada, Ottawa K1A 0T6.
(annual) 1973. 4 vols.
Contents:
Part I Rates and regulations (Can$1.05)
Part II Motive fuel sales (Can$0.70)
Part III Registrations (Can$0.70)
Part IV Revenues (Can$0.70)
Time factor: the 1973 edition, with data for that year, was published in 1975.
§ En, Fr.

¶   H.ii,   continued

695   Passenger bus and urban transit statistics   (Statistics Canada)
           Publications Distribution, Statistics Canada, Ottawa K1A 0T6.
           1974-   1974.   Can$1.05.   41 p.
           The results of surveys, containing statistics of intercity bus establishments, urban transit establishments,
               and other carriers.
           Time factor: the 1974 issue, published mid-1976, has data for 1974.
           §   En,   Fr.

696   Road and street length and financing   (Statistics Canada)
           Publications Distribution, Statistics Canada, Ottawa K1A 0T6.
           (annual)   1976.   Can$0.70.   31 p.
           Contains a broad range of statistics, the results of surveys.
           Time factor: the 1976 issue was published in 1979 and will be the final issue as the surveys have been
               cancelled.
           §   En,   Fr.

697   Motor vehicle traffic accidents   (Statistics Canada)
           Publications Distribution, Statistics Canada, Ottawa K1A 0T6.
           1973-   1975.   Can$1.40.   c 70 p.
           Time factor: the 1975 issue, published in 1976, has data for 1975.
           §   En,   Fr.

698   Motor carriers - freight and household goods movers, 1975   (Statistics Canada)
           Publications Distribution, Statistics Canada, Ottawa K1A 0T6.
                             Can$2.10.   137 p.
           The results of a census of motor carriers - freight and a census of household goods movers.
           Time factor: the results of the censuses were published in 1978.
           §   En,   Fr.

699   Road motor vehicles: registrations   (Statistics Canada)
           Publications Distribution, Statistics Canada, Ottawa K1A 0T6.
           1977-   1977.   Can$0.70.   18 p.
           Contains data on registrations, drivers' licenses, and dealers' permits.
           Time factor: the 1977 issue, published 1979, has data for the 1977 licence year.
           §   En,   Fr.

       iii.   Rail

700   Railway transport   (Statistics Canada)
           Publications Distribution, Statistics Canada, Ottawa K1A 0T6.
           1961-   1976.   6 vols.
           Contents:
               Part I   Comparative summary statistics   (Can$1.05)
               Part II   Financial statistics   (Can$0.70)
               Part III   Equipment, track and fuel statistics (Can$0.70)
               Part IV   Operating and traffic statistics (Can$0.70)
               Part V   Freight carried (Can$2.10)
               Part VI   Employee statistics (Can$0.70)
           Time factor: the volumes of the 1976 edition were published in 1977 and 1978 and have data for 1976,
               except Part I which covers 1972 to 1976.
           §   En,   Fr.

¶   H.iii,   continued

701   Railway operating statistics   (Statistics Canada)
            Publications Distribution, Statistics Canada, Ottawa K1A 0T6.
            1921-   monthly.   Can$0.30 or Can$3 yr.
            Contains selected financial and traffic statistics, and statistics pertaining to six major Class I and
                Class II Railways operating in Canada.
            Time factor: each issue has data for the month of the issue and is published about three months later.
            §   En,   Fr.

702   Canadian National Railways and Canadian Pacific Limited   (Statistics Canada)
            Publications Distribution, Statistics Canada, Ottawa K1A 0T6.
            1973/77-   1973-1977.   Can$0.70.   26 p.
            Summarises the principal statistics relating to the two major Canadian railway systems.
            Time factor: the 1973-1977 issue, published early 1979, has data for the five years 1973 to 1977.
            §   En,   Fr.

            Note: earlier summary data was published in 'Canadian National Railways, 1923-1971' and 'Canadian
                Pacific Limited, 1923-1971'.

703   Railway freight traffic   (Statistics Canada)
            Publications Distribution, Statistics Canada, Ottawa K1A 0T6.
            1970-   1977.   Can$2.80.   353 p.
            Contains a summary by province, and revenue freight carried by railways within Canada, and revenue
                freight by province.   Part I gives the data in short tons and part II in metric tonnes.
            Time factor: the 1977 issue, published late 1978, has data for 1977.
            §   En,   Fr.

704   Railway freight traffic   (Statistics Canada)
            Publications Distribution, Statistics Canada, Ottawa K1A 0T6.
            1923-   quarterly.   Can$1.05 or Can$4.20 yr.
            Contains revenue freight traffic statistics by commodity and by geographic area.
            Time factor: each issue has data for the quarter of the issue and is published about six months later.
            §   En,   Fr.

    iv.   Air

705   Airport activity statistics   (Statistics Canada)
            Publications Distribution, Statistics Canada, Ottawa K1A 0T6.
            1968-   1975.   Can$1.05.   62 p.
            Detailed statistical information about Canada's 25 leading airports.
            Time factor: the 1975 issue, published late 1976, has data for 1975 and some earlier years.
            §   En,   Fr.

706   Air carrier operations in Canada   (Statistics Canada)
            Publications Distribution, Statistics Canada, Ottawa K1A 0T6.
            1970-   quarterly.   Can$1.40 or Can$5.60 yr.
            Contains operating and financial statistics for the entire Canadian air transport industry.
            Time factor: each issue has data for the quarter of the issue and the year to date and is published about
                six months later.
            §   En,   Fr.

CANADA, continued

¶ H.iv, continued

707 Transcontinental and regional air carrier operations (Statistics Canada)
Publications Distribution, Statistics Canada, Ottawa K1A 0T6.
1941- monthly. Can$0.40 or Can$4 yr.
Statistics of operations and finances of the seven largest Canadian scheduled air carriers.
Time factor: each issue has data for that month and cumulated figures for the year to date, and is
published about six months later.
§ En, Fr.

708 International air charter statistics (Statistics Canada)
Publications Distribution, Statistics Canada, Ottawa K1A 0T6.
1971- quarterly. Can$1.05 or Can$4.20 yr.
Contains data on commercial air carriers performing charter services into and out of Canada.
Time factor: each issue has data for each month of the quarter of the issue and is published about six
months later.
§ En, Fr.

709 Air carrier traffic at Canadian airports (Statistics Canada)
Publications Distribution, Statistics Canada, Ottawa K1A 0T6.
1976- 1977. Can$2.80. 215 p.
Time factor: the 1977 issue, published mid-1978, has data for 1977.
§ En, Fr.

Note: there is also a quarterly with the same title (Can$1.75 or Can$7 yr). Both the quarterly and
the annual continue 'Airport activity statistics'.

710 Air carrier financial statements (Statistics Canada)
Publications Distribution, Statistics Canada, Ottawa K1A 0T6.
(annual) 1974. Can$1.05. 41 p.
Time factor: the 1974 issue, published in 1975, has data for 1974.
§ En, Fr.

711 Aviation in Canada, 1971: a statistical handbook of Canadian civil aviation (Statistics Canada)
Publications Distribution, Statistics Canada, Ottawa K1A 0T6.
Can$2. 167 p.
Time factor: published in 1972.
§ En.

712 Air passenger origin and destination: domestic report (Statistics Canada)
Publications Distribution, Statistics Canada, Ottawa K1A 0T6.
1946- 1974. Can$3.50. 264 p.
Time factor: the 1974 issue, published in 1975, has data for 1973 and 1974.
§ En, Fr.

713 Air passenger origin and destination: Canada - United States report (Statistics Canada)
Publications Distribution, Statistics Canada, Ottawa K1A 0T6.
1946- 1976. Can$9. 622 p.
Time factor: the 1976 issue, published late 1977, has data for 1975 and 1976.
§ En, Fr.

¶   H,   continued

v.   Telecommunications and postal services

714   Telephone statistics   (Statistics Canada)
        Publications Distribution, Statistics Canada, Ottawa K1A 0T6.
        1974-   1976.   Can$1.05.   46 p.
        The results of an annual survey, including numbers of calls, telephones, telegraph systems, exchanges,
            miles of lines, etc.   Also finances, equipment, etc.
        Time factor   the 1976 issue, published in 1978, has data for 1976.
        §   En,   Fr.

        Note: also published is 'Telephone statistics – preliminary report on large telephone systems' (Can$0.35)

715   Telephone statistics   (Statistics Canada)
        Publications Distribution, Statistics Canada, Ottawa K1A 0T6.
        1949-   monthly.   Can$0.15 or Can$1.50 yr.
        Mainly textual, but has a page or more of statistics on operating revenue and expenses, and number of
            telephones by type of service, etc.
        Time factor: each issue is published about two months later.
        §   En,   Fr.

716   Telecommunications   (Statistics Canada)
        Publications Distribution, Statistics Canada, Ottawa K1A 0T6.
        1972-   1977.   Can$0.70.   16 p.
        Contains statistical data on operating, property, employment, finance, construction and repair.
        Time factor: the 1977 issue, published early 1979, has data for 1977.
        §   En,   Fr.

        Note: continues 'Telegraph and cable statistics'.

717   Radio and television broadcasting   (Statistics Canada)
        Publications Distribution, Statistics Canada, Ottawa K1A 0T6.
        1956-   1977.   Can$1.05.   42 p.
        The report of an annual survey, with data on revenue, expenses, employees in the industry, finance,
            property and plant, salaries and wages, etc.
        Time factor: the 1977 issue, published in 1979, has data for 1977.
        §   En,   Fr.

        Note: there is also 'Cable television' published from 1967 (Can$0.70).

718   Radio broadcasting   (Statistics Canada)
        Publications Distribution, Statistics Canada, Ottawa K1A 0T6.
        1977-   monthly.   Can$0.15 or Can$1.50 yr.
        A monthly survey of radio broadcasting stations.
        Time factor: each issue has data for that month and is published three months later.
        §   En,   Fr.

There is no central statistical office on the Cayman Islands, but enquiries concerning statistical matters regarding the islands may be made to the Administrator's Office on Grand Cayman or to the Department of Finance and Development, Administration Building, George Town, Grand Cayman.   There is also a Customs Department on Grand Cayman.

Statistical publications

719   Statistical abstract of the Government of the Cayman Islands   (Department of Finance and Development)
          Department of Finance and Development, Administration Building, George Town, Grand Cayman.
          1975-   Vol I No.2, 1979.   CI$5 or £2.85.   56 p.
          Main sections:
                    Area and climate   Foreign trade
                    Population and vital statistics   Tourism
                    Agriculture and animal husbandry   Prices
                    Manufacturing   Financial statistics
                    Labour and employment   Education and health
                    Construction and housing   Planning statistics
                    Transport and communication
          Time factor: Volume I, No.2, which is the second edition to be published, was issued in 1979 and has
                    data for several years to 1977.   It is intended to issue the publication annually, with the assistance
                    of automation from 1979 onwards.
          §   En.

720   Report for the year...   (Department of Finance and Development)
          Department of Finance and Development, Administration Building, George Town, Grand Cayman.
          1918-   1977.   not priced.   89 p.
          Mainly textual, but includes some statistics.   Subjects covered include climate and weather, finance
                    and development, agriculture and natural resources, health, education, social services, communica-
                    tions, works, local administration, tourism, aviation and trade, and court statistics.
          Time factor: the 1977 report was published in 1978.
          §   En.

   ¶   B   -   Production

          Refer to 719, 720.

   ¶   C   -   External trade

          Refer to 719, 720.

   ¶   D   -   Internal distribution and service trades

          Refer to 719, 720.

   ¶   E   -   Population

721   Census of population
          1881-   1970.

          Refer to 258 for the 1970 census of population for the Commonwealth Caribbean, which includes data for
                    the Cayman Islands, and to 719 and 720 for other population statistics.

CAYMAN ISLANDS, continued

¶ F - Social

Refer to 719, 720.

¶ G - Finance

Refer to 719, 720.

ii. Public finance

722 Estimates of gross domestic product and related aggregates (Department of Finance and Development)
Department of Finance and Development, Grand Cayman.
1972- 1972. CI$1. 16 p.
Time factor: the 1972 issue, published mid-1975, has data for 1972.
§ En.

¶ H - Transport and communications

Refer to 719, 720.

Central statistical office

723   Instituto Nacional de Estadísticas   [National Institute of Statistics],
        Casilla 7597 - correo 3,
        Santiago.
        t 3 3744.   tg DIGEDISTICA

        The National Institute of Statistics was created in 1970 out of the Office of Statistics and Censuses, the responsibilities of the institute being to collect, analyse and publish statistical information, to organise official censuses and surveys, and to study the methodology of the collection and use of statistics. Unpublished data can be supplied when available, the cost of extraction of the information being charged to the enquirer.

Libraries

        The Instituto de Estadísticas (see above) has a library which is open to the public who wish to consult statistical publications.

Libraries and information services abroad

        Statistical publications of Chile are available for reference at Chile's embassies abroad, including:

        United Kingdom   Chilean Embassy, 12 Devonshire Street, London W1 (t 01-580 6392)
        Canada   Chilean Embassy, 801-56 Sparks Street, Ottawa (t 235-4402)
        USA   Chilean Embassy, 1732 Massachusetts Ave NW, Washington DC (t (202) 785-1746)

Bibliographies

724   Guía de publicaciones estadísticas, 1970   [Guide to statistical publications, 1970]   (Instituto Nacional de Estadísticas)   free on request.

725   Catálogo de series estadísticas   [Catalogue of statistical series]   (Instituto Nacional de Estadísticas)   published 1977.   E$48;   US$10.

726   Boletín informativo   [Information bulletin]   (Instituto Nacional de Estadísticas)   a sales list issued free at intervals.

Statistical publications

¶   A - General

727   Chile anuario estadístico   [Statistical yearbook for Chile]   (Instituto Nacional de Estadísticas)
        Instituto Nacional de Estadísticas, Casilla 7597 - correo 3, Santiago.
        1976- 1976.   Ch$60; US$18.   365 p.
        Main sections:
            Demography (population and vital   National accounts
              statistics)   Agriculture
            Housing   Industry and construction
            Employment (and wages)   Trade (internal and external)
            Education, culture & communications   Transport, retail trade, and communications
              media   (including tourism)
            Health   Finance
            Other demographic and social statistics   Prices
        Time factor: the 1976 edition, published in 1978, has data for 1974 or 1975.
        §   Es.

        Note: an Anuario estadístico de Chile' was published from 1860 to 1937.

CHILE, continued

¶ A, continued

728 Sinopsis [Synopsis] (Instituto Nacional de Estadísticas)
　　　Instituto Nacional de Estadísticas, Casilla 7597 - correo 3, Santiago.
　　　1880- 1971-72.　Ch$36; US$8.　165 p.
　　　Main sections:

Population and demography	Transport
Agriculture and livestock	Public finance
Aviculture	Employment and social security
Forestry	Health
Manufacturing industry	Education
Minerals	Police
Construction	

　　　Time factor: the 1971-72 edition has data for 1971 or 1971/72 and some earlier years in some tables.
　　　§　Es.

729 Compendio estadístico [Statistical compendium] (Instituto Nacional de Estadísticas)
　　　Instituto Nacional de Estadísticas, Casilla 7597 - correo 3, Santiago.
　　　1971- 1978.　Ch$36; US$8.　318 p.
　　　Main sections:

Demography	National accounts and balances
Housing	Agriculture
Employment	Minerals, industry & construction
Education, culture & communications media	Trade
Health	Transport and communications
Other demographic and social statistics	Finance
	Prices

　　　Time factor: the 1978 edition, published in 1978, has data for 1977 and also a few earlier years in some tables.
　　　§　Es.

730 Sintesis estadística [Statistical survey] (Instituto Nacional de Estadísticas)
　　　Instituto Nacional de Estadísticas, Casilla 7597 - correo 3, Santiago.
　　　1943- 2-monthly.　free.
　　　Contains data on demography and social statistics, employment, cattle markets, minerals, manufacture, foreign trade, buildings, price indices, retail prices in Santiago, wholesale prices, transport, finance, money and banking, indices of nominal sales of internal trade, wholesale trade indices, retail trade indices, and special tables on wages, employment, etc.
　　　Time factor: each issue has data to about two months prior to the date of the issue.
　　　§　Es.

731 Informativo estadístico [Statistical information] (Instituto Nacional de Estadísticas)
　　　Instituto Nacional de Estadísticas, Casilla 7597 - correo 3, Santiago.
　　　1976- irreg (3 or 4 a year)　Ch$18; US$5 each issue.
　　　Contains general indicators, social statistics (demography, population, employment, recreation, police), and economic statistics (minerals, manufacturing industry, electricity, construction, internal trade, foreign trade, transport, finance, and prices).
　　　Time factor: each issue has data for several years and months to about three months prior to the date of issue.
　　　§　Es.

732 Estadística Chilena [Chilean statistics] (Instituto Nacional de Estadísticas)
　　　1928- 2-monthly.
　　　Contained data on demography, agricultural production, fisheries, mining, industry and construction, prices, transport, foreign trade, money and finance, employment, social assistance and insurance.
　　　Time factor: ceased publication with the January-February 1961 issue.
　　　§　Es.

¶ A, continued

733 Boletín mensual [Monthly bulletin] (Banco Central de Chile)
Banco Central de Chile, casilla 967, Santiago.
1928- Ch$150 or Ch$1500 yr; US$5 or US$50 yr.
Includes a statistical section with data on monetary operations; financial operations; foreign trade, exchange and gold; national accounts; public finance; production; prices, wages and salaries; population and occupations.
Time factor: each issue has data for the month of issue and runs of earlier figures and is published about two months later.
§ Es.

Note: "Memoria anual del Banco Central de Chile" [Annual report...] includes some statistics on Chile's economy, finance and banking and is free to subscribers to the monthly bulletin.

734 Informe económico [Economic report] (Oficina de Planificación Nacional - ODERPLAN)
Oficina de Planificación Nacional, Santiago.
1973- monthly. not priced.
Contains data on the monetary and financial situations, foreign trade, minerals, employment and wages, and prices.
Time factor: each issue contains long runs of figures to the latest available.
§ Es.

¶ B - Production

i. Mines and mining

735 Minería [Mining] (Instituto Nacional de Estadísticas)
Instituto Nacional de Estadísticas, Casilla 7597 - correo 3, Santiago.
1911- 1973-74. Ch$36; US$8. c 50 p.
Contains data on mining companies, production, petroleum and gas, employment, accidents, exports, and international trade.
Time factor: the 1973-74 issue, published in 1975, has data for 1974 and 1973 and some earlier years.
§ Es.

Refer also to 728, 730.

ii. Agriculture, fisheries, forestry, etc.

736 Censo nacional agropecuario [National census of agriculture] (Instituto Nacional de Estadísticas)
Instituto Nacional de Estadísticas, Casilla 7597 - correo 3, Santiago.
1929/30- 5th, 1975-1976.
A volume titled 'Adelanto de cifras - tabulaciones manuales. Por regions' [Advance figures - manual tabulations. By regions] (Ch$36 or US$8) has been published.
§ Es.

Note: the results of the 4th census for 1964/65 were published in 26 regional volumes.

737 Encuesta agropecuario [Agricultural survey] (Instituto Nacional de Estadísticas)
Instituto Nacional de Estadísticas, Casilla 7597 - correo 3, Santiago.
1966/67- 1976/77. Ch$18; US$5. c 100 p.
The results of an annual survey of agriculture and livestock.
Time factor: the report of the 1976/77 crop year survey was published in 1978.
§ Es.

¶　B.ii,　continued

738　Agricultura e industria agropecuaria　[Agriculture and the agricultural industries]　(Instituto Nacional de
　　　　　Estadísticas)
　　　　Instituto Nacional de Estadísticas, Casilla 7597 - correo 3, Santiago.
　　　　1911/12-　1973/74-1974/75.　Ch$36;　US$8.　c 60 p.
　　　　Contains data on the production of cereal crops and livestock, on farms and ranches, and on the
　　　　　agricultural and livestock industries.
　　　　Time factor: the 1973/74-1974/75 issue has data for both those crop years.
　　　　§　Es.

739　Encuesta nacional de mataderos y feria de animales　[Survey of the slaughter and marketing of livestock]
　　　　　(Instituto Nacional de Estadísticas)
　　　　Instituto Nacional de Estadísticas, Casilla 7597 - correo 3, Santiago.
　　　　　　half-yearly.　Ch$18;　US$5 each issue.
　　　　Time factor: each issue has data for the period of the issue and is published some months later.
　　　　§　Es.

740　Existencia de ganado vacuna, 1972-1977　[Stocks of bovine livestock]　(Instituto Nacional de Estadísticas)
　　　　Instituto Nacional de Estadísticas, Casilla 7597 - correo 3, Santiago.
　　　　　　　　　Ch$18;　US$5.
　　　　Time factor: published in 1978.
　　　　§　Es.

741　Anuario estadístico de pesca　[Statistical yearbook of fisheries]　(Ministerio de Agricultura: Servicio Agricola
　　　　　y Ganadero: Division de Protección Pesquera)
　　　　Ministerio de Agricultura, Santiago.
　　　　1951-　1976.　not priced.　90 p.
　　　　Contains data on catch by type, utilisation, catch by town, value, industrial production, and foreign
　　　　　trade (imports and exports).
　　　　Time factor: the 1976 edition, published in 1978, has data for 1976 generally, and for 1967 to 1976 for
　　　　　the tables on catch by type.
　　　　§　Es.

　　　　Refer also to 727, 728, 730.

　　iii.　Industry

742　Censo nacional de manufacturas　[National census of industry]　(Instituto Nacional de Estadísticas)
　　　　Instituto Nacional de Estadísticas, Casilla 7597 - correo 3, Santiago.
　　　　1937-　1967.　Ch$36;　US$8 for 3 vols.　3 vols.
　　　　Contents:
　　　　　　Vol I　　Establishments of 5 or more persons, classified by branch of activity
　　　　　　Vol II　　Power used in establishments of 5 or more persons
　　　　　　Vol III　Earlier data. Results by geographic area, size and branch of activity in establishments of
　　　　　　　　　5 or more persons.
　　　　Time factor: the results of the 1967 census, collected in 1968, were published in 1970.　A census is
　　　　　taken every ten years.
　　　　§　Es.

743　Industrias manufactureras [Manufacturing industry]　(Instituto Nacional de Estadísticas)
　　　　Instituto Nacional de Estadísticas, Casilla 7597 - correo 3, Santiago.
　　　　1911-　1972.　Ch$36;　US$8.　114 p.
　　　　Contains data on manufacturing industry by type of industry, by occupations, by regions and provinces,

[continued next page]

¶   B.iii,   continued

743,   continued

> and by regions and type of industry; indexes of industrial production; and the production of electric energy.
> Time factor: the 1972 edition, published in 1975, has data for 1972.
> §   Es.
>
> Note: from 1911 to 1956 the title was "Industrias" and included the mining industry.

744   Indice de producción industrial manufacturera   [Index numbers of industrial manufacturing production] (Instituto Nacional de Estadísticas)
> Instituto Nacional de Estadísticas, Casilla 7597 - correo 3, Santiago.
> 1958-   monthly.   free.
> §   Es.
>
> Refer also to 727, 728, 730.

iv.   Construction

745   Boletín de edificación   [Construction bulletin]   (Instituto Nacional de Estadísticas)
> Instituto Nacional de Estadísticas, Casilla 7597 - correo 3, Santiago.
>   monthly.   Ch$18;   US$5.
> §   Es.
>
> Refer also to 727, 728, 730.

v.   Energy

746   Producción y consumo de energia en Chile   [Production and consumption of energy in Chile]   (Empresa Nacional de Electricidad SA)
> ENDESA-ODIC, Santa Rosa 76, 7° piso, Santiago.
> 1973- 1977.   free.   108 p.
> Time factor: the 1977 edition, published in 1978, has data for 1977 and some earlier years.
> §   Es.

¶   C - External trade

747   Comercio exterior   [Foreign trade]   (Instituto Nacional de Estadísticas)
> Instituto Nacional de Estadísticas, Casilla 7597 - correo 3, Santiago.
> 1915-   1973-1974.   Ch$36;   US$8.   2 vols.
> Vol I is devoted to statistics of imports and Vol II to exports.   Main tables show detailed trade by commodity subdivided by countries of origin and destination.
> Time factor: the 1973-1974 issue, with figures for both 1973 and 1974, was published early 1976.
> §   Es.

748   Sistema importaciones cuadro estadistico item/pais   [Statistical tables of imports arranged by commodity subdivided by countries]   (Banco Central de Chile: Dirección de Comercio Exterior)
> Banco Central de Chile, Santiago.
>   1977.   not priced.   2 vols.
> Computer printout.
> §   Es.
>
> Refer also to 727, 730.

¶ D - Internal distribution and service trades

749 Comercio interior y servicios [Internal trade and service] (Instituto Nacional de Estadísticas)
Instituto Nacional de Estadísticas, Casilla 7597 - correo 3, Santiago.
1958/59/60- 1970. Ch$36; US$8. 89 p.
Covers the wholesale and retail trades and service trades. Includes data on employees, by occupation; sales and indirect taxes; investment in new and established concerns; expenditure by activity; average sales by employees; wages; consumer price indix; retail prices of selected items in cities; wholesale price index, etc.
Time factor: the 1970 issue has data for 1970.
§ Es.

750 Estadísticas de turismo y movimiento internacional de viajeras [Statistics of tourism and international movement of travellers] (Instituto Nacional de Estadísticas)
Instituto Nacional de Estadísticas, Casilla 7597 - correo 3, Santiago.
1965- 1971. Ch$36; US$8. 87 p.
Contains statistics of all entries and departures, foreigners entries and departures, tourists' entries and departures, tourist hotels, and communications (posts, telegraphs, telecommunications, radio diffusion, and television).
Time factor: the 1971 issue has data for 1971.
§ Es.

751 Indice de precios al por mayor [Index of wholesale prices] (Instituto Nacional de Estadísticas)
Instituto Nacional de Estadísticas, Casilla 7597 - correo 3, Santiago.
1947- monthly. Ch$44; US$6, yr.
§ Es.

Refer also to 727, 730.

¶ E - Population

752 Censo nacional de población y vivienda [National census of population and housing] (Instituto Nacional de Estadísticas)
Instituto Nacional de Estadísticas, Casilla 7597 - correo 3, Santiago.
1854- 1970.
Contents:
Población, resultados definitivos [Population, final results] 25 provincial and one national volume (Ch$36; US$8 each volume)
Vivienda hogares y familias [Houses, households and families] 25 provincial and one national volume (Ch$36; US$8 each volume)
Localidades pobladas [Villages, etc] 25 volumes, one for each province (not priced)
Muestra de adelanto de cifras censales [Sample of advance census figures] 12 provincial and one national volume (not priced)
§ Es.

753 Demografia [Demography] (Instituto Nacional de Estadísticas)
Instituto Nacional de Estadísticas, Casilla 7597 - correo 3, Santiago.
1909- 1971. Ch$36; US$8. c 70 p.
Contains data on births, marriages and deaths.
Time factor: the 1971 issue has data for 1971.
§ Es.

¶ E, continued

754 Perspectivas de crecimiento de la población Chilena, 1970-1985 [Projections of the increase in population, 1970-1985] (Corporación de Fomento de la Producción)
Corporación de Fomento de la Producción, Santiago.
not priced. 55 p.
Time factor: published in 1970.
§ Es.

755 Proyecciones de población por sexo y grupos de edad (1970-2000). Total pais y sus regions [Projections of population by sex and age groups (1970-2000). Total for the country and for regions] (Instituto Nacional de Estadísticas)
Instituto Nacional de Estadísticas, Casilla 7597 - correo 3, Santiago.
Ch$48; US$10. 59 p.
Time factor: published in 1975.
§ Es.

756 Perfiles de la población de 65 y más ãnos de edad [Profiles of the population of 65 or more years of age] (Instituto Nacional de Estadísticas)
Instituto Nacional de Estadísticas, Casilla 7597 - correo 3, Santiago.
Ch$48; US$10. 38 p.
Time factor: published in 1977.
§ Es.

757 Encuesta nacional del emploi, 1976 [National survey of employment, 1976] (Instituto Nacional de Estadísticas)
Instituto Nacional de Estadísticas, Casilla 7597 - correo 3, Santiago.
Ch$18; US$5. 2 vols.
Contains statistics of employment for the nation and by regions.
§ Es.

758 Proyección de población por provincia, departamento y comunas del 30 de junio al 31 diciembre de 1976 [Projection of the population by provinces, departments and communes from 30th June to 31st December 1976] (Instituto Nacional de Estadísticas)
Instituto Nacional de Estadísticas, Casilla 7597 - correo 3, Santiago.
Ch$18; US$5. 17 p.
Time factor: published in 1976.
§ Es.

759 Población total pais, regiones, provincias y comunas: estimaciones de población, 1960-75 [Population: total country, regions, provinces and communes: estimates of population] (Instituto Nacional de Estadísticas)
Instituto Nacional de Estadísticas, Casilla 7597 - correo 3, Santiago.
not priced. 232 p.
The basic volume is up-dated at intervals.
§ Es.

Refer also to 727, 728, 729, 730.

CHILE,   continued

¶   F - Social

i.   Standard of living

760   Indice de salarios y sueldos   [Index of salaries and wages]   (Instituto Nacional de Estadísticas)
        Instituto Nacional de Estadísticas, Casilla 7597 - correo 3, Santiago.
        1959-   quarterly.   Ch$44;   US$6 yr.
        §   Es.

761   Indice de precios al consumidor   [Index of consumer prices]   (Instituto Nacional de Estadísticas)
        Instituto Nacional de Estadísticas, Casilla 7597 - correo 3, Santiago.
        1958-   monthly.   Ch$44;   US$6 yr.
        §   Es.

762   Encuesta nacional sobre ingresos familiares, Marzo-Junio 1968   [National survey of family incomes,
            March-June 1968]   (Instituto Nacional de Estadísticas)
        Instituto Nacional de Estadísticas, Casilla 7597 - correo 3, Santiago.
                        Ch$12;   US$4.
        §   Es.

        Refer also to 730.

    ii.   Health and welfare

763   Estadísticas de salud   [Health statistics]   (Instituto Nacional de Estadísticas)
        Instituto Nacional de Estadísticas, Casilla 7597 - correo 3, Santiago.
        1965-   1973.   Ch$60;   US$18 each volume.   2 volumes.
        Vol I deals with resources and care of patients and Vol II with discharges from hospitals.
        Time factor: the 1973 issue, published in 1975, has data for 1973.
        §   Es.

        Refer also to 727, 728, 729.

    iii.   Education and leisure

764   Educación y cultura   [Education and culture]   (Instituto Nacional de Estadísticas)
        Instituto Nacional de Estadísticas, Casilla 7597 - correo 3, Santiago.
        1967-   1975.   Ch$36;   US$8.   126 p.
        Contains data on numbers of establishments, teachers, pupils, classes, etc, in pre-primary, primary,
            secondary, adult, scientific-humanities, and university education.   Also data on libraries and
            publishing.
        Time factor: the 1975 issue, published late 1977, has data for 1975.
        §   Es.

        Note: from 1911 to 1966 title was 'Educación y justicia'.   A census of education was taken in 1933.

765   Estadísticas de educación extraescolar   [Statistics of post-school education]   (Instituto Nacional de
            Estadísticas)
        Instituto Nacional de Estadísticas, Casilla 7597 - correo 3, Santiago.
        1976-   1977.   Ch$18;   US$5.   27 p.
        Contains data on matriculates, etc.
        Time factor: the 1977 issue, published in 1977, has data for that year.
        §   Es.

        Refer also to 727, 728, 729.

155

CHILE,   continued

¶   F,   continued

iv.   Justice

766   Justicia y policia   [Justice and police]   (Instituto Nacional de Estadísticas)
            Instituto Nacional de Estadísticas, Casilla 7597 - correo 3, Santiago.
            1967-   1975.   Ch$36; US$8.   125 p.
            Contains statistical data on the administration of justice and the police.
            Time factor: the 1975 issue, published in 1977, has data for 1975.
            §   Es.

            Note: earlier title was 'Educación y justicia', from 1911 to 1966.

            Refer also to 728.

¶   G   -   Finance

767   Finanzas, bancos y cajas sociales   [Finance, banking and social savings]   (Instituto Nacional de Estadísticas)
            Instituto Nacional de Estadísticas, Casilla 7597 - correo 3, Santiago.
            1911-   1975.   Ch$36; US$8.   c 150 p.
            Contains data on national accounts, public finance, banking and money etc.
            Time factor: the 1975 issue, published in 1977, has data for several years to 1975 or 1974.
            §   Es.

            Note: cover title is 'Finanzas anuario'.

            Refer also to 727, 730.

ii.   Public finance

768   Cuentas nacionales de Chile   [National accounts of Chile]   (Oficina de Planificación National)
            ODERPLAN, Santiago.
            1965/72-   1960-1975.   not priced.   92 p.
            Contains statistics of national accounts for the years 1960 to 1974 and estimates for 1975.
            Time factor: published late 1976.
            §   Es.

769   Balanza de pagos   [Balance of payments]   (Banco Central de Chile)
            Banco Central de Chile, Casilla 967, Santiago.
            1942-   1975.   Ch$70; US$3.   99 p.
            Time factor: the 1975 issue, published in 1977, has data for several years to 1975.
            §   Es.

            Refer also to 728.

¶   H   -   Transport and communications

            Refer to 727, 728, 730.

156

COLOMBIA - COLOMBIE - KOLUMBIEN

Central statistical office

770   Departamento Administrativo Nacional de Estadística (DANE) [National Administrative Department of
            Statistics],
        Via El Dorado,
        Bogotá.
        † 2693802 & 2693803 & 2445510 & 2445513.

The Department is, by law, the only compiler of official statistics in Colombia, and is a department of
the Centro Administrativo Nacional (CAN) [National Administration Centre].   Unpublished statistical
information can be supplied if available, a charge being made based on the amount of work done and the
administrative costs.

Libraries

DANE has a library which is open to the public for reference.   The collection includes statistical
publications of other countries as well as those relating to Colombia.   Banco Datos DANE, Apartado 88043,
Bogotá († 2445351) provides personal-telephonic and written statistical data.   Some Colombian statistical
publications are also available in public libraries in Colombia.

Libraries and information services abroad

Colombian embassies abroad have some of the official statistical publications published by DANE; the
embassies including:
        United Kingdom   Colombian Embassy, 3 Hans Crescent, London SW1.   † 01-589 9177.
        USA   Colombian Embassy, 2118 Leroy Place NW, Washington DC. († (202) 387 5828)
        Canada   Colombian Embassy, 140 Wellington Street, Ottawa.   † 235 8803.

Bibliographies

There is no detailed bibliography of Colombian statistical publications but DANE issues a sales list in
both Spanish and English editions from time to time.

Statistical publications

¶   A - General

771   Anuario general de estadística   [General statistical yearbook]   (DANE)
        DANE, via El Dorado, Bogotá.
        1915- 1968.   prices vary between Col$20 and $40 each volume.   5 vols.
        Contents:
            Vol I   Population, social assistance and health
            Vol II   Culture
            Vol III   Transport and communications
            Vol IV   Price indices, employment and wages
            Vol V   Justice
        Time factor: the 1968 edition was the last to be published, being continued by separate titles for each
            subject (refer to 787, 791, 793 and 798).   The 1968 edition contains data for 1968 and some
            earlier years.
        §   Es.

¶   A,   continued

772   Anuario estadístico de Bogotá   [Statistical yearbook of Bogotá]   (DANE)
          DANE, Via El Dorado, Bogotá.
          1964-   1972-1974.   Col$150;   US$5.   272 p.
          Contains data relating to the city of Bogotá, with similar subject coverage to 771.
          Time factor: the 1972-1974 edition, with data for those years, was published in 1978.
          §   Es.

          Note: also available are Anuario estadístico de Antioquia (Departamento Administrativo de Planeación,
              Gobernación de Antioquia), Medellin en cifras, 1965-1975 (DANE), Panorama estadístico de
              Cordoba, 1973-1975 (regional de Medallin (DANE), and Economia antioqueña en cifras, 1974-1975
              (DANE).

773   Boletín mensual de estadística   [Monthly bulletin of statistics]   (DANE)
          DANE, Via El Dorado, Bogotá.
          1951-   Col$30 or Col$430 yr;   US$1.50 or US$14 yr.
          Contains data on socio-economic indicators, demography and social affairs, production and transport,
              money and finance, prices and wages, external economy, and the public sector.   Preliminary
              results of the many censuses taken by DANE are published in the bulletin.
          Time factor: each issue has the latest data available at the time of compilation.
          §   Es.

774   Revista del Banco de la República   [Review of the Banco de la República]
          Banco de la República, Bogotá.
          1927-   monthly.   not priced.
          A monthly summary of the economic conditions in Colombia, including monetary accounts, credit and
              banking system, money and banking, market prices, external finance, public finance, production,
              prices, etc.
          §   Es.

775   Informe anual del Gerente a la Junta Directiva   [Annual report of the Board]   (Banco de la República)
          Banco de la República, Bogotá.
          1924-   1976.   not priced.   358 p.
          Contains data on the administration of the bank and also on the national economy, the monetary situation,
              financial institutions, production, prices, and employment.
          Time factor: the 1976 report, published in 1977, has data for several years to 1976.
          §   Es.

¶   B   -   Production

ii.   Agriculture, fisheries, forestry, etc.

776   Censo nacional agropecuario   [National agricultural census]   (DANE)
          DANE, Via El Dorado, Bogotá.
          1960-   1970-1971.   Col$30;   US$1.50 each volume.   8 vols.
          There is a national summary volume and regional volumes for Caldas-Quindío-Risaralda (former Caldas),
              Atlantico-Bolivar-Sucre, Boyacá-Meta, Cundinamarca-Tolima-Huila, Magdalena Cesar,
              Santander-Norte de Santander, Valle-Cauca-Nariño, and Antioquia-Cordoba.
          §   Es.

777   Encuesta agropecuario nacional   [National survey of agriculture]   (DANE)
          DANE, Via El Dorado, Bogotá.
          1965-   1969.   Col$15.
          An annual survey on area cultivated, crops, livestock, employees, etc.
          Time factor: ceased publication with the survey for 1969.
          §   Es.

¶   B.ii,   continued

778   Prognosticos y estimaciones agropecuarias   [Agricultural forecasts and estimates]   (DANE)
            DANE, Via El Dorado, Bogotá.
            1971-   half-yearly.   US$1 each issue.
            Time factor: each issue is published about three months after the date of the issue.
            §   Es.

        iii.   Industry

779   Censo industrial   [Industrial census]   (DANE)
            DANE, Via El Dorado, Bogotá.
            1945-   3rd, 1970.   US$3.50.   111 p.
            Contains data on establishments, employment, production, consumption of raw materials, sales, wages,
                etc, by areas.
            Time factor: the results of the census were published in 1972.
            §   Es.

            Note: an industrial directory was also issued (US$2.50).

780   Industria manufacturera nacional   [Manufacturing industry of Colombia]   (DANE)
            DANE, Via El Dorado, Bogotá.
            1966-   1975.   Col$120; US$4.   114 p.
            Contains detailed statistics of products manufactured or improved, by product and department of country;
                and employment by industry and department.
            Time factor: the 1975 issue, with data for that year, was published in 1978.
            §   Es.

781   Industria manufacturera   [Manufacturing industry]   (DANE)
            DANE, Via El Dorado, Bogotá.
            1966-   1975.   US$2.50.   122 p.
            Contains preliminary results of the above.
            Time factor: the 1975 issue, published in May 1977, has data for 1975.
            §   Es.

            Refer also to 773, 774.

        v.   Energy

782   Censo de energía eléctrica   [Census of electrical energy]   (DANE)
            DANE, Via El Dorado, Bogotá.
            1970-   1970.   not priced.   25 p.
            Contains data on employment, wages, capacity of generators, equipment installed, number and capacity
                of plants, value of electricity generated, number of consumers, income, operations, etc.
            Time factor: the results of the census were published in 1972.
            §   Es.

783   La electrificación en Colombia   [Electrification in Colombia]   (Ministerio de Minas y Energía: Instituto
                Colombiano de Energía Eléctrica)
            Ministerio de Minas y Energía, Cra.13, No 27-oo P./., Bogotá.
            1973/74-   1974/75.   not priced.   unpaged.
            Contains data on the structure of the electrical sector, a description of the principal projects, a plan of
                the system, data on rural electrification, finances, and projections to the future.
            Time factor: the 1974/75 issue, with data for 1972, 1973 and 1974, was published in 1975.
            §   Es.

¶   C - External trade

784   Anuario de comercio exterior   [Yearbook of external trade]   (DANE)
         DANE, Via El Dorado, Bogotá.
         1916-   1975.   Col$100;   US$3.   273 p.
         Main tables show detailed statistics of imports and exports arranged by commodity and subdivided by
             countries of origin and destination.
         Time factor: the 1975 issue, with data for 1975, was published late 1976.
         §   Es.

¶   E - Population

785   Censo nacional de población y edificios y viviendas   [National census of population and buildings and
             houses]   (DANE)
         DANE, Via El Dorado, Bogotá.
         1780-   1975 (14th census of population, 3rd of buildings and houses)
         and
         1951-
         Advance sample results, by states, have been published (Col$1.50)
         §   Es.

         Note: the 1964 census resulted in the publication of four main volumes on population, for the country
             and each of the states, and a general summary volume for the country and each of the states
             concerning buildings and houses.

786   Projections of the rural and urban populations of Colombia, 1965 to 2000   (US Bureau of the Census)
         Government Printing Office, Washington DC 20402, USA.
                         US$1.20.   33 p.
         Time factor: published in December 1975.
         §   En.

787   Anuario demografico, 1968-1969   [Demographic yearbook]   (DANE)
         DANE, Via El Dorado, Bogotá.
                         US$3.   184 p.
         Time factor: published in 1974.
         §   Es.

788   Encuesta nacional de fecundidad colombiana, 1976: resultados generales [National survey of Colombian
             fecundity, 1976: general results]   (DANE)
         DANE, Via El Dorado, Bogotá.
                         not priced.   491 p.
         Time factor: published in 1978.
         §   Es.

789   Encuesta de hogares, 1970   [Household survey]   (DANE)
         DANE, Via El Dorado, Bogotá.
         There is a report for the whole country (Col$50 or US$2) and reports for the states (Col$10 each).
         Time factor: published in 1971.
         §   Es.

790   Encuesta de hogares: trabajo   [Household survey: labour force]   (DANE)
         DANE, Via El Dorado, Bogotá.
         1970-   1975.   US$2.50.
         An annual series of reports on the labour force, based on the data collected in the 1970 household survey.
         §   Es

         Refer also to 771, 772, 773.

COLOMBIA,   continued

¶   F - Social

i.   Standard of living

791   Anuario de precios y costos   [Yearbook of prices and costs]   (DANE)
        DANE, Via El Dorado, Bogotá.
        1970-   1971-1972.   US$1.   46 p.
        Includes consumer price indices nationally and for the main towns.
        Time factor: the 1971-1972 issue, with data for those years, was published in 1974.
        §   Es.

        Refer also to 771, 772.

ii.   Health and welfare

        Refer to 771, 772.

iii.   Education and leisure

792   Censo de establecimientos educativos, 1968   [Census of educational establishments]   (DANE)
        DANE, Via El Dorado, Bogotá.
                        Col$40.   230 p.
        Includes data on all types of educational establishments, official and private.
        Time factor: the results of the census were published in 1970.
        ·§   Es.

        Refer also to 771, 772.

iv.   Justice

793   Justicia [Justice]   (DANE)
        DANE, Via El Dorado, Bogotá.
        1968-   1974.   US$5.
        Time factor: the 1974 issue was published in 1976.
        §   Es.

        Refer also to 771, 772.

¶   G - Finance

794   Información financiera   [Financial information]   (Asociación Bancaria de Colombia)
        Asociación Bancaria de Colombia, Bogotá.
        1963-   monthly.   not priced.
        Includes a statistical appendix containing economic indicators and banking and monetary statistics.
        §   Es.

        Refer also to 773, 774, 775.

ii.   Public finance

795   Anuario de fiscales y financieras   [Yearbook of public finance]   (DANE)
        DANE, Via El Dorado, Bogotá.
        1960/62-   1972-1973.   US$2.50.   261 p.
        Contains national, departmental, administrative and inspectorate, and municipal financial statistics,
            employment in the public sector, company statistics, etc.
        Time factor: ceased publication with the 1972-1973 issue, which has data for the years 1972 and 1973.
        §   Es.

¶   G,   continued

796   Cifras fiscales del Gobierno nacional y de las entidades descentralizadas nacionales   [Financial figures of
            the national government and of the national decentralised organisations]   (Contraloría General de
            la República de Colombia)
            Contraloría General de la República de Colombia, Bogotá.
            1964/71-   4th, 1965-1974.   not priced.   493 p.
            Time factor: the 1965-1974 issue, with figures for those years, was published in 1975.
            §   Es.

797   Informe financiero   [Financial report]   (Contraloría General de la República de Colombia)
            Contraloría General de la República de Colombia, Bogotá.
            1967-   1974.   not priced.   829 p.
            Contains data on public finance.
            Time factor: the 1974 issue, published in 1975, has data for 1974.
            §   Es.

¶   H   -   Transport and communications

798   Anuario de transportes y comunicaciones   [Yearbook of transport and communications]   (DANE)
            DANE, Via El Dorado, Bogotá.
            1968-   1974.   not priced.   56 p.
            Contains data on rail transport, national and international air transport, road transport, the port of
                Magdalena, coastal transport, international sea transport, oil transport, urban passenger transport
                by town, and communications (post, telegraph, telex, telephone).
            Time factor: the 1974 edition, published in 1976, has data for 1972 and 1973.
            §   Es.

            Refer also to 771, 772, 773.

Central statistical office

799   Dirección General de Estadística y Censos   [General Office of Statistics and Censuses],
Apartado 10163,
San José.
† 21-05-77.   Cables: DIRGENESTAC.

The Dirección General de Estadística y Censos, which is within the Ministerio de Económia, Industria y Comercio [Ministry of Economy, Industry and Commerce], is responsible for the collection, co-ordination, analysis and publications of the official economic statistics of Costa Rica.   Unpublished statistical information may be provided to enquirers if it is available, and no fee is charged.

Libraries

The Dirección General de Estadística y Censos (see above) has a library which is open to the public for reference to statistical publications.   The Instituto Centroamericano de Estadística [Central-American Statistical Institute] of the University of Costa Rica, San Pedro de Montes de Oca, San José († 25-55-55), also has a library with similar material, as has the Library of the Banco Central de Costa Rica, San José.

Libraries and information services abroad

Statistical publications of Costa Rica are available for reference in Costa Rican embassies abroad, including:
United Kingdom   Costa Rican Embassy, 39 Gloucester Place Mews, London W1.
USA   Costa Rican Embassy, 2112 S Street NW, Washington DC. († (202) 234 2945)

Bibliographies

800   Inventario de las estadísticas nacionales   [Inventory of national statistics] (Dirección General de Estadística y Censos)
          1966-   2nd ed, 1970.
A subject index to official statistics published by all Costa Rica government departments.

Statistical publications

¶   A - General

801   Anuario estadístico de Costa Rica   [Statistical yearbook of Costa Rica] (Dirección General de Estadística y Censos)
          Dirección General de Estadística y Censos, Apartado 10163, San José.
          1883- 1975. not priced.   c 200 p.
          Main sections:

Geography and climate	Industry
Population	Internal trade & services
Housing	Foreign trade
Education	Transport
Health	Employment
Social security	Price indices
Judicial	Money and banking
Accidents in transit	Public finance
Tourism	Balance of payments & national accounts
Agriculture and livestock	Direct taxes

Time factor: the 1975 edition, published in 1977, has data for 1975.
§   Es.

¶   A,   continued

802   Boletín estadístico   [Statistical bulletin]   (Banco Central de Costa Rica)
        Banco Central de Costa Rica, San José.
        1950-   monthly.   not priced.
        Contains data on money, credit and banking; foreign trade; production; indices (prices, wages, etc);
            and public finance.
        Time factor: each issue has runs of figures, both annual and monthly, to the date of the issue and is
            published six months or more later.
        §   Es.

        Note: the bank also publishes 'Informe anual' on the activities of the bank, and 'Memoria...'
            [Report...] which includes a few bank and general statistics at the end of the report.

¶   B   -   Production

ii.   Agriculture, fisheries, forestry, etc.

803   Censo agropecuario   [Agricultural census]   (Dirección General de Estadística y Censos)
        Dirección General de Estadística y Censos, San José.
        1950-   1973.   not priced.   2 vols.
        Issued as volumes 3 & 7 of the national census, the first volume includes numbers of estates by class of
            product; distribution by province, canton and district; and the second volume contains regional data.
        Time factor: the report of the 1973 census was published in 1975.
        §   Es.

804   Boletin estadístico agropecuario M A G   [Statistical bulletin of agriculture]   (Dirección de Planeamiento,
            Departamento de Económia y Estadística Agropecuario)
        Departamento de Económia y Estadística Agropecuario, San José.
        1970-   quarterly.   not priced.
        Contains data on agricultural credit, prices of products, export trade in products, numbers of heads of
            cattle, etc, slaughtered and sold, imports of agricultural products, use of fertilisers, etc.
        Time factor: each issue is published about six months after the end of the period covered.
        §   Es.

805   Encuesta agricola por muestreo en las regiones agricolas de Costa Rica: arroz, frijol, maiz   [Survey of
            agriculture of the agricultural regions of Costa Rica: rice, beans, maize]   (Dirección General de
            Estadística y Censos)
        Dirección General de Estadística y Censos, Apartado 10163, San José.
        1965-   1971.   not priced.   12 p.
        Time factor: the results of the 1971 survey were published in 1972.
        §   Es.

806   Encuesta pecuaria   [Survey of livestock]   (Dirección General de Estadística y Censos)
        Dirección General de Estadística y Censos, Apartado 10163, San José.
        1970-   1971.   not priced.   20 p.
        Time factor: the results of the 1971 survey were published late 1971.
        §   Es.

        Refer also to 801.

¶   A.iii,   Industry

807   Censo industrias manufactureras [Census of manufacturing industry] (Dirección General de Estadística y Censos)
        Dirección General de Estadística y Censos, Apartado 10163, San José.
        1950-   4th, 1975.   not priced.   3 vols.
        Vol 1 has general results, Vol 2 has results by industry, and Vol 3 has data on employment and on value
            of production.
        Time factor: the results of the census were published in 1977 and 1978.
        §   Es.

808   Encuesta industrial   [Industrial survey]   (Dirección General de Estadística y Censos)
        Dirección General de Estadística y Censos, Apartado 10163, San José.
        1959-   1965.   not priced.   20 p.
        Contains data on the number of establishments, number of employees, wages, capital, production, etc.
        Time factor: the results of the 1965 survey were published in 1967.   A survey is taken only occasionally.
        §   Es.

809   Cifras sobre producción industrial, 1957-1977   [Industrial production figures]   (Banco Central de Costa Rica)
        Banco Central de Costa Rica, San José.
                            not priced.   not paged.
        Contains data on gross value and aggregated value of production by groups, divisions, percentage of
            participants, and percentage increase; and wages of employees.
        Time factor: published in 1978.
        §   Es.

        Refer also to 801, 802.

    v.   Energy

810   Estadística eléctrica: Costa Rica   [Electricity statistics: Costa Rica]   (Servicio Nacional de Electricidad)
        Servicio Nacional de Electricidad, San José.
        1967-   1973.   not priced.   101 p.
        Contains data on services provided to the public.
        Time factor: the 1973 issue, published in 1974, has data for 1973.
        §   Es.

¶   C -   External trade

811   Anuario de comercio exterior   [Yearbook of foreign trade]   (Dirección General de Estadística y Censos)
        Dirección General de Estadística y Censos, Apartado 10163, San José.
        1886-   1976.   not priced.   405 p.
        Main tables show detailed statistics of imports and exports arranged by commodites and subdivided by
            countries of origin and destination.
        Time factor: the 1976 issue, published in 1978, has data for 1976.
        §   Es.

        Note: to 1975 the title was 'Comercio exterior - Costa Rica'.

812   Estadísticas económicas: comercio exterior, movimiento marítimo internacional y construcciones   [Economic
            statistics: foreign trade, international shipping and construction]   (Dirección General de
            Estadística y Censos)
        Dirección General de Estadística y Censos, Apartado 10163, San José.
        1966-   2 a year.   not priced.
        Contains values of imports & exports by country & commodity, as well as shipping & construction statistics.
        Time factor: ceased publication with the issue for the first half of 1974.
        §   Es.

        Refer also to 801, 802.

¶   D   -   Internal distribution and service trades

813   Censo de comercio y servicios   [Census of commerce and services]   (Dirección General de Estadística y
            Censos)
         Dirección General de Estadística y Censos, Apartado 10163, San José.
         1950/51-   1975.   not priced.
         §   Es.

         Note: the results of the 1975 census were to be published in 1978.   The previous census, taken in
               1964, contained data on number of establishments by activity, province, value of trade, employees
               and wages, etc.

814   Indice de precios al por menor   [Index of retail prices]   (Dirección General de Estadística y Censos)
         Dirección General de Estadística y Censos, Apartado 10163, San José.
         1960-   2-monthly.   not priced.
         Retail price indices for the metropolitan area of San José, Valle Central, Golfito, Quepos and Limón.
         Time factor: each issue has data for the two months of the issue and is published about five months later.
               The title ceased publication from 1973 until 1975.
         §   Es.

         Refer also to 801.

¶   E   -   Population

815   Censo de población   [Census of population]   (Dirección General de Estadística y Censos)
         Dirección General de Estadística y Censos, Apartado 10163, San José.
         1864-   1973.   not priced.
         Contents:
               Población [Population]   (2 vols)
               Población: area metropolitan [Population: metropolitan area]   (2 vols)
               Vivienda: area metropolitan [Housing: metropolitan area]   (2 vols)
               Ciudades capitales de provincia... [Capital cities of provinces]
               Vivienda y población: cuidades capitales [Housing & population: capital cities]   (2 vols)
               Población total, urbana y rural, por provincias, cantones y distritos   [Total population, urban and
                   rural, by provinces, cantons and districts]
         Time factor: the results of the census were published between 1974 and 1977.
         §   Es.

815   Evaluación del censo de 1973 y proyección de la población por sexo y grupos de edades, 1950-2000
               [Evaluation of the 1973 census and projections of the population by sex and age groups, 1950-2000]
               (Dirección General de Estadística y Censos and Centro Latinoamericano de Demografía)
         Dirección General de Estadística y Censos, Apartado 10163, San José.
                         not priced.   105 p.
         Time factor: published in June 1976.
         §   Es.

817   Población total de Costa Rica, por provincias, cantones y distrites   [Total population of Costa Rica by
               provinces, cantons and districts]   (Dirección General de Estadística y Censos)
         Dirección General de Estadística y Censos, Apartado 10163, San José.
         1966-   quarterly.   not priced.
         Time factor: each issue has data to the month of the issue and is published the following month.
         §   Es.

¶   E,   continued

818   Estadística vital   [Vital statistics]   (Dirección General de Estadística y Censos)
          Dirección General de Estadística y Censos, Apartado 10163, San José.
          1966- 6-monthly and annual.   not priced.
          Contains data on population, births, marriages, divorces, deaths.
          Time factor: each issue is published about 18 months after the end of the period covered.
          §   Es.

819   Encuesta de hogares por muestreo   [Survey of households]   (Dirección General de Estadística y Censos)
          Dirección General de Estadística y Censos, Apartado 10163, San José.
          1966/67-   5th, 1971.   not priced.   45 p.
          Time factor: the results of the 1969 survey were published in 1971, and mainly deal with employment
              and unemployment.
          §   Es.

820   Encuesta nacional de hogares, empleo y desempleo   [National survey of households, employment and
              unemployment]   (Dirección General de Estadística y Censos)
          Dirección General de Estadística y Censos, Apartado 10163, San José.
          1976-   quarterly.   not priced.
          Time factor: the results of each quarterly survey are published about six months later.
          §   Es.

          Refer also to 801.

    ¶   F - Social

          Refer to 801.

    ¶   G - Finance

          Refer to 801, 802.

    ¶   H - Transport and communications

821   Accidentes de tránsito en Costa Rica   [Traffic accidents in Costa Rica]   (Dirección General de Estadística
              y Censos and Instituto Nacional de Seguros)
          Dirección General de Estadística y Censos, Apartado 10163, San José.
          1969- 6-monthly.   not priced.
          §   Es.

          Refer also to 801.

822   Comité Estatal de Estadísticas   [State Committee for Statistics],
Almendares y Desague,
Ciudad de la Habana.
† 70 2586 & 79 6506.

In November 1976 a law was passed creating the Comité Estatal de Estadísticas which is responsible for the collection, analysis and publication of the official statistics of Cuba.   Unpublished statistical information will be provided to enquirers if it is available.

Libraries

The Comité Estatal de Estadísticas has a library but it is not open to the public.   Cuban statistical publications are, however, available in the national library, Biblioteca Nacional 'José Marti'.

Libraries and information services abroad

Copies of the publications of the Comité Estatal de Estadísticas are available for reference in Cuban embassies abroad, including:
United Kingdom   Cuban Embassy, 57 Kensington Court, London W8. († 01-937 8226)
Canada   Cuban Embassy, 388 Main, Ottawa. († 563-0141)

Bibliographies

823   The Comité Estatal de Estadísticas does not issue a sales list, but in November 1977 it produced a publication, 'Organización y desarrollo de la estadística en Cuba' [Organisation and development of statistics in Cuba], which describes the work which is to be done.

Statistical publications

824   Anuario estadístico de Cuba   [Statistical yearbook of Cuba] (Dirección Central de Estadística: Junta Central de Planificación)
        Comité Estatal de Estadísticas, Almendares y Desague, Ciudad de la Habana.
        1966/67- 1974.   not priced.   318 p.
        Main sections are:
            Area, climate, population
            Global indicators, etc.
            Economic sector (agriculture, fisheries, industry, construction, transport, communications, internal trade, foreign trade)
            Social services (education, cultural activities, public health, recreation and sport)
        Time factor: the 1974 edition, published in 1976, has data for several years to 1974.
        §   Es.

825   Statistical yearbook compendium of the Republic of Cuba   (Central Statistical Division, National Planning Board)
        Comité Estatal de Estadísticas, Almendares y Desague, Ciudad de la Habana.
        1974- 1974.   not priced.   70 p.
        A summary of the contents of the statistical yearbook (see 824 above).
        Time factor: the 1974 edition was published in 1976.
        §   En.   There are also Russian and Spanish editions (see 829).

826   Cuba 1968: a supplement to the 'Statistical abstract of Latin America' (University of California. Latin
          American Center)
       University of California, Latin American Center, Los Angeles, California, USA.
       Time factor: published in 1970.
       §   En.

827   Boletín estadístico [Statistical bulletin] (Dirección Central de Estadística)
       Comité Estatal de Estadísticas, Almendares y Desague, Ciudad de la Habana.
       1965-   1970.   free.   287 p.
       Contains data on area and climate, demography, employment, agriculture, industry, construction and
          investment, transport, communications, internal trade, foreign trade, education, cultural services,
          public health, sports and recreation.
       Time factor: the 1970 issue, which appears to be the latest issued, has data for 1970 and some earlier
          years.
       §   Es.

828   Statistical yearbook: member states of the Council for Mutual Economic Assistance   (Soviet Ekonomicheskoi
          Vzaimopomoshchi, Sekretariat)
       IPC Industrial Press Ltd, Dorset House, Stamford Street, London SE1 9LU.
       1974-   1977.   £20.   502 p.
       Contains data on area and population, a summary section (indices), capital investment, construction,
          agriculture, forestry, transport and communications, internal trade, foreign trade, labour and wages,
          education, culture, art, public health and social services.   An English translation of the
          COMECON's 'Statisticheskii ezhegodnik' which includes data for Cuba.
       Time factor: the 1977 edition, published in 1978, has data for several years to 1976.
       §   En.

829   Compendio del anuario estadístico de la República de Cuba   [Compendium of the statistical yearbook of the
          Republic of Cuba] (Comité Estatal de Estadísticas)
       Comité Estatal de Estadísticas, Almendares y Desague, Ciudad de la Habana.
       1965-   1976.   not priced.   71 p.
       Main sections:

       Area, climate and population   Foreign trade
       Global chapter (index of production,   Employment and wages
          development of the national economy)   Education
       Industry   Culture and art (libraries, theatres, films,
       Construction   publishing, zoos, etc)
       Agriculture - forestry   Public health
       Transport and communications   Recreation and sports
       Internal trade

       Time factor: the 1976 edition has data for several years to 1976.
       §   Es.

830   Guia estadística [Statistical guide] (Comité Estatal de Estadísticas)
       Comité Estatal de Estadísticas, Almendares y Desague, Ciudad de la Habana.
                     not priced.   14 p.
       Contains statistics on the subjects included in 829 above, but has only total figures for very broad sections
          of the subject in each case.
       Time factor: Contains data for 1970, 1975 and 1977.
       §   Es.

831   La economia cubana (Comité Estatal de Estadísticas)
       Comité Estatal de Estadísticas, Almendares y Desague, Ciudad de la Habana.
       1975-   quarterly.   not priced.
       Mainly textual but includes some current statistics on various subjects, updating the annual publications.
       §   Es.

CUBA,   continued

¶   B   -   Production

832   Cuba azúcar   [Cuban sugar]   (Ministerio de la Industria Azucarera)
          Instituto Cubana del Libro, Apartado 605, La Habana 7.
          1970-   quarterly.   US$6 yr.
          Mainly textual but includes sugar statistics.
          §   Es.

          Refer also to 824, 827, 828, 829.

¶   C   -   External trade

833   Comercio exterior de Cuba   [Foreign trade of Cuba]   (Dirección Central de Estadística)
          Comité Estatal de Estadísticas, Almendares y Desague, Ciudad de la Habana.
          1926-   1965.   not priced.   2 vols.
          One volume relates to imports and the other to exports.
          §   Es.

          Refer also to 824, 827, 828, 829.

¶   D   -   Internal distribution and service trades

          Refer to 824, 827, 828, 829.

¶   E   -   Population

834   Censo de población y viviendas   [Census of population and housing]   (Junta Central de Planificación)
          Comité Estatal de Estadísticas, Almendares y Desague, Ciudad de la Habana.
          1899-   1970.   not priced.   1055 p.
          Time factor: the results of the census were published in 1975.
          §   Es.

835   Resumen de estadísticas de población   [Summary of population statistics]   (Dirección Central de Estadística)
          Comité Estatal de Estadísticas, Almendares y Desague, Ciudad de la Habana.
          No 1, 1965-   No 5, 1965-70.   not priced.
          Time factor: the 1965-70 edition was published in 1971.
          §   Es.

          Refer also to 824, 827, 828, 829.

¶   F   -   Social

i.   Standard of living

836   Encuesta rural: nivel de vida, 1957-1966 (mujeres)   [Rural survey: cost of living, 1957-1966 (women)]
          (Comisión de Estudios Sociales)
          Comisión de Estudios Sociales, La Habana.
                          not priced.   68 p.
          §   Es.

¶ F.i,   continued

837   Encuesta rural: nivel de vida, 1957-1966 (hombres)   [Rural survey: cost of living, 1957-1966 (men)]
          (Comisión de Estudios Sociales)
        Comisión de Estudios Sociales, La Habana.
                  not priced.   70 p.
       §   Es.

ii.   Health and welfare

      Refer to 824, 827, 828, 829.

iii.   Education and leisure

838   Estadísticas de la educación   [Education statistics]   (Ministerio de Educación)
        Ministerio de Educación, Ciudad Libertad, Marionao, La Habana.
        1962/63- 1965/66.   not priced.   780 p.
        Contains data on numbers of students, courses, examinations, establishments, etc, in primary, medium
           (general, technical, etc), higher (university), special, and adult education.
        Time factor: the 1965/66 issue has data for the academic year 1965/66.
       §   Es.

      Refer also to 824, 827, 828, 829.

¶   G - Finance

      Refer to 828.

¶   H - Transport and communications

      Refer to 824, 827, 828, 829.

Central statistical office

839   Statistics Section,
       Ministry of Finance,
       Government Headquarters,
       Roseau.
       t   2401-2409.

       The Statistics Section, Ministry of Finance is responsible for the collection, analysis and publication
of statistics for Dominica.   Unpublished statistical information can be supplied if available and a fee is not
usually charged.

Statistical publications

840   Annual statistical digest   (Statistical Department)
       Statistical Section, Government Headquarters, Kennedy Avenue, Roseau.
       1963- 1969.   EC$2.   95 p.
       Main sections:
           Climate   Industrial production
           Population and vital statistics   Land, agriculture, forestry and fishing
           Migration and tourism   Public finance
           Labour and employment   National accounts
           Justice and crime   External trade
           Social conditions (health, education,   Miscellaneous (co-operative societies, credit unions,
             electorate, social assistance, housing)   post office savings, government savings bank,
           Transport and communications   public library)
       Time factor: published every three years, the 1969 edition has data for a number of years to 1967 or 1968.
       §   En.

¶   B   -   Production

     Refer to 840.

¶   C   -   External trade

841   Annual overseas trade report   (Statistics Department)
       Statistics Section, Government Headquarters, Kennedy Avenue, Roseau.
       1920-   1969.   EC$4.   122 p.
       Main tables show imports, exports and re-exports arranged by commodity and subdivided by countries
           of origin and destination.
       Time factor: the 1969 edition, published in 1970, has data for 1969.
       §   En.

       Refer also to 840.

¶   E   -   Population

842   Population census   (Division of Statistics, Ministry of Finance, Trade & Industry)
       Ministry of Finance, Trade and Industry, Government Headquarters, Kennedy Avenue, Roseau.
       1881-   1970.
       A preliminary report (provisional) was published in 1971 (EC$2)

       Refer also to 840.

DOMINICA, continued

¶ F - Social

ii. Health and welfare

Refer to 840.

iii. Education and leisure

Refer to 840.

iv. Justice

Refer to 840.

¶ G - Finance

Refer to 840.

¶ H - Transport and communications

Refer to 840.

Central statistical office

843   Oficina Nacional de Estadísticas y Censos   [National Statistics and Census Office],
           Avenida Mexico,
           Santa Domingo.
           † 689 3396.

           The Oficina Nacional de Estadísticas y Censos is responsible for the collection, analysis and publication
   of the official statistics of the Republic.   Unpublished statistical information may be supplied to enquirers
   if it is available.

Libraries

      The Oficina Nacional de Estadísticas y Censos has a library which is open to the public for reference
during office hours, 7.30 to 13.30, Monday through Friday.

Libraries and information services abroad

      The Dominican Republic's embassies abroad have available for consultation the statistical publications of
the country, including:
      United Kingdom   Embassy of the Dominican Republic, 4 Braemar Mansions, Cornwall Gardens,
                             London SW7. († 01-589 8751)
      USA   Embassy of the Dominican Republic, 1715 22nd Street NW, Washington DC.
                             († (202) 332 6280)

Statistical publications

¶   A - General

844   República Dominicana en cifras [Dominican Republic in figures] (Oficina Nacional de Estadísticas y Censos)
        Oficina Nacional de Estadísticas y Censos, Avenida Mexico, Santo Domingo.
        1964-   Vol VI, 1971.   not priced.   198 p.
        Main sections:
              Climate   Transport and communications
              Population   Other economic aspects
              Education   National finances
              Agriculture   Money and banking
              Fisheries   Prices
              Minerals   Wages
              Manufactures   Social situation
              Electricity   Co-operatives
              Internal trade   Consumption
              Foreign trade   National product and income
        Time factor: the 1971 edition, published in 1973, has data for 1970 and 1971 and also for some earlier
              years in some tables.
        §   Es.

845   Boletín mensual   [Monthly bulletin]   (Banco Central de la República Dominicana)
        Banco Central de la República Dominicana, Santo Domingo.
        1948-   not priced.
        Includes statistics of money and banking, foreign trade, direction of trade, finances, prices, and
              industrial and agricultural production.
        Time factor: each issue has data to the previous month or the latest available and is published about
              three months later.
        §   Es.

¶ B - Production

ii. Agriculture, fisheries, forestry, etc

846 Censo nacional agropecuario [National agricultural census] (Oficina Nacional de Estadísticas y Censos)
Oficina Nacional de Estadísticas y Censos, Avenida Mexico, Santo Domingo.
1920- 1971. not priced. c 300 p.
Contains the final results of the 6th agricultural and livestock census.
§ Es.

847 Boletín estadistico [Statistical bulletin] (Instituto del Tabaco de la República Dominicana: Secretaría de
Estado de Agricultura)
Instituto del Tabaco de la República Dominicana, Santiago de los Caballeros.
1964- 1974. $28. 49 p.
Contains data on production, sales, exports, prices, etc, of tobacco and cigarillos.
Time factor: the 1974 issue, published in 1975, has data for 1974 and some earlier years.
§ Es.

Refer also to 844, 845.

iii. Industry

848 Estadística industrial de la República Dominicana [Industrial statistics of the Dominican Republic] (Oficina
Nacional de Estadísticas y Censos)
Oficina Nacional de Estadísticas y Censos, Avenida Mexico, Santo Domingo.
1950- 1974. not priced. 116 p.
Contains data on industrial production generally, the sugar industry, rural industries, showing production
statistics, numbers of establishments, employment, etc.
Time factor: the 1974 issue, published late 1977, has data for 1974.
§ Es.

849 Indice de la producción industrial manufacturera [Index of industrial manufacturing production] (Oficina
Nacional de Estadísticas y Censos)
Oficina Nacional de Estadísticas y Censos, Avenida Mexico, Santo Domingo.
1950/63- 1963-1974. not priced. 36 p.
Contains indices for manufacturing generally and the manufacture of foodstuffs; beverages and tobacco;
clothing, except footwear and moulded rubber and plastic; paper and printing; glass and glassware;
manufactures of other non-metallic minerals; and machinery. Issued in the series 'Monografias
estadísticas'.
Time factor: the 1963-1974 issue, with data for 1963 to 1974, was published in 1977.
§ Es.

Refer also to 844, 845.

v. Energy

850 Memoria [Report] (Corporación Dominicana del Electricidad)
Corporación Dominicana del Electricidad, Santo Domingo.
1974. not priced. 95 p.
Contains text on electrification plans, production and sales, administration and finance, and includes
a small statistical section.
Time factor: the 1974 issue, published in 1975, has data for 1974 and 1973.
§ Es.

Refer also to 844.

¶   C   -   External trade

851   Comercio exterior de la República Dominicana   [Foreign trade of the Dominican Republic]   (Oficina
            Nacional de Estadísticas y Censos)
        Oficina Nacional de Estadísticas y Censos, Avenida Mexico, Santo Domingo.
        1953-   1978.   not priced.   412 p.
        Main tables show detailed statistics of imports and exports arranged by commodity subdivided by countries
            of origin and destination.
        Time factor: the 1978 issue, published in 1979, has data for 1978.
        §   Es.

        Refer also to 844, 845.

¶   D   -   Internal distribution and service trades

        Refer to 844.

¶   E   -   Population

852   Censo nacional de población y habitación   [National census of population and housing]   (Oficina Nacional
            de Estadísticas y Censos)
        Oficina Nacional de Estadísticas y Censos, Avenida Mexico, Santo Domingo.
        1930-   1970.   not priced.
        'Boletín censal No 3', published in June 1970, has preliminary official figures.   The first two bulletins
            dealt with methodology and instructions relating to the census.
        §   Es.

853   Estadística demografica   [Demographic statistics]   (Oficina Nacional de Estadísticas y Censos)
        Oficina Nacional de Estadísticas y Censos, Avenida Mexico, Santo Domingo.
        1943/46-   1972.   not priced.   105 p.
        Contains population statistics, vital statistics, migration statistics and tourism statistics.
        Time factor: the 1972 issue, published in 1974, has data for 1972.
        §   Es.

854   Encuesta nacional de fecundidad: informe general   [National survey of fertility: general report]   (Consejo
            Nacional de Población y Familia)
        Consejo Nacional de Población y Familia, Santo Domingo.
                    not priced.   611 p.
        Time factor: published in 1976, the report refers to the year 1974.
        §   Es.

        Refer also to 844.

¶   F   -   Social

i.   Standard of living

855   Encuesta de ingresos y gastos de los familias en la ciudad de Santo Domingo, 1969   [Survey of income and
            expenses of families in the city of Santo Domingo, 1969]   (Oficina Nacional de Estadística)
        Oficina Nacional de Estadística, Calle Mercedes No 27, Santo Domingo.
        §   Es.

iii.   Education and leisure

        Refer to 844.

DOMINICAN REPUBLIC,   continued

¶ F,   continued

iv.   Justice

   Refer to 844.

¶   G   -   Finance

i.   Banking

   Refer to 844, 845.

ii.   Public finance

856   Cuentas nacionales: producto nacional bruto [National accounts: gross national product]   (Banco Central de
      la República Dominicana)
      Banco Central de la República Dominicana, Santo Domingo.
      1950/64-   1970-1976.   not priced.   205 p.
      Time factor: the 1970-1976 issue was published mid-1977 and has data for the years 1970 to 1976.
      §   Es.

   Refer also to 844, 845.

¶   H   -   Transport and communications

   Refer to 844.

Central statistical office

857   Instituto Nacional de Estadística y Censos   [National Institute of Statistics and Censuses],
           10 de Agosto 229,
           Quito.
           † 211126 - 212402.   Cables: INEC QUITO-ECUADOR.

The Institute is a division of the Junta Nacional de Planificación y Coordinación [National Council of Economic Planning and Co-ordination].   It is responsible for the collection, analysis and publication of economic statistics of Ecuador and for taking various censuses.   Unpublished statistical information may be supplied to enquirers when it is available.

Libraries

The Institute has a library which specialises in national and international publications and is open to the public for reference.   The central bank (Banco Central del Ecuador) in Quito also has a library with statistical publications which is open to the public for reference.

Libraries and information services abroad

Statistical publications of the Institute and the central bank are available for reference at Ecuadorian embassies and consulates abroad, including:
           United Kingdom   Embassy of Ecuador, 3 Hans Crescent, London SW1.   († 01-584 1367)
           USA   Embassy of Ecuador, 2535 15th Street NW, Washington DC.   († (202) 234 7426)
           Canada   Embassy of Ecuador, 320 Queen Street, Ottawa.   († 238 5032)

Statistical publications

¶   A - General

858   Anuario de estadística, 1963-68   [Statistical yearbook, 1963-68]   (Instituto Nacional de Estadística)
           Instituto Nacional de Estadística, 10 de Agosto 229, Quito.
           Includes data on population, vital statistics, industry, external trade, social statistics, etc.
           Time factor: covers the years 1963 to 1968.
           §   Es.

859   Serie estadística   [Statistical series]   (Instituto Nacional de Estadística)
           Instituto Nacional de Estadística, 10 de Agosto 229, Quito.
                     1967-1972.   not priced.   203 p.
           Main sections:
                     Population   Electric energy
                     Housing and construction   Internal trade
                     Vital   Service trades
                     Hospital   Foreign trade
                     Education   Transport & communications
                     Agriculture and livestock   Money & banking
                     Manufacturing & mineral industry   Indexes of employment, wages & prices
                     Oil exploitation   Climate
           Time factor: the 1967-1972 issue, with data for those years, was published in 1974.
           §   Es.

¶ A, continued

860 Boletín - anuario [Annual bulletin] (Banco Central del Ecuador)
Banco Central del Ecuador, Quito.
1978- 1978. free. 229 p.
Main sections:

Monetary statistics	Indices of foreign trade
Exchange statistics	Sector indicators (agriculture, industry, etc)
Public finance	Population, employment & wages
Prices (consumer price indices; prices	Housing
of cocoa, coffee, bananas and oil)	Education
Balance of payments and foreign trade	

Time factor: the 1978 edition, published in July 1978, has data for the years 1966 to 1977.
§ Es.

861 Boletín [Bulletin] (Banco Central del Ecuador)
Banco Central del Ecuador, Quito.
1928- quarterly. free.
Contains data on money, exchanges, public finances, foreign trade, oil and prices.
Time factor: each issue has data for two or three years and the last 24 months to the end of the period
of the issue, and is published about three months later.
§ Es.

862 Quito y sus estadísticas [Quito and its statistics] (Instituto de Investigaciones Económicas y Financieras:
Universidad Central del Ecuador)
Universidad Central del Ecuador, Quito.
1965- No 4, 1968-1969-1970. not priced. 122 p.
Contains general and meteorological information, demography, social and assistance, education and
culture, and economic statistics (agriculture, industry, commerce, consumption and production,
transport, communications, money, prices, finance, and services).
Time factor: the 1968-1969-1970 edition, covering those years, was published in 1972.
§ Es.

¶ B - Production

863 Encuesta de manufactura y minera [Survey of the manufacturing and mining industries] (Instituto Nacional
de Estadística y Censos)
Instituto Nacional de Estadística y Censos, 10 de Agosto 229, Quito.
1964- 1973. not priced. 173 p.
Contains data on employment, wages, social grants, raw materials, production, income and expenditure,
consumption of electric energy and water, the value of principal raw materials consumed and the
value of principal products manufactured.
Time factor: the 1973 edition, published in 1975, has data for 1973.
§ Es.

Refer also to 859, 860 862.

ii. Agriculture, fisheries, forestry, etc

864 Censo agropecuario nacional [Census of agriculture and livestock] (Instituto Nacional de Estadística y
Censos)
Instituto Nacional de Estadística y Censos, 10 de Agosto 229, Quito.
2nd, 1974.
Publications include: provisional results S/:40, national summary ['Distribución de la tierra']
S/:60 or US$4, and final results for regions S/:120 or US$8 each volume).
§ Es.

¶   B,   continued

865   Producción estimativa de los principales cultivos agrícoles del Ecuador   [Estimated production of the
            principal agricultural products of Ecuador]   (Ministerio de Agricultura y Ganadería)
        Ministerio de Agricultura y Ganadería, Quito.
        1962- 1966.   not priced.   20 p.
        §   Es.

    iii.   Industry

        Refer to 863.

    iv.   Construction

866   Encuesta de edificaciones (permisos de construcción)   [Survey of buildings (construction permits)]   (Instituto
            Nacional de Estadística y Censos)
        Instituto Nacional de Estadística y Censos, 10 de Agosto 229, Quito,
        1969- 1974.   not priced.   25 p.
        Contains data on numbers of permits conceded by type of material, place, floors, type of building, etc.
        Time factor: the 1974 edition, with data for 1974, was published in 1975.
        §   Es.

    v.   Energy

867   Censo nacional de electrificación   [National census of electrification]   (Dirección General de Recursos
            Hidraulicos y Electrificación)
        Dirección General de Recursos Hidraulicos y Electrificación, Quito.
        1962/63- 1962-1963.   not priced.   91 p.
        Contains data on installations functioning, by province, and potential installations.
        Time factor: the results of the 1962-1963 census were published in 1964.
        §   Es.

    ¶   C - External trade

868   Anuario de comercio exterior   [External trade yearbook]   (Departamento de Estadística del Ministerio de
            Finanzas)
        Departamento de Estadística, Ministerio de Finanzas, Quito.
        1957- 1975.   not priced.   732 p.
        Main tables show detailed statistics of imports and exports arranged by commodities and subdivided by
            countries of origin and destination.
        Time factor: the 1975 issue, published in 1977, has data for 1975.
        §   Es.

869   Comercio exterior ecuatoriano   [Foreign trade of Ecuador]   (Banco Central del Ecuador)
        Banco Central del Ecuador, Quito.
        1947- monthly.   not priced.
        Contained data on licences granted to export and import certain commodities, and data on movement
            at the ports.
        Time factor: ceased publication in 1964.
        §   Es.

        Refer also to 859, 860, 861.

¶   D   -   Internal distribution and service trades

870   Encuesta anual de comercio interno   [Annual survey of internal trade]   (Instituto Nacional de Estadística y
             Censos)
             Instituto Nacional de Estadística y Censos, 10 de Agosto 229, Quito.
             1972- 1973.   not priced.   97 p.
             A survey of the trading activities of over 2000 firms, by province and on a national basis.   Includes
                  numbers of establishments, employees, class of trade, income and expenditure, etc.
             Time factor: the results of the 1973 survey were published in December 1975.

871   Encuesta anual de restaurantes, hoteles y servicios   [Annual survey of restaurants, hotels and service trades]
                  (Instituto Nacional de Estadística y Censos)
             Instituto Nacional de Estadística y Censos, 10 de Agosto 229, Quito.
             1972- 1973.   not priced.   50 p.
             Contains data on the numbers of restaurants, hotels and services, numbers of employees, income and
                  expenditure, etc.
             Time factor: the results of the 1973 survey were published in September 1975.
             §   Es.

             Refer also to 859.

¶   E   -   Population

872   Censo de población   [Census of population]   (Instituto Nacional de Estadística y Censos)
             Instituto Nacional de Estadística y Censos, 10 de Agosto 229, Quito.
             1950-   3rd, 1974.
             Provisional results were published in 1974 (31 p).
             Final results:
                  Resumen nacional   [National summary]   S/:60 or US$4.
                  Final results for each city are also being published   S/:100 or US$8 each volume.
             §   Es.

873   Encuesta de población y ocupación   [Survey of population and occupation]   (Instituto Nacional de Estadística
             y Censos)
             Instituto Nacional de Estadística y Censos, 10 de Agosto 229, Quito.
             (annual)   not priced.
             §   Es.

874   Censo de vivienda: resultados definitivos: resumen nacional   [Housing census: final results: national summary]
                  (Instituto Nacional de Estadística y Censos)
             Instituto Nacional de Estadística y Censos, 10 de Agosto 229, Quito.
             1950- 1974.   S/:50 or US$4.
             Time factor: published in 1977.
             §   Es.

875   Anuario de estadísticas vitales   [Yearbook of vital statistics]   (Instituto Nacional de Estadística y Censos)
             Instituto Nacional de Estadística y Censos, 10 de Agosto 229, Quito.
             1960- 1972.   not priced.   227 p.
             Contains data on births, marriages, divorces, and mortality rates.
             Time factor: the 1972 issue, with data for 1972, was published in 1974.
             §   Es.

¶   E,   continued

876   Encuestas de fecundidad de las ciudades de Quito y Guayaquil   [Survey of fertility in the cities of Quito
            and Guayaquil]   (Dirección de Estadística y Censos)
            Instituto Nacional de Estadística y Censos, 10 Agosto 229, Quito.
                                        c 200 p.
            Time factor: published in 1969.
            §   Es.

877   Estadísticas del trabajo: indices de empleo y remuneraciones   [Statistics of work: indices of employment
            and wages]   (Instituto Nacional de Estadística y Censos)
            Instituto Nacional de Estadística y Censos, 10 de Agosto 229, Quito.
            1965-   quarterly.   not priced.
            Time factor: each issue has data for several months, quarters and years to the end of the period of the
                issue, and is published many months later.
            §   Es.

       Refer also to 858, 859, 860.

    ¶   F - Social

    i.   Standard of living

878   Indices de precios al consumidor: Quito, Guayaquil y Cuenca   [Consumer price indices: Quito, Guayaquil
            and Cuenca]   (Instituto Nacional de Estadística y Censos)
            Instituto Nacional de Estadística y Censos, 10 de Agosto 229, Quito.
            1954-   monthly.   not priced.
            Time factor: each issue has indices for nine or more months up to the month of the issue, and is published
                about two months later.
            §   Es.

       Refer also to 859, 860.

    ii.   Health and welfare

879   Anuario de estadísticas hospitalarias   [Yearbook of hospital statistics]   (Instituto Nacional de Estadística y
            Censos)
            Instituto Nacional de Estadística y Censos, 10 de Agosto 229, Quito.
            1965-   1974.   not priced.   163 p.
            Contains statistical data on hospitals, clinics and patients.
            Time factor: the 1974 issue, published in 1976, has data for 1974.
            §   Es.

880   Encuesta de actividades y recursos de salud   [Survey of health resources and activities]   (Instituto Nacional
            de Estadística y Censos)
            Instituto Nacional de Estadística y Censos, 10 de Agosto 229, Quito.
            (annual)   1973.   not priced.
            §   Es.

       Refer also to 858, 859.

ECUADOR,   continued

¶ F,   continued

iii. Education

881   Anuario de estadísticas educacionales   [Statistical yearbook of Education]   (Instituto Nacional de Estadística
         y Censos)
         Instituto Nacional de Estadística y Censos, 10 de Agosto 229, Quito.
         (annual)   1971-1972.   not priced.   2 vols.
         One volume deals with primary education and the other with secondary education, both having data on
            establishments, types of education, classes, staff, pupils/students, finance, etc.
         §   Es.

      Refer also to 858, 859, 860.

¶ G - Finance

      Refer also to 860, 861.

i. Banking

882   Información estadística el Ecuador ha sido, es y sera pais amazonico   [Statistical information]   (Banco Central
         del Ecuador)
         Banco Central del Ecuador, Quito.
         1928-   monthly.   free.
         Contains data on the activities of the bank, of private banks, and of the Banco Nacional de Fomento.
         Time factor: each issue has long runs of monthly and annual figures to the month of the issue and is
            published the following month.
         §   Es.

      Note: "Memoria del Gerente General...Banco Central del Ecuador" [Report of the Chairman...] also
         includes banking statistics.

883   Indicadores financieros   [Financial indicators]   (Junta Nacional de Planificación y Coordinación)
         Junta Nacional de Planificación y Coordinación, Quito.
                  monthly.   not priced.
         Contains statistical indicators of banking activities in both the public and private sector.
         Time factor: each issue has data to the date of the issue but is not published for about twelve months.
         §   Es.

      Refer also to 859.

iv. Investment

884   Recopilación y clasificación de datos sobre inversiones extranjeras en el Ecuador (incluyendo operaciones de
         muto, venta de acciones, etc) en los anos de 1970-1971-1972-1973   [Compilation and classification
         of data on foreign investment in Ecuador (including loan operations, selling of shares, etc]
         (Superintendencia de Bancos: Dirección de Asesoria de Integración)
                  not priced.
         Time factor: published in February 1974.
         §   Es.

¶ H - Transport and communications

885 Anuario de estadísticas de transporte [Yearbook of transport statistics] (Instituto Nacional de Estadística y Censos)
Instituto Nacional de Estadística y Censos, 10 de Agosto, 229, Quito.
1965/66- 1974/75. not priced. 182 p.
Contains data on vehicle licences, national and by provinces; accidents in transit; rail traffic; international air traffic; ships registered - coast and river; international maritime traffic.
Time factor: the 1974-1975 issue, published in 1977, has data for 1975 or 1974 if later figures are not available.
§ Es.

Refer also to 859.

i. Ships and shipping

886 Boletín estadístico: puertos ecuatorianos [Statistical bulletin: Ecuadorian ports] (Dirección de la Marina Mercante y del Literal: Systema Portuario Ecuatoriano)
Dirección de la Marina Mercante y del Literal, Quito.
1976- 1977. not priced. 75 p.
Contains data on the movement of ships, cargoes, nationally and by port, including principal products, net tonnage, imports and exports, etc.
Time factor: published for the first half-year and annually, the 1977 issue, published mid-1978, has data for 1970 to 1977 nationally and from 1974 or 1975 to 1977 by port. There is also a half-yearly up-dating issue.
§ Es.

There is no central statistical office in the territory.

Statistical publications

887   Falkland Islands and dependencies: report for the year... (Foreign and Commonwealth Office)
        H M Stationery Office, PO Box 569, London SE1 9NH.
        1919-   1972 & 1973.   £1.15.   70 p.
        Mainly textual, but includes some statistics on population, employment, etc.
        Time factor: the report is issued biennially, and the 1972 & 1973 report was published in 1975.
        §   En.

¶   E   -   Population

888   Report of the census... (Census Supervisor)
        Government Printing Office, Stanley, Falkland Islands.
        1881-   1962.   not priced.   16 p.
        Time factor: the report of the 1962 census was published in 1962.
        §   En.

Central statistical office

889   Institut National de la Statistique et des Etudes Economiques   [National Institute for Statistics and
            Economic Research),
        18 boulevard Adolphe Pinard,
        75675 Paris Cedex 14, France.
        t 540 01 12 & 540 12 12.   tx 204924 INSEE

        INSEE is the central organisation for economic information on France and it also collects and publishes
information on French overseas territories.   It is concerned with economic and social information.   There
is a departmental service in French Guiana - Institut National de la Statistique et des Etudes Economiques,
Service Départemental de Guyane, 47 avenue du Général de Gaulle, (BP 757), 97305 Cayenne (t 31 12 79:
telex PREFEGU 532 FG).

        Statistical publications

    ¶   A - General

890   Annuaire statistique de la Guyane   [Statistical yearbook of Guiana]   (Institut National de la Statistique et
            des Etudes Economiques)
        INSEE, 18 boulevard Adolphe Pinard, 75675 Paris Cedex 14, France.
        1947/52-   1961/1970.   not priced.   168 p.
        Main sections:
            Geography and climate   Production
            Demography   Foreign trade
            Active population   Transport and communications
            Health and social aid   Prices, wages, social security
            Education   Money and credit
            Justice   Public finance
            Political and administrative organisation   Central Spacial Organisation
        Time factor: the 1961-1970 edition, with data for those years, was published in 1971.
        §   Fr.

    ¶   B - Production

        Refer to 890.

    ¶   C - External trade

        Refer to 890.

    ¶   D - Internal distribution and service trades

        Refer to 890.

    ¶   E - Population

891   Résultats statistiques du recensement général de la population de 1967: Guyane. 1ère partie: tableaux
            statistiques   [Statistical results of the general census of population of Guyane, 1967. 1st part:
            statistical tables]   (INSEE)
        INSEE, 18 boulevard Adolphe Pinard, 75675 Paris Cedex 14, France.
        1877-   not priced.   172 p.
        §   Fr.

        Refer also to 890.

¶   F - Social

      Refer to 890.

i.   Standard of living

892   Enquête sur les dépenses des ménages: Guyane, 1967   [Survey of the expenditure of households: Guyana]
          (INSEE)
        INSEE, 18 boulevard Adolphe Pinard, 75675 Paris Cedex 14, France.
                FrF4.
      §   Fr.

893   Une enquête sur les consommations des ménages dans le département de la Guyane, 1968   [Survey of
          consumption in households in Guyane, 1968]   (INSEE)
        INSEE, 18 boulevard Adolphe Pinard, 75675 Paris Cedex 14, France.
                not priced.   21 p.
      §   Es.

¶   G - Finance

      Refer to 890.

¶   H - Transport and communications

      Refer to 890.

894   Until independence on 1st May, 1979, statistics for Greenland were collected, analysed and published
by Danmarks Statistik [the Danish central ststistical office] Seirøgade 11, Postboks 2250, 2100 København
(† (01) 29 82 22).

        Statistical publications

    ¶   A   -   General

895   Statistisk årbog [Statistical yearbook]   (Danmarks Statistik)
        Danmarks Statistik, Seirøgade 11, 2100 København Ø, Denmark.
        1887- 1977   DKr45.   592 p.
        Pages 456-483 refer to Greenland, with data on metrological conditions, population, vital statistics,
            housing, business, agriculture and fisheries, sales, foreign trade, transport and communications,
            wages, consumer price index, finance and banking, and public accounts.
        Time factor: the 1977 edition, published in 1977, has data for 1975 and also earlier years in some tables.
        §   Da,   En.

    ¶   B   -   Production

        Refer to 895.

    ¶   C   -   External trade

896   Danmarks vareindførsel og- udførsel. Bind 1   [Foreign trade of Denmark. Volume 1]   (Danmarks Statistik)
        Danmarks Statistik, Seirøgade 11, 2100 København ¢, Denmark.
        1883- 1977. DKr32.   327 p.
        Includes data on trade of Greenland with the rest of Denmark and with foreign countries, pages 211-225).
        Time factor: the 1977 issue, published in 1978, has data for 1977.
        §   Da,   En.

897   Månedsstatistik over udenrigshandelen   [Monthly bulletin of foreign trade]   (Danmarks Statistik)
        Danmarks Statistik, Seirøgade 11, 2100 København Ø, Denmark.
        1910-
        Includes statistical tables on trade of Denmark proper with Greenland (values only).
        Time factor: published about one month after the end of the month to which the figures relate.
        §   Da,   tables of contents and main headings also in En.

        Refer also to 895.

    ¶   D   -   Internal distribution and service trades

        Refer to 895.

    ¶   E   -   Population

898   Folke- og boligtællingen [Census of population and housing] (Danmarks Statistik)
        Danmarks Statistik, Seirøgade 11, 2100 København Ø, Denmark.
        1801- 1970.   DKr16. each volume.
        Includes one voiume on the population and housing census for Greenland, including data on births,
            marriages and deaths.
        Time factor: a census is taken every 10 years.
        §   Da,   table of contents and headings also in En.

¶   E,   continued

899   Befolkningens bevægelser   [Vital statistics]   (Danmarks Statistik)
          Danmarks Statistik, Seirøgade 11, 2100 København Ø, Denmark.
          1931/33-   1976.   DKr20.55.   219 p.
          Includes a section on Greenland (pages 208-212).
          Time factor: the 1976 issue, published in 1978, has data for 1976.
          §   Da, ' En.

          Refer also to 895.

¶   F   -   Social

          Refer to 895.

¶   G   -   Finance

          Refer to 895.

¶   H   -   Transport and communications

          Refer to 895.

Grenada is self-governed in association with Britain, which retains powers and responsibilities for defence and external affairs.   Enquiries concerning statistics for the island can be made to the Minister of Finance, Trade and Production, at St George's, or to the Grenada Chamber of Commerce, PO Box 129, St George's.

Statistical publications

¶   A   -   General

900   Grenada: report for the year   (Foreign and Commonwealth Office)
HM Stationery Office, PO Box 569, London SE1 9NH.
1955/56-   1965 & 1966.   £0.50.   64 p.
Mainly textual, but contains some statistics on population, employment, commerce, tourism, production, finance, etc.
Time factor: published in 1969.
§   En.

901   Economic survey and projections   (British Development Division in the Caribbean)
not priced.   45 p.
Deals with the economy of Grenada and has a statistical appendix showing projections for exports, construction and engineering, hotels, government and other sectors.
Time factor: published in 1967.
§   En.

¶   B   -   Production

Refer to 900, 901.

¶   C   -   External trade

902   Annual overseas trade report   (Government of Grenada)
Government Printer, St George's, Grenada.
1921-   1973. $15.   222 p.
Main tables show detailed statistics of imports and exports arranged by commodities and subdivided by countries of origin and destination.
Time factor: the 1973 issue, published in 1975, has data for 1973.
§   En.

903   Quarterly overseas trade report   (Government of Grenada)
Government Printer, St George's, Grenada.
not priced.
Main tables show statistics of imports and exports arranged by commodities and subdivided by countries of origin and destination.
Time factor: each issue has data for that quarter and cumulated figures for the year to date.   Ceased publications with the 1968 issues.
§   En.

¶   D   -   Internal distribution and service trades

Refer to 900, 901.

¶   E   -   Population

904   Census of population
            1881-   1970.
            Refer to 258 for details of the 1970 census, part of the census of the Commonwealth Caribbean.

            Refer also to 900.

¶   G   -   Finance

            Refer to 900.

Central Statistical office

905   Institut National de la Statistique et des Etudes Economiques: Service Départemental de Guadeloupe
           [National Institute of Statistics and Economic Studies: Departmental Service for Guadeloupe],
       Boîte Postale 96,
       Basse-terre.

       INSEE is the central organisation for information on France and its overseas territories and departments.
It is concerned with social and economic demography, consumption, prices, income, national accounts, and
national and regional economic planning.

Statistical publications

¶   A - General

906   Annuaire statistique de la Guadeloupe   [Statistical yearbook of Guadeloupe]   (Institut National de la
           Statistique et des Etudes Economiques)
       INSEE, 18 boulevard Adolphe Pinard, 75675 Paris Cedex 14, France.
       1949/53- 1967-1970.   Fr 30.   113 p.
       Main sections:
           Area and administration   Production (agriculture, fisheries, land, industry,
           Climate   construction, electricity, tourism)
           Population (& migration & employment) Transport & communications
           Health and social assistance   Foreign trade
           Education   Prices, wages, social security
           Housing   Money and credit
           Justice   Public finance
           Elections
       Time factor: the 1967-1970 edition, with data for those years, was published in 1972.
       §   Fr.

907   Comptes économiques de la Guadeloupe   [Economic accounts of Guadeloupe]   (Institut National de la
           Statistique et des Etudes Economiques)
       INSEE, 18 boulevard Adolphe Pinard, 75675 Paris Cedex 14, France.
       1965/67- 1971-1972-1973.   Fr 7.   49 p.
       Contains textual data on the economy of Guadeloupe and statistical tables of resources and the use of
           goods and services, industrial production, enterprises, foreign trade, etc.
       Time factor: the 1971-1972-1973 edition was published in 1977.
       §   Fr.

908   Bulletin de statistique [Statistical bulletin] (INSEE, Service Départemental de Guadeloupe)
       INSEE, BP 96, Basse-terre.
       1969-   monthly.   Fr 3 each issue .
       Contains data on demography, agriculture, industry, transport, foreign trade, tourism, prices, wages,
           social security, money and credit.
       Time factor: each issue has data for the month of the issue and is published some two months later.
       §   Fr.

909   Informations rapides   [Rapid information]   (INSEE, Service Départemental de Guadeloupe)
       INSEE, BP 96, Basse-terre.
       1971-   monthly.   Fr 3 each issue.
       Contains data on population, agriculture, industry, agro-food, energy, construction materials, transport,
           foreign trade, wages, public finance, price indices, evolution of price indices.
       §   Fr.

¶   B   -   Production

Refer to 906, 907, 908, 909.

¶   C   -   External trade

Refer to 906, 908, 909.

¶   D   -   Internal distribution and service trades

910   Données statistiques sur le tourisme en Guadeloupe, 1968-1972   [Statistics of tourism in Guadeloupe]
            (INSEE, Service Départemental de Guadeloupe)
        INSEE, BP 96, Basse-terre.
                        not priced.   49 p.
        Contains data on migratory movements, hotel activity and hotel clientele.
        Time factor: published in 1972.

        Refer also to 906, 907, 908.

¶   E   -   Population

911   Démographie et emploi en Guadeloupe: informations disponsibles...   [Demography and employment in
            Guadeloupe: information]   (INSEE, Service Départemental de Guadeloupe)
        INSEE, Service Départemental de Guadeloupe, BP 96, Basse-terre.
        1956-   2nd, 1976.   Fr10.   19 p.
        Time factor: published in 1978.
        §   Fr.

912   Le logement dans le Département de la Guadeloupe en 1961   [Housing in the Department of Guadeloupe]
            (Institut National de la Statistique et des Etudes Economiques)
        INSEE, 18 boulevard Adolphe Pinard, 75675 Paris Cedex 14, France.
                        not priced.   63 p.
        Time factor: published in 1964.
        §   Fr.

        Refer also to 906, 908, 909.

¶   F   -   Social

Refer to 906, 908, 909.

¶   G   -   Finance

Refer to 906, 908, 909.

¶   H   -   Transport and communications

Refer to 906, 908, 909.

Central statistical office

913 Dirección General de Estadística [General Statistical Office],
    8a calle 9-55, zona 1, Edificio América, 20 nivel,
    Ciudad de Guatemala.
    t 514456.

    The Office is a part of the Ministerio de Economía [Ministry of the Economy] and its functions are to collect, analyse and publish official statistics which may be required, including the taking of censuses of population, industry, agriculture, etc. Unpublished statistical information can be provided to enquirers if it is available.

Libraries

    The Dirección General de Estadística, referred to above, has a library in which there is a collection of Guatemalan statistical publications. The library is open to the public and the staff speak Spanish and English.

    The Secretaría Permanente del Tratado General de Integración Económica Centroaméricana, 4a Avenue 10-25, zona 14, Guatemala also has a library (Centro de Documentación e Información) where members of the public may consult statistical publications of the Central American Common Market and individual member countries, other individual countries, and the United Nations. The library is open from 8.00 to 12.00 and from 14.00 to 17.30, Monday through Friday, except between 16 and 31 December; the staff speak Spanish and English.

Libraries and information services abroad

    Guatemalan embassies abroad receive copies of Guatemalan statistical publications, including:
     USA Guatemalan Embassy, 2220 R Street NW, Washington DC. (t (202) 332 2865)

Bibliographies

    The Dirección General de Estadística issues a catalogue of its publications at intervals.

Statistical publications

¶ A - General

914 Anuario estadístico [Statistical yearbook] (Dirección General de Estadística)
    Dirección General de Estadística, 8a calle 9-55, zona 1, Edificio América, 20 nivel, Ciudad de
     Guatemala.
    1970- 1974. Q3.50. 226 p.
    Contents:
     I Geographical
     II Demography
     III Economic (agriculture and livestock, industrial production, foreign trade, price indices, balance
       of payments, national accounts, public finance, municipal finance, transport)
     IV Social (social security, hospitals, justice)
     V Culture and education
     VI Housing
    Time factor: the 1974 edition, published in 1976, has data for ten years to 1974 or 1973/74.
    § Es.

    Note: supersedes "Guatemala en cifras' [Guatemala in figures] which was published from 1955 to 1969.

¶   A,   continued

915   Boletín estadístico [Statistical bulletin] (Dirección de Estadística)
       Dirección General de Estadística, 8a calle 9-55, zona 1, Edificio América, 20 nivel, Ciudad de
           Guatemala.
       1946-   Q2 each issue.
       Contains data on area, demography, industrial production and consumption, foreign trade, transport,
           finance, banking and insurance, prices, social, and judicial.
       Time factor: started as a quarterly ("Trimestro estadístico") it became normal for only one issue a year
           to appear, but with statistics for each quarter, and the last two issues have been for two years each.
           The 1973-1974 issue, published in 1976, has annual and monthly figures for those two years and also
           annual figures for 1970 to 1972.
       §   Es.

916   Informador estadístico   [Statistical information]   (Dirección General de Estadística)
       Dirección General de Estadística, 8a calle 9-55, zona 1, Edificio América, 20 nivel, Ciudad
           Guatemala.
       1962-   weekly.   free.
       Each issue has brief statistics on one important subject such as industrial production, construction,
           external trade, agriculture, demography, crime, hospitals, etc.
       §   Es.

917   Boletín estadístico   [Statistical bulletin] (Banco de Guatemala)
       Banco de Guatemala, 7a Avenue 22-01, zona 1, Guatemala.
       1948-   quarterly.   not priced.
       Contains data on money and banking, public finance, foreign trade, price indices, other economic
           indicators (index of industrial production, production of selected articles, property – conveyancing
           – taxation, rail – cargo carried, construction), and national accounts.
       Time factor: each issue has long runs of annual and monthly figures and includes data up to three months
           prior to publication.
       §   Es.

       Note: the bank also issues "Informe económico" annually, which is mainly textual with some tables in
           the text.

918   Estudio económico y memoria de labores   [Economic study and report of activities] (Banco de Guatemala)
       Banco de Guatemala, 7a Avenue 22-01, zona 1, Guatemala.
       1946-   1976.   not priced.   215 p.
       Contains information on the national economic situation, balance of payments international, the money
           and banking situation, and the public finance situation, as well as the operations and accounts of
           the bank.   Includes text and tables.
       Time factor: the 1976 edition, published in 1977, has data for 1975 and 1976.
       §   Es.

919   Sector externo, 1965-1975 [Foreign sector] (Banco de Guatemala)
       Banco de Guatemala, 7a Avenue 22-01, zona 1, Guatemala.
                   not priced.   31 p.
       Contains data on the balance of payments, imports and exports (summary data), prices, etc.
       Time factor: published in 1976.
       §   Es.

¶   B   -   Production

ii.   Agriculture, fisheries, forestry, etc.

920   Censo agropecuario   [Agricultural census]   (Dirección General de Estadística)
      Dirección General de Estadística, 8a calle 9-55, zona 1, Edificio América, 20 nivel, Ciudad de
          Guatemala.
      1950-   2nd, 1964.   Q2 each volume.   5 vols.
      Vol I   Summary
      Vol II   Use of land, cultivation
      Vol III Livestock
      Vol IV   Poultry, aviculture, agricultural products, machinery and vehicles, power used, etc.
      Vol V   Panorama of the agricultural structure of Guatemala.
      §   Es.

921   Estadísticas agropecuarias continuas...   [Agricultural statistics continuing...]   (Dirección General de
          Estadística)
      Dirección General de Estadística, 8a calle 9-55, zona 1, Edificio América, 20 nivel, Ciudad de
          Guatemala.
      1965/66-   1976.   Q2.   c 50 p.
      Contains estimates of agricultural production, conditions of cultivation and crops, livestock production,
          and prices.
      Time factor: the 1976 edition, published in 1977, has data for 1976.
      §   Es.

922   Encuesta agricolas de granos basicos   [Survey of basic agricultural crops]   (Dirección General de Estadística)
      Dirección General de Estadística, 8a calle 9-55, zona 1, Edificio América, 20 nivel, Ciudad de
          Guatemala.
      1967/68-   1975/76.   Q2.
      Contains preliminary statistics on maize, beans, rice, wheat and other crops.
      Time factor: the 1975/76 report was published in 1977.
      §   Es.

923   Encuestas pecuaria   [Survey of cattle]   (Dirección General de Estadística)
      Dirección General de Estadística, 8a calle 9-55, zona 1, Edificio América, 20 nivel, Ciudad de
          Guatemala.
      1967/68-   1974.   Q2.
      Time factor: the final report for 1974 was published in 1976.   Preliminary results for 1975-1976-1977
          have also been published.
      §   Es.

      Refer also to 914, 916.

  iii.   Industry

924   Censo de industria   [Industrial census]   (Dirección General de Estadística)
      Dirección General de Estadística, 8a calle 9-55, zona 1, Edificio América, 20 nivel, Ciudad de
          Guatemala.
      1946-   4th, 1965.   Q2 each volume.   2 vols.
      Published as volumes V and VI of the economic census, and including data on number of establishments,
          materials used, employment, wages, production, capital invested, finances, etc.
      Time factor: published in 1972.
      §   Es.

¶ B.iii, continued

925 Encuesta industrial [Industrial enquiry] (Dirección General de Estadística)
Dirección General de Estadística, 8a calle 9-55, zona 1, Edificio América, 20 nivel, Ciudad de
Guatemala.
1971- 4th, 1974. not priced. 563 p.
Contains data on production, sales, other income, employment, expenditure on operations, general
expenditure, income and finance for manufacturing industry.
Time factor: the report of the 1974 survey was published mid-1977.
§ Es.

Note: "Directorio industrial" [Industrial directory] in two volumes (Q3 each) were published in 1975
and 1976.

926 Encuesta trimestral de la industria manufacturera fabril [Quarterly enquiry on industrial manufacturing]
(Dirección General de Estadística)
1974- Q2 each issue.
Contains similar information to that in 925 above.
§ Es.

Refer also to 914, 915, 916.

¶ C - External trade

927 Anuario de comercio exterior [Yearbook of foreign trade] (Dirección General de Estadística)
Dirección General de Estadística, 8a calle 9-55, zona 1, Edificio América, 20 nivel, Ciudad de
Guatemala.
1952- 1973. Q3. c 300 p.
Main tables show imports and exports arranged by commodity and subdivided by countries of origin and
destination.
Time factor: the 1973 issue, with data for 1972, was published in 1975.
§ Es.

Refer also to 914, 915, 919.

¶ D - Internal distribution and service trades

928 Censo de comercios [Commercial census] (Dirección General de Estadística)
Dirección General de Estadística, 8a calle 9-55, zona 1, Edificio América, 20 nivel, Ciudad de
Guatemala.
1959- 2nd, 1965. Q2 each volume. 2 vols.
Published as volumes II & IV of the economic census, and including data on number of establishments,
employees, income and expenditures, etc, for commercial firms.
Time factor: the volumes were published in 1968 and 1971.
§ Es.

929 Censo de servicios [Census of service trades] (Dirección General de Estadística)
Dirección General de Estadística, 8a calle 9-55, zona 1, Edificio América, 20 nivel, Ciudad de
Guatemala.
1965- 1965. Q2 each volume. 2 vols.
Published as volumes I & III of the economic census, and including data on number of firms, employment,
income and expenditure, etc, of service trades.
Time factor: the report of the census was published in 1971.
§ Es.

¶   D,   continued

930   Estadísticas de turismo   [Statistics of tourism]   (Instituto Guatemalteco de Turismo)
           Instituto Guatemalteco de Turismo, Ciudad de Guatemala.
           1964-   1976.   not priced.   29 p.
           Contains data on tourists by country, nationality, month of arrival, finances, exits, etc.
           Time factor: the 1976 issue has data for 1976 and also some earlier years in some tables.
           §   Es.

           Refer also to 915.

¶   E - Population

931   Censo de población   [Census of population]   (Dirección General de Estadística)
           Dirección General de Estadística, 8a calle 9-55, zona 1, Edificio América, 20 nivel, Ciudad de
                 Guatemala.
           1824-   8th, 1973.
           The final results are issued in two volumes (Q4 each), and there is also a volume on Guatemala City
                 [Ciudad capital (municipio de Guatemala)].
           Time factor: the results of the 1973 census were published in 1977.
           §   Es.

932   Guatemala: evaluación del censo de 1973 y proyección de la población por sexo y edad, 1950-2000
                 [Guatemala: evaluation of the census of 1973 and projections by sex and age, 1950-2000]   (Juan
           Chackiel)
           Dirección General de Estadística, 8a calle 9-55, zona 1, Edificio América, 20 nivel, Ciudad de
                 Guatemala.
                          Q2.
           Time factor: published in 1976.
           §   Es.

933   Censo de vivienda   [Census of housing]   (Dirección General de Estadística)
           Dirección General de Estadística, 8a calle 9-55, zona 1, Edificio América, 20 nivel, Ciudad de
                 Guatemala.
           1949-   3rd, 1973.   Q2.
           Contains data on construction materials, type of site, number of households, type of tenancies, etc.
           Time factor: the final results of the 1973 census were published in 1975.
           §   Es.

934   Censo de habitación   [Census of dwellings]   (Dirección General de Estadística)
           Dirección General de Estadística, 8a calle 9-55, zona 1, Edificio América, 20 nivel, Ciudad de
                 Guatemala.
           1949-   3rd, 1973.   Q4.50 each volume.   3 vols.
           Volumes I and II have final data for the Republic of Guatemala as a whole and volume III has data for
                 Guatemala City.
           Time factor: the results of the 1973 census were published in 1977.
           §   Es.

           Refer also to 914, 915, 916.

GUATEMALA,   continued

¶   F   -   Social

935   Indice de precios al consumidor en la Republica de Guatemala   [Consumer price indices in the Republic of
            Guatemala]   (Dirección General de Estadística)
            Dirección General de Estadística, 8a calle 9-55, zona 1, Edificio América, 20 nivel, Ciudad de
            Guatemala.
                    monthly.   Q1.50.
            §   Es.

        Refer also to 914, 915, 916.

¶   G   -   Finance

i.   Banking.

936   Boletín de estadísticas bancarias   [Bulletin of banking statistics]   (Superintendencia de Bancos)
            Superintendencia de Bancos, Ciudad de Guatemala.
            1958-   quarterly.   free.
            Contains the condensed balance of the banks, financial statistics, credit, etc.
            Time factor: each issue has data for four quarters to the date of the issue and is published three months
                later.
            §   Es.

        Refer also to 915, 917, 918.

ii.   Public finance

        Refer to 914, 915, 917, 918.

v.   Insurance

937   Boletín de estadisticas de seguros y fianzas   [Statistical bulletin on insurance]   (Superintendencia de Bancos)
            Superintendencia de Bancos, Ciudad de Guatemala.
            1951-   1977.   not priced.   80 p.
            Time factor: the 1977 issue, published in 1978, has data for 1973 to 1977.
            §   Es.

        Refer also to 915.

¶   H   -   Transport and communications

        Refer also to 914, 915.

ii.   Road

938   Accidentes de transito   [Road accidents]   (Dirección General de Estadística)
            Dirección General de Estadística, 8a calle 9055, zona 1, Edificio América, 20 nivel, Ciudad de
            Guatemala.
            1974-   1974.   Q1.50.   27 p.
            Time factor: the 1974 issue, published in 1975, has data for 1972, 1973 and 1974.
            §   Es.

GUYANA - GUYANE - GUAYANA

Central statistical office

939   Statistical Bureau,
           Ministry of Economic Development,
           Avenue of the Republic,
           Georgetown.
           t 4764.

           The Statistical Bureau of the Ministry of Economic Development is the organisation responsible for the
           collection, analysis and publication of statistics of Guyana.

Statistical publications

940   Annual statistical abstract   (Statistical Bureau: Ministry of Economic Development)
           Statistical Bureau, Ministry of Economic Development, Avenue of the Republic, Georgetown.
           1970-   1974. $4 Guyana.   308 p.
           Main sections:
               Agriculture   Miscellaneous (electricity production, houses erected,
               Banking, insurance and finance   imports of building materials, consumer price indexes,
               Crime and justice   production of specific commodities)
               Education   National accounts and balance of payments
               External trade   Population and vital statistics
               Labour   Transport and communications
               Migration   Weather
               Mining
           Time factor: the 1974 edition, published in 1976, has data for 1973 and 1974 and several earlier years in
               some tables.   A 1973 edition of the abstract was not published.
           §   En.

941   Quarterly statistical digest   (Statistical Bureau: Ministry of Economic Development)
           Statistical Bureau, Ministry of Economic Development, Avenue of the Republic, Georgetown.
           1960- $2 Guyana each issue.
           Contains data on weather, population and vital statistics, consumer price indices, foreign trade, building
               statistics (imports of building materials), internal trade (retail sales, retail sales index), transport
               and communications, (new registration of motor vehicles), industrial production (including electricity
               production and labour statistics).   December issues also have balance of payments and national
               income, and crime statistics.
           Time factor: each issue has runs of several years, quarters and months to the end of the quarter of the
               issue, and is published some six months later.
           §   En.

942   Economic survey of Guyana   (Statistical Bureau: Ministry of Economic Development)
           Statistical Bureau, Ministry of Economic Development, Avenue of the Republic, Georgetown.
           1965-   1975/1976. $3 Guyana.   100 p.
           Main sections:
               General review   Investment
               National income and product   Construction
               Agriculture (sugar, rice, livestock)   Banking and finance
               Mining   Retail sales and prices
               Manufacturing   Public finance
               Electricity production   Population and migration
               External trade   Prospect for the future
               Balance of payments
           Each of the above chapters has statistics interspersed with the text.
           Time factor: the 1975/1976 edition, published in 1978, has data for 1976 or 1975.
           §   En.

¶   B   -   Production

i.   Mines and mining

943   Annual report   (Geological Surveys and Mines Department, Ministry of Energy and Natural Resources)
       Geological Surveys and Mines Department, PO Box 1028, Georgetown.
       1949-   1975.   not priced.   36 p.
       Includes some statistics of mining production, etc.
       Time factor: the 1975 report was published in 1977.
       §   En.

       Refer also to 940, 942.

ii.   Agriculture, fisheries, forestry, etc

       Refer to 940, 942.

iii.   Industry

944   Indices of production, employment, hours and earnings   (Statistical Bureau: Ministry of Economic Development)
       Statistical Bureau, Ministry of Economic Development, Avenue of the Republic, Georgetown.
       1968/70-   1969/1975. $1.50 Guyana.   23 p.
       Outlines the methodology used in calculations, as well as including calculated indexes.
       Time factor: the 1969-1975 issue, with data for those years, was published in 1977.
       §   En.

       Refer also to 940, 941, 942.

iv.   Construction.

       Refer to 940, 942.

v.   Energy

       Refer to 940, 941, 942.

¶   C   -   External trade

945   Annual account relating to external trade   (Statistical Bureau: Ministry of Economic Development)
       Statistical Bureau, Ministry of Economic Development, Avenue of the Republic, Georgetown.
       1879-   1974. $3 Guyana.   439 p.
       Main tables show imports and exports arranged by commodity and sub-divided by countries of origin and
           destination.
       Time factor: the 1974 issue, published in 1977, has data for 1974.
       §   En.

946   Monthly account relating to external trade   (Statistical Bureau: Ministry of Economic Development)
       Statistical Bureau, Ministry of Economic Development, Avenue of the Republic, Georgetown.
       1955- $1.50 Guyana each issue.
       Main tables show imports and exports arranged by commodity and subdivided by countries of origin and
           destination.
       Time factor: each issue has data for that month and cumulative figures for the year to date, and is
           published about six months later.
       §   En.

GUYANA,   continued

¶   C,   continued.

947   Quarterly external trade with CARICOM and CARIFTA territories   (Statistical Bureau: Ministry of Economic
         Development)
         Statistical Bureau, Ministry of Economic Development, Avenue of the Republic, Georgetown.
         1968- $0.75 Guyana each issue.
         Contains details of trade with individual countries in the Caribbean Community and Caribbean Free Trade
             Area.
         Time factor: each issue has data for the quarter of the issue and cumulated figures for the year to date,
             and is published about six months after the end of that period.
         §   En.

         Refer also to 940, 941, 942.

¶   D   -   Internal distribution and service trades

         Refer to 941, 942.

¶   E   -   Population

948   Census of population

         Refer to 258 for the 1970 census of population of the Commonwealth Caribbean.   (Censuses have been
             taken since the 1840's).

949   Population and vital statistics report (Statistical Bureau, Ministry of Economic Development)
         Statistical Bureau, Ministry of Economic Development, Avenue of the Republic, Georgetown.
         1885-   1967. $1.50 Guyana.
         Contains data on births, marriages, deaths and other characteristics of the population.
         §   En.

950   International migration report   (Statistical Bureau: Ministry of Economic Development)
         Statistical Bureau, Ministry of Economic Development, Avenue of the Republic, Georgetown.
         1969-   1970. $1.50 Guyana.   53 p.
         Time factor: the 1970 report, published in 1972, has data for 1970.
         §   En.

         Refer also to 940, 941, 942.

¶   F   -   Social

i.   Standard of living

951   Household expenditure survey, 1969/70   (Ministry of Economic Development)
         Ministry of Economic Development, Avenue of the Republic, Georgetown.
                         not priced.   2 vols.
         The report of a survey that was aimed to develop a weighting pattern and market basket items for the
             consumer price index.   Includes consumer price index for 1970 to 1973.
         Time factor: published in 1975.
         §   En.

         Refer also to 940, 941.

¶   F,   continued

iii.   Education and leisure

952   A digest of educational statistics   (Planning Unit, Ministry of Education and Social Development)
         Ministry of Education and Social Development, 21 Brickdam, Georgetown.
         1966/67-   8th, 1973/74.   not priced.   207 p.
         Time factor: the 1973-1974 issue, published late 1975, has data for the 1973/74 academic year and also
              a ten-year review.
         §   En.

         Refer also to 940.

iv.   Justice

         Refer to 940.

¶   G   -   Finance

953   Quarterly review of financial statistics   (Statistical Bureau: Ministry of Economic Development)
         Statistical Bureau, Ministry of Economic Development, Avenue of the Republic, Georgetown.
         1966- $1 Guyana each issue.
         Contains data on public finance, banking and currency, insurance, co-operatives and credit.
         Time factor: each issue has annual and quarterly figures for several years to the quarter of the issue,
              and is published about six months later.
         §   En.

954   Economic bulletin   (Bank of Guyana)
         Bank of Guyana, PO Box 658, Georgetown.
         1967-   monthly.   not priced.
         Contains data on the activities of the bank, commercial banks, the banking system, other financial
              institutions, the securities market, public finance, balance of payments, and general economic
              conditions.
         Time factor: each issue has long runs of annual, quarterly and monthly figures to about two months prior
              to the date of the issue.
         §   En.

         Note: the 'annual report' of the bank contains a statistical annex with similar data to that published in
              the 'Economic bulletin'.

         Refer also to 940, 941, 942.

¶   H   -   Transport and communications

955   Report of the Transport & Harbours Department
         Transport and Harbours Department, Georgetown.
         1971-   1974.   not priced.   46 p.
         The report includes statistical data on the accounts, revenues and receipts of the department, and also
              statistics of traffic, etc.
         Time factor: the 1974 issue, published in 1975, has data for 1974.
         §   En.

         Refer also to 940, 941.

Central statistical office

956   Institut Haitien de Statistique   [Haitian Institute of Statistics],
Cité de l'Exposition,
Boulevard Harry Truman,
Port-au-Prince.

The Institute is the main collector and disseminator of economic and social statistics of Haiti.
Unpublished statistical data may be provided on request if available.

Libraries

The Institut Haitien de Statistique has a library which is open to the public.

Libraries and information centres abroad

Copies of the Institute's quarterly bulletin are sent to embassies abroad, including:

USA   Haitian Embassy, 4400 17th Street NW, Washington DC   (t (202) 723 7000)
Canada   Haitian Embassy, 150 Driveway N, Ottawa (t 232-2855)

Statistical publications

¶   A - General

957   Bulletin trimestriel de statistique   [Quarterly bulletin of statistics] (Institut Haitien de Statistique)
Institut Haitien de Statistique, Cité de l'Exposition, Boulevard Harry Truman, Port-au-Prince.
1951-   not priced.
Main sections:

Climate	Finance
Demography	Prices and cost of living
Tourism	Consumption
Housing	Employment, revenue & social security
Energy	Conflicts & accidents at work
Industrial production	Police & justice
Industrial & commercial establishments	Social & cultural affairs
Foreign trade	Miscellaneous (accidents, ministers, etc)
Transport & communications	

Time factor: each issue has runs of statistics to the end of that quarter and is published about eight or
nine months later.
§   Fr.

958   Guide économique de la République d'Haiti   [Economic guide to the Haitian Republic] (Institut Haitien de
Statistique)
Institut Haitien de Statistique, Cité de l'Exposition, Boulevard Harry Truman, Port-au-Prince.
                not priced.   515 p.
Contains data on climate, demography, tourism, housing, health, education, energy, agriculture and
fisheries, mines and quarries, industrial production, industrial and commercial establishments,
internal trade and services, foreign trade, national accounts, transport and communications, finance,
banking, insurance, prices and cost of living, consumption, employment, wages, social security,
conflicts at work, police and justice, social and cultural affairs, etc.
Time factor: this edition was published in December 1971 and has long runs of figures to 1970.   An
earlier edition was published in 1964.
§   Fr.

¶ A, continued

959 Bulletin trimestriel [Quarterly bulletin] (Secrétairerie d'Etat du Commerce et de l'Industrie)
    Secrétairerie d'Etat du Commerce et de l'Industrie, Port-au-Prince.
    1975-   not priced.
    Includes statistical tables on cost of living index for Port-au-Prince, wholesale prices of certain foodstuffs,
        industrial production, foreign trade, balance of payments, and air traffic.
    Time factor: each issue includes the latest data available.
    § Fr.

960 Recensement général de la République d'Haiti [General census of the Republic of Haiti] (Institut Haitien
    de Statistique)
    Institut Haitien de Statistique, Cité de l'Exposition, Boulevard Harry Truman, Port-au-Prince.
    1950- 1950.   not priced.   5 vols.
    Contains data on demography, economy, family and housing, agriculture and livestock.
    § Fr.

961 Enquête socio-économique, (avril 1970) [Socio-economic survey, April 1970)] (Institut Haitien de
    Statistique)
    Institut Haitien de Statistique, Cité de l'Exposition, Boulevard Harry Truman, Port-au-Prince.
               not priced.   60 p.
    Contains the first results of the survey on housing, population, agriculture, livestock, family expenditure
        for the country, for metropolitan areas, and for rural zones.
    Time factor: the first results of the survey were published in 1975.
    § Fr.

962 Dossier d'information économique: Haiti [Dossier of economic information: Haiti] (Service des études et
    questions internationales, Ministère de la Coopération)
    Ministère de la Coopération, 27 rue Oudinot, Paris 7me, France.
               not priced.   179 p.
    Includes a statistical annex on population, education, household, finance, production, etc.
    Time factor: published late 1976, the publication contains data for several years to 1972 or 1973.
    § Fr.

¶ B - Production

    Refer to 957, 958, 959, 960.

¶ C - External trade

963 Annuaire du commerce extérieur d'Haiti: importations, exportations [Foreign trade yearbook for Haiti:
    imports, exports] (Administration Générale des Douanes)
    Administration Générale des Douanes, Port-au-Prince.
    1955- 1975/76.   not priced.   173 p.
    Main tables show imports and exports arranged by commodity and subdivided by countries of origin and
        destination.
    Time factor: the 1975/76 issue, published late 1977, has data for the fiscal year 1975/76.
    § Fr.

    Refer also to 957, 959.

HAITI,   continued

¶   D   -   Internal distribution and service trades

Refer to 957, 958.

¶   E   -   Population

Refer to 957, 958, 960.

¶   F   -   Social

Refer to 957, 958, 961, 962.

¶   G   -   Finance

964   Estimations et projections sectorielles de l'investissement   [Estimates and projections of investment]   (Institut
Haitien de Statistique)
Institut Haitien de Statistique, Cité de l'Exposition, Boulevard Harry Truman, Port-au-Prince.
not priced.   82 p.
Time factor: published in November 1975.
§   Fr.

Refer also to 957, 958.

¶   H   -   Transport and communications

Refer to 957, 958, 959.

HONDURAS

Central statistical office

965   Dirección General de Estadística y Censos   [General Office of Statistics and Census],
Avenida Centenario 6Y8 Calles,
Comayaguela DC.
† 22-8448 22-8450.

The Dirección General de Estadística y Censos is responsible for the collection, analysis and publication of the official statistics of Honduras.

Libraries

The Dirección General de Estadística y Censos has a library which is open to the public for reference to statistical publications.

Libraries and information services abroad

The publications of the Dirección General de Estadística are sent to Honduras embassies abroad, including:

United Kingdom Embassy of Honduras, 48 George Street, London W1. († 01-486 3380)
USA   Embassy of Honduras, 4301 Connecticut Avenue NW, Washington DC.
        († (202) 966 7700)

Bibliographies

966   Inventario estadístico nacional al 31 diciembre de 1969   [National inventory of statistics as at 31 December 1969] (Dirección General de Estadística y Censos)
Published in 1970 this detailed publication includes a list of organisations then producing statistics and a list of the statistics produced, arranged by general subject subdivided by the organisation responsible, details of tables, and title of publication.

The Dirección General de Estadistica y Censos also issues a list of its publications from time to time.
Publications are not priced but a charge of £2 or US$1 is made to cover postage outside Honduras.

Statistical publications

¶ A - General

967   Anuario estadístico   [Statistical yearbook] (Dirección General de Estadística y Censos)
Dirección General de Estadística y Censos, Avenida Centenario 6Y8 Calles, Comayaguela.
1952- 1976. not priced. 220 p.
Main sections:

Climate	Banking and money
Population	Income & expenditure of central government
Vital statistics	Electrical energy and construction
Social security	Agriculture and livestock
Public health	Tourism
Education	Transport and communications
Consumer price indices	

Time factor: the 1976 edition, published in 1978, has data for 1976 and earlier years in a few tables.
§ Es.

¶   A,   continued

968   Compendio estadístico   [Statistical compendium]   (Dirección General de Estadística y Censos in collaboration
            with Consejo Superior de Planificación Económica)
        Dirección General de Estadística y Censos, Avenida Centenario 6Y8 Calles, Comayaguela.
        1966- 1967/68.   not priced.   266 p.
        Contains data on demography, housing, public health and social assistance, education, national accounts,
            banking and money, public sector, external trade, agriculture, industry, electricity, and transport.
        Time factor: the 1967/68 edition, published in 1970, has long runs of figures to 1967.
        §   Es.

969   Honduras en cifras   [Honduras in figures]   (Banco Central de Honduras)
        Banco Central de Honduras, Tegucigalpa.
        1971/73- 1972-1974.   not priced.   26 p.
        Contains data on demography, cooperatives, tourism, national product and consumption, electricity and
            water, transport and communications, education, balance of payments and foreign trade, money,
            public finance, and consumer prices.
        Time factor: the 1973-1974 edition, published in 1974, has data for the years 1972, 1973 and estimates
            for 1974.
        §   Es.

970   Boletín estadístico   [Statistical bulletin]   (Banco Central de Honduras)
        Banco Central de Honduras, Tegucigalpa.
        1951- monthly.   not priced.
        Includes statistical tables on money and banking, public finance, foreign trade, national accounts, and
            balance of payments.
        Time factor: each issue has runs of figures to about three months prior to the date of the issue.
        §   Es.

    ¶   B   -   Production

    ii.   Agriculture, fisheries, forestry

971   Censo nacional agropecuario   [National agricultural census]   (Dirección General de Estadística y Censos)
        Dirección General de Estadística y Censos, Avenida Centenario 6Y8 Calles, Comayaguela.
        1952- 3rd, 1974.   not priced.
        Volumes published are:
            Cifras preliminares: superficie sembrada y producción de maíz, frijol, arroz y maicillo, ganada,
                bovino y porcino por departamento y municipio [Preliminary figures: production of crops and
                livestock by department, and municipality]
            Encuesta de pronóstico de granos básicos [Survey of predictions for basic cereals]
            Encuesta nacional de tasas ganaderas [National survey of livestock prices]
            Esquema del plan nacional de estadísticas agropecuarias continuas [Plan for continuing agricultural
                and livestock statistics]
            Censo nacional agropecuario. Tomo V: cultivos permanentes [Vol V: permanent crops]
            Censo nacional agropecuario. Tomo VI: ganados [Vol VI: livestock]
        Time factor: published between 1975 and 1977.
        §   Es.

972   Información agropecuaria: precios recibidos por el productor e indices de precios   [Agricultural information:
            prices received by the producer and price indices]   (Dirección General de Estadística y Censos)
        Dirección General de Estadística y Censos, Avenida Centenario 6Y8 Calles, Comayaguela.
        1950/58- quarterly.   not priced.
        Time factor: ceased publication with the issue for the 1st quarter of 1964.
        §   Es.

        Refer also to 967, 968.

¶   B,   continued

iii.   Industry

973   Censo: la industria en Honduras   [Census of industry in Honduras]   (Dirección General de Estadística y Censos)
        Dirección General de Estadística y Censos, Avenida Centenario 6Y8 Calles, Comayaguela.
        1966- 1966.   not priced.   188 p.
        Contains data on manufacturing establishments, including the number of establishments, number of
            employees, occupations of employees, wages and salaries, the value of materials used, power used,
            production and sales, etc.
        Time factor: published in 1969.
        §   Es.

974   Investigación industrial   [Industrial enquiry]   (Dirección General de Estadística y Censos)
        Dirección General de Estadística y Censos, Avenida Centenario 6Y8 Calles, Comayaguela.
        1956/57- 1975.   not priced.   c 150 p.
        Contains data on number of establishments; materials used; value of production; value of buildings,
            machinery, vehicles, etc; sales; depreciation; reserves, etc.
        Time factor: the 1975 issue, published in 1977, has data for 1975.
        §   Es.

        Note: an earlier title 'Estadísticas industriales' was published from 1950 to 1956.

        Note 2: an industrial directory 'Directorio industrial' has also been published annually since 1960, the
            latest issue being for 1977.

        Refer also to 968.

iv.   Construction

        Refer to 967.

v.   Energy

975   Datos estadísticos   [Statistical data]   (Empresa Nacional de Energía Electrica)
        Empresa Nacional de Energía Electrica, Comayaguela.
        1973- 1976.   not priced.   71 p.
        Contains data on capacity installed, production and distribution of energy; investment, and economic-
            financial information.
        Time factor: the 1976 issue, published in 1977, has data for 1976.
        §   Es.

        Refer also to 967, 968, 969.

¶   C - External trade

976   Comercio exterior   [Foreign trade]   (Dirección General de Estadística y Censos)
        Dirección General de Estadística y Censos, Avenida Centenario 6Y8 Calles, Comayaguela.
        1955- 1976.   not priced.   2 vols.
        Main tables show detailed statistics of imports and exports arranged by commodities and subdivided by
            countries of origin and destination.
        Time factor: the 1976 issue, published in 1977, has data for 1976.
        §   Es.

¶ C, continued

977 Avances de comercio exterior [Advance figures of foreign trade] (Dirección General de Estadística y Censos)
    Dirección General de Estadística y Censos, Avenida Centenario 6Y8 Calles, Comayaguela.
    1961-   quarterly.   not priced.
    Time factor: not published every quarter.   Each issue published has cumulated figures for the year to the date of the issue, and is published some six months later.
    § Es.

978 Comercio exterior de Honduras con Centroamérica [Foreign trade of Honduras with Central America] (Dirección General de Estadística y Censos)
    Dirección General de Estadística y Censos, Avenida Centenario 6Y8 Calles, Comayaguela.
    1958/61- 1970.   not priced.
    Time factor: the 1970 issue, published in 1972 has data for 1970.
    § Es.

979 Numeros indices de comercio exterior [Index numbers of foreign trade] (Dirección General de Estadística y Censos)
    Dirección General de Estadística y Censos, Avenida Centenario 6Y8 Calles, Comayaguela.
    1957/58- 1969/70.   not priced.
    § Es.

    Refer also to 968, 969, 970.

¶ D - Internal distribution and service trades

980 Investigación comercial [Commercial enquiry] (Dirección General de Estadística y Censos)
    Dirección General de Estadística y Censos, Avenida Centenario 6Y8 Calles, Comayaguela.
    1954/57- 1965.   not priced.
    Contains data on the number of establishments, value of sales, finances, etc.
    § Es.

    Note: a commercial directory, 'Directorio comercial', was also issued for 1960, 1963, and 1965, and a directory of services, 'Directorio de servicios' in 1960.

    Refer also to 967.

¶ E - Population

981 Censo nacional de población y vivienda [Census of population and housing] (Dirección General de Estadística y Censos)
    Dirección General de Estadística y Censos, Avenida Centenario 6Y8 Calles, Comayaguela.
    1881- 1974.   not priced.
    Volumes published are:
        Cifras preliminares [Preliminary figures]
        Resultados muestra [Sample results]
        Población y vivienda por departamento y municipio [Population and housing for departments and municipalities]
        Censo nacional de población, Tomo I: resúmen por departamento y municipio [National census of population, Vol I: summary for departments and municipalities]
        Censo nacional de población, Tomo II: sumaria [National census of population, Vol II: abstract]
        Censo nacional de vivienda, [National census of housing (3 vols)]
        Area approximada de los municipios, número de habitantes y número de viviendas de la República de Honduras [Approximate area of the municipalities, numbers of inhabitants and number of habitations in the Republic of Honduras]
    Time factor: reports published between 1974 and 1977.
    § Es.

¶   E,   continued

982   Estadísticas vitales   [Vital statistics]   (Dirección General de Estadística y Censos)
          Dirección General de Estadística y Censos, Avenida Centenario 6Y8 Calles, Comayaguela.
          1966-   1972.   not priced.
          Time factor: the 1972 issue, published in 1972, has data for 1971.
          §   Es.

          Refer also to 967, 968, 969.

¶   F   -   Social

i.   Standard of living

983   Encuesta de ingresos y gastos familiares, 1967-1968   [Survey of family incomes and expenditure, 1967-1968]
          (Dirección General de Estadística y Censos)
          Dirección General de Estadística y Censos, Avenida Centenario 6Y8 Calles, Comayaguela.
          Time factor: published in 1970.
          §   Es.

          Refer also to 967.

ii.   Health and welfare

          Refer to 967, 968.

iii.   Education and leisure

984   Estadísticas educacionales   [Educational statistics]   (Dirección General de Estadística y Censos)
          Dirección General de Estadística y Censos, Avenida Centenario 6Y8 Calles, Comayaguela.
          1956-   1970.   not priced.
          Contains data on numbers of establishments, pupils, teachers, finances, etc, for all levels of education.
          Time factor: the 1970 issue, published in 1972, has data for 1970.
          §   Es.

          Refer also to 967, 968, 969.

¶   G   -   Finance

985   Memoria   [Report]   (Banco Central de Honduras)
          Banco Central de Honduras, Tegucigalpa.
                 1973.   not priced.   139 p.
          Contains mainly financial and banking statistics, but also has a few economic statistics, particularly
                 foreign trade.
          Time factor: the 1973 report, published late 1974, has data to 1973.
          §   Es.

          Refer also to 967, 968, 969, 970.

¶   H   -   Transport and communications.

          Refer to 967, 968, 969.

Central statistical office

986   Department of Statistics,
      9 Swallowfield Road,
      Kingston 5.
      † 93.62175.

The Department of Statistics is the organisation responsible for the collection, analysis and publication of most of the economic statistics of Jamaica. Available but unpublished statistical information can be supplied and there is no charge involved, except in cases where the volume of data requested is great.

Libraries

The Department of Statistics has a reference library which is open to the public Mondays to Thursdays, 8.30 to 17.00, and Fridays, 8.30 to 16.00 hours. The collection includes publications of Jamaica, of other countries, and of international organisations. The library also has available for consultation unpublished tables from the 1970 census of population.

A number of public, government and educational libraries in Jamaica receive publications of the Department of Statistics.

Libraries and information services abroad

Publications of the Department of Statistics are available for reference in the office of the Jamaican information services in various countries, including those at the following addresses:
    United Kingdom High Commissioner for Jamaica, 50 St James's Street, London SW1A 1JS
                                                 († 01-499 8600)
    Canada   High Commissioner for Jamaica, 85 Range Road, Ottawa (†233 9311)

Bibliographies

The Department of Statistics issues a sales list of its current publications from time to time.

Statistical publications

¶ A - General

987   Statistical yearbook of Jamaica (Department of Statistics)
        Department of Statistics, 9 Swallowfield Road, Kingston 5.
        1973- 5th, 1977. J$20. 690 p.
        Main sections:

Physiography	External trade
History and government	Price indices
Population and vital statistics	Economic aggregates
Health and sanitation	Banking and credit
Pensions	Central and local government expenditure
Education	Labour and employment
Justice and crime	Electricity and water supply
Transport and communications	Agriculture, forestry, and fisheries
Housing and construction	Mineral industry
Tourism	Manufacturing industry

        Time factor: the 1977 edition, published in 1978, has the latest data available at the time of publication.
        § En.

988   Statistical abstract   (Department of Statistics)
        Department of Statistics, 9 Swallowfield Road, Kingston 5.
        1947-   1977.   J$3.   197 p.
        Main sections:

Demography	Social security
Migration	Electricity and water
Labour and employment	Tourism
Education	Banking and finance
Justice and crime	Production
Transport and communications	Indices of consumer prices and trade
Health and sanitation	External trade
Housing	Economic aggregates

        Time factor: the 1977 edition, published early 1978, has data for 1977 or the latest available and one
           or two retrospective years.
        §   En.

989   Quarterly abstract of statistics   (Department of Statistics)
        Department of Statistics, 9 Swallowfield Road, Kingston 5.
        1947-   J$1.20 or J$4.80 yr.
        Contains data on climate, demography, health, housing, labour and employment, tourism, transport and
           communications, banking and finance, indices of consumer prices, production, and external trade.
           Supplements the 'Statistical abstract' (988) and the 'Statistical yearbook...' (987).
        Time factor: each issue has data for the quarter of the issue and a few earlier figures and is published
           some nine months later.
        §   En.

990   Facts on Jamaica   (Department of Statistics)
        Department of Statistics, 9 Swallowfield Road, Kingston 5.
                 not priced.   8 vols.
        A series of reports containing information from the first 'Statistical yearbook' (987).   Titles of the
           volumes are Trade and price indices, Tourism, Population and vital statistics, Physiography, Mineral
           production, History and government, Electricity and water supply, and Education.
        Time factor: published in 1973 the volumes contain data for several years to 1972.
        §   En.

991   Pocketbook of statistics   (Department of Statistics)
        Department of Statistics, 9 Swallowfield Road, Kingston 5.
        1977-   1977.   J$2.   125 p.
        A handy reference guide of abridged statistical information on major areas of interest, such as population,
           education, migration, labour, and employment.
        Time factor: the 1977 edition, published early 1978, has data for 1976 and one or two earlier years.
        §   En.

992   Economic and social survey, Jamaica   (National Planning Agency)
        National Planning Agency, 39 Barbados Avenue, Kingston.
        1957-   1974.   not priced.   278 p.
        Includes statistical tables in the text covering national accounts, balance of payments and external trade,
           banking and finance, central government expenditure and receipts, consumer prices, labour force -
           employment and industrial relations, agriculture, mineral industry, tourism, manufacturing and
           processing, construction and installation, utilities - communications and transport, population and
           migration, social development and welfare, social defence, health, housing, education and training,
           and scientific research.
        Time factor: the 1974 edition, published in 1976, has data for 1973 and earlier years in some tables.
        §   En.

¶   A,   continued

993   Statistical digest   (Bank of Jamaica)
         Bank of Jamaica, PO Box 621, Kingston.
         1969-   monthly.   not priced.
         Contains data on money and banking, public finance, foreign trade and international payments, and
              general statistics (consumer price indices, production of selected commodites, other production).
         Time factor: each issue has long runs of annual and monthly figures to about three months prior to the
              date of the issue.
         §   En.

994   Monthly review   (Bank of Jamaica)
         Bank of Jamaica, PO Box 621, Kingston.
                             not priced.
         Contains selected economic indicators on banking, money and credit, non-bank financial institutions,
              financial survey, money and capital markets, public finance, external assets, external trade,
              tourism and remittances, consumer prices, production, labour market, instalment credit, other
              credit, international currency and international developments.   Statistics and statistical tables
              are included in the text.
         Time factor: each issue has data to about two months prior to the date of the issue.
         §   En.

         Note: the bank also issues a quarterly 'Bulletin' which is mainly textual but includes a few tables in the
              text, and 'Report and statement of accounts' which deals mainly with the activities of the bank in
              the past year but also has a few economic statistics.

¶   B   -   Production

995   Production statistics   (Department of Statistics)
         Department of Statistics, 9 Swallowfield Road, Kingston 5,
         1972-   1977.   J$1.   75 p.
         Contains statistics on the volume and value of production in large establishments in some sectors of the
              economy, indices of production, value of production by sectors, volume and value of production by
              product, production - volume (agriculture, mining, manufacturing, electricity, and construction).
         Time factor: the 1977 issue, published mid-1978, has data for the years 1968 to 1977, or for 1976 and
              1977 in some tables.
         §   En.

         Note: there is also a 4-page quarterly bulletin (J$0.20   or   J$0.80 yr) which to some extent up-dates
              the annual.

i.   Mines and mining

         Refer to 987, 990, 992.

ii.   Agriculture, fisheries, forestry, etc

996   Census of agriculture   (Department of Statistics)
         Department of Statistics, 9 Swallowfield Road, Kingston 5.
         1943-   1968/69.   J$0.60 each vol.   4 vols in 8.
         The report of the census includes data on climate, area and number of farms, employment, land tenure
              and ownership, land utilisation, agricultural techniques, and production.
         Time factor: the results were published in 1973 and relates to the 1968/69 crop year.
         §   En.

JAMAICA,   continued

¶   B.ii,   continued

997   Annual report   (Ministry of Agriculture)
          Ministry of Agriculture, Kingston.
          1952-   1974/75.   not priced.   97 p.
          Contains some tables in the text, including agriculture, soil, crops, livestock, fisheries, forestry, etc.
          Time factor: the 1974/75 report has data for 1974 or 1974/75 and one or two earlier years.
          §   En.

998   Report of the Coconut Industry Board: Jamaica.
          Coconut Industry Board, 18 Waterloo Road, Kingston.
          (annual)   1974/75.   not priced.   28 p.
          Includes data on crops as well as the accounts of the Board.
          Time factor: the 1974/75 report has data for several years to the 1974/75 crop year, and was published in
              1976.
          §   En.

999   Sample survey of the fishing industry in Jamaica, 1973   (Agriculture Planning Board, Ministry of Agriculture)
          Ministry of Agriculture, Kingston.
                            not priced.   not paged.
          Contains data on fish caught and catch per unit effort, average retail prices, number of fishing trips,
              quantity caught by type of fish, etc.
          Time factor: published mid-1975.
          §   En.

1000   Annual report   (Forest Department)
          Agricultural Information Service, Ministry of Agriculture, Kingston.
          1965/66-   1975.   not priced.   20 p.
          Includes a few statistics on forest development, as well as information relating to the Department.
          Time factor: the 1975 report was published late 1975.
          §   En.

          Refer also to 987, 992.

    iii.   Industry

          Refer to 987, 988, 989, 992.

    iv.   Construction

1001   Abstract of building and construction statistics   (Department of Statistics)
          Department of Statistics, 9 Swallowfield Road, Kingston 5.
          (annual)   1977.   J$1.50.   32 p.
          Section I has indicators of output, dwellings completed, gross domestic product of the construction
              industry, etc.   Section II has indices of output - building materials, materials imported, labour
              force, mortgages, bank loans, quantity and value of production of building materials.
          Time factor: the 1977 issue, published 1978, has data for 1977 and some earlier years.
          §   En.

1002   Building activity in Jamaica   (Department of Statistics)
          Department of Statistics, 9 Swallowfield Road, Kingston 5.
          1961/65-   4th, 1967-1975.   J$0.70.   60 p.
          Includes data on permits granted, dwellings completed, new mortgages, imports of building materials,
              labour force, etc.
          Time factor: the 1967-1975 issue, with data for those years, was published in 1976.
          §   En.

¶   B.iv,   continued

Refer also to 992.

v.   Energy

Refer to 987, 988, 989.

¶   C   -   External trade

1003   External trade   (Department of Statistics)
Department of Statistics, 9 Swallowfield Road, Kingston 5.
1947-   1977 (provisional)   J$2.50.   364 p.
Main tables show statistics of imports, exports and re-exports arranged by commodity and subdivided by
    countries of origin and destination.
Time factor: the 1977 issue, published mid-1978, has provisional data for 1977.
§   En.

1004   External trade   (Department of Statistics)
Department of Statistics, 9 Swallowfield Road, Kingston 5.
1954-   quarterly.   J$1.75 or J$7 yr.
Main tables show imports, exports and re-exports arranged by commodity and sub-divided by countries of
    origin and destination.
Time factor: each issue has cumulated figures for the year to the end of that quarter and is published
    about six months later.
§   En.

1005   External trade...summary tables (preliminary)   (Department of Statistics)
Department of Statistics, 9 Swallowfield Road, Kingston 5.
1947-   monthly.   J$0.50 or J$6 yr.
Main tables show imports, exports and re-exports arranged by commodity and subdivided by countries of
    origin and destination.
Time factor: each issue has data for that month and cumulated figures for the year to date, and is
    published four or five months later.
§   En.

Note: there is also a 2-page monthly bulletin titled 'External trade' (J$0.20 or J$2.40 yr).

1006   Indices of external trade   (Department of Statistics)
Department of Statistics, 9 Swallowfield Road, Kingston 5.
1966-   1969-1977.   J$0.70.   38 p.
Contains indicators of movement of imports and exports, of their relative prices and values,
Time factor: the 1969-1977 issue, with data for those years, was published early 1978.
§   En.

Refer also to 987, 989, 990, 994.

¶   D   -   Internal distribution and service trades

1007   Travel statistics - Jamaica   (Jamaica Tourist Board)
         Jamaica Tourist Board, 80 Harbour Street, Kingston.
         1968- 1976.   not priced.   35 p.
         Contains data on number of visitors, finances, long and short stays, cruise passengers, armed forces,
             stop-overs (air and sea), permanent residents, number of hotels, etc.
         Time factor: the 1976 issue, published early 1977, has data for 1976 and several earlier years, including
             some monthly figures.
         §   En.

1008   Visitors statistics   (Jamaica Tourist Board)
         Jamaica Tourist Board, 80 Harbour Street, Kingston.
         A 5-page updating of the above.

         Refer also to 987, 988, 990.

¶   E   -   Population

1009   Population census   (Department of Statistics)
         Department of Statistics, 9 Swallowfield Road, Kingston 5.
         1881- 1970.
         A number of preliminary reports were issued by the Department, such as 'Preliminary report by parish,
             sex and age; households by parish and size', 'Preliminary report by constituencies and type of house-
             hold' but for the final reports refer to 258.

1010   Population trends and housing needs   (Department of Statistics)
         Department of Statistics, 9 Swallowfield Road, Kingston 5.
                        J$0.70.   43 p.
         A brief review abstracted from the population censuses of 1960 and 1970.
         Time factor: published in 1974.
         §   En.

1011   Demographic statistics   (Department of Statistics)
         Department of Statistics, 9 Swallowfield Road, Kingston 5.
         1970- 1977.   J$1.   45 p.
         Contains annual and quarterly data on the demographic characteristics of the population - births, deaths,
             marriages and divorces.   Also includes data on external migration, end of year population estimates,
             and family planning statistics.
         Time factor: the 1977 issue, published early 1978, has data for 1977.
         §   En.

1012   Population and vital statistics: Jamaica, 1832-1964: a historical perspective   (Kalman Tekse)
         Department of Statistics, 9 Swallowfield Road, Kingston 5.
                        J$6.   340 p.
         Contains data on population for 1844-1964 and vital statistics for 1879-1964.
         Time factor: the volume was published in 1974.
         §   En.

¶   E,   continued

1013   The labour force   (Department of Statistics)
            Department of Statistics, 9 Swallowfield Road, Kingston 5.
            1972-   1977.   J$0.70.   133 p.
            Contains data on population, the employed, the unemployed by occupations, hours worked, etc.
            Time factor: the 1977 issue, published mid-1978, has data for 1977 and two or three earlier years.
            §   En.

1014   Employment, earnings and hours in large establishments   (Department of Statistics)
            Department of Statistics, 9 Swallowfield Road, Kingston 5.
            1963/64-   1977.   J$1.   45 p.
            Contains data on employment, earnings and hours worked in large establishments in the mining,
                manufacturing, electricity and private construction sectors; and also for the distribution, transport
                and other selected service sectors.
            Time factor: the 1977 issue, published in 1978, has data for 1977 and also for 1976 in some tables.
            §   En.

            Note: a quarterly 4-page bulletin titled 'Employment, earnings in large establishments' is also available
                (J$0.20 or J$0.80 yr).

            Refer also to 987, 988, 989, 990.

    ¶   F   -   Social

    i.   Standard of living

1015   Consumer price indices: annual review   (Department of Statistics)
            Department of Statistics, 9 Swallowfield Road, Kingston 5.
            1972-   1977.   J$1.   54 p.
            Time factor: the 1977 issue, published mid-1978, has data for 1977.
            §   En.

1016   Consumer price indices   (Department of Statistics)
            Department of Statistics, 9 Swallowfield Road, Kingston 5.
            1968-   monthly.   J$0.50 or J$6 yr.
            Time factor: each issue has data to the month of the issue and is published the following month.
            §   En.

            Note: there is also a 2-page up-dating monthly bulletin with the same title (J$0.20 or J$2.40 yr).

1017   Consumer price indices: percentage movements   (Department of Statistics)
            Department of Statistics, 9 Swallowfield Road, Kingston 5.
            1970/75-   2nd, 1970-1978.   J$1.75.   211 p.
            Monthly consumer price indices, composite and by areas, on the January 1975 base.
            Time factor: the 1970-1978 issue was published mid-1978.
            §   En.

            Refer also to 987, 988, 989, 992.

    ii.   Health and welfare

            Refer to 987, 988, 989.

¶   F.iii.   Education and leisure

1018   Education statistics: an annual review of the education sector   (Ministry of Education)
          Ministry of Education, PO Box 498, Kingston.
          1974/75-   1975-76.   not priced.   114 p.
          Contains statistics of plants, teachers, students, curricula, examinations, and finances.
          Time factor: the 1975-76 issue, published in 1977, has data for the academic year 1975/76.
          §   En.

          Note: the annual report of the Ministry also includes some statistics.

          Refer also to 987, 988, 990, 991.

    iv.   Justice

          Refer to 987, 988.

¶   G   -   Finance

1019   Monetary statistics   (Department of Statistics)
          Department of Statistics, 9 Swallowfield Road, Kingston 5.
          1966-   1977.   J$1.   61 p.
          Contains annual, quarterly and monthly data on the major financial institutions operating in Jamaica.
             There are five sections - banking, non-banking, money and the capital market, government
             financing, and miscellaneous.
          Time factor: the 1977 issue, published mid-1978, has data for 1977 and a few earlier years.
          §   En.

          Note: this title was issued quarterly until the 1972 issue.

1020   Cost output and investment survey programme   (Department of Statistics)
          Department of Statistics, 9 Swallowfield Road, Kingston 5.
          A 'massive' survey started in 1965.   Volumes of results published so far are:
             Vol 1   Sources and uses of funds in corporate establishments (flow of funds accounts) 1962-1966
                (J$1)
             Vol 2.1   Production costs and output in large establishments manufacturing (provisional report) 1964
                (J$1.50)
             Vol 2.2   Production cost and output in large and small agriculture (provisional report) 1964.   (J$1)
             Vol 2.3   Production costs and output in construction and installation and real estate, 1964-66.   (J$1)
          and there are to be other reports covering mining, small manufacture, investment in non-corporate
             establishments, and a general report.
          §   En.

          Refer also to 987, 988, 989, 992, 993, 994.

    ii.   Public finance

1021   National income and product   (Department of Statistics)
          Department of Statistics, 9 Swallowfield Road, Kingston 5.
          1958-   1977.   J$1.50.   78 p.
          Contains estimates of the national accounts, including gross domestic product, gross national product, per
             capita indicators, etc.
          Time factor: the 1977 issue, published mid-1978, has data for 1977 and some earlier years.
          §   En.

          Note: there is also a preliminary report (J$1).

JAMAICA, continued

¶ G.ii, continued

1022 Balance of payments (Bank of Jamaica)
        Bank of Jamaica, PO Box 621, Kingston.
        1961- 1977. not priced. 69 p.
        Time factor: the 1977 issue, published mid-1978, has data for 1976, preliminary figures for 1977, and
           also for some earlier years.
        § En.

¶ H - Transport and communications

    Refer to 987, 988, 989, 992.

Central Statistical office

1023   Institut National de la Statistique et des Etudes Economiques   [National Institute for Statistics and
                Economic Research],
        Pointe de Jaham Schoelcher, (BP 605),
        97261 Fort-de-France Cedex.
        t 71.71.79.

        INSEE in Martinique is a departmental service of the French INSEE.   It is concerned with the collection,
analysis and publication of social and economic statistics relating to Martinique.

Libraries

        INSEE, referred to above, in Martinique has a library which is open for reference from Mondays to Fridays
from 7.00 to 13.00 and also on Mondays to Thursdays from 14.30 to 17.30 hours.

Statistical publications

¶   A - General

1024   Annuaire statistique la Martinique   [Statistical yearbook of Martinique]   (Institut National de la Statistique
                et des Etudes Economiques)
        INSEE, BP 605, 97261 Fort-de-France Cedex.
        1952/56-   1969/72.   Fr 30.   170 p.
        Main sections:

Geography	Fisheries
Climate	Industry
Demography	Transport and communications
Population	Foreign trade
Health and social aid	Prices, wages & social security
Education	Money, credit
Justice	Public finance
Elections	Economic accounts
Agriculture-forestry-livestock	

        Time factor: the 1969/72 edition, published in 1973, has data for the years 1969 to 1972 and also some
                earlier years in some tables.   A 1973-1976 edition is in preparation.
        §   Fr.

1025   Comptes définitifs de la Martinique   [Final accounts of Martinique]   (Institut National de la Statistique et
                des Etudes Economiques)
        INSEE, BP 605, 97261 Fort-de-France Cedex.
        1965/67-   1968 à 1973.   Fr 3.   24 p.
        Contains textual information on the economy of Martinique and statistical tables of resources and the use
                of goods and services; analysis of production by industry; statistical data on enterprises, administration
                and houses; and foreign trade.
        Time factor: the 1968-1973 edition, with data for those years, was published in 1975.
        §   Fr.

1026   Informations statistiques rapides   [Rapid statistical information]   (INSEE, Service Départemental de Martinique)
        INSEE, BP 605, 97261 Fort-de-France Cedex.
        1970-   monthly.   Fr 3 each issue.
        §   Fr.

¶ A,   continued

1027   Bulletin de statistique [Statistical bulletin] (INSEE, Service Départemental de Martinique)
          INSEE, BP 605, 97261 Fort-de-France Cedex.
          1960-   quarterly.   Fr 3 each issue.
          Contains data on climate, demography, agriculture, energy, building and public works, transport,
               tourism, enterprises, prices, wages, social security and assistance, finance, and foreign trade.
          Time factor: each issue has data for the last six months and monthly averages for the last two years up
               to the date of the issue.   Currently there is a delay before publication of over six months but it is
               hoped to reduce the gap shortly.
          §   Fr.

¶   B - Production

          Refer to 1024, 1025, 1026.

¶   C - External trade

          Refer to 1024, 1025, 1026.

¶   D - Internal distribution and service trades

          Refer to 1025, 1026.

¶   E - Population

1028   L'emploi en Martinique: résultats des enquêtes de 1971 et 1972   [Employment in Martinique: results of surveys
               of 1971 and 1972]   (Institut National de la Statistique et des Etudes Economiques)
          INSEE, PO Box 605, 97261 Fort-de-France Cedex.
          1974.   Fr 20.   134p.
          §   Fr.

          Refer also to 1024, 1027.

¶   F - Social

          Refer to 1024, 1027.

     i.   Standard of living

1029   Les revenues des ménages en Martinique: résultats des enquêtes de 1971 et 1972   [Household incomes in
               Martinique: results of the surveys of 1971 and 1972]   (Institut National de la Statistique et des Etudes
               Economiques)
          INSEE, BP 605, 97261 Fort-de-France Cedex.
                              Fr 20.   54 p.
          Time factor: the results of the survey were published in 1974.
          §   Fr.

1030   Les salaires à la Martinique en 1971   [Wages in Martinique in 1971]   (Institut National de la Statistique et
               des Etudes Economiques)
          INSEE, BP 605, 97261 Fort-de-France Cedex.
                              not priced. 41 p.
          Time factor: the report was published in 1973
          §   Fr.

MARTINIQUE,   continued

¶   F.i,   continued

1031   Salaires et pouvoir d'achat en Martinique depuis 1966   [Wages and purchasing power in Martinique since
            1966] (Institut National de la Statistique et des Etudes Economiques)
          INSEE, BP 605, 97261 Fort-de-France Cedex.
                          Fr 5.   25 p.
          Time factor: covers the years 1966 to 1973.
          §   Fr.

¶   G - Finance

        Refer to 1024, 1027.

¶   H - Transport and communications

        Refer to 1024, 1027.

Central statistical office

1032   Dirección General de Estadística   [Central Office of Statistics],
          Secretaría de Programación y Presupuesto   [Secretariat of Programme and Budget],
          Dr Erazo no 85,
          Despacho 411,
          México 1, DF.
          t 761-36-84 & 761-38-25.

          The Secretaría de Programación y Presupuesto is by law the national statistical office, the work of
          collection, analysis and publication being conducted by the Dirección General de Estadística.

Libraries

          The Secretaría de Programación y Presupuesto has a library at Balderas 71, México 1, (t 585-01-48)
          which is open to the public for reference from 9.00 to 14.30 and from 16.00 to 19.00, Monday to Friday,
          except for vacation periods from 15th to 30th May and 15th to 30th December each year.   The library has
          statistical publications of Mexico, approximately 62 other countries and the most important international
          organisations.   The staff of the library speak Spanish.

Libraries and information services abroad

          Mexican embassies abroad are provided with the principal statistical publications of the Dirección General
          de Estadística, including:
          United Kingdom   Mexican Embassy, 8 Halkin Street, London SW1X 8QY   (t 01-235 6393)
          USA   Mexican Embassy, 2829 16th Street NW, Washington DC 20009 (t 234-6000)
          Canada   Mexican Embassy, 130 Albert Street, Despacho 206, K1P 5G4, Ottawa (t 233-8988)

Bibliographies

1033   The Dirección General de Estadística issues a 'Catalogo de estadísticas y publicaciones de la DGE'
          from time to time, the latest issue covering the years 1970-1976 (advance 1977).   More comprehensive
          bibliographies were issued in 1942 and 1966 ('Inventario de estadística nacionales').

Statistical publications

¶   A - General

1034 Anuario estadístico de los Estados Unidos Mexicanos   [Statistical yearbook of the United States of Mexico]
          (Dirección General de Estadística)
      Dirección General de Estadística, Balderas 71, México 1, DF.
      1893-   1972-1974.   not priced.   c 350 p.
      Main sections:

Population	Hunting and fishing
Buildings and housing	Irrigation
Assistance	Industry
Health and social security	Communications and transport
Education and culture	Internal trade
Justice	External trade
Employment	Finance
Agriculture	National product and balance of payments
Forestry	

      Time factor: the 1973-1974 edition, published in 1978, has data for the years 1972 to 1974 and also
          earlier years in some tables.
      §   Es.

¶ A,   continued

1035   Anuario estadístico compendiado de los Estados Unidos Mexicanos   [Annual statistical compendium of the
                United States of Mexico]   (Dirección General de Estadística)
            Dirección General de Estadística, Balderas 71, México 1, DF.
            1941- 1970.   not priced.   382 p.
            Contains data on physical characteristics of the country, population, demography, migration, tourism,
                housing, health, social assistance and security, education and culture, justice, employment,
                agriculture, livestock, forestry, fisheries, irrigation, industry (mineral, oil, electricity, construction,
                transformation), communications and transport, internal trade (prices), foreign trade, finance, gross
                national product and balance of payments.
            Time factor: the 1970 edition, published in 1971, has data for 1970 generally.
            §   Es.

1036   Revista de estadística   [Review of statistics]   (Dirección General de Estadística)
            Dirección General de Estadística, Balderas 71, México 1, DF.
            1933- monthly.   not priced.
            Contains data on area and climate, population, social assistance and health, agriculture, industry
                (transformation, mineral, oil, electric energy), communications and transport, internal trade
                (consumption and sales, price indices, cost of living), foreign trade, finance, and trading
                corporations and co-operatives.
            Time factor: each issue has annual quarterly and monthly figures to about seven months prior to the date
                of publication.
            §   Es.

1037   Boletín mensual de información económica   [Monthly bulletin of economic information]   (Secretaría de
                Programación y Presupuesto)
            Secretaría de Programación y Presupuesto, Articulo 123, no 88 - 2° pisa, México 1, DF.
            1977-   not priced.
            Includes statistical data on production, employment, sales and investment; prices; economic relations
                with other countries (balance of payments, external trade, etc); money and banking; and public
                finance.
            Time factor: each issue has annual and monthly figures to four or five months prior to the date of the
                issue.
            §   Es.

1038   Indicadores económicos   [Economic indicators]   (Banco de Mexico SA)
            Banco de Mexico SA, Condesa 6, 4° piso, México 1, DF.
            1973- monthly.   Mex $30 or Mex $330 yr; US$30 yr.
            Contains data on fiscal and financial accounts, production, prices, foreign trade and tourism.
            Time factor: each issue has long runs of monthly and annual figures to about three months prior to the
                date of the issue.
            §   Es.

1039   Review of the economic situation of Mexico   (Banco Nacional de México SA)
            Banco Nacional de México SA, Isabel da Católica 44, México 1, DF.
            1926- monthly.   not priced.
            Includes some tables in the text on the economy, farming, industry, trade, external trade, and has a
                very small statistical section with price indices and industrial production indices.
            §   En.

1040   México...hechos, cifras, tendencias   [Mexico...facts, figures, trends]   (Banco Nacional de Comercio
                Exterior SA)
            Banco Nacional de Comercio Exterior SA, Venustiano Carranza no 32 - 4° piso, México 1, DF.
            1960- 7th, 1976.   not priced.   c 250 p.

[continued next page]

¶ A, continued

1040, continued

> Compiled for the general reader, with some statistics and statistical tables in the text. Contains data on the national economy, society and culture.
> Time factor: the 1976 issue, publi-'ed in 1976, has data for several years to 1975.
> § Es.

1041 Principales indicadores económicos [Principal economic indicators] (Dirección General de Estadística)
> Dirección General de Estadística, Balderas 71, México 1, DF.
> monthly. not priced.
> Indices of volume of production, foreign trade, mineral and metal goods, oil and petrochemicals, industrial production, electric energy, tourism.
> Time factor: each issue has cumulated figures for the year to date and comparative figures for the last four years.
> § Es.

1042 Agenda estadística México [Statistical notebook of Mexico] (Dirección General de Estadística)
> Dirección General de Estadística, Balderas 71, México 1, DF.
> 1970- 1976. not priced. 270 p.
> Contains data on population and housing, education and culture, social assistance and security, agriculture, livestock, forestry, fisheries, industry, communications and transport, foreign trade, finance, national product and investment, and international statistical indicators.
> Time factor: the 1976 issue, published in 1976, has data for 1974 and 1975.
> § Es.

1043 Informe anual [Annual report] (Banco de México SA)
> Banco de México SA, Condesa 6, 4° piso, México 1, DF.
> 1922- 1977. not priced. 134 p.
> Includes a statistical appendix with data on consumer price indices, wholesale price index, banking, balance of payments, foreign trade, etc.
> Time factor: the 1977 report, published early 1978, has data for 1977 and also earlier years in some tables.
> § Es.

1044 La economía mexicana... The Mexican economy (Secretaría de Economía)
> Secretaría de Economía, México 1, DF.
> 1956- 1974. not priced. 448 p.
> A statistical review of agriculture, manufacturing industries, transport, mining, petroleum, finance, domestic and foreign trade. Tables are included in the text.
> Time factor: the 1974 edition, published in 1975, has data for 1973 and 1974.
> § En, Es.
>
> Note: the 1974 edition is headed 'Análisis - 74'.

¶ B - Production

1045 Censos económicos: censo industrial [Economic censuses: industrial census] (Dirección General de Estadística)
> Dirección General de Estadística, Balderas 71, México 1, DF.
> 1930- 10th, 1976. not priced.
> Preliminary and advance data were published in 1976, the final summary data [Resumen general] in two volumes in 1977. Includes data on the number of establishments, number of employees by occupation and industry, raw materials and power used, finances, etc.
> Time factor: the census is taken every five years.
> § Es.

¶   B,   continued

i. Mines and mining

1046   Anuario estadístico de la minera Mexicana   [Statistical yearbook of Mexican mining]   (Consejo de Recursos
            Naturales no Renovables)
        Consejo de Recursos Naturales no Renovables, México 1, DF.
        1969- 1971.   not priced.   133 p.
        Contains data on production, economics of the mining industry, exports and imports, index numbers, etc.
        Time factor: the 1971 issue, published in 1972, has data for 1971.
        §   Es.

1047   Estadística minerometalurgica, producción y exportación   [Mineral/metal statistics, production and export]
            (Dirección General de Estadística)
        Dirección General de Estadística, Balderas 71, México 1, DF
        1971- 1972.   not priced.
        Time factor: the 1972 issue was published in 1977.
        §   Es.

        Refer also to 1035, 1036.

ii.   Agriculture, fisheries, forestry, etc

1048   Censo agricola - ganadero y ejidal   [Census of agriculture - livestock and land]   (Dirección General de
            Estadística)
        Dirección General de Estadística, Balderas 71, México 1, DF.
        1930- 5th, 1970.   not priced.   377 p.
        Time factor: the results of the censuses were published in 1975.
        §   Es.

1049   Boletín mensuel de la Dirección General de Economía Agricola   [Monthly bulletin of the General Office of
            Agricultural Economics]
        Dirección General de Economía Agricola, México 1, DF.
        Contains preliminary statistical data on production, internal and foreign trade.
        1926-   not priced.
        §   Es.

        Refer also to 1034, 1035, 1036.

iii.   Industry

1050   Estadístico industrial anual   [Annual industrial statistics]   (Dirección General de Estadística)
        Dirección General de Estadística, Balderas 71, México 1, DF.
        1963- 1975.   not priced.
        Contains data on production, stocks, finances, sales, employment, wages, raw materials used, etc.
        Time factor: the 1975 issue, published in 1977, has data for 1975.
        §   Es.

1051   Boletín de estadísticas industriales   [Bulletin of industrial statistics]   (Dirección General de Estadística)
        Dirección General de Estadística, Balderas 71, México 1, DF.
        1964- monthly.   not priced.
        Contains data on plant and machinery, mineral and metal production, energy production (natural gas, oil
            and derivatives, electric energy), and manufacturing production.
        Time factor: each issue has data for that month and cumulated figures for the year to date, or in some
            tables quarterly figures, and is published about three months later.
        §   Es.

¶   B.iii,   continued

Refer also to 1034, 1035, 1036.

iv.   Construction

1052   Construcción de viviendas de interes social   [Construction of houses of social interest]   (Dirección General
de Estadística)
Dirección General de Estadística, Balderas 71, México 1, DF.
1973-   1977.   not priced.
Time factor: published every two years.
§   Es.

Refer also to 1034, 1035.

¶   C   -   External trade

1053   Anuario estadístico del comercio exterior de los Estados Unidos Mexicanos   [Statistical yearbook of the
foreign trade of Mexico]   (Dirección General de Estadística)
Dirección General de Estadística, Balderas 71, México 1, DF.
1896/97-   1975.   not priced.   c 800 p.
Main tables show detailed statistics of imports and exports arranged by commodity and subdivided by
countries of origin and destination.
Time factor: the 1975 issue, published in 1977, has data for 1975.
§   Es.

1054   Anuario estadístico del comercio exterior de los Estados Unidos Mexicanos con los países de la ALALC
[Statistical yearbook of foreign trade of Mexico with the countries of ALALC]   (Dirección General
de Estadistica)
Dirección General de Estadística, Balderas 71, México 1, DF.
1964-   1975.   not priced.
Time factor: the 1975 issue, published in 1977, has data for 1975.
§   Es.

1055   Boletín de comercio exterior   [Bulletin of foreign trade]   (Dirección General de Estadística)
Dirección General de Estadística, Balderas 71, México 1, DF.
1967-   monthly.   not priced.
Contains statistics of trade of Mexico arranged by commodity, and arranged by countries of origin and
destination.
Time factor: each issue has cumulated figures for the year to the date of the issue and corresponding
figures for the previous year, and is published some six months later.
§   Es.

1056   Comercio exterior de México   [Foreign trade of Mexico]   (Banco Nacional de Comercio Exterior)
Banco de Comercio Exterior SA, Avenida Chapultapec 230, 2° piso, México 7, DF.
1951-   monthly.   free.
A journal which includes a statistical summary of exports by country and of exports by commodity.
§   En & Fr versions with the Spanish title, are abbreviated forms of the Spanish edition.

1057   Anuario del exportador   [Export annual]   (Instituto Mexicano de Comercio Exterior)
Instituto Mexicano de Comercio Exterior, Ave Alphonso Reyes Nûm 30, Col Condesa, México 11, DF.
1974-   1976.   not priced.   407 p.
Mainly directory information but also contains data on foreign trade and economic indicators.
Time factor: the 1976 edition, published in 1976, has data for 1972, 1973 & 1974.
§   Es.

¶   C,   continued

Refer also to 1034, 1035, 1036.

¶   D - Internal distribution and service trades

1058 Censo comercial: resumen general   [Commercial census: general summary]   (Dirección General de
          Estadística)
      Dirección General de Estadística, Balderas 71, México 1, DF.
      1940-   7th, 1976.   not priced.   c 400 p.
      Contains data on the principal characteristics of the commerce of Mexico by various groupings, employment,
          employment, income from sales, etc.
      Time factor: the census is taken every five years and the 1976 census report, referring to 1975, was
          published in 1977.
      §   Es.

1059 Censo de servicios: resumen general   [Census of service trades: general summary]   (Dirección General de
          Estadística)
      Dirección General de Estadística, Balderas 71, México 1, DF.
      1940-   7th, 1976.   not priced.   c 200 p.
      Includes data on services connected with recreation, hotels and motels, education, finance, medicine,
          hairdressers, laundries, restaurants and bars, law, garages, agents, undertakers, photographers, etc.
      Time factor: the census is taken every five years and the 1976 census report, referring to 1975, was
          published in 1977.
      §   Es.

1060 Encuesta de turismo receptivo, 1970/1975   [Survey of incoming tourists, 1970/1975]   (Banco de México SA)
      Banco de México SA, Condesa 6, 4° piso, México 1, DF.
                        not priced.   77 p.
      An analysis of tourism, including data on numbers of visitors, nights, methods of travel, home countries,
          etc.
      Time factor: contains monthly and annual data for the years 1970 to 1975.
      §   Es.

      Refer also to 1034, 1035, 1036, 1067.

¶   E - Population

1061 Censo general de población   [General census of population]   (Dirección General de Estadística)
      Dirección General de Estadística, Balderas 71, México 1, DF.
      1895-   9th, 1970.   not priced.
      Volumes published are:
          Datos preliminares   [Preliminary data]
          Resumen general   [General summary]
          Resumen general abreviado   [Abbreviated general summary]
          Datos sobre la vivienda   [Data on housing]
          Localidades por entidad federativa y municipio con algunas caracteristicas de su población y vivienda
          [General characteristics of the population and housing by state and municipality]   (3 vols and
          annex to vol 1).
            and 32 volumes; one for each 'federativa' or state.
          Time factor: the results of the census were published between 1970 and 1973.
            §   Es.

¶   E,   continued

1062   Proyecciones de población [Population projections] (Dirección General de Estadistica)
        Dirección General de Estadística, Balderas 71, México 1, DF.
        1960/80-   1975-2000.   not priced.   c 250 p.
        Time factor: the 1975-2000 projections were published in 1977.
        §   Es.

1063   Estadísticas vitales: imagen demografica, 1960-1973 (Vital statistics: demographic images, 1960-1973]
                (Dirección General de Estadística)
        Dirección General de Estadística, Balderas 71, México 1, DF.
                        not priced.
        Time factor: published in 1975.
        §   Es.

1064   Estadísticas de natalidad, 1975 [Statistics of births, 1975] (Dirección General de Estadística)
        Dirección General de Estadística, Balderas 71, México 1, DF.
                        not priced.
        Time factor: published in 1977.
        §   Es.

1065   Estadísticas de mortalidad general, 1975 [Statistics of deaths] (Dirección General de Estadística)
        Dirección General de Estadística, Balderas 71, México 1, DF.
                        not priced.
        Time factor: published in 1977.
        §   Es.

        Note: 'Niveles de mortalidad, 1960-74' has earlier figures.

1066   Proyecciones de la mortalidad para México, 1970-2000   [Mortality projections for Mexico, 1970-2000]
                (Dirección General de Estadística)
        Dirección General de Estadística, Balderas 71, México 1, DF.
                        not priced.
        Time factor: published in 1975.
        §   Es.

1067   Migración y turismo, 1969-1973 [Migration and tourism, 1969-1973] (Dirección General de Estadística)
        Dirección General de Estadística, Balderas 71, México 1, DF.
        Time factor: published in 1976.
        §   Es.

1068   Estadística de trabajo y salarios industriales... [Statistics of industrial employment and wages] (Dirección
                General de Estadística)
        Dirección General de Estadística, Balderas 71, México 1, DF.
        1938-   1975.   not priced.
        The results of an annual survey taken at the end of October each year.
        Time factor: the 1975 issue, published in 1977, relates to 1975.
        §   Es.

1069   Estadística laboral, 1969-1974 [Work statistics, 1969-1974] (Dirección General de Estadística)
        Dirección General de Estadística, Balderas 71, México 1, DF.
        Time factor: published in 1977.
        §   Es.

        Refer also to 1034, 1035, 1036.

MEXICO,   continued

¶   F - Social

i.   Standard of living

1070   Ingresos y egresos de las familias en la República Mexicana, 1969-1970   [Income and expenditure of Mexican
            families, 1969-1970]   (Dirección General de Estadística)
            Dirección General de Estadística, Balderas 71, México 1, DF.
                        not priced.
            Time factor: published in 1971.
            §   Es.

            Refer also to 1036.

ii.   Health and welfare

1071   Estadísticas hospitalarias   [Hospital statistics]   (Dirección General de Estadística)
            Dirección General de Estadística, Balderas 71, México 1, DF.
            1972- 1975.   not priced.
            Time factor: the 1975 issue, published in 1977, has data for 1975.
            §   Es.

            Refer also to 1034, 1035, 1036.

iii.   Education and leisure

1072   Estadísticas educativas   [Education statistics]   (Dirección General de Estadística)
            Dirección General de Estadística, Balderas 71, México 1, DF.
            1968/73- 1969-1974.   not priced.
            Time factor: the 1969-1974 issue was published in 1977.
            §   Es.

1073   Estadísticas de espectaculos publicos, 1950-1974   [Statistics of public entertainments, 1950-1974]   (Dirección
            General de Estadística)
            Dirección General de Estadística, Balderas 71, México 1, DF.
                        not priced.
            Time factor: published in 1977.
            §   Es.

            Refer also to 1034, 1035.

iv.   Justice

            Refer to 1034, 1035.

1074   Censo de transportes   [Census of transport]   (Dirección General de Estadística)
            Dirección General de Estadística, Balderas 71, México 1, DF.
            1940- 8th, 1976.   not priced.
            Contains data on the number of firms, locations, type of service, employment, wages, capital invested,
                income and expenditures, passengers and cargo transported, equipment used.
            Time factor: a census of transport is taken every five years, and the 1976 results for 1975 were published
                in 1977.
            §   Es.

            Refer also to 1034, 1035, 1036.

The present Constitution came into force on January 1st, 1960, whereby the territory of Montserrat is governed by a Governor and has its own Executive and Legislative Councils.   Early in 1967 when other East Caribbean Islands adopted 'associated status' vis-à-vis the United Kingdom, Montserrat decided to remain a colony until separate arrangements, more suitable to her requirements, could be worked out.

Enquiries of a statistical nature should be made to the Chief Statistician, Statistics Office, PO Box 292, Plymouth, Montserrat.

Libraries

A library of statistical publications, for reference only, is kept within the Statistics Office (see above). The collection includes statistical publications from the 1970 population census for the Commonwealth Caribbean.

Statistical publications

1075   Statistical digest   (Statistics Office)
        Statistics Office, Plymouth.
        1973-   1977. $6.   100 p.
        Main sections:

Population	Prices and incomes
Migration and tourism	Banking
Labour	Public finance
Agriculture	Housing
Overseas trade	Education
Cargo movements and international traffic	Medical
	Crime
Infrastructure (water, telephones, electricity)	Traffic
	Meteorology

        Time factor: the 1977 edition, published in 1978, has data from 1962 or 1969 to 1976.
        §   En.

1076   Montserrat: report for the year...   (Foreign and Commonwealth Office)
        HM Stationery Office, PO Box 569, London SE1 9NH.
        1955/56-   1967 to 1972.   £0.45.   36 p.
        Mainly textual, but includes some statistics of population, labour, banking, production, commerce, etc.
        Time factor: the 1967 to 1972 edition was published in 1974.
        §   En.

    ¶   B   -   Production

    ii.   Agriculture, fisheries, forestry, etc.

1077   Agricultural census report   (Statistics Office)
        Statistics Office, Plymouth.
        1959-   1972.   not priced.
        Time factor: the results of the 1972 census were to be published in 1976.
        §   En.

        Refer also to 1075.

¶ C - External trade

1078 Overseas trade (Statistics Office)
Statistics Office, Plymouth.
1967- 1976. $6. 78 p.
Main tables show statistics of imports and exports arranged by commodity and subdivided by countries of
origin and destination.
Time factor: the 1976 issue, published late 1977, has data for 1976.
§ En.

Refer also to 1075.

¶ D - Internal distribution and service trades

1079 Bulletins of the 1977 visitors survey (Statistics Office)
Statistics Office, Plymouth.
not priced.
Time factor: the bulletins were to be published in 1978.
§ En.

Refer also to 1075.

¶ E - Population

1080 Census of population
1911- 1970.

Refer to 258 for details of the 1970 population census of the Commonwealth Caribbean.

1081 Report on vital statistics for the year... (Statistics Office)
Statistics Office, Plymouth.
1936- 1977. not priced. 12 p.
Contains population estimates and vital statistics.
Time factor: the 1977 issue published in 1978, has data for 1977.
§ En.

Refer also to 1075, 1076.

¶ F - Social

i. Standard of living

1082 Montserrat's price index (Government of Montserrat)
Government of Montserrat, Plymouth.
(monthly) not priced.
§ En.

Refer also to 1075.

ii. Health and welfare

Refer to 1075.

¶ F, continued

iii. Education and leisure

Refer to 1075.

iv. Justice

1083 Annual report on the Prison Department
Superintendent of Prisons, HM Prison, Plymouth.
1966- 1976. not priced. 10 p.
Includes some statistical data on prisons, prisoners, crimes, etc.
Time factor: the 1976 report, published in 1978, has data for 1976.
§ En.

Refer also to 1075.

¶ G - Finance

Refer to 1075, 1076.

¶ H - Transport and communications

Refer to 1075.

Central statistical office

1084   Bureau voor de Statistiek   (Statistical Office),
         Fort Amsterdam,
         Curaçao.
         ɫ 11335.

         The Office is responsible for the collection, analysis and publication of the official economic statistics
         of the Netherlands Antilles (Aruba, Bonaire, Curaçao and St Maarten).

Statistical publications

¶   A - General

1085   Statistisch jaarboek: Nederlandse Antillen   [Statistical yearbook: Netherlands Antilles]   (Bureau voor de
             Statistiek)
         Bureau voor de Statistiek, Fort Amsterdam, Curaçao.
         1956.   1974.   NAf 10.   148 p.
         Main sections:

Area & climate	Transport & communications
Population	Money & banking
Public health	National accounts
Housing	Balance of payments
Religion & politics	Public finance
Education	Incomes
Economically active population,	Prices
employment & unemployment	Social affairs (social security, social insurance, wages)
Agriculture	Justice and prisons
Manufacturing	International data
Foreign trade	

         Time factor: the 1974 edition, published in 1975, has data for 1973 and some earlier years.   The year-
             book was not published in 1972 or 1973.
         §   En,   Es,   Nl.

1086   Statistische mededelingen: Nederlandse Antillen [Statistical information: Netherlands Antilles] (Bureau voor
             de Statistiek)
         Bureau voor de Statistiek, Fort Amsterdam, Curaçao.
         1954-   monthly.   NAf 24 yr.
         Contents include data on climate, population, public health, housing, agriculture, industry, foreign trade,
             traffic and transport, banking, public finance, prices, social affairs, justice and prisons, and
             international data.
         Time factor: each issue has long runs of monthly and annual figures to the month of the issue and is
             published about three months later.
         §   En,   Es,   Nl.

¶   B - Production

         Refer to 1085, 1086.

   ¶   C - External trade

1087   Kwartaalstatistiek van der in- en uitvoer per goederensoort van Curaçao en Aruba   [Quarterly statistics of imports and exports by commodity of Curaçao and Aruba]   (Bureau voor de Statistiek)
      Bureau voor de Statistiek, Fort Amsterdam, Curaçao.
      1954-   NAf 20 or NAf 30 yr.
      Contains detailed statistics of imports and exports arranged by commodity and subdivided by countries of origin and destination.   Separate figures are given for Curaçao and Aruba.
      Time factor: each issue has data for that quarter and cumulated figures for the year to date and is published about 12 months later.
      §   NI.

1088   Kwartaalstatistiek van de in- en uitvoer per land van Curaçao en Aruba   [Quarterly statistics of imports and exports by country of Curaçao and Aruba]   (Bureau voor de Statistiek)
      Bureau voor de Statistiek, Fort Amsterdam, Curaçao.
      1954-   NAf 20 or NAf 30 yr.
      Contains detailed statistics of imports and exports arranged by countries of origin and destination, subdivided by commodities.   Separate figures are given for Curaçao and Aruba.
      Time factor: each issue has data for that quarter and cumulative figures for the year to date and is published about 12 months later.
      §   NI.

1089   In- en uitvoer Bonaire   [Imports and exports of Bonaire]   (Bureau voor de Statistiek)
      Bureau voor de Statistiek, Fort Amsterdam, Curaçao.
      1954-   1975.   not priced.   unpaged.
      Contains detailed statistics of imports and exports of Bonaire arranged by commodity and subdivided by countries of origin and destination.
      Time factor: the 1975 issue has data for the year 1975 and was published about 12 months later.
      §   NI.

      Refer also to 1085, 1086.

   ¶   D - Internal distribution and service trades

1090   De ontwikkeling van het toerisme op de Nederlandse Antillen...   [The development of tourism in the Netherlands Antilles]   (Bureau voor de Statistiek)
      1964-   1964-1974.   NAf 1.   17 p.
      Includes statistical data on resorts; hotels and beds; cruise tourism; and ships, planes in tourism and their passengers.
      Time factor: the 1964-1974 edition, with data for those years, was published in 1974.
      §   NI.

   ¶   E - Population

1091   Algemene volks- en woningtelling Nederlandse Antillen   [General population and housing census of the Netherlands Antilles]   (Bureau voor de Statistiek)
      Bureau voor de Statistiek, Fort Amsterdam, Curaçao.
      1960-   1972.   NAf 25 a set.   4 vols.
      Deel A [Vol A] is in 10 parts, dealing with methods, totals, and population statistics for each island.
      Time factor: the parts of Vol A were published late 1972.   No other parts have been traced.
      §   NI.

¶   E,   continued

1092   De ontwikkeling van de beroepsbevolking van 15-64 jaar tot 1985 op Aruba, Bonaire en Curaçao:
            budgettonderzoek 1974   [The development of the economically active population of the 15-64 years
            olds till 1985 in Aruba, Bonaire and Curaçao: budget survey 1974]   (Bureau voor de Statistiek)
        Bureau voor de Statistiek, Fort Amsterdam, Curaçao.
                        NAf 20.
        Time factor: published in 1974.
        §   NI.

1093   De werkgelegenheid op de Nederlandse Antillen ten tijde van de volks- en woningtelling, 1972, Deel 1
            [Employment in the Netherlands Antilles during the population and housing census, 1972, Vol 1]
            (Bureau voor de Statistiek)
        Bureau voor de Statistiek, Fort Amsterdam, Curaçao.
                        NAf 5.
        Time factor: published in 1972.
        §   NI.

1094   Statistiek arbeidsvolume en loonsommen en 1972.   [Statistics of labour and wages in 1972]   (Economische
            Ontwikkeling)
        Economische Ontwikkeling, Aruba.
                        not priced.   48 p.
        Time factor: published mid-1974.
        §   NI.

        Refer also to 1085, 1086.

¶   F - Social

        Refer to 1085, 1086.

¶   G - Finance

1095   Quarterly bulletin   (Bank van de Nederlandse Antillen)
        Bank van de Nederlandse Antillen, Fort Amsterdam 4, Curaçao.
        1973-   not priced.
        Includes a statistical bulletin with data on foreign transactions, monetary authorities, commercial banks,
            giro system, monetary survey, non-monetary institutions, interest rates, public finance and develop-
            ment aid, indices (consumer price indices for the Leeward Islands; production), tourism, and foreign
            trade.
        Time factor: each issue contains long runs of monthly, quarterly and annual figures to about three months
            prior to the date of the issue.
        §   En & NI eds.

        Refer also to 1085, 1086.

¶   H - Transport and communications

        Refer to 1085, 1086.

Central statistical office

1096   Ministerio de Economía, Industria y Comercio,
        Managua, DN
        t 21-701.

        The Ministry works with the Banco Central de Nicaragua to collect, analyse and publish economic
        statistics of Nicaragua, other than foreign trade statistics, which are handled solely by the bank.

Libraries

        The Banco Central de Nicaragua, (Apartado 2252), Managua (t 21-801) has a library which includes the
        statistical publications of Nicaragua.

Statistical publications

¶   A - General

1097   Anuario estadístico [Statistical yearbook] (Banco Central de Nicaragua and Ministerio de Economía,
            Industria y Comercio)
        Ministerio de Economía, Industria y Comercio, Managua.
        1942- 1975.   not priced.   393 p.
        Main sections:
            Area and climate   Construction
            Population   Transport & communications
            Education   Agriculture, livestock & agricultural reform
            Health and social assistance   Manufacturing industry
            Employment & wages   Prices
            Family protection   Banking, finance, gross national product, balance of
            Justice   payments, foreign trade
            Public services
        Time factor: the 1975 edition, published in 1977, has data for the years 1971 to 1975.
        §   Es.

1098   Boletin semestral [Half-yearly bulletin] (Banco Central de Nicaragua)
        Banco Central de Nicaragua, Apartado 2252, Managua.
        1929-   not priced.
        Includes a statistical section on money and banking, balance of payments, and foreign trade, public
            finance, national accounts.
        Time factor: each issue has annual and monthly figures to either July or December and is published some
            months later.
        §   Es.

1099   Compendio estadístico [Statistical compendium] (Banco Central de Nicaragua and Ministerio de Economía,
            Industria y Comercio)
        Ministerio de Economía, Industria y Comercio, Managua.
            1965-1974.   not priced.   487 p.
        Main sections:
            Area & climate   Public services
            Population   Building activity
            Education   Transport & communications
            Health & social security   Agriculture, livestock & agricultural reform
            Employment & wages   Manufacturing industry
            Family protection   Banking, finance, gross national product, balance of
            Justice   payments, and foreign trade
        Time factor: the 1965-1974 edition, with data for those years, was published in 1976.
        §   Es.

¶   A,   continued

1100   Indicadores económicos   [Economic indicators]   (Departamento de Estudios Económicos)
        Departamento de Estudios Económicos, Apartado 2252-2253, Managua, DN.
        1975-   No 3, 1976.   C$7 each issue.
        Contains indicators of population, employment and prices, gross internal product; money and banking;
            public finance; foreign trade and balance of payments; agricultural activity; exploitation of natural
            resources; industrial activity; construction; and services (electricity and water).
        Time factor: each issue has long runs of fiscal year figures and the last 18 months to about three months
            prior to publication.
        §   Es.

¶   B   -   Production

ii.   Agriculture, fisheries, forestry, etc.

1101   Censo agropecuario   [Census of agriculture and livestock]   (Dirección General de Estadística y Censos)
        Dirección General de Estadística y Censos, Ministerio de Economía, Managua, DN.
                1963.   not priced.   1 volume.
        §   Es.

        Refer also to 1097, 1099, 1100

iii.   Industry

        Refer to 1097, 1099, 1100.

iv.   Construction

        Refer to 1097, 1099, 1100.

v.   Energy

        Refer to 1100.

¶   C   -   External trade

1102   Comercio exterior de Nicaragua por productos y países   [Foreign trade of Nicaragua by products and countries]
            (Banco Central de Nicaragua)
        Banco Central de Nicaragua, Managua.
        1968-   1976.   not priced.   315 p.
        Contains summary tables and detailed statistics of imports and exports arranged by commodity subdivided by
            countries of origin and destination, and detailed statistics of imports and exports arranged by country
            of origin and destination subdivided by commodities.
        Time factor: the 1976 issue, with data for 1976, was published in 1977.
        §   Es.

1103   Indicadores del comercio exterior de Nicaragua   [Indicators of foreign trade of Nicaragua]   (Banco Central
            de Nicaragua)
        Banco Central de Nicaragua, Managua.
                quarterly.   not priced.
        Time factor: each issue has data for the year to the date of the issue and for the previous year and is
            published about three months later.
        §   Es.

        Refer also to 1097, 1098, 1099, 1100.

¶ E - Population

1104 Censo de población [Census of population] (Dirección General de Estadística y Censos)
Dirección General de Estadística y Censos, Ministerio de Economía, Managua.
1920- 1963. not priced. 5 vols.
Contents:
Vol I General characteristics of the population by departments and towns
Vol II Educational characteristics of the population by departments and towns
Vol III Economic characteristics of the population by departments and principal cities
Vol IV Demographic characteristics of the population by departments and principal cities
Vol V Economic characteristics of the population by principal cities
§ Es.

Note: a census of population was taken in 1971.

1105 Censo de vivienda [Census of housing] (Dirección General de Estadística y Censos)
Dirección General de Estadística y Censos, Ministerio de Economía, Managua.
1963- 1971. not priced. 592 p.
Time factor: the results of the 1971 census were published in 1974.
§ Es.

Refer also to 1097, 1099, 1100.

¶ F - Social

Refer to 1097, 1099.

¶ G - Finance

1106 Informe anual [Annual report] (Banco Central de Nicaragua)
Banco Central de Nicaragua, Apartado 2252, Managua, DN.
1961- 1977. not priced. 237 p.
Mainly concerned with data on the operations of the bank, but also includes some statistics of industrial
production, etc.
Time factor: the 1977 report was published in 1978.
§ Es.

Refer also to 1097, 1098, 1099, 1100.

¶ H - Transport and communications

Refer to 1097, 1099.

Central statistical office

1107   Dirección de Estadística y Censo   [Office of Statistics and Census]
        Ave Balboa y Calle Federico Boyd,
        Apartado 5213,
        Panamá 5,
        t   64-3734.

        The Dirección de Estadística y Censo, a part of the Contraloria General de la República, is responsible
        for the collection, analysis and publication of the official statistics of the country.   Unpublished statistical
        information may be supplied to enquirers if it is available and is usually free of charge, although a charge,
        based on the work done, is made for special analyses.

Libraries

        The Dirección de Estadística y Censo, referred to above, has a library which is open to the public for
        reference.   The library has statistical publications of Panama, other countries and international organisations.

        Some university and public libraries have statistical bulletins available for reference.

Libraries and information services abroad

        Panama's statistical publications are sent to Panamanian embassies abroad, including:

        United Kingdom   Panamanian Embassy, 109 Jermyn Street, London SW1Y 6HA
        USA   Panamanian Embassy, 2862 McGill Terrace NW, Washington DC 20008.
                          (t 483-1407)

Bibliographies

1108   Inventario estadístico nacional   [National statistical inventory]   (Dirección de Estadística y Censo)

1109   The Dirección Estadística y Censo issues a sales list of publications at intervals.

Statistical publications

¶   A   -   General

1110   Panamá en cifres [Panama in figures]   (Dirección de Estadística y Censo)
        Dirección de Estadística y Censo, Apartado 5213, Panamá 5.
        1958/62-   1972-1976.   B/0.25 (B/0.35 abroad)   227 p.
        Main sections:
            Economic and social indicators
            Physical situation
            Demography (population, vital statistics, migration)
            Economic situation (agriculture, fisheries, industrial structure, manufacturing production, construction,
              electricity and gas, trade (mainly foreign), services, transport, communications, balance of pay-
              ments, national accounts, public finance, banking, prices, and consumption)
            Social situation (housing, social security, social assistance, employment and wages, and accidents
              in transit)
            Political, administrative and justice situation
        Time factor: the 1972-1976 edition, published late 1977, has data for the years 1972 to 1976.
        §   Es.

PANAMA,   continued

¶   A,   continued

1111   Indicadores económicos y sociales   [Economic and social indicators]   (Dirección de Estadística y Censo)
          Dirección de Estadística y Censo, Apartado 5213, Panamá 5.
          1966-   quarterly and annual: 1975 - 1976.   B/0.20 (B/0.30 abroad) each.   27 p.
          Contains tables showing trends in the economic situation of Panama.   Published in the series 'Estadistica
              Panameña'.
          Time factor: each issue is published some months after the end of the period covered; the 1975 - 1976
              annual issue was published in 1977, and has data for the years 1975 and 1976.
          §   Es.

          Note: also available are retrospective volumes covering 1972-1976 and 1965-1970 titled 'Indicadores
              económicos y sociales de Panamá'.

1112   Compendio estadístico   [Statistical compendium]   (Dirección de Estadística y Censo)
          Dirección de Estadística y Censo, Apartado 5213, Panamá 5.
                              not priced.   9 vols.
          Contains social and economic statistics for each province of Panamá, one volume for each province.
          Time factor: published in 1973, the volumes relate to 1970 and some earlier years.
          §   Es.

     ¶   B   -   Production

     ii.   Agriculture, fisheries, forestry, etc

1113   Censos nacionales: censo agropecuario   [Census of agriculture and livestock]   (Dirección de Estadística y
          Censo)
          Dirección de Estadística y Censo, Apartado 5213, Panamá 5.
          1950-   3rd, 1971.   free.   5 vols.
          Contents:
                    Vol I   Agricultural production
                    Vol II   Livestock production
                    Vol III   Characteristics of agricultural exploitations
                    Vol IV   General compendium
                    Vol V   Methodological information
          Time factor: the volumes were published between 1974 and 1976.
          §   Es.

1114   Producción agropecuario   [Agricultural production]   (Dirección de Estadística y Censo)
          Dirección de Estadística y Censo, Apartado 5213, Panamá 5.
          1941-   1971.   B/0.20 (B/0.30 abroad)
          Presents the results of agricultural surveys.
          §   Es.

1115   Situación económica: producción pecuaria   [Economic situation: livestock production]   (Dirección de
              Estadística y Censo)
          Dirección de Estadística y Censo, Apartado 5213, Panamá 5.
          1966-   1976.   B/0.20 (B/0.30 abroad)   32 p.
          Contains data on the numbers in existence, slaughtered, prices, and consumption of cattle, pigs and
              poultry.   Also data on milk and eggs.   Issued in the series 'Estadística Panameña'.
          Time factor: the 1976 issue, published in 1976, has data for 1975 and the first quarter of 1976.
          §   Es.

¶ B.ii, continued

1116 Situación económico: superficie sembrada y cosecha de café, tabaco y caña de azúcar, año agricola...
        [Economic situation: area sown and harvested of coffee, tobacco, cane sugar, crop year] (Dirección
        de Estadística y Censo)
        Dirección de Estadística y Censo, Apartado 5213, Panamá 5.
        1966/67- 1975-1976. B/0.20 (B/0.30 abroad) 30 p.
        Issued in the series 'Estadística Panameña'.
        Time factor: the 1975-1976 issue, published in 1976, has data for the crop year 1975/76 and some
            earlier years.
        § Es.

1117 Situación económica: superficie sembrada y cosecha de arroz, maíz y frijol de bejuco, año agrícola...
        [Economic situation: area sown and harvested of rice, maize and beans] (Dirección de Estadística
        y Censo)
        Dirección de Estadística y Censo, Apartado 5213, Panamá.
        1966/67- 1975-1976. B/0.20 (B/0.30 abroad) 30 p.
        Issued in the series 'Estadística Panameña'.
        Time factor: the 1975-1976 issue, published in 1976, has data for the crop year 1975/76 and some
            earlier years.
        § Es.

1118 Situación económica: precios recibidos por el productor agropecuario [Economic situation: prices received
        by agricultural producers] (Dirección de Estadística y Censo)
        Dirección de Estadística y Censo, Apartado 5213, Panamá.
        1960- 2-monthly issues and annual compendium. B/0.20 (B/0.30 abroad) each issue.
        Issued in the series 'Estadística Panameña .
        Time factor: the 1977 issue, published in May 1978, has data for 1977 and 1976.
        § Es.

1119 Situación económica: precios pagados por el productor agropecuario [Economic situation: prices paid to
        agricultural producers] (Dirección de Estadística y Censo)
        Dirección de Estadística y Censo, Apartado 5213, Panamá 5.
        1970- 1975-1976. B/0.20 (B/0.30 abroad) 19 p.
        Prices paid in different areas of the country.   Issued in the series 'Estadística Panameña'.
        § Es.

        Refer also to 1110.

iii. Industry

1120 Censos nacionales: censos economicos. Vol I Industria manufacturera, construcción y electricidad [Economic
        census. Vol I Manufacturing industry, construction, and electricity] (Dirección de Estadística y
        Censo)
        Dirección de Estadística y Censo, Apartado 5213, Panamá 5.
        1960- 2nd, 1972. free. 175 p.
        Results of the census (Vol II refers to commerce and services - see 1125).
        Time factor: published in 1976.
        § Es.

        Note: there is also a methodological volume relating to Vol I & II.

¶   B.iii,   continued

1121   Situación económica: industrias   [Economic situation: industries]   (Dirección de Estadística y Censo)
           Dirección de Estadística y Censo, Apartado 5213, Panamá 5.
           1955-   1975.   B/0.20 (B/0.30 abroad)   83 p.
           Contains the results of annual surveys relating to manufacturing industry and electricity production.
                Issued in the series 'Estadística Panameña'.
           Time factor: the 1975 issue, published mid-1977, has data for several years to 1975.
           §   Es.

1122   Situación económica: industria   [Economic situation: industry]   (Dirección de Estadística y Censo)
           Dirección de Estadística y Censo, Apartado 5213, Panamá 5.
           1940-   quarterly and annual.   B/0.20 (B/0.30 abroad)
           Presents statistical data on the production of principal manufactures, electricity, gas, water,
                construction, fisheries, licences and declared capital of economic activities.   Issued in the series
                'Estadística Panameña'.
           Time factor: each issue has data for the period of the issue and is published about six months later.
                The 1977 annual issue, with data for 1977, was published in July 1978.
           §   Es.

           Refer also to 1110.

      iv.   Construction

           Refer to 1110.

      v.   Energy

           Refer to 1110.

¶   C   -   External trade

1123   Situación económica: comercio exterior   [Economic situation: foreign trade]   (Dirección de Estadística y
           Censo)
           Dirección de Estadística y Censo, Apartado 5213, Panamá 5.
           1907-   1975.   B/2. (B/2.50 abroad)   835 p.
           Main tables show detailed statistics of imports and exports arranged by commodity and subdivided by
                countries of origin and destination.   Issued in the series 'Estadística Panameña'.
           Time factor: the 1975 issue, published in 1978, has data for 1975.
           §   Es.

1124   Situación económica: comercio exterior - preliminar   [Economic situation: foreign trade - preliminary]
           Dirección de Estadística y Censo)
           Dirección de Estadística y Censo, Apartado 5213, Panamá 5.
           1975-   1976.   B/0.50 (B/0.75 abroad)   203 p.
           Preliminary data on foreign trade, with main tables arranged by commodity and subdivided by countries
                of origin and destination.   Issued in the series 'Estadística Panameña'.
           Time factor: the 1976 issue, with data for 1976, was published in 1978.
           §   Es.

           Refer also to 1110.

PANAMA,   continued

¶   D   -   Internal distribution and service trades

1125   Censos nacionales: censos económicos. Vol II Comercio y servicios   [Economic census. Vol II commerce and
services]   (Dirección de Estadística y Censo)
Dirección de Estadística y Censo, Apartado 5213, Panamá 5.
1960-   2nd, 1972.   free.   104 p.
Results of the census.   (Vol I refers to manufacturing industry, construction and electricity - see 1120).
Time factor: published in 1976.
§   Es.

Note: there is a methodological volume relating to Vols I & II.

Refer also to 1110.

¶   E   -   Population

1126   Censos nacionales: población y vivienda   [Census of population and housing]   (Dirección de Estadística y
Censo)
Dirección de Estadística y Censo, Apartado 5213, Panamá 5.
1911-   7th, 1970.   free.   6 vols.
Contents:
Vol   I   Population by geographical location
Vol   II   Housing
Vol   III   General compendium on population
Vol   IV   General characteristics of education, internal migration, fertility and homes
Vol   V   Economic characteristics
Vol   VI   Census sectors (districts of Panama, San Miguelito and Colon)
Time factor: published between 1973 and 1976.
§   Es.

Note: Also published were a methodological volume, results of a pilot census (Ensayos censales),
preliminary results (Cifras preliminares), advance final tabulations (Avance de tabulacciones finaies),
and brief results (Resultados generals).

1127   Población de Panamá por divisiones geograficas: resultados censales y proyecciones hasta 1980   [Population
of Panama by geographic division: census results and projections to 1980]   (Dirección de Estadística
y Censo)
Dirección de Estadística y Censo, Apartado 5213, Panamá 5.
free.   20 p.
Time factor: published in 1975, the volume covers the years 1960 to 1980.
§   Es.

1128   Situación demografica: estadisticas vitales   [Demographic situation: vital statistics]   (Dirección de Estadística
y Censo)
Dirección de Estadística y Censo, Apartado 5213, Panamá 5.
1950-   1974.   B/0.20   (B/0.30 abroad)   232 p.
Contains statistics of births, marriages, divorce, and deaths.   Issued in the series 'Estadística Panameña'.
Time factor: the 1974 issue, published in 1976, has data for 1974.
§   Es.

1129   Situación demografica: estadísticas vitales - cifras preliminares   [Demographic situation: vital statistics -
preliminary figures]   (Dirección de Estadística y Censo)
Dirección de Estadística y Censo, Apartado 5213, Panamá 5.
1967-   2 a year.   B/0.20   (B/0.30 abroad)
Issued in the series 'Estadística Panameña'.
Time factor: published about six months after the end of the period covered, which is the first six months
of the year and the annual data.
§   Es.

¶   E,   continued

1130   Situación demografica: migración internacional   [Demographic situation: international migration]   (Dirección
            de Estadística y Censo)
        Dirección de Estadística y Censo, Apartado 5213, Panamá 5.
        1965-   1975.   B/0.20   (B/0.30 abroad)
        Contains data on the entry to and exit from the country, by passengers by air, sea and road.   Issued in
            the series 'Estadística Panameña'.
        Time factor: the 1975 issue, published in 1976, has data for 1975.
        §   Es.

1131   Situación sociales: estadisticas del trabajo   [Social situation: employment statistics]   (Dirección de Estadística
            y Censo)
        Dirección de Estadística y Censo, Apartado 5213, Panamá 5.
        1965-   1975.   B/0.20   (B/0.30 abroad)   144 p.
        Contains data on manpower, by area, sex, occupation, etc; wages; and employment by province, sex,
            work, etc.   Issued in the series 'Estadística Panameña'.
        Time factor: the 1975 issue, published in 1976, has data for 1975.
        §   Es.

        Refer also to 1110.

    ¶   F   -   Social

    i.   Standard of living

1132   Situación económica: indice de precios al por mayor y al consumidor   [Economic situation: wholesale and
            consumer price indices]   (Dirección de Estadística y Censo)
        Dirección de Estadística y Censo, Apartado 5213, Panamá 5.
        1941-   quarterly and annual.   B/0.20   (B/0.30 abroad)
        Issued in the series 'Estadística Panameña'.
        Time factor: each quarterly issue covers the quarter of the issue, the previous quarter and the correspond-
            ing quarter of the previous year and is published three or four months later.   The 1977 annual issue,
            with data for 1977 and earlier years in some tables, was published in May 1978.
        §   Es.

    ii.   Health and welfare

1133   Situación social: asistencia social   [Social situation: social assistance]   (Dirección de Estadística y Censo)
        Dirección de Estadística y Censo, Apartado 5213, Panamá 5.
        1965-   1974.   B/0.20   (B/0.30 abroad)
        Contains data on the numbers of health institutions, doctors, dentists, laboratory technicians, auxiliaries,
            beds in hospitals, and medical centres in the Republic; also the movement of patients in the general
            and special hospitals in Panama Province.   Issued in the series 'Estadística Panameña'.
        Time factor: the 1974 issue, published in 1976, has data for 1974 and 1973/74.
        §   Es.

        Refer also to 1110.

    iii.   Education and leisure

1134   Situación cultural: Educación   [Cultural situation: education]   (Dirección de Estadística y Censo)
        Dirección de Estadística y Censo, Apartado 5213, Panamá 5.
        1965-   1975.   B/0.20   (B/0.30 abroad)   51 p.
        Contains data on primary, supplementary, and university education, including numbers of students, staff,
            examination results, etc.   Issued in the series 'Estadística Panameña'.
        Time factor: the 1975 issue, published in 1977, has data for 1975.
        §   Es.

¶   F.iii, continued

1135   Estadísticas de educación [Statistics of education] (Ministerio de Educación: Departamento de Estadística)
           Ministerio de Educación, Panamá.
           1946- 1977.   not priced.
           Titles and contents vary with each issue.   A 'Suplemento provincial' [Provincial supplement] was
                published in 1976, and in 1971 there was 'Compendio, 1959-60 a 1968'.   More usually there is
                a sub-title 'analisis estadístico'.
           Time factor: the 1977 issue was published in 1977 and contains the latest figures available.
           §   Es.

1136   Estadísticas de educación: avance de cifras [Education statistics: advance figures] (Dirección de Estadística
                y Censo)
           Dirección de Estadística y Censo, Apartado 5213, Panamá 5.
           1971-   monthly.   not priced.
           A single sheet (two sides) with new statistical data on education in the Republic.
           §   Es.

1137   Estadísticas de la ciencia y la tecnologia [Statistics of science and technology] (Dirección de Estadística y
                Censo)
           Dirección de Estadística y Censo, Apartado 5213, Panamá 5.
                              not priced.   31 p.
           Contains data on institutions, personnel, graduates, entrants, and projects started and realised.
           Time factor: published in 1976, the data is for 1975.
           §   Es.

      iv.   Justice

1138   Situación politica, administrativa, y justicia: justicia [Political, administrative and justice situation: justice]
                (Dirección de Estadística y Censo)
           Dirección de Estadística y Censo, Apartado 5213, Panamá 5.
           1965-   B/0.20 (B/0.30 abroad).

           Refer also to 1110.

   ¶   G - Finance

      ii.   Public finance

1139   Situación económica: cuentas nacionales [Economic situation: national accounts] (Dirección de Estadística
                y Censo)
           Dirección de Estadística y Censo, Apartado 5213, Panamá 5.
           1944- 1974 & 1976.   B/0.20 (B/0.30 abroad)   34 p.
           Contains data relative to the income and product, both national and per capita of Panama, together with
                statistical tables on the economy of Panama in general.   Issued in the series 'Estadística Panameña'.
           Time factor: the 1974 & 1976 issue, published in 1977, has data for 1974, 1975 and 1976.
           §   Es.

1140   Situación económica: hacienda pública y finanzas [Economic situation: the Treasury and finance] (Dirección
                de Estadística y Censo)
           Dirección de Estadística y Censo, Apartado 5213, Panamá 5.
           1966-   1974.   B/0.20 (B/0.30 abroad)   169 p.
           Contains data on the budget, income and expenditure, internal and external national debt, etc.   Issued
                in the series 'Estadística Panameña'.
           Time factor: the 1974 issue, published in 1975, has data for 1974.
           §   Es.

PANAMA,   continued

.ii,   continued

1141   Situación económica: balanza de pagos   [Economic situation: balance of payments]   (Dirección de Estadística
            y Censo)
        Dirección de Estadística y Censo, Apartado 5213, Panamá 5.
        1960/66-   1975 - 1976.   B/0.20 (B/0.30 abroad)   41 p.
        Issued in the series 'Estadística Panameña'.
        Time factor: the 1975 and 1976 issue, published in 1978 has data for 1976 and 1975.
        §   Es.

1142   Informe del Contralor General de la República   [Report of the Controller General of the Republic]
        Contraloría General, Apartado 5231, Panamá 5.
        1966-   1975.   not priced.   325 p.
        Includes statistical data on public finance.
        Time factor: the 1975 report, published in 1975, has data for 1974 or the fiscal year 1974/75.
        §   Es.

        Refer also to 1110.

¶   H   -   Transport and communications

1143   Situación económica: transportes y comunicaciones   [Economic situation: transport and communications]
            (Dirección de Estadística y Censo)
        Dirección de Estadística y Censo, Apartado 5213, Panamá 5.
        1962-   1976.   B/0.20 (B/0.30 abroad)   41 p.
        Contains statistics relative to road transport (motor vehicles registered, in circulation, etc), maritime
            transport (ships registered, types, etc), rail transport (passengers and cargo); air transport (companies,
            personnel, traffic, passengers and cargo), and communications (telephone, television, radio, etc).
        Issued in the series 'Estadística Panameña'.
        Time factor: the 1976 issue, published in 1977, has data for 1975.
        §   Es.

1144   Situación social: accidentes de tránsito   [Social situation: accidents in transit]   (Dirección de Estadística y
            Censo)
        Dirección de Estadística y Censo, Apartado 5213, Panamá 5.
        1958-   1976.   B/0.20 (B/0.30 abroad)
        Time factor: the 1976 issue, published in 1977, has data for 1976.
        §   Es.

        Refer also to 1110.

There is no central statistical office and it is recommended that enquiries be addressed to the Panama Canal Information Office, Balboa Heights, Canal Zone.

Statistical publications

¶   A   -   General

1145   Panama Canal Company and Canal Zone Government: annual report
        The Panama Canal Information Office, Balboa Heights, Canal Zone.
        1951/52-   1975-76. $2.   154 p.
        The two separate reports are published in one volume, the Governor of the Canal Zone also being the
            President of the Panama Canal Company.   The Panama Canal Company report includes statistical
            data on finance, shipping, water supply, dredging operations, electrical power generated, cargo
            handled across piers, vessels serviced, marine bunkering, and railroad operations.   The Canal
            Zone Government report includes statistics on hospital occupancy, school enrolment, police statistics,
            fire service statistics, postal service statistics, and customs activities.
        Time factor: in the 1975/76 edition, the data for the Canal Company covers the period 1973 to 1976 and
            the data for the Government covers 1975 and 1976.
        §   En.

¶   C   -   External trade

        Refer to 1123 and 1124, which includes foreign trade for the Canal Zone.

¶   E   -   Population

1146   Census of population   (US Bureau of the Census)
        Government Printing Office, Washington DC 20402, USA.
        1912-   1970.   various prices.
        Vol 1. Characteristics of the population, part 57 has data for the Panama Canal Zone.   It is in four
            parts, which were initially available separately -
            PC(1)-A: number of inhabitants;
            PC(1)-B: general population characteristics;
            PC(1)-C: general, social and economic characteristics; and
            PC(1)-D: detailed characteristics.
        Time factor: the results of the census were published between 1971 and 1974.
        §   En.

1147   Census of housing   (US Bureau of the Census)
        Government Printing Office, Washington DC 20402.
        1940-   1970.   prices vary
        Vol 1. Housing characteristics for states, cities and counties, part 57 has data for the Panama Canal Zone.
            It is in two parts -
            HC(1)-A: General housing characteristics;
            HC(1)-B: Detailed housing characteristics.
        Time factor: the results of the census were published between 1971 and 1974.
        §   En.

¶   F   -   Social

        Refer to 1145, 1491.

¶   G   -   Finance

Refer to 1145.

¶   H   -   Transport and communications

Refer to 1145.

PARAGUAY

Central statistical office

1148   Dirección General de Estadística y Censos   [General Office of Statistics and Censuses],
        Humaitá 473,
        Asunción.
        † 47900.

        The Dirección General de Estadística y Censos has, as one of its duties, the compilation and publication
        of national statistics, and the organisation of the censuses of population and housing.   Unpublished statistical
        information can be provided in certain cases, when available.

Libraries

        The Dirección General de Estadística y Censos has a library which is open to the public for reference to
        statistical publications.

Libraries and information services abroad

        Paraguayan embassies abroad have statistical publications of Paraguay, including:

        United Kingdom   Braemar Lodge, Cornwall Gardens, London SW7   † 01-937 1253.
        USA   2400 Massachusetts Avenue NW, Washington DC.   † (202) 483 6960.

Statistical publications

¶   A - General

1149   Anuario estadístico del Paraguay   [Statistical yearbook of Paraguay]   (Dirección General de Estadística y
                Censos)
        Dirección General de Estadística y Censos, Humaitá 473, Asunción.
        1886-   1974.   not priced.   103 p.
        Main sections:
                Area and climate   Banking and public finance
                Population   Trade (internal and foreign)
                Education   Transport and communications
                Health and social services   Services (electric energy, water)
                Justice and employment   Municipal statistics
                Economy (agriculture, forestry,   Miscellaneous (agricultural registration, accidents in
                    livestock, industry)   transit)
        Time factor: the 1974 edition, published in 1976, has data for 1974 and also for earlier years in some
                tables.
        §   Es.

1150   Boletín estadístico del Paraguay   [Statistical bulletin of Paraguay]   (Dirección General de Estadística y
                Censos)
        Dirección General de Estadística y Censos, Humaitá 473, Asunción.
        1957-   quarterly.   not priced.
        Contains data on climate, demography, tourism, transport and communications, education, finance and
                banking, foreign trade, electricity, consumer price indexes, etc.
        Time factor: each issue contains the latest data available and is usually about six months earlier than the
                date of the publication.
        §   Es.

  ¶   A,   continued

1151   Boletín estadístico   [Statistical bulletin]   (Banco Central del Paraguay)
        Banco Central del Paraguay, 15 de Agosto y Estrella (altos), Asunción.
        1948-   monthly.   not priced.
        Contains data on banking, foreign trade, finance, production, balance of payments, consumer price
            indices, and insurance.
        Time factor: each issue has long runs of annual and monthly figures up to the month of the issue and is
            published about three months later.
        §   Es.

1152   Memoria...   [Report...]   (Banco Central del Paraguay)
        Banco Central del Paraguay, 15 de Agosto y Estrella (altos), Asunción.
        1944-   1971.   not priced.
        Apart from the report of the bank's activities for the year, the volume includes data on banking and
            finance, foreign trade, cost of living, agriculture, and various basic industries.
        §   Es.

1153   Manual estadístico del Paraguay   [Statistical manual for Paraguay]   (Ministerio de Agricultura y Ganadería)
        Ministerio de Agricultura y Ganadería, Asunción.
        1951/57-   1962/1969.   not priced.   157 p.
        Contains data on population, communications, transport, education, climate, industrial production,
            agriculture, livestock, forestry, banking and finance, foreign trade, prices, and general indices.
        Time factor: the 1962/1969 issue has information for the years 1962 to 1969.
        §   Es.

  ¶   B - Production

  ii.   Agriculture, fisheries, forestry, etc

1154   Censo agropecuario   [Agricultural census]   (Ministerio de Agricultura y Ganadería)
        Ministerio de Agricultura y Ganadería, Asunción.
        1860-   1956.   not priced.   697 p.
        §   Es.

        Note: a sample census was taken in 1961.

1155   Boletín estadístico   [Statistical bulletin]   (Ministerio de Agricultura y Ganadería)
        Ministerio de Agricultura y Ganadería, Asunción.
        1965-   monthly.   not priced.
        §   Es.

        Note: no recent issues of this publication have been located.

        Refer also to 1149, 1153.

  iii.   Industry

1156   Censo industrial   [Industrial census]   (Ministerio de Industria y Comercio)
        Ministerio de Industria y Comercio, Asunción.
        1955-   2nd, 1963.   not priced.   298 p.
        Contains data on industry, including general aspects, employment, wages, machinery, value of raw
            materials and power consumed, value of production.
        Time factor: published in 1966.
        §   Es.

¶   B.iii,   continued

1157   Censo económico   [Economic census]   (Ministerio de Industria y Comercio)
       Ministerio de Industria y Comercio, Asunción.
       1955- 1963.   not priced.   298 p.
       This volume contains the final results of an industrial census, a commercial census, a census of service
          industries, and a directory of industrial and commercial establishments.
       Time factor: published in 1966.
       §   Es.

       Refer also to 1151, 1152, 1153.

¶   C - External trade

1158   Boletín estadístico de comercio exterior   [Statistical bulletin of foreign trade]   (Dirección General de
          Estadística y Censos)
       Dirección General de Estadística y Censos, Asunción.
       1963/64- 1966.   not priced.   253 p.
       Main tables show detailed statistics of imports and exports arranged by commodity subdivided by countries
          of origin and destination.
       Time factor: the 1966 issue, published in 1968, has data for 1966.
       §   Es.

       Refer also to 1149, 1150, 1151, 1152, 1153.

¶   D - Internal distribution and service trades

       Refer to 1149, 1150, 1157.

¶   E - Population

1159   Censo nacional de población y viviendas   [National census of population and housing]   (Dirección General
          de Estadística y Censos)
       Dirección General de Estadística y Censos, Humaitá 473, Asunción.
       1793- 1972.   not priced.
       Publications issued so far are sub-titled
          (muestra del 10%)   [10% sample]   56p.   published in 1974.
          (cifras provisionales) [provisional figures] 32p   published in 1973.
       §   Es.

       Refer also to 1149, 1150, 1153.

¶   F - Social

       Refer to 1149, 1150, 1153.

¶   G - Finance

1160   Cuentas nacionales   [National accounts] (Banco Central del Paraguay)
       Banco Central del Paraguay, 15 de Agosto y Estrella (altos), Asunción.
       1955/57- 1962/1975.   not priced.
       Time factor: the 1962/75 issue, with data for those years, was published in 1976.
       §   Es.

       Refer also to 1149, 1151, 1152, 1153.

¶   H - Transport and communications

       Refer to 1149, 1150, 1153.

253

PERU - PEROU

Central statistical office

1161   Instituto Nacional de Estadística [National Institute of Statistics],
            Avenida 28 de Julio 1056,
            Lima 1.
            † 32-0237

            The Institute is responsible for the collection, analysis and publication of economic and social statistics
of Peru.   Unpublished information may be supplied to enquirers if available, and no charge is made for
this service.

Libraries

            The Instituto Nacional de Estadística has a library which is open to the public for reference to statistical
publications.   Such material is also available for reference in the libraries of the national universities and
in the National Library of Peru.

Libraries and information services abroad

            Peruvian embassies abroad have some statistical material, particularly the'Statistical yearbook', and
these embassies include:
            United Kingdom   Peruvian Embassy, 52 Sloane Street, London SW1   † 01-235 1917.
            USA   Peruvian Embassy, 1700 Massachusetts Avenue NW, Washington DC   † (202) 833 9860.
            Canada   Peruvian Embassy, 539 Island Park Drive, Ottawa   † 722 7186.

Statistical publications

¶   A - General

1162   Anuário estadístico del Peru   [Statistical yearbook of Peru] (Dirección General de Estadística y Censos)
        Instituto Nacional de Estadística, Avenida 28 de Julio 1056, Lima 1.
        1919- 1971.   not priced.   3 vols.
        Vol 1 contains economic and financial statistics, including agriculture, livestock, forestry, hunting,
            fisheries, minerals, petroleum, manufactures, electricity, construction, transport, internal trade,
            foreign trade, banking, public finance, national accounts, balance of payments, and external public
            debt.   Vol 2 is concerned with social statistics and vol 3 with geographical statistics.
        Time factor: only vol 1 has been examined and this has data from 1968 to 1971 or the latest data
            available.
        §   Es.

1163   Boletín del Banco Central de Reserva del Perú   [Bulletin of the Bank...]
        Banco Central de Reserva del Perú, Lima.
        1931-   monthly.   not priced.
        Includes a statistical section on banking, foreign exchange, foreign trade, and the cost of living.
        Time factor: each issue has long runs of figures to the month prior to the date of the issue.
        §   Es.

1164   Reseña económica y financiera   [Economic and financial review] (Banco Central de Reserva del Perú)
        Banco Central de Reserva del Perú, Lima.
        1944-   1970 & Jan-June 1971.   not priced.
        Includes statistics in the text and also contains a statistical annex, with data on production, monetary
            developments, balance of payments, principal exports, imports, public finance, and economic
            indicators.
        §   Es.

¶   A,   continued

1165   Memoria [Report] (Superintendencia de Banco y Seguros)
        Superintendencia de Banco y Seguros, Jr Huancavelica 240, Apartado No 775, Lima.
        (annual)   1976.   not priced.   526 p.
        Includes a statistical annex with data on the activities of the bank and other banks, finance, foreign
            trade, production, price indices, agriculture and fisheries, mineral production, etc.
        Time factor: the 1976 issue, published in 1977, has data from 1972 to 1976.
        §   Es.

¶   B - Production

i.   Mines and mining

1166   Anuário de la minería   [Mining yearbook]   (Ministerio de Energía y Minas)
        Ministerio de Energía y Minas, Lima.
        1969-   1974.   not priced.   125 p.
        Contains statistical data on production, exports, employment, finances, etc.
        Time factor: the 1974 edition, published in 1976, has data for 1974 or the latest available (1972 or 1973).
        §   Es.

1167   Censo nacional económico: resultados de censo de minería y directorio   [National economic census: mining
            results and directory]   (Dirección Nacional de Estadística y Censos)
        Instituto Nacional de Estadística, Avenida 28 de Julio 1056, Lima 1.
        1963-   1963.   not priced.
        §   Es.

        Refer also to 1162, 1165.

ii.   Agriculture, fisheries, forestry, etc

1168   Censo nacional agropecuario   [National census of agriculture and livestock]   (Oficina Nacional de
            Estadística y Censos)
        Instituto Nacional de Estadística, Avenida 28 de Julio 1056, Lima 1.
        1961-   2nd, 1972.   not priced.
        The final summary results are published in 'Resultados definitivos: nivel nacional: Perú', and there are
            also 31 volumes relating to the 23 departments of Peru and one volume on the Prov. Const. del
            Callao.
        Time factor: the results were published between 1973 and 1975.
        §   Es.

1169   Estadística agraria   [Agricultural statistics] (Oficina de Estadística: Ministerio de Agricultura)
        Ministerio de Agricultura, Lima.
        1963-   1971.   not priced.   366 p.
        Contains data on crops, livestock, forestry, fisheries, etc.
        Time factor: the 1971 issue, published late 1972, has data for 1971.
        §   Es.

        Refer also to 1162, 1165.

PERU, continued

¶ B.iii. Industry

1170 Censo nacional económico [National economic census] (Dirección Nacional de Estadística y Censos)
Instituto Nacional de Estadística, Avenida 28 de Julio 1056, Lima 1.
1963- 1963. not priced.
The census covered both industry and commerce. The volumes concerned with industry are 'Industria manufacturera' and 'Industria manufacturera: suplemento' which include data on the number of establishments, employees, wages, raw materials consumed, production, etc.
§ Es.

1171 Estadística industrial [Industrial statistics] (Dirección de Estadística y Información: Ministerio de Industria y Turismo)
Ministerio de Industria y Turismo, Lima.
1965- 1972. not priced. 76 p.
Contains data on the numbers of establishments, value of goods produced, employment, etc nationally, by department and by region.
Time factor: the 1972 issue, published in 1974, has data for 1970, 1971 and 1972.
§ Es.

1172 Indices del sector manufacturero: boletín estadístico trimestral - industria [Indices of the manufacturing sector: quarterly statistical bulletin - industry] (Dirección de Estadística y Información, Ministerio de Industria y Turismo)
Ministerio de Industria y Turismo, Lima.
Time factor: each issue is published about three months after the end of the period covered.
§ Es.

Refer also to 1162, 1164, 1165.

iv. Construction

1173 Censo nacional económico: construcción [National economic census: construction] (Dirección Nacional de Estadística y Censos)
Instituto Nacional de Estadística, Avenida 28 de Julio 1056, Lima.
1963- 1963. not priced. 31 p.
§ Es.

Refer also to 1162

v. Energy

1174 Anuário de estadística eléctrica [Statistical yearbook of electricity] (Ministerio de Energía y Minas)
Ministerio de Energía y Minas, Lima.
1971- 1974. not priced. 186 p.
Contains data on installations, production, consumption, indices and projections, systems, tariffs, etc.
Time factor: the 1974 edition, published in 1975 has data mainly for 1974.
§ Es.

1175 Estadística petrolera del Perú [Petroleum statistics for Peru] (Ministerio de Energía y Minas)
Ministerio de Energía y Minas, Lima.
1949- 1975. not priced. 109 p.
Contains data on world production of crude oil, world performance, national production of crude oil and of natural gas, refining, and commercial operations.
Time factor: the 1975 issue, published in 1976, has data for 1975 and in some tables from 1966 to 1975.
§ Es.

PERU,   continued

¶   B.v,   continued

1175,   continued

> Note: the 1975 issue was published in the 'Boletín oficial de la Dirección General de Hidrocarburos',
> 26th year, No 26.

> Refer also to 1162.

¶   C   -   External trade

1176   Estadística del comercio exterior   [Statistics of foreign trade]   (Dirección General de Aduanas, Ministerio
> de Comercio)
> Dirección General de Aduanas, Ministerio de Comercio, Lima.
> 1891- 1974.   not priced.   784 p.
> Contains detailed statistics of imports and exports arranged by commodities and subdivided by countries
> of origin and destination, and of imports and exports arranged by countries of origin and destination
> subdivided by commodity numbers.
> Time factor: the 1974 issue, published in 1976, has data for 1974.
> §   Es.

1177   Estadísticas de importación y exportación   [Statistics of imports and exports]   (Instituto Nacional de
> Estadística)
> Instituto Nacional de Estadística, Avenida 28 de Julio 1056, Lima.
> 1975- 1976.   not priced.   not pages (reduced computer printout)
> Contains detailed statistics arranged by commodities, and summary data by country of origin and
> destination.
> Time factor: the 1976 issue, published in 1978, has data for each month of 1976.
> §   Es.

1178   Boletín estadístico de comercio exterior   [Statistics bulletin of foreign trade]   (Ministerio de Comercio)
> Ministerio de Comercio, Lima.
> 1972- half-yearly.   not priced.
> Contains data on imports and exports for January to June and January to December, imports and exports
> being issued in separate volumes.
> Time factor: each issue, is published three to six months after the end of the period covered.
> §   Es.

> Refer also to 1162, 1163, 1164, 1165.

¶   D   -   Internal distribution and service trades

1179   Censo nacional económico   [National economic census]   (Dirección General de Estadística y Censos)
> Instituto Nacional de Estadística, Avenida 28 de Julio 1056, Lima.
> 1963- 1963.   not priced.
> The census covered both industry and commerce.   The volume concerning internal distribution and
> services is 'Censo de comercio y de servicios' which includes data on the number of establishments
> in the various retail and service trades, employees, wages, sales figures, etc.
> §   Es.

1180   Estadística del turismo en el Perú, 1971   [Statistics of tourism in Peru, 1971]   (Ministerio de Industria y
> Comercio: Dirección General de Turismo)
> Ministerio de Comercio, Lima.
> §   Es.

> Refer also to 1162.

¶   E   -   Population

1181   Censos nacionales...de población...[y] de vivienda   [National census of population and housing]   (Oficina
              Nacional de Estadística y Censos)
              Instituto Nacional de Estadística, Avenida 28 de Julio 1056, Lima.
              1836-   1972.   not priced.
              The summary of final results is published as 'Resultados definitivos: nivel nacional' in two volumes.
                    There are also between one and four volumes for each of the departments of Peru with more detailed
                    data.
              Time factor: the results of the 1972 census were published in 1974.
              §   Es.

1182   Boletín de análisis demográfico   [Bulletin of demographic analysis]   (Instituto Nacional de Estadística)
              Instituto Nacional de Estadística, Avenida 28 de Julio 1056, Lima.
              1965-   irregular.   not priced.
              Each issue is devoted to a separate subject and some include a few statistics, whilst others have more.
                    Issue No 16, published late 1975, has projections of the population of Peru from 1960 to 2000.
              §   Es.

              Refer also to 1162.

¶   F   -   Social

1183   Indice de precios al consumidor, base 1973=100.00, Lima metropolitana   [Consumer price index, base
              1973=100.00, metropolitan Lima]   (Instituto Nacional de Estadística)
              Instituto Nacional de Estadística, Avenida 28 de Julio 1056, Lima.
              1962-   monthly.   not priced.
              Time factor: each issue has long runs of monthly figures to the date of the issue and is published some
                    months later.
              §   Es.

              Refer also to 1162, 1163.

¶   G   -   Finance

1184   Cuentas nacionales del Perú   [National accounts of Peru]   (Banco Central de Reserva del Perú)
              Banco Central de Reserva del Perú, Lima.
              1950/65-   1960-1974.   not priced.   44 p.
              Time factor: the 1960-1974 issue, published in 1976, has data for 1960, 1963, and 1967 to 1974.
              §   Es.

1185   Cuentas financieras del Perú   [Financial accounts of Peru]   (Banco Central de Reserva del Perú)
              Banco Central de Reserva del Perú, Lima.
                         quarterly.   not priced.
              §   Es.

              Refer also to 1162, 1163, 1164, 1165.

¶   H   -   Transport and communications

              Refer to 1162.

PUERTO RICO

Central statistical office

1186   Planning Board. Junta de Planificación,
North Building,
Box 41119,
Santurce, Puerto Rico 00940.
t 726 6200.

The Planning Board is the main source of economic statistics on Puerto Rico, other than those published by the United States Department of Commerce, Bureau of the Census.

Statistical publications

1187   Anuario estadístico   Statistical yearbook: Puerto Rico (Planning Board)
      Planning Board, North Building, Box 41119, Santurce, Puerto Rico 00940.
      1960- 1968.   not priced.   224 p.
      Contains data on population, demography, climate, public health and welfare, crime and delinquency, education, labour force, employment and payroll, national accounts and related economic statistics, agricultural production and related subjects, industry, prices, distribution of products and services, construction and housing, transport and communications, passenger movement and tourism, banking, finance, insurance, public accounts, and foreign trade.
      Time factor: the 1968 edition, published in 1970, has data for 1967 and 1968, and some earlier years.
      §   En,   Es.

1188   Estadísticas socioeconómicas de Puerto Rico...   Socioeconomic statistics of Puerto Rico... (Bureau of Statistics, Planning Board)
      Bureau of Statistics, Planning Board, North Building, Box 41119, Santurce, Puerto Rico 00940.
      1940/73-   1940, 1950, 1960, 1963-1976.   not priced.   14 p.
      Contains data on gross product, national income, vital statistics, education, labour, agriculture, construction, tourism, transport, communications, passenger movement, foreign trade, banking, and other (consumer price indices, electric energy, highway maintenance, beer production, bottled rum production, sales of petrol, water supply, etc).
      Time factor: the 1940-76 issue was published in 1977.
      §   En,   Es.

1189   Compendio estadísticas sociales [Compendium of social statistics] (Planning Board)
      Planning Board, North Building, Box 41119, Santurce, Puerto Rico 00940.
                   not priced.   129 p.
      Contains data on population, health, accidents, human resources, education, housing, communications, transport, social benefits, protection, culture, recreation, crime and delinquency.
      Time factor: published in 1973, the compendium has long runs of statistics to 1972 or 1971/72.
      §   Es.

1190   Indicadores económicos mensuales de Puerto Rico : Monthly economic indicators of Puerto Rico (Bureau of Statistics, Planning Board)
      Bureau of Statistics, Planning Board, North Building, Box 41119, Santurce, Puerto Rico 00940.
      1964-   not priced.
      Indicators of production, employment, manufacture, construction, tourism, transport, foreign trade, banking, public finance, personal consumption, and consumer price index.
      Time factor: each issue has indicators covering two fiscal years and the three latest months.
      §   En,   Es.

1191   Economy and finances: Puerto Rico   (Department of the Treasury)
            Department of the Treasury, PO Box 4515, San Juan, Puerto Rico 00905.
            1970- 1975. not priced.   35p.
            Mainly textual but contains brief statistics of economic activity.
            Time factor: the 1975 issue, published in 1976, has data for 1975 and some earlier years.
            §   En.

            Refer also to 1324.

    ¶   B - Production

    ii.   Agriculture, fisheries, forestry, etc

1192   Anuario de estadísticas agricolas de Puerto Rico   [Statistical yearbook of agriculture: Puerto Rico]   (Oficina
            de Estadística Agricolas, Departamento de Agricultura)
            Departamento de Agricultura, Apartado 10163, Santurce, Puerto Rico 00908.
            1968/69- 1973/74.   not priced.   113 p.
            Contains data on use of land, livestock statistics, aviculture, sugar cane, other (coffee, tobacco, etc),
                agricultural income and sales, foreign trade, population of agricultural workers, etc.
            Time factor: the 1973/74 issue, published late 1975, has data for 1974 or crop year 1973/74 and some
                earlier years.
            §   Es.

1193   Boletín mensual de estadísticas agricolas   [Monthly bulletin of statistics of agriculture]   (Oficina de
            Estadística Agricolas, Departamento de Agricultura)
            Departamento de Agricultura, Apartado 10163, Santurce, Puerto Rico 00908.
            1961-   not priced.
            Contains data on sugar, shipments, labour force, sales, prices, livestock, wages, climate.
            Time factor: each issue has data to the previous month.
            §   Es.

1194   Facts and figures on Puerto Rico's agriculture   (Office of Agricultural Statistics and Economic Studies,
            Department of Agriculture)
            Departamento de Agricultura, Apartado 10163, Santurce, Puerto Rico 00908.
            1969/70- 1974/75-1975/76.   not priced,   113 p.
            Contains data on land in farms, livestock statistics, dairy statistics, poultry statistics, sugar statistics,
                field crops, other crops, marketing and agricultural income, imports and exports, labour statistics
                and population, and miscellaneous (fertilisers, etc).
            Time factor: the 1974/75-1975/76 issue, published late 1977, has data for several years to 1975/76
                crop year.
            §   En.

            Refer also to 1187, 1342, 1350.

    iii.   Industry

1195   Censo de industrias manufactureras de Puerto Rico: Census of manufacturing industries of Puerto Rico   (Bureau
            of Labour Statistics)
            Negociado de Estadísticas del Trabajo, Departamento de Trabajo, Santurce, Puerto Rico.
            1946- 1976.   not priced.   13 p.
            Results of an annual census of employment in the manufacturing industries, including numbers of
                establishments and employees by major industry groups, as well as hours of work, earnings, etc.
            Time factor: the 1976 issue, published early 1977, has data for 1976.   The 1973 issue was a more
                substantial one.
            §   En,   Es.

PUERTO RICO, continued

¶   B.iii,   continued

1196   Economic census of outlying areas: vol 4: Puerto Rico; manufactures   (US Bureau of the Census)
            Government Printing Office, Washington DC 20402.
            1946-   1972.   US$2.90.
            Contains data on numbers of establishments, employees, finances, production, etc, by industry, by area,
                and local and non-local ownership.
            Time factor: the results of the 1972 census were published in 1974/75.
            §   En,   Es.

            Refer also to 1187, 1190.

    iv.   Construction

1197   Economic census of outlying areas: vol 3; Puerto Rico; construction industry   (US Bureau of the Census)
            Government Printing Office, Washington DC 20402, USA.
            1972-   1972.   US$2.
            Contains data by kind of business.
            Time factor: the results of the 1972 census were published in 1974/75.
            §   En,   Es.

            Refer also to 1187, 1188, 1190.

    v.   Energy

            Refer to 1188.

¶   C   -   External trade

1198   External trade statistics   (Planning Board)
            Planning Board, North Building, Box 41119, Santurce, Puerto Rico 00940.
            1969-   1975.   not priced.   696 p.
            Contains statistical data on shipments from the USA to Puerto Rico, by commodity; shipments to the USA
                from Puerto Rico, by commodity; imports and exports of Puerto Rico, commodity by country; imports
                and exports of Puerto Rico, by country; and shipments of merchandise between Puerto Rico and the
                Virgin Islands, by commodity.
            Time factor: the 1975 issue, published mid-1977, has data for 1975.
            §   En,   Es.

            Refer also to 1187, 1188, 1190, 1413, 1421.

¶   D   -   Internal distribution and service trades

1199   Economic census of outlying areas: vol 1-2: Puerto Rico; retail trade, wholesale trade and selected service
                industries   (US Bureau of the Census)
            Government Printing Office, Washington DC 20402.
            1939-   1972.   Vol 1 US$2.65; Vol 2 US$3.50.   2 vols.
            Volume 1 is an area report, with data by varied kind-of-business detail on number of establishments, sales
                or receipts, payroll, employment, and working partners and proprietors.   Data is given for Puerto
                Rico, each municipio, and place with 2500 inhabitants or more.   Vol 2 is a subject report, with
                data for Puerto Rico by sales or receipts, size, employment size, and legal forms of organisation; for
                retail trade, by merchandising lines; and for wholesale trade, by class of customer.
            Time factor: the results of the 1972 census were published in 1974/75.
            §   En,   Es.

¶ D,   continued

1200   The tourism industry of Puerto Rico: selected statistics   (Tourism Company of Puerto Rico)
Tourism Company, GPO Box BN, San Juan , Puerto Rico.
1970/71- 1976/77.   not priced.   87 p.
Contains data on passenger movement, numbers and expenditure of visitors, growth and occupancy rates
of hotels, employment in the industry.
Time factor: the 1976/77 issue, published early 1978, has monthly and annual data for several years to
mid-1977.
§   En.

Note: 'Selected statistics on the visitors and hotel industry in Puerto Rico' for 1967/68 and 1968/69 were
prepared by the Office of Economic Research in co-ordination with the Department of Tourism.

Refer also to 1187, 1188, 1190.

¶   E - Population

1201   Census of population   (US Bureau of the Census)
Government Printing Office, Washington DC 20402, USA.
1850- 1970.   various prices.
Vol 1 Characteristics of the population, part 53 has data for Puerto Rico.   It is in four parts, which
were initially available separately -
PC(1)-A: number of inhabitants;
PC(1)-B: general population characteristics;
PC(1)-C: general, social and economic characteristics; and
PC(1)-D: detailed characteristics.
Time factor: the results of the 1970 census were published between 1971 and 1974.
§   En.

1202   Informe anual de estadisticas vitales : Annual vital statistics report   (Departamento de Salud. Department of
Health)
Departamento de Salud, San Juan, Puerto Rico.
1968- 1976.   not priced.   100 p.
Contains data on demography, population, births, deaths, violent deaths, infant deaths, maternity deaths,
marriages and divorces.
Time factor: the 1976 issue, published late 1977, has data for 1976.
§   En,   Es.

1203   Emploi, horas y salarios en los establecimientos manufactureros promovidos por la administración de fomento
económico o la compañia de fomento industrial de Puerto Rico: Employment, hours and earnings in
the manufacturing establishments promoted by the economic development administration or the Puerto
Rican industrial development company   (Departamento del Trabajo y Recursos Humanos.   Department
of Labor and Human Resources).
Departamento del Trabajo y Recursos Humanos, San Juan.
1950- monthly.   not priced.
Time factor: each issue has data for the month and some earlier figures, and is published about three
months later.
§   En,   Es.

1204   Employment and unemployment in Puerto Rico   (Department of Labor)
Department of Labor, 414 Barbosa Avenue, Hato Rey, Puerto Rico 00917.
1970- monthly and annual.   not priced.
Time factor: each issue has data to about three months prior to the date of the issue.
§   En,   Es.

Refer also to 1187, 1188, 1189, 1190, 1195.

¶   E,   continued

1205   Estado de empleo de la población civil no institucional   State of employment of the civilian non-institutional
            population   (Bureau of Labor Statistics)
        Departamento de Trabajo, 414 Barbosa Avenue, Hato Rey, Puerto Rico 00917.
        1974-   monthly.   not priced.
        Time factor: each issue has data for that month and is published about a month later.
        §   En,   Es.

1206   Census of housing   (US Bureau of the Census)
        Government Printing Office, Washington DC 20402, USA.
        1960-   1970.
        The following volumes have been published:
            Census of housing. Vol 1: housing characteristics for states, cities and counties. Part 53: Puerto
            Rico   (US$4.50) which includes -
                HC(1)-A: General housing characteristics: Puerto Rico
                HC(1)-B: Detailed housing characteristics: Puerto Rico.
        Time factor: the reports were published in 1973 and 1972.
        §   En,   Es.

¶   F   -   Social

i.   Standard of living

1207   Consumer price index for wage earners' families in Puerto Rico   (Bureau of Labor Statistics)
        Department of Labor, 414 Barbosa Avenue, Hato Rey, Puerto Rico 00917.
        1966-   monthly.   free.
        Time factor: each issue has data to the month of the issue.
        §   En,   Es.

1208   Income and expenditure of the families, Puerto Rico   (Bureau of Labor Statistics)
        Department of Labor, 414 Barbosa Avenue, Hato Rey, Puerto Rico 00917.
        1953-   2nd, 1963.   not priced.   9 vols.
        Time factor: the 1963 volumes were published in 1967.
        §   En,   Es.

        Refer also to 1188, 1190.

ii.   Health and welfare

1209   Informe anual de estadísticas de salud   [Annual report on health statistics]   (Departamento de Salud)
        Departamento de Salud, San Juan, Puerto Rico.
        1971/72-   1975/76.   not priced.   72 p.
        Contains data on hospitals, public health, staffing, etc.
        Time factor: the 1975/76 issue, published in 1977, has data for the years 1975/76.
        §   Es.

        Refer also to 1187, 1189.

iii.   Education

        Refer to 1187, 1188, 1189.

¶   G   -   Finance

1210   Puerto Rico: business review   (Government Development Bank for Puerto Rico)
            Government Development Bank for Puerto Rico, PO Box 42001, San Juan, Puerto Rico 00940; or
                140 Broadway, New York, BY NY 10005, USA.
            1976-   monthly.   not priced.
            Includes statistics in the features and articles but has no regular tables.
            §   En.

1211   Balanza de pagos, Puerto Rico   Balance of payments   (Junta de Planificación)
            Junta de Planificación, North Building, Box 41119, Santurce, Puerto Rico 00940.
            1961-   1975.   not priced.   60 p.
            Time factor: the 1975 issue, published mid-1976, has long runs of figures to 1975.
            §   En,   Es.

1212   Ingreso y producto: Puerto Rico: income and products   (Planning Board)
            Junta de Planificación, North Building, Box 41119, Santurce, Puerto Rico 00940.
            1956-   1972.   not priced.   73 p.
            Time factor: the 1972 issue, published early 1973, has data for 1940, 1950, 1960 to 1972.
            §   Es,   En.

            Refer also to 1187, 1188, 1190, 1496.

¶   H   -   Transport and communications

        Refer to 1187, 1188, 1189, 1190, 1519.

There is no central statistical office on the islands but enquiries for statistical information could be made to the Minister of Finance, Trade, Development and Tourism, Basseterre, St Kitts, or to St Kitts-Nevis Chamber of Commerce, Basseterre, St Kitts.

Statistical publications

1213   St Kitts-Nevis - Anguilla: report   (Foreign and Commonwealth Office)
          HM Stationery Office, PO Box 569, London SE1 9NH.
          1955/56- 1959-1962.   £0.32½.   74 p.
          Contains a few tables in the text which covers population, occupations, wages, public finance and
              taxation, currency and banking, commerce, production, social services, justice, police, prisons, etc.
          Time factor: the 1959-1962 report was published in 1966.
          §   En.

   ¶   B - Production   Refer to 1213.

   ¶   C - External trade

1214   External trade report   (Ministry of Finance: Statistics Department)
          Ministry of Finance, Basseterre, St Kitts.
          1953- 1973. $10.   326 p.
          Main tables show statistics of imports and exports arranged by commodity and subdivided by countries of
              origin and destination.
          Time factor: the 1973 issue, published in 1975, has data for 1973.
          §   En.

1215   External trade report (summary tables)   (Ministry of Finance: Statistics Department)
          Ministry of Finance, Basseterre, St Kitts.
          1975- 1975. $5.   38 p.
          Main tables show statistics of imports and exports arranged by commodity and subdivided by countries of
              origin and destination.   This volume was produced because of delay in publication of the final
              reports (see above).
          Time factor: the 1975 issue, with data for 1975, was issued early 1978.
          §   En.

          Refer also to 1213.

   ¶   D - Internal distribution and service trades   Refer also to 1213.

   ¶   E - Population

1216   Census of population
          1921- 1970.

          Refer to 258 for details of the 1970 population census of the Commonwealth Caribbean.

          Refer also to 1213.

   ¶   F - Social   Refer to 1213.

   ¶   G - Finance   Refer to 1213.

ST LUCIA

Central statistical office

1217   Development, Planning and Statistics Division,
            Premier's Office,
            Post Office Building,
            Castries.
            t   2611 ext 155 or 154.

            The Development, Planning and Statistics Division collects, analyses and publishes economic and social
        statistics of St Lucia.   Unpublished statistical information is supplied on request when available and no fee
        is charged.

        Statistical publications

    ¶   A   -   General

1218   Annual statistical digest   (Development, Planning and Statistics Division)
            Development, Planning and Statistics Division, Premier's Office, Post Office Building, Castries.
            1966-   1975. $6.   57 p.
            Main sections:
                    Population   Foreign trade
                    Manpower   Prices and wages
                    Agriculture   Banking and finance
                    Forestry and timber   Education
                    Industrial production   Health
                    Energy   Justice
                    Building and construction   Social
                    Transport and communications   Meteorological
            Time factor: the 1975 edition, published late 1976, has data for 1974 or 1975 and two or three earlier
                    years.
            §   En.

    ¶   B   -   Production

            Refer to 1218.

    ¶   C   -   External trade

1219   Overseas trade of St Lucia   (Development, Planning and Statistics Division)
            Development, Planning and Statistics Division, Premier's Office, Post Office Building, Castries.
            1951-   Part I: 1974 $10 each vol.   2 vols.
                    Part II: 1973
            Part I contains detailed statistics of imports and exports arranged by commodities and subdivided by
                    countries of origin and destination; part II contains summary tables.
            Time factor: part I for 1974, with data for that year, was published in 1975; part II for 1973, with data
                    for that year, was published in 1976.
            §   En.

1220   Preliminary summary tables of external trade: tables...   (Ministry of Trade, Industry and Tourism)
            Ministry of Trade, Industry and Tourism, Castries.
            1974-   1976.   45 p.
            Contains data on trade by commodities (SITC sections and divisions), trade by country, and trade with
                    CARIM countries.
            Time factor: the 1976 issue, published in 1977, has data for 1974, 1975 and 1976, plus earlier years in
                    some tables.
            §   En.

¶   C,   continued

1221   Quarterly overseas trade report   (Ministry of Trade, Industry and Tourism)
            Ministry of Trade, Industry and Tourism, Castries.
            1960-   not priced.
            Contains data on imports and exports arranged by commodity and sub-divided by countries of origin and
                destination.
            Time factor: each issue has data for the quarter of the issue, the latest being for the 1st quarter of 1976.
            §   En.

            Refer also to 1218.

¶   E   -   Population

1222   Census of population
            1891-   1970.
            Refer to 258 for details of the 1970 population census of the Commonwealth Caribbean.

            Refer also to 1218.

¶   F   -   Social

            Refer to 1218.

¶   G   -   Finance

            Refer to 1218.

¶   H   -   Transport and communications

            Refer to 1218.

Central statistical office

1223   Institut National de la Statistique et des Etudes Economiques   [National Institute for Statistics and
              Economic Research],
         18 boulevard Adolphe Pinard,
         75675 Paris Cedex 14,
         France.
         t 555 92 20   telex 207.28 Inseedir Paris.

         INSEE is the central organisation for economic information on France and it also collects and publishes
     information on French overseas territories, of which St Pierre et Miquelon is one.   It is concerned with social
     and economic demography, consumption, prices, income, national accounts, and national and regional
     economic planning.

Statistical publications

¶   A   -   General

1224   Annuaire statistique des territoires d'outre-mer   [Statistical yearbook of overseas territories]   (Institut
              National de la Statistique et des Etudes Economiques)
         INSEE, 18 boulevard Adolphe Pinard, 75675 Paris Cedex 14, France.
         1959-   1969-1971.   not priced.   406 p.
         Contains data on physical aspects, climate, demography, active population, health, education, production,
              prices, wages, transport and communications, foreign trade, money and credit, public finance,
              economic accounts, for French overseas territories, including St Pierre et Miquelon.
         Time factor: published in 1973.
         §   Fr.

¶   B   -   Production

         Refer to 1224.

¶   C   -   External trade

1225   Statistique du commerce et de la navigation de Saint Pierre et Miquelon   [Foreign trade statistics of St Pierre
              et Miquelon]   (Direction des Douanes)
         Direction des Douanes, St Pierre et Miquelon or INSEE, 18 boulevard Adolphe Pinard, 75675 Paris
              Cedex 14, France.
         1961-   1974.   Fr 4.   26 p.
         Main tables included show detailed statistics of imports and exports arranged by commodity and subdivided
              by countries of origin and destination.
         Time factor: the 1974 issue, with data for 1974, was published in 1975.
         §   Fr.

         Refer also to 1224.

¶   E   -   Population

1226   Recensement de la population du territoire de Saint Pierre et Miquelon   [Census of population for the territory
              of St Pierre et Miquelon]   (Institut National de la Statistiques et des Etudes Economiques)
         INSEE, 18 boulevard Adolphe Pinard, 75675 Paris Cedex 14, France.
         1962-   3rd, 1974.   Fr 5.   c 36 p.
         Contains data on the population of the territory by sex, age, matrimonial conditions, nationality, families
              and housing.
         Time factor: published in 1974.
         §   Fr.
[continued next page]

¶   E,   continued

1226,   continued

Refer also to 1224.

¶   F - Social

Refer to 1224.

¶   G - Finance

Refer to 1224.

¶   H - Transport and communications

Refer to 1224.

ST VINCENT

Central statistical office

1227   Statistical Office,
            Ministry of Finance & Information,
            Kingstown.
            t 61111 ext 19/20.

            The Statistical Office is responsible for the collection, analysis and publication of statistical information
            concerning St Vincent, except for foreign trade statistics, which are the responsibility of the Customs Depart-
            ment of the Ministry of Trade, Agriculture and Tourism.

Statistical publications

¶   A - General

1228   Digest of statistics (Statistical Office)
            Government Printing Office, Kingstown.
            1959- 1975.   not priced.   46 p.
            Main sections:
                    Area & climate   Finance and banking
                    Population and vital statistics   Consumption and production
                    Transport and communications   Prices (retail price index)
                    Education   External trade
                    Crime   Tourism
            Time factor: the 1975 edition, published in 1977, has data for 1975 and some earlier years.
            §   En.

¶   B - Production

            Refer to 1228.

¶   C - External trade

1229   Annual trade report   (Customs Department)
            Government Printing Office, Kingstown.
            1954- 1967.   EC$2.   166 p.
            Main tables show detailed statistics of imports and exports arranged by commodities and subdivided by
                    countries of origin and destination.
            Time factor: the 1967 issue, published in 1969, has data for 1967.
            §   En.

1230   Quarterly overseas trade report   (Customs Department)
            Government Printing Office, Kingstown.
            1965-   not priced.
            Contains detailed statistics of imports and exports arranged by commodity and subdivided by countries of
                    origin and destination.
            Time factor: each issue has data for the quarter of the issue, cumulated figures for the year to date and
                    corresponding figures for the previous year.   Oct-Dec 1972 is the latest issue published.
            §   En.

            Refer also to 1228.

¶   D - Internal distribution and service trades

            Refer to 1228.

¶ E - Population

1231 Census of population
1891- 1970.
Refer to 258 for details of the 1970 population census of the Commonwealth Caribbean.

Refer also to 1228.

¶ F - Social

Refer to 1228.

¶ G - Finance

Refer to 1228.

¶ H - Transport and communications

Refer to 1228.

Central statistical office

1232   Dirección General de Estadística y Censos   [General Office of Statistics and Censuses],
            Calle Arce no 973,
            San Salvador.
            t   225011 & 216173.

        The Office is responsible for the taking of 10-yearly censuses of population and housing, and 5-yearly
        censuses of agriculture, industry and commerce, as well as the collection, analysis and publication of
        statistics relating to El Salvador on a monthly, quarterly and annual basis.   Unpublished data is supplied on
        request if available, and is usually in the form of computer printout.

Libraries

        The Dirección General de Estadística y Censos (see above) has a library which is open to the public.
        The more important statistical publications are also available for reference in the national library and the
        university library in San Salvador.

Statistical publications

1233   Anuario estadístico   [Statistical yearbook]   (Dirección General de Estadística y Censos)
            Dirección General de Estadística y Censos, Calle Arce no 973, San Salvador.
            1911- 1976.   free distribution.   5 vols.
            Contents:
                Vol   I   Foreign trade (Section 1 deals with imports and section 2 with exports.   The main tables
                        in both volumes show detailed trade by commodity subdivided by countries of origin and
                        destination)
                Vol II   Population, demography, migration, tourism, medical assistance & health.
                Vol III   Industry, commerce, and service trades
                Vol IV   Climate, agricultural production, game and fisheries, manufacturing production, construction,
                        internal trade, transport, communications, public finance, banking, and prices.
                Vol V   Labour, education, other cultural aspects (publishing, radio, recreation), justice, accidents
                        in transit, registration of property.
            Time factor: the 1976 edition, with data for that year and earlier years also in some tables, was published
                        from 1977 onwards.
            §   Es.

1234   Boletín estadístico   [Statistical bulletin]   (Dirección General de Estadística y Censos)
            Dirección General de Estadística y Censos, Calle Arce no 973, San Salvador.
            1935-   quarterly.   free.
            Contains data on population, demography, migration, manufacturing production, construction, foreign
                trade, internal trade, transport, public finance, banking, prices, other aspects of culture (publishing,
                television and radio, spectacles, etc), justice, and accidents in transit.
            Time factor: each issue has data for the quarter of the issue and also monthly figures for that period, and
                is published about six months later.
            §   Es.

1235   El Salvador en graficas   [El Salvador in figures]   (Dirección General de Estadística y Censos)
            Dirección General de Estadística y Censos, Calle Arce no 973, San Salvador.
            1956- 1975.   free.   89 p.
            Main sections:
                Population   Prices
                Demography   Construction
                Health   Electricity
                Transport   Tourism

[continued next page]

EL SALVADOR, continued

1235, contd Communications   Social services
            Roads   Social security
            Education   Finance
            Culture   Banking
            Justice   Foreign trade
            Agriculture   Climate
            Livestock   Special tables
            Industry
            Time factor: the 1975 edition, published late 1975, has provisional data for 1974 and final data for
                several earlier years.
            § Es.

1236   Indicadores económicos y sociales [Economic and social indicators] (Ministerio de Planificación y
                Coordinación del Desarrollo Económico y Social)
            Ministerio de Planificación y Coordinación del Desarrollo Económico y Social, Casa Presidencial, San
                Salvador.
                    quarterly.   not priced.
            Contains statistical indicators on population, migration, housing, national accounts, agriculture and
                fisheries, manufacture, trade, electric energy, transport and communications, investment, public
                finance, foreign trade, money and banking, education, labour, and health.
            Time factor: each issue has annual and monthly data for several years to the date of the issue and is
                published some months later.
            § Es.

1237   Revista mensual [Monthly review] (Banco Central de Reserva de El Salvador)
            Banco Central de Reserva de El Salvador, San Salvador.
            1968-   not priced.
            Contains data on money and banking, foreign trade, public finance, production and prices.
            Time factor: each issue has annual and monthly data to about one month prior to the date of the issue.
            § Es.

            Note: the bank also issues an annual 'Memoria' [annual report] which is devoted to activities of the
                bank.

1238   Boletín estadístico industrial [Statistical bulletin of industry] (Dirección General de Estadística y Censos)
            Dirección General de Estadística y Censos, Calle Arce no 973, San Salvador.
            1975- quarterly.   free.
            Includes data on agriculture, livestock, forestry, hunting, fisheries, industry, foreign and internal trade,
                services, transport, communications, tourism, prices, wages, consumption, etc.
            Time factor: each issue has data for the quarter or cumulated figures for the year to date, and is published
                about six months later.
            § Es.

    ¶ B - Production

1239   Censos nacionales: censos económicos [National censuses: economic censuses] (Dirección General de
                Estadística y Censos)
            Dirección General de Estadística y Censos, Calle Arce no 973, San Salvador.
            1950/51- 1972. not priced. 3 vols.
            Contents:
                Vol I   Manufacturing: data on firms employing 5 or more persons, and data on firms employing
                        4 or less persons.
                Vol II Agricultural industry (cotton, sugar, coffee), construction, electricity, and commercial
                        land transport.
                Vol III Trade, commerce, and service trades
            Time factor: the results of the censuses were published in 1977.
            § Es.

¶   B,   continued

1240   Económia salvadoreña   [Economics of El Salvador]   (Universidad de El Salvador: Facultad de Ciencias
            Económicas)
            Universidad de El Salvador, San Salvador.
            1952-   January-December 1973.   not priced.   80 p.
            Includes a statistical annex with data on the structure of agricultural, mineral and industrial production.
            Time factor: the 1973 issue includes data from 1961 to estimated figures for 1974.
            §   Es.

     ii.   Agriculture, fisheries, forestry, etc

1241   Censo agropecuario   [Agricultural census]   (Dirección General de Estadística y Censos)
            Dirección General de Estadística y Censos, Calle Arce no 973, San Salvador.
            1950-   3rd, 1971.   not priced.   2 vols.
            Contains data on numbers of farms, employees on the land, acreages of land, crops and livestock.
            Time factor: the results of the 1971 census were published in 1975.
            §   Es.

1242   Estadísticas agropecuarias continuas   [Continuing statistics of agriculture and livestock]   (Ministerio de
            Agricultura y Ganadería)
            Ministerio de Agricultura y Ganadería, San Salvador.
            1960-   1966/67.   not priced.
            §   Es.

            Refer also to 1233, 1235, 1236.

    iii.   Industry

            Refer to 1233, 1234, 1235, 1236, 1237.

    iv.   Construction

            Refer to 1233, 1234, 1235.

    v.   Energy

1243   Estadística de las empresas eléctricas de servicio pública y privado de la República de El Salvador   [Statistics
            of the electric companies of El Salvador]   (Ministerio de Económia: Inspección General de Empresas
            y Servicios Electricos)
            Ministerio de Económia, San Salvador.
            1972-   1975.   not priced.   65 p.
            Contains data on the various electric companies.
            Time factor: the 1975 issue, published in 1976, has data for 1975.
            §   Es.

1244   Estadística eléctrica   [Electricity statistics]   (Ministerio de Económia: Inspección General de Empresas y
            Servicios Eléctricos)
            Ministerio de Económia, San Salvador.
            (annual)   1977.   not priced.   44 p.
            Contains data on various electricity companies, distribution, etc.
            Time factor: the 1977 issue, with data for 1977, was published in 1978.
            §   Es.

            Refer also to 1235.

EL SALVADOR,   continued

¶   C   -   External trade

1245   Boletín estadistico de comercio exterior   [Statistical bulletin of foreign trade]   (Instituto Salvadoreño de
            Comercio Exterior)
        Instituto Salvadoreño de Comercio Exterior, Paseo General Escalon 4122, (BP 19) San Salvador.
        1977-   1977.   not priced.   67 p.
        Contains basic information about El Salvador, balance of payments and commerce, imports and exports
            arranged by commodity, and exports and imports arranged by area and countries of origin and
            destination.
        Time factor: the 1977 issue, published mid-1978, has data for 1977.
        §   Es.

        Refer also to 1233, 1234, 1235, 1236, 1237.

¶   D   -   Internal distribution and service trades

        Refer to 1233, 1234, 1235.

¶   E   -   Population

1246   Censo nacional de población   [National census of population]   (Dirección General de Estadística y Censos)
        Dirección General de Estadística y Censos, Calle Arce no 973, San Salvador.
        1930-   4th, 1971.   not priced.   2 vols.
        Vol I contains data on general characteristics, educational characteristics, and fecundity; vol II has
            economic characteristics.
        Time factor: the results of the 1971 census were published in 1974.
        §   Es.

1247   Censo nacional de vivienda   [National census of housing]   (Dirección General de Estadística y Censos)
        Dirección General de Estadística y Censos, Calle Arce no 973, San Salvador.
        1950-   3rd, 1971.   not priced.   435 p.
        Time factor: the results of the 1971 census were published in 1974.
        §   Es.

        Refer also to 1233, 1234, 1235, 1236.

¶   F   -   Social

1248   Indice de precios al consumidor abrero (San Salvador, Mejicanos y Delgado)   [Index of consumer prices]
            (Dirección General de Estadística y Censos)
        Dirección General de Estadística y Censos, Calle Arce no 973, San Salvador.
            monthly.   not priced.
        §   Es.

1249   Encuesta de ingresos y gastos familiares (familias de ingresos menores de seiscientos colones $600): area
            metropolitana   [Survey of family income and expenditure (families with incomes of less than colones
            $600)...]   (Dirección General de Estadística y Censos)
        Dirección General de Estadística y Censos, Calle Arce no 973, San Salvador.
            free.   110 p.
        Time factor: the survey refers to 1949 and was published in 1972.
        §   Es.

        Refer also to 1233, 1234, 1235, 1236.

275

¶   G   -   Finance

1250   Estadísticas seguros, fianzas, capitalización   [Statistics of insurance, finance, capital]   (Junta Monetaria)
      Junta Monetaria, San Salvador.
      §   Es.

      Refer also to 1233, 1234, 1235, 1236, 1237.

¶   H   -   Transport and communications

      Refer to 1233, 1234, 1235, 1236.

Central statistical office

1251   Algemeen Bureau voor de Statistiek   [General Bureau of Statistics],
Dr S Redmondstraat 118,
Paramaribo.
t 73927.

The Bureau is responsible for the collection, analysis and publication of the official economic statistics
for Surinam, many of which are issued in the series "Suriname in cijfers" [Surinam in figures].

Statistical publications

¶ A - General

1252   Jaarcijfers voor Suriname.   Statistical yearbook of Surinam   (Algemeen Bureau voor de Statistiek)
Algemeen Bureau voor de Statistiek, Dr S Redmondstraat 118, Paramaribo.
1956/60- 1958/62.   not priced.   172 p.
Contains data on area, soil and climate; population; public health; housing; religion; education; adult
education and recreation; economically active population, employment and unemployment; establishments; agriculture and fisheries; manufacture; foreign trade; traffic and transport; money and banking;
national accounts; balance of payments; public finance; income and wealth; consumption; prices;
social affairs; justice; miscellaneous.
Time factor: Issued as Suriname in cijfers, no 34', the 1958/62 yearbook has data for those years and
was published in 1965.
§   En, NI.

1253   Statistische berichten [Statistical bulletin] (Algemeen Bureau voor de Statistiek)
Algemeen Bureau voor de Statistiek, Dr S Redmondstraat 118, Paramaribo.
1956- monthly.   not priced.
Each issue is devoted to a different subject: prices, balance of payments, shipping, finance, money, etc.
§   NI, En.

1254   Verslag [Report] (Centrale Bank van Suriname)
Centrale Bank van Suriname, Paramaribo.
(annual) 1971.   not priced.   106 p.
Contains text and tables on the economy, agriculture, fisheries, forestry, minerals, industrial production,
building activity, trade and tourism.
Time factor: the 1971 issue, published in 1972, has data for 1971 and some earlier years.
§   NI.

1255   Suriname in vogelvlucht [A bird's eye view of Surinam] (Algemeen Bureau voor de Statistiek)
Algemeen Bureau voor de Statistiek, Dr S Redmondstraat 118, Paramaribo.
                not priced.   42 p.
Contains data on population, meterology, education, consumer price index, production, national income,
finance, agriculture, construction, shipping, motor vehicle tax, etc.
Time factor: published in 1977 as "Suriname in cijfers, no 83", the volume has data for 1975 and some
earlier years in some tables.
§   NI.

¶ B - Production

ii. Agriculture, fisheries, forestry, etc

1256   Landbouwtelling Suriname [Census of agriculture for Suriname] (Algemeen Bureau voor de Statistiek)
            Algemeen Bureau voor de Statistiek, Dr S Redmondstraat 118, Paramaribo.
                    2nd, 1959.   not priced.
            §   NI.

            Refer also to 1252, 1254, 1255.

iii. Industry

1257   Bedrijfs- en beroepstelling.   Census of industries and occupations (Algemeen Bureau voor de Statistiek)
            Algemeen Bureau voor de Statistiek, Dr S Redmondstraat 118, Paramaribo.
            1961- 1961.   not priced.   10 vols.
            The reports include volumes for each of the districts, for Paramaribo, for Surinam, and a summary volume.
                Data include the number of persons employed and wages by major industry group; occupations and
                wages; number of establishments, by size; number of persons employed, by district; etc.
            Time factor: published in 1962.
            §   NI,   En.

1258   Statistiek van de industriële produktie [Statistics of industrial production] (Algemeen Bureau voor de
                Statistiek)
            Algemeen Bureau voor de Statistiek, Dr S Redmondstraat 118, Paramaribo.
            1965- 1973.   not priced.   14 p.
            Contains data on production of commodities.
            Time factor: the 1973 issue, published in 1974, has data for 1973 and some earlier years.
            §   NI.

            Refer also to 1252, 1254, 1255.

iv. Construction

1259   Bouwaktiviteiten [Building activity] (Algemeen Bureau voor de Statistiek)
            Algemeen Bureau voor de Statistiek, Dr S Redmondstraat 118, Paramaribo.
            1964- 1964.   not priced.   32 p.
            Time factor: published as 'Suriname in cijfers' no 36 of 1966).
            §   NI.

            Refer also to 1254, 1255.

¶ C - External trade

1260   In- en uitvoer [Imports and exports] (Algemeen Bureau voor de Statistiek)
            Algemeen Bureau voor de Statistiek, Dr S Redmondstraat 118, Paramaribo.
            1953- 1964.   not priced.
            Contains data on imports and exports arranged by commodity subdivided by countries of origin and
                destination.
            Time factor: the 1964 issue, published in 1966, has data for 1964.
            §   NI,   En.

            Refer also to 1252.

¶   E   -   Population

1261   Volkstelling   [Population census]   (Algemeen Bureau voor de Statistiek)
       Algemeen Bureau voor de Statistiek, Dr S Redmondstraat 118, Paramaribo.
       1950-   4th, 1972.   not priced.
       A preliminary report was issued in the 'Suriname in cijfers' series, no 60, in 1972.
       §   Nl,   En.

       Refer also to 1252, 1255.

¶   F   -   Social

i.   Standard of living

1262   Prijs indexcijfers van de gezinsconsumptie   [Consumer price indexes]   (Algemeen Bureau voor de Statistiek)
       Algemeen Bureau voor de Statistiek, Dr S Redmondstraat 118, Paramaribo.
       1973-   monthly.   not priced.
       Time factor: each issue has data for the month of issue, the previous month, and corresponding periods
           for the previous year.
       §   Nl.

1263   Prijsontwikkeling   [Price development]   (Algemeen Bureau voor de Statistiek)
       Algemeen Bureau voor de Statistiek, Dr S Redmondstraat 118, Paramaribo.
                            not priced.   27 p.
       Text and statistics on $12\frac{1}{2}$ years of price development.
       Time factor: published in 1966.
       §   Nl.

       Refer also to 1255.

ii.   Health and welfare

       Refer to 1252.

iii.   Education and leisure

1264   Statistiek van het algemeen vormend onderwijs   [Statistics of general education]   (Algemeen Bureau voor de
           Statistiek)
       Algemeen Bureau voor de Statistiek, Dr S Redmondstraat 118, Paramaribo.
       1957-   1963.   not priced.
       Time factor: the 1963 issue, published in the series 'Suriname in Cijfers', was issued in 1965.
       §   Nl.

       Refer also to 1252, 1255.

iv.   Justice

       Refer to 1252.

¶   G   -   Finance

       Refer to 1252, 1255.

¶   H   -   Transport and communications

       Refer to 1252.

Central statistical office

1265   Central Statistical Office,
         1 Edward Street
         Port of Spain.
         † 52759 or 53813.

The Central Statistical Office collects, analyses and publishes all the official statistics of Trinidad and Tobago, and has also been involved in carrying out censuses of population for Trinidad, Tobago and some other parts of the West Indies.   The Office also issues a series of research papers.

Libraries

The Central Statistical Office, referred to above, has a library which is open to the public for reference to statistical publications.   Hours of business are Mondays to Thursdays, 8.00 to 12.00 and 13.00 to 16.15 hours; Fridays from 8.00 to 12.00 and 13.00 to 16.00 hours.   Language spoken by the staff is English.   The collection includes statistical data of Trinidad and Tobago, of other countries, and of international organisations.

Libraries and information services abroad

A number of university, government and other libraries throughout the world, and particularly in the West Indies and the American continent receive copies of publications of the Central Statistical Office; Trinidad and Tobago embassies abroad which receive the publications include:

United Kingdom   High Commission for Trinidad and Tobago, 42 Belgrave Square, London SW1
                 † 01-245 9351.
USA   Embassy of Trinidad and Tobago, 1708 Massachusetts Avenue NW, Washington DC
                 † (202) 467 6490.
Canada   High Commission, 75 Albert Street, Ottawa   † 232-2418

Bibliographies

The Central Statistical Office issues a sales list of its publications at intervals.   The 1978/79 edition is the latest.

Statistical publications

¶   A - General

1266   Annual statistical digest   (Central Statistical Office)
        Government Printer, 2 Victoria Avenue, Port of Spain.
        1935/51-   1974/75.   TT$3.   272 p.
        Main sections:
            Area and climate   National accounts
            Population and vital statistics   Production, agriculture, forestry, mining, industry
            Social conditions (education, health,   Prices, retail and industrial
               housing, justice and crime, pensions) Banking and finance
            Labour and employment   Public finance
            Transport and communications   Miscellaneous (fire losses, revenue and receipts of
            Overseas trade   postal services)
        Time factor: the 1974/75 edition, published late 1977, has the latest available data for the years 1970 to
               1975.
        §   En.

¶   A,   continued

1267   Quarterly economic report   (Central Statistical Office)
        Government Printer, 2 Victoria Avenue, Port of Spain.
        1950-   TT$1.50 a copy.
        Contains data on overseas trade, wages, prices, retail sales, agriculture, fisheries, industrial production,
            employment, petroleum production, transport and communications, finance, banking, population,
            and vital statistics.
        Time factor: each issue has data for about six years, five quarters to the quarter of the issue, and is
            published about six months later.
        §   En.

1268   Statistical bulletin (new series)   (Central Statistical Office)
        Government Printer, 2 Victoria Avenue, Port of Spain.
        1972-   irreg.   not priced.
        Intended to provide some preliminary information as soon as such data becomes available on various
            statistical series, such as overseas trade, travel, labour, wages, education, tourism, transport,
            agriculture, and a series of indices of domestic production and industrial sales.
        §   En.

1269   Economic indicators   (Central Statistical Office)
        Government Printer, 2 Victoria Avenue, Port of Spain.
        1974-   quarterly.   TT$1 each issue.
        Contains indicators of prices, retail sales, domestic production, employment, productivity, wages and
            earnings.
        Time factor: each issue has data for about seven years and nine or ten quarters to the quarter of the issue,
            and is published about six months later.
        §   En.

1270   Statistical digest   (Central Bank of Trinidad and Tobago)
        Central Bank of Trinidad and Tobago, Port of Spain.
        1968-   monthly.   not priced.
        Contains data on banking and money; public finance; foreign trade and balance of payments; index of
            retail prices; and production, sales and exports of selected items (petroleum based products, crude
            petroleum, sugar, cocoa and coffee beans, fertilisers, cement, bricks and blocks, motor vehicles
            locally assembled, radio and television, gas cookers and refrigerators).
        Time factor: each issue has runs of annual and monthly figures to about three months prior to the date of
            the issue.
        §   En.

1271   Annual report...   (Central Bank of Trinidad and Tobago)
        Central Bank of Trinidad and Tobago, Port of Spain.
        1965-   1976.   not priced.   80 p.
        A review of the national economy (supply of goods, demand, prices, labour, employment and wages,
            government finance, credit, money and capital markets, balance of visible trade, foreign trade, the
            oil trade, direction of trade, international payments) and reports on the activities of the bank.
            Tables are interspersed with the text.
        Time factor: the 1976 report, published mid-1977, has data for 1976.
        §   En.

        Note: the bank also publishes a 'Quarterly economic bulletin' which is not statistical.

¶   A,   continued

1272   Trinidad and Tobago today   (Central Statistical Office)
            Government Printer, 2 Victoria Avenue, Port of Spain.
                        TT$3.   52 p.
            'A graphic presentation of social and economic statistics', including population; the economic structure;
                employment, income and prices; and level of living and social conditions.
            Time factor: the revised edition, No 2, was published in 1972 and covers the years 1957 to 1971.
            §   En.

1273   Business surveys, 1974/75   (Central Statistical Office)
            Government Printer, 2 Victoria Avenue, Port of Spain.
                        not priced.   95 p.
            Contains data on sugar manufacture, petroleum industry, manufacturing industry, construction industry,
                distribution industry, hotels and restaurants industry, transport, storage and communications industry,
                other service industries.   Includes data on establishments, employment, finance, use of materials,
                capital formation, etc.
            Time factor: published in 1978.
            §   En.

    ¶   B   -   Production

    ii.   Agriculture, fisheries, forestry, etc

1274   Agricultural census   (Central Statistical Office)
            Government Printer, 2 Victoria Avenue, Port of Spain.
            1946-   1963.   out of print.   2 vols in 4.
            Vol I is a report on procedure and methodology, together with summary tables.   Vol II is in 3 parts:
                Part A has data on the holder and his holdings; Part B is on land utilisation; and Part C shows
                production and sales of crops by county, holding size, land utilisation, production size and tenure.
            §   En.

1275   Quarterly agricultural report   (Central Statistical Office)
            Government Printer, 2 Victoria Avenue, Port of Spain.
            1974-   TT$1 each issue.
            Contains up to date information on agriculture, including citrus, copra and copra products; tobacco; and
                fisheries.
            Time factor: each issue has data for about six years and 15 months or 5 quarters to the quarter of the issue,
                and is published about six months later.
            §   En.

1276   Agricultural pig survey, 1975-1977   (Central Statistical Office)
            Government Printer, 2 Victoria Avenue, Port of Spain.
                        not priced.
            Time factor: the results of the survey were published in 1978.
            §   En.

            Note: A census of pig farms was taken in June 1971 and the results published in 1972.

1277   Survey of broiler industry in Trinidad and Tobago   (Central Statistical Office)
            Government Printer, 2 Victoria Avenue, Port of Spain.
            1969/71-   2nd, 1973.   TT$2.   c 40 p.
            Contains data on broiler production, cost of production of broilers, and the control of the poultry industry.
            Time factor: the 1973 survey report was published in 1974.
            §   En.

            Refer also to 1266, 1267, 1268.

¶   B,   continued

iii.   Industry

1278   Survey of business establishments   (Central Statistical Office)
        Government Printer, 2 Victoria Avenue, Port of Spain.
        1966/68-   1974/75.   TT$2.
        Contains data on the number of establishments, employment, wages, operating expenditure, receipts,
            inventory changes and capital formation by economic sector.
        Time factor: the 1974/75 report, published in 1977, has data for the financial year 1974/75.
        §   En.

1279   Census of manufacturing   (Central Statistical Office)
        Government Printer, 2 Victoria Avenue, Port of Spain.
        1969/70-   1969 and 1970.   TT$1.   109 p.
        Contains data on the size, structure and output of manufacturing establishments employing 10 or more
            persons.
        Time factor: the results of the census were published in March 1974.
        §   En.

        Note: surveys of industrial establishments were carried out in 1957 and 1963, the results being published
            but now out of print.

        Refer also to 1266, 1267, 1269, 1270.

iv.   Construction

1280   Index of retail prices of building materials, 1968-1971   (Central Statistical Office)
        Government Printer, 2 Victoria Avenue, Port of Spain.
                        not priced (restricted circulation)

v.   Energy

1281   Monthly bulletin: petroleum industry   (Ministry of Petroleum and Mines)
        Ministry of Petroleum and Mines, Port of Spain.
        1964-   not priced.
        Contains preliminary statistics of production, imports, refining, drilling, and natural gas sales.
        Time factor: each issue has data for the month of the issue and is published about two months later.
        §   En.

1282   T & TEC annual report   (Trinidad and Tobago Electricity Commission)
        Trinidad and Tobago Electricity Commission, 63 Frederick Street, Port of Spain.
        1966-   1972.   not priced.   55 p.
        Contains data on generation, consumption, cost, employment, and finance in the industry.
        Time factor: the 1972 report, with data for 1972, was published in 1973.
        §   En.

        Refer also to 1267, 1270.

¶   C   -   External trade

1283   Overseas trade   (Central Statistical Office)
       Government Printer, 2 Victoria Avenue, Port of Spain.
       1951-   1976.   Part A   TT$3.50
                       Part B   TT$2.   2 vols.
       Part A contains some summary tables and detailed statistics of imports and exports arranged by commodity
          and subdivided by countries of origin and destination.   Part B also has some summary tables and a
          review of the year's trade.
       Time factor: Part A for 1976 was published in March 1978 and Part B in July 1978.   Both parts have
          data for 1976.
       §   En.

1284   Overseas trade: bi-monthly report - revised series - SITC (revised)   (Central Statistical Office)
       Government Printer, 2 Victoria Avenue, Port of Spain.
       1951-   TT$3.50 or TT$20 yr.
       Contains provisional data on monthly overseas trade, the main tables showing imports and exports arranged
          by commodity and subdivided by countries of origin and destination.
       Time factor: each issue has data for the month of the issue and cumulated figures for the year to date, and
          is published about six months later.
       §   En.

       Note: there is also a 4-page preliminary bulletin giving values of imports and exports.

       Refer also to 1266, 1267, 1270, 1271.

¶   D   -   Internal distribution and service trades

1285   Distributive trades and other services - survey of distribution, transport and other services   (Central Statistical
         Office)
       Government Printer, 2 Victoria Avenue, Port of Spain.
       1957-   1957.   out of print.   2 vols.
       Vol I contains tables; vol II an analytical report.
       §   En.

1286   International travel report   (Central Statistical Office)
       Government Printer, 2 Victoria Avenue, Port of Spain.
       1955-   1976.   TT$1.50.   70 p.
       Contains data on travellers arriving and departing by air and sea, according to age, sex and occupation,
          by category (i.e hotel holiday visitor, business visitor, etc), and by country of normal residence.
       Time factor: the 1976 issue, published in September 1977, has data for 1976.
       §   En.

1287   Monthly travel   (Central Statistical Office)
       Government Printer, 2 Victoria Avenue, Port of Spain.
       1955-   TT$0.50 each issue.
       Provides preliminary monthly data on passenger movement, by category of passenger, county of embarcation
          or disembarcation, and country of normal residence.
       Time factor: each issue has data for the month of the issue and latest quarter and is published about six
          months later.
       §   En.

       Refer also to 1266, 1267, 1268, 1269, 1270.

¶   E - Population

1288   Census of population   (Central Statistical Office)
            Central Statistical Office, 2 Victoria Avenue, Port of Spain.
            1861-   1970.
            The CSO has issued two population census bulletins - No 1 in 1971 on population by sex and administra-
                tion areas, etc (TT$0.25) and No 1A with summary figures in 1974.   The main results are published
                in the reports of the Commonwealth of the Caribbean census (258).

1289   Population abstract, 1960-1970, including projections, 1970-1985   (Central Statistical Office)
            Government Printer, 2 Victoria Avenue, Port of Spain.
                        TT$2.   68 p.
            Contains data on the demographic situation for the period 1960 to 1970 and also population and school
                age projections to 1985.
            Time factor: published in 1973.
            §   En.

1290   Population and vital statistics   (Central Statistical Office)
            Government Printer, 2 Victoria Avenue, Port of Spain.
            1884-   1975.   TT$3.   157 p.
            Contains data on births, deaths and marriages.
            Time factor: the 1975 issue, published May 1978, has data for 1975 and a historical appendix with data
                from 1882.
            §   En.

1291   Continuous sample survey of population   (Central Statistical Office)
            Government Printer, 2 Victoria Avenue, Port of Spain.
            1963-   irreg.   L F I reports   TT$1.50
                                Special report   TT$2.50
            Reports designed to give a description of the labour force of Trinidad and Tobago since 1963.   There are
                two series - L F I-1 tables show employed and unemployed classified by age, industry, occupation
                and type of worker; and L F I-2 includes similar tables by administrative area, educational attainment,
                hours worked, interval of time since last worked for the unemployed.   Supplementary data, intended
                mainly for use in research, is published in 'Special labour force 1', a 5-part report published in 1978.
            §   En.

1292   Employment in Trinidad and Tobago   (International Bank for Reconstruction and Development)
            World Bank, 1818 H Street NW, Washington DC 20433, USA.
                        not priced.   various pagings.
            A report based on the findings of an economic mission that visited Trinidad and Tobago in April/May 1972.
                A large statistical appendix has data on the population and labour force, national accounts,
                agricultural statistics, other (petroleum production, employment, tourism, etc) statistics, prices and
                wages, transport and communications, education, etc.
            Time factor: published in 1973, the report has data from 1960 or later to 1970 or 1971.
            §   En.

1293   Manpower reports   (Central Statistical Office)
            Central Statistical Office, 2 Victoria Avenue, Port of Spain.
            1972-   irregular.   TT$2 each issue.
            A series of reports based on the 1970 census of population results.
            §   En.

¶   E,   continued

1294   Work permits report   (Central Statistical Office)
         Central Statistical Office, 2 Victoria Avenue, Port of Spain.
         1974-   1975.   TT$1.   40 p.
         Contains data on the number of permits granted by sex, occupational group; professional, technical and
             related workers as well as various other types of workers.
         Time factor: the 1975 issue, published in 1977, has data for 1975.
         §   En.

         Refer also to 1266, 1267.

¶   F   -   Social

1295   Social indicators   (Central Statistical Office)
         Government Printer, 2 Victoria Avenue, Port of Spain.
                         TT$2.   106 p.
         Contains a breakdown on population, health and nutrition, education, employment, earnings, prices and
             household expenditure patterns, housing and levels of living, public order, and leisure.
         Time factor: 'a pioneering effort' published in 1975 and including data for many years to 1970 or 1972.
         §   En.

    i.   Standard of living

1296   Household budgetary survey   (Central Statistical Office)
         Government Printer, 2 Victoria Avenue, Port of Spain.
         1971/72-   2nd, 1975/76.
         Contents include:
             Bulletin No 1 (TT$0.50)   (shows preliminary data on characteristics of households)
             HBS Report No 1 (TT$2.50)   (description of method)
         Time factor: the above reports were published in 1977 and there will be more reports to come.
         §   En.

    ii.   Health and welfare

         Refer to 1266.

    iii. Education and leisure

1297   Education digest   (Central Statistical Office)
         Government Printer, 2 Victoria Avenue, Port of Spain.
         1958-   1971/1972.   TT$1.50.   165 p.
         Contains data on primary, intermediate and secondary schools, technical and vocational schools, and
             university.   Data includes numbers and geographical distribution of establishments, enrolments,
             classes and teachers' qualifications.
         Time factor: the 1971/72 issue has data for the academic year 1971/72.
         §   En.

         Note: prior to the 1971/72 issue title was 'A digest of statistics in education'.

¶   F.iii,   continued

1298   Report on enrolment in educational institutions   (Central Statistical Office)
         Government Printer, 2 Victoria Avenue, Port of Spain.
         1973/74-   1973/74.   TT$1.
         Contains data on enrolments by age, sex and class in junior secondary, government secondary and assisted
              secondary schools, technical and vocational colleges, teacher training colleges, the Eastern Caribbean
              Institute of Agriculture and Forestry, and the University of the West Indies.
         Time factor: the 1973/74 report, published in 1978, has data for the academic year 1973/74.
         §   En.

1299   Awards and scholarships report, 1967-1972 (Central Statistical Office)
         Government Printer, 2 Victoria Avenue, Port of Spain.
                        TT$1.50.   221 p.
         Contains data on development scholarships, study leave, educational assistance, commonwealth
              scholarships, commonwealth bursaries, loans, etc.
         Time factor: the report was published in 1975.
         §   En.

1300   Enrolments in primary schools   (Central Statistical Office)
         Government Printer, 2 Victoria Avenue, Port of Spain.
         1975/76-   1975/76.   TT$0.50.
         Time factor: published as 'Education bulletin no 1' in 1978, the 1975/76 issue has data for the academic
              year 1975/76.
         §   En.

         Refer also to 1266, 1268.

¶   G   -   Finance

1301   Financial statistics (Central Statistical Office)
         Government Printer, 2 Victoria Avenue, Port of Spain.
         1966-   1975/76.   TT$1.50.   81 p.
         Summarises the financial operations of central and other government organisations as well as commercial
              banks and other private and public institutions.
         Time factor: the 1975/76 issue, published April 1978, has data from 1969 or 1970 to 1976.
         §   En.

1302   Quarterly economic report   (Royal Bank of Trinidad and Tobago)
         Royal Bank of Trinidad and Tobago, 3b Chancery Lane, Port of Spain.
         1973-   not priced.
         Mainly financial news, including statistical tables, but also has data on the economy of Trinidad and
              Tobago.
         §   En.

    i.   Banking

         Refer to 1266, 1267, 1270, 1271.

¶   G.ii.   Public finance

1303   National income of Trinidad and Tobago   (Central Statistical Office)
        Government Printer, 2 Victoria Avenue, Port of Spain.
        1951/54-   1952-1962.   TT$1.
        Includes data on domestic product, national income, capital account, government account, and external
            transactions.
        Time factor: the 1952-1962 issue, the latest to be published, has data for those years.
        §   En.

1304   The gross domestic product, 1966-1976   (Central Statistical Office)
        Government Printer, 2 Victoria Avenue, Port of Spain.
                        TT$2.
        Time factor: published in 1977.
        §   En.

1305   An analysis of government revenue and expenditure, 1966-1971   (Central Statistical Office)
        Government Printer, 2 Victoria Avenue, Port of Spain.
                        TT$1.   33 p.
        Time factor: published in 1974.
        §   En.

1306   Flow of funds for Trinidad and Tobago   (Central Statistical Office)
        Government Printer, 2 Victoria Avenue, Port of Spain.
        1966/74-   1966-1976.   TT$3.
        Time factor: issued as 'Financial statistics report no 2' in May 1977.
        §   En.

1307   Balance of payments   (Central Statistical Office)
        Government Printer, 2 Victoria Avenue, Port of Spain.
        1959-   1975.   TT$1.50.   29 p.
        Time factor: the 1975 issue, published May 1977, has data for 1975 and some earlier years.
        §   En.

        Refer also to 1266, 1267, 1270.

¶   H   -   Transport and communications

        Refer to 1266, 1267, 1268.

There is no central government statistical office in the Turks and Caicos Islands. Enquiries concerning statistical data for the tourist industry should be addressed to the Ministry of Tourism and Development, Grand Turk; other statistical enquiries should be addressed to the Chief Secretary's Office, Grand Turk, Turks and Caicos Islands.

Statistical publications

¶   A - General

1308   Turks & Caicos Islands: report for the year   (Foreign and Commonwealth Office)
         HM Stationery Office, PO Box 569, London SE1 9NH.
         1920-   1967 to 1970.   £1.35.   93 p.
         Includes some statistics of population, demography, wages, cost of living, public finance and taxation,
            currency and banking, foreign trade, tourism, production (mainly salt), social services, public
            health, justice, crime, registration of motor vehicles, traffic accidents, education, and rainfall.
         Time factor: the report for 1967 to 1970 was published in 1976.
         §   En.

¶   E - Population

Refer to 258 for details of the 1970 population census for the Commonwealth Caribbean.

Central statistical office

1309   Bureau of the Census,
            Department of Commerce,
            Suitland, Maryland 20233.
            t (202) 655 4000.

      The Bureau of the Census is responsible for arranging periodical censuses of population, housing, agriculture, irrigation, mineral industries, transport and government for which it collects, analyses and publishes the statistical data.   It is also responsible for current population reports and projections, distribution of consumer income and buying intentions, wholesale and retail trade, construction, manufacturing activity, foreign trade, etc.   The Bureau also provides special services whereby users of statistics may obtain information at an earlier date than the release of the published reports, or may obtain data in greater detail than that available in the statistics regularly released.   The entire cost of extra work or duplication of data is charged to the subscriber.

Some other important organisations publishing statistics

1310   Bureau of International Commerce,
            Department of Commerce,
            Washington DC 20230.
            t (202) 377 2000.

      The Bureau is concerned with foreign economic trends and their implications for the United States.

1311   Economic Research Service,
            Department of Agriculture,
            Washington DC 20250.

      The organisation is responsible for research into agricultural economics.

1312   Bureau of Labor Statistics,
            Department of Labor,
            441 G Street NW,
            Washington DC 20212.
            t (202) 655 4000.

      The Bureau is the principal data-gathering agency of the federal government in the field of labour economics.

1313   National Center for Educational Statistics,
            400 Maryland Avenue SW,
            Washington DC 20202.
            t (202) 245 8704.

      Designs, directs, co-ordinates and executes all statistical programmes for the Office of Education.

1314   National Center for Health Statistics,
            3700 East West Highway,
            Hyattsville, Maryland.
            t (202) 436 8500.

      The national centre for general purpose vital and health statistics.

Libraries

The Library of the Bureau of the Census, Room 2451, Federal Office Building No 3, Suitland, Maryland (t 301 763 5042) may be consulted for research purposes during office hours.   Other government departments in Washington also have libraries.   In New York, there is the New York Public Library and the Statistics Library in the United Nations main building.   Other university and public libraries throughout the country have selected items of United States statistical publications.

Libraries and information services abroad

A selection of United States statistical publications are available for reference in US embassies abroad, including:

United Kingdom   United States Embassy, Grosvenor Square, London W1A 1AE   t 01-499 9000.
Canada   United States Embassy, 100 Wellington Street, Ottawa   t 238 5335.
Australia   United States Embassy, State Circle, Yarralumla, Canberra   t 733 711

Bibliographies

1315   Statistical services of the United States government   (Statistical Policy Division, Executive Office of the
             President)
        Government Printing Office, Washington DC 20402.
        The latest revision of this work was published in 1975 (US$3.40. 234 p).   Designed to serve as a basic
             reference document on the statistical programme of the US government, it describes the system of
             federal government, gives brief descriptions of the principal economic and social statistical series
             collected by government agencies, and contains a brief statement of the statistical responsibilities
             of each agency and a list of principal statistical publications.

        Note: 'Statistical reporter: current developments in federal statistics' (Office of Management and
             Budget) is a monthly publication which is prepared primarily for interchange of information among
             government employees engaged in statistical and research activities.   It includes news about new
             publications and release dates for principal federal economic indicators and is available from the
             Government Printing Office (US$0.85 or US$9.70 yr (US$13 yr abroad)).

1316   Bureau of the Census catalog   (Bureau of the Census)
        Government Printing Office, Washington DC 20402.
        A quarterly, cumulating to an annual volume, and with 12 monthly supplements (US$14.40 yr or US$18
             yr abroad).   It is in two parts - part I: Publications; part II: Data files and special tabulations.

1317   Business service checklist: a bi-weekly guide to Department of Commerce publications, plus key economic
             indicators (Department of Commerce)
        Government Printing Office, Washington DC 20402.
        A guide to new publications of the Department (US$9.70 yr or US$12.15 yr abroad)

1318   American statistics index: a comprehensive guide to the statistical publications of the US government
             (Congressional Information Service)
        Congressional Information Service, 7101 Wisconsin Avenue, Washington DC 20014; or Government
             Printing Office, Washington DC 20402.
        1973-   monthly with cumulative annual indexes.
        Arranged by source, with entries including abstracts, geographical and time coverage; a separate index
             gives subject, name, category and title access.

1319   Statistics sources   (Paul Wasserman and Jacqueline Bernero)
        Gale Research Company, Book Tower, Detroit, Michigan 48226, USA.
        A subject guide to data on industrial, business, social, educational, financial and other topics for the
             United States.   The 5th edition was published in 1977 (US$58).

Bibliographies, continued

1320   Fact finder for the nation   (Bureau of the Census)
            Subscriber Service Section (Publications), Bureau of the Census, Department of Commerce, Suitland,
            Maryland 20233.
            A series of topical brochures, each describing a range of census materials available on a given subject and
            suggesting some uses.   Geared to the general reader as well as the potential user of census data.
            Each covers some particular aspect of the Bureau's work, such as minority statistics, records about
            individuals, agriculture statistics, history and organisation of the Bureau, housing statistics,
            population statistics, geographical tools, construction statistics, statistics on service industries,
            statistics on mineral industries, statistics on governments, retail trade statistics, and wholesale trade
            statistics.   (US$2 yr; prices for individual issues vary).

1321   Guide to foreign trade statistics   (Bureau of the Census)
            Government Printing Office, Washington DC 20402.
            Issued annually (US$5.05), the guide contains a description of the foreign trade statistics programme,
                published foreign trade reports, foreign trade reference material, a list of classification schedules,
                and availability of special services.

1322   Guide to industrial statistics   (Bureau of the Census)
            Government Printing Office, Washington DC 20402.
            Published in 1978 (US$2.75) the volume describes the industrial statistics programme, etc.

1323   Directory of federal statistics for local areas: a guide to sources   (Bureau of the Census)
            Government Printing Office, Washington DC 20402.
            The first edition, dated 1976, was published in 1978 (US$5.50).

Statistical publications

¶   A - General

1324   Statistical abstract of the United States   (Bureau of the Census)
            Government Printing Office, Washington DC 20402.
            1878-   1977.   US$11   cloth   1072 p.
                                        US$8.50 paper
            Main sections:

Population	Banking, finance and insurance
Vital statistics	Business enterprise
Immigration and naturalization	Communications
Health and nutrition	Energy
Education	Science
Law enforcement, federal courts and prisons	Transportation - land
	Transportation - air and water
Geography and environment	Agriculture
Public lands, parks, recreation and travel	Forests and forest products
	Fisheries
Federal government finances and employment	Mining and mineral products
	Construction and housing
State and local government finances and employment	Manufactures
Social insurance and welfare services	Domestic trade and services
National defence and veterans' affairs	Foreign commerce and aid
Labour force, employment and earnings	Outlying areas under the jurisdiction of the United States (Puerto Rico)
Income, expenditures and wealth	Comparative international statistics
Prices	Guide to sources of statistics
Elections	Guide to State statistical abstracts

[continued next page]

¶   A,   continued

1324,   continued

>   Time factor: the 1977 edition, published late 1977, has data for long periods to 1975 or 1976.
>   §   En.
>
>   Note: supplements to the 'Statistical abstract...' are the 'County and city databook' (see 1327),
>   'Historical statistics of the United States' (see 1325), 'Pocket data book, USA' (see 1326), 'USA
>   statistics in brief', 'Congressional district data book', 'Congressional district data, CDD',
>   'Directory of non-federal statistics for state and local areas'.

1325   Historical statistics of the United States: colonial times to 1970   (Bureau of the Census)
>   Government Printing Office, Washington DC 20402.
>   US$26 for 2 vols.   2 vols.
>   Part 1 contains data on population, vital and health medicare, migration, labour, prices and price
>   indices, national income and wealth, consumer income and expenditure, social statistics, land,
>   water and climate, agriculture, forestry and fisheries, and minerals.   Part 2 contains data on
>   construction and housing, manufactures, transportation, communications, energy, distribution and
>   services, international transactions and foreign commerce, business enterprise, productivity and
>   technological development, financial markets and institutions, government, and colonial and pre-
>   federal statistics.
>   Time factor: published in 1975, this is the 3rd volume of its kind, the earlier titles being for the periods
>   1789 to 1945 and from colonial times to 1957.
>   §   En.

1326   Pocket data book, USA   (Bureau of the Census)
>   Government Printing Office, Washington DC 20402.
>   1967-   5th, 1976.   US$4.   444 p.
>   A compact selection of statistics on all major facets of the social, economic and political structure of
>   the US.   Covers population, vital statistics, immigration, land, environment, recreation,
>   government, elections, national defence, veterans, law enforcement, labour, health, education,
>   welfare, income, prices, agriculture, forestry, fisheries, business enterprise, manufacturing, mining,
>   construction and housing, transport, communications, science, energy, finance and insurance,
>   distribution and services, foreign commerce.   Is a supplement to the 'Statistical abstract of the
>   United States' (1324).
>   Time factor: issued biennially, the 1976 edition was published early 1977 and contains the latest data
>   available in 1976.
>   §   En.

1327   County and city data book   (Bureau of the Census)
>   Government Printing Office, Washington DC 20402.
>   1949-   9th, 1977.   not priced.   956 p.
>   In four sections – regions, divisions and states; counties; metropolitan areas; and cities.   Data included
>   is on area, population, vital statistics, civilian labour force, employment, school enrolment, health,
>   income, family income, banking, housing, government finance, manufactures, internal trade,
>   agriculture, etc.
>   Time factor: the 1977 edition, published in 1978, has the latest data available, usually 1970, 1972 or
>   1974.
>   §   En.

1327a   Economic indicators   (Council of Economic Advisers)
>   Government Printing Office, Washington DC 20402.
>   1948-   monthly.   US$0.85 or US$10.10 yr plus $2.55 for foreign mailing.
>   Contains data on total output, income & spending; employment, unemployment & wages; production and
>   business activity; prices; money, credit & security markets; federal finance; & international statistics.
>   Time factor: each issue has long runs of annual and monthly figures to the month prior to the date of the
>   issue.
>   §   En.

¶   A,   continued

Statistical yearbooks or abstracts are also available for individual States:

1328 AL   Economic abstract of Alabama, 1977. (University of Alabama: Center for Business & Economic Research).

1328 AK   The Alaska economy, 1978.   (Department of Commerce & Economic Development, Juneau).

1328 AZ   Statistical abstract of Arizona, 1976.   (University of Arizona, Tucson).

1328 AZ   Arizona statistical review, 1978.   (Valley National Bank, Phoenix).

1328 AR   Arkansas almanac, 1976.   (Arkansas Almanac Inc, Little Rock).   (final edition).

1328 CA   California statistical abstract, 1978.   (Department of Finance, Sacramento).

1328 CO   Statistical abstract of Colorado, 1978-1979.   (Transrep/bibliographics, Denver).

1328 CT   Connecticut market data, 1976.   (Connecticut Department of Commerce, Hartford).

1328 DE   Dimensions on Delaware, 1977.   (Delaware Office of Management, Budget and Planning, Dover).

1328 DC   District of Columbia data, 1976.   (D.C. Municipal Planning Office).

1328 FL   Florida statistical abstract, 1978.   (University of Florida, Gainsville).

1328 GA   Georgia statistical abstract, 1978.   (University of Georgia, Athens).

1328 HI   The State of Hawaii data book 1978: a statistical abstract.   (Department of Planning and Economic Development, Honolulu).

1328 ID   Idaho statistical abstract, 1971.   (University of Idaho, Moscow).   (Updated by a quarterly 'Centerpoint: focus on business and economics').

1328 IL   Illinois State and regional economic data book, 1976.   (Department of Business and Economic Development, Springfield).

1328 IN   Indiana fact book, 1979.   (Indiana State Planning Services Agency, Indianapolis).

1328 IA   Statistical profile of Iowa.   (Iowa Development Commission, Des Moines).

1328 KS   Kansas statistical abstract, 1977.   (University of Kansas, Lawrence).

1328 KY   Kentucky deskbook of economic statistics, 1978.   (Department of Commerce, Frankfurt).

1328 LA   Statistical abstract of Louisiana, 1977.   (University of New Orleans).

1328 ME   Facts about industrial Maine.   (Maine State Development Office, Augusta).   (updated continuously).

1328 MD   Maryland statistical abstract, 1977.   (Department of Economic and Community Development, Annapolis).

1328 MA   Massachusetts fact book, 1978.   (Department of Commerce and Development, Boston).

1328 MI   Michigan statistical abstract, 1978.   (Michigan State University, East Lansing).

1328 MN   Minnesota statistical profile, 1978.   (Minnesota Department of Economic Development, Saint Paul).

1328 MS   Mississippi statistical abstract, 1977.   (Mississippi State University).

1328 MO   Data for Missouri counties, 1970.   (University of Missouri, Columbia).   (loose-leaf volume, updated periodically).

¶   A,   continued

Statistical yearbooks for individual States,   continued

1328 MT   Montana data book, 1970.   (Montana State Division of Research and Information Systems, Helena).
(loose-leaf volume, updated periodically.   Published in similar fashion are the separate county
reports and regional summaries, 'Montana county profiles').

1328 NE   Nebraska statistical handbook, 1978-1979.   (Department of Economic Development, Lincoln).

1328 NV   Nevada statistical abstract, 1977.   (State Planning Coordinator's Office, Carson City).

1328 NH   New Hampshire economic indicators, 1974.   (Department of Resources and Economic Development,
Concord).

1328 NJ   County data summary, 1977.   (Office of Demographic and Economic Analysis, Trenton, New Jersey).

1328 NM   New Mexico statistical abstract, 1979.   (University of New Mexico, Albuquerque).

1328 NY   New York statistical yearbook, 1977.   (Division of Budget, Albany, State of New York).

1328 NC   North Carolina State government statistical abstract (and supplement 'North Carolina statistical guide')
1978.   (Department of Administration, Raleigh).

1328 ND   North Dakota growth indicators, 1978.   (Business and Industrial Development Department, Bismarck).

1328 OH   Statistical abstract of Ohio, 1978.   (Department of Economic and Community Development, Columbus).

1328 OK   Statistical abstract of Oklahoma, 1978.   (University of Oklahoma, Norman).

1328 OR   Oregon economic statistics, 1977.   (University of Oregon, Eugene).

1328 PA   Pennsylvania statistical abstract, 1978.   (Department of Commerce, Harrisburg).

1328 RI   Rhode Island basic economic statistics, 1977-1978.   (Department of Economic Development, Providence).

1328 SC   South Carolina statistical abstract, 1977.   (Budget and Control Board, Columbia).

1328 SD   South Dakota facts, 1976.   (South Dakota State Planning Bureay, Pierre).

1328 TN   Tennessee statistical abstract, 1977.   (University of Tennessee, Knoxville).

1328 TX   Texas almanac, 1978-1979.   (Dallas Morning News, Dallas).

1328 UT   Statistical abstract of Utah, 1979.   (University of Utah, Salt Lake City).

1328 VT   Vermont facts and figures, 1975.   (Department of Budget and Management, Montpelier).

1328 VA   Data summary.   (Department of Planning and Budget, Richmond, Virginia).   (a series of separate
county and city reports, each updated triennially).

1328 WA   State of Washington pocket data book, 1977.   (Washington State Office of Financial Management,
Olympia).

1328 WV   Statistical handbook.   (West Virginia Research League Inc, Charleston).

1328 WI   Wisconsin statistical abstract, 1977.   (Department of Administration, Madison).

1328 WY   Wyoming data book, 1972.   (University of Wyoming, Laramie).

¶ A,   continued

1329   Economic report of the President to the Congress
          Government Printing Office, Washington DC 20402.
          1947-   1978.   not priced.   385 p.
          An annual review of the national economy with some charts and tables in the text and a statistical
             appendix with tables relating to income, employment and production, etc.
          Time factor: published in January 1978, the report has long runs of annual and monthly figures to
             December 1977.
          §   En.

1330   The handbook of basic economic statistics   (Bureau of Economic Statistics Inc)
          Bureau of Economic Statistics Inc, Box 10163, Washington DC 20018.
          1947-   monthly.   US$96 yr.
          'A manual of basic economic data on industry, commerce, labour and agriculture...'   A new fully
             cumulative and up-to-date handbook is issued each month, covering employment and earnings of
             labour; production, labour productivity and labour cost; profits and working capital; prices; general
             business indicators; social security operations; federal financial operations; national product and
             national income.
          Time factor: each issue has long runs of figures back to 1913 or the earliest date thereafter and is
             published shortly after the end of the latest month covered.
          §   En.

          Note: there are also a 'Quarterly handbook and monthly supplement service' (US$48 yr) and an 'Annual
             handbook and monthly supplement service' (US$24 yr).

1331   OECD economic surveys: United States   (Organisation for Economic Co-operation and Development)
          OECD, 2 rue André-Pascal, 75775 Paris Cedex 16, France; or from sales agents.
          1962-   1978.   £1.50 or US$3 or FrF 12.   65 p.
          An analysis of the economic policy of the country which includes statistics showing recent developments
             in demand, production, wages and prices, conditions in the money and capital markets, and
             developments in the balance of payments.
          Time factor: the 1978 issue was published mid-1978 and has data to 1977 and the first half of 1978.
          §   En,   Fr.

1332   Survey of current business   (Bureau of Economic Analysis: Department of Commerce)
          Government Printing Office, Washington DC 20402.
          1921-   monthly.   US$1.60 or US$19 yr domestic
                                       US$2 or US$23.75 yr foreign
          Contains more than 2,500 statistical series and significant articles analysing economic developments.
             Includes national income and product, balance of payments, plant and equipment expenditures,
             regional personal income, and input-output tables.
          Time factor: each issue has runs of figures to one or two months prior to the date of the issue.
          §   En.

          Note: 'Business statistics: a weekly supplement to the survey of current business' (US$15 domestic;
             US$18.75 yr foreign) has also been issued since 1954.   See also 1333 below.

1333   Business statistics   (Bureau of Economic Analysis: Department of Commerce)
          Government Printing Office, Washington DC 20402.
          1932-   20th, 1975.   US$5.15.   281 p.
          A basic reference volume containing historical data for the series included in 'Survey of current business'
             (see 1332)
          Time factor: the 1975 edition, published in 1976, has long runs of data to 1974 and 1975.
          §   En.

¶   A,   continued

1334   Defense indicators   (Bureau of Economic Analysis: Department of Commerce)
        Government Printing Office, Washington DC 20402.
        1968-   monthly.   US$1.50 or US$17.90 yr (US$1.90 or US$22.40 yr abroad).
        Brings together the principal time series on defence activity which influence short-term changes in the
            national economy.   Includes series on obligations, contracts, orders, shippings, inventories,
            expenditures, employment, and earnings.
        Time factor: each issue has long runs of figures to about one month prior to the date of the issue.
        §   En.

1335   Statistical indicators of scientific and technical communications, 1960-1980. Volume 1, a summary report for
            National Science Foundation, Division of Science Information   (D W King)
        Government Printing Office, Washington DC 20402.
                    US$2.05.   99 p.
        Time factor: published in 1976.
        §   En.

1336   Business conditions digest   (Bureau of Economic Analysis: Department of Commerce)
        Government Printing Office, Washington DC 20402.
        1961-   monthly.   US$3.50 or US$40 yr domestic
                                US$4.50 or US$50 yr foreign
        Contents:
            Part   I   Cyclical indicators
            Part II   Other important economic measures (National income and product; prices, wages and
                        productivity; labour force, employment and unemployment; government activities; US
                        international transactions; and international comparisons)
            Part III   Appendices
        Time factor: each issue has data to the month prior to the date of the issue.
        §   En.

        Note: a 'Handbook of cyclical indicators' was issued as a supplement in May 1977.

1337   A guide to consumer markets   (Helen Axel)
        Conference Board Inc, 845 Third Avenue, New York, NY 10022.
        1971/72-   1977/1978.   US$10 to associates and educational establishments;   295 p.
                                US$30 to others
        Contains data on population, employment, income (national and personal), expenditure, production and
            distribution, prices (consumer price index, purchasing value of the dollar, wholesale price index,
            family budgets, intercity comparisons of living costs.
        Time factor: the 1977/78 edition, published late 1977, has data for 1976 and 1975 and some earlier years.
        §   En.

1338   County business patterns   (Bureau of the Census)
        Government Printing Office, Washington DC 20402.
        1946-   1976.   various prices.   52 vols.
        Contains data on employment, number and employment size of establishments, and payrolls for most
            economic sectors (i.e, agriculture, mining, construction, manufacturing, transport, public utilities,
            wholesale trade, retail trade, finance, insurance, real estate and services.   One volume covers
            the US as a whole and there is one volume for each of the States.
        Time factor: the 1976 issue, published in 1978, has data for 1976.
        §   En.

¶   A,   continued

1339   US industrial outlook   (Industry and Trade Administration: Department of Commerce)
        Government Printing Office, Washington DC 20402.
        1960-   1978.   US$6.75.   480 p.
        Contains data on building and forest products; metals; chemicals, rubber and allied products; transporta-
            tion; distribution and marketing; consumer goods; communications; machinery; instrumentation;
            power and electrical equipment; business and consumer services.
        Time factor: the 1978 issue, published early 1978, has data for several years to 1978 and also a 5-year
            projection for 200 industries.
        §   En.

¶   B   -   Production

i.   Mines and mining

1340   Census of mineral industries: subject, industry and area statistics   (Bureau of the Census)
        Government Printing Office, Washington DC 20402.
        1850-   1972.   not priced.   911 p.
        The one-volume issue has limited distribution, being intended only for internal use by the Bureau of the
            Census.   More generally available are the individual reports:
            series MIC 72 (1) - 10A to 14E   Industry series
                    MIC 72 (1) - 1   to 6   Subject series
                    MIC 72 (2) - 1   to 9   Area series
        Time factor: the one-volume edition was published in 1976; the individual reports in 1974 and 1975.
        §   En.

        Note: for production indexes of mineral industries, refer to the Census of Manufactures (1352).

1341   Minerals yearbook   (Bureau of Mines)
        Government Printing Office, Washington DC 20402.
        1882-
        Recent volumes relating to the United States are:
            Vol 1 1975.   Metals, minerals and fuels (US$13.75)
            Vol 2 1974.   Area reports - domestic (US$9.75)
            Vol 3 is titled 'Area reports - international' (see 067).
            Vol 1 has data for the US on metals, minerals and fuels, including production, shipping, sales,
                consumption, etc.   Vol 2 has chapters on the mineral industries for each state.
        Time factor: Vol 1 1975 was published in February 1978 and Vol 2 1974 in August 1978, both volumes
            having data for the year in the title.   Preprints of the 1976 volumes are now being issued by the
            Bureau of Mines.
        §   En.

1342   Mineral commodity summaries   (Bureau of Mines)
        Bureau of Mines, 4800 Forbes Avenue, Pittsburgh, Pa 15213.
        (annual)   1979.   not priced.   190 p.
        An up-to-date summary of 90 mineral commodities, including data on domestic production, imports and
            exports, consumption, prices, producer stocks, recycling, world mine production and reserves, etc.
        Time factor: the 1979 issue, published early 1979, has data for 1978 and some earlier years.
        §   En.

¶   B.i,   continued

1343   Aluminium statistical review   (Aluminium Association)
        Aluminium Association, 818 Connecticut Avenue NW, Washington DC 20006.
        1968-   1975.   not priced.   67 p.
        Contains the most important available data on the industry, including production, capacity, shipments to
           major markets (users).
        Time factor: the 1975 issue, with long runs of data to 1975, was published in 1976.

        Refer also to 1324, 1325, 1326.

   ii.   Agriculture, fisheries, forestry, etc

1344   Census of agriculture   (Bureau of the Census)
        Government Printing Office, Washington DC 20402.
        1840-   1974.
        Final reports are:
             Vol   I   State and country data (54 separate reports, one for each state, the US as a whole, Puerto
                   Rico, Guam and the Virgin Islands) (prices vary)
             Vol   II Statistics by subject
             Vol   III Agricultural services (US$2.50)
             Vol   IV Special reports
                  1. Graphic summary
                  2. Ranking by counties and states
                  3. Coverage evaluation
                  4. Procedural history
        Time factor: the census is taken every five years, and the results of the 1974 census were published in
           1977.
        §   En.

1345   Agricultural statistics   (Department of Agriculture)
        Government Printing Office, Washington DC 20402.
        1936-   1977.   US$5.75.   623 p.
        Contains data on agricultural production, supplies, consumption, facilities, costs and returns for grains;
           cotton, sugar and tobacco; oilseeds, fats and oils; vegetables and melons; fruits, treenuts and
           horticultural specialities; hay, seeds, and minor field crops; cattle, hogs and sheep.   Also dairy
           and poultry production; farm resources, income and expenditure; taxes, insurance, co-operatives
           and credit; stabilisation and price-support; agricultural conservation and forestry statistics;
           consumption and family living; and miscellaneous (foreign trade, weather, commodity futures,
           fishery statistics, refrigeration statistics, and Alaska statistics).
        Time factor: the 1977 edition, published mid-1978, has data for 1977 for the first items and for 1974,
           1975 and 1976 for the later ones.
        §   En.

1346   Agricultural outlook   (Department of Agriculture)
        Government Printing Office, Washington DC 20402.
        1947-   monthly.   US$17 yr (US$21.25 yr abroad)
        Includes a section of statistical indicators on farm income, farm prices, producer and retail prices, farm-
           retail price spreads, transport, livestock and products, crops and products, general economic data.
        Time factor: each issue has data for the three crop years and subsequent months to about two months prior
           to the date of the issue.
        §   En.

UNITED STATES OF AMERICA,   continued

¶   B.ii,   continued

1347   Meatfacts: a statistical summary about America's largest food industry   (American Meat Institute)
American Meat Institute, PO Box 3556, Washington DC 20007.
1971-   1977.   not priced.   26 p.
Contains data on the numbers of animals on farms, livestock prices, slaughter of animals, meat production, meat plants, etc.
Time factor: the 7th edition, published in June 1977, has data for 1977 and 1976 and some earlier years.
§   En.

1348   Commodity yearbook   (Commodity Research Bureau Inc)
Commodity Research Bureau Inc, One Liberty Plaza, New York, NY 10006.
1939-   1978.   US$24.95.   385 p.
Data on trends in demand, supply and prices of 110 basic commodities.   Mainly concerned with the USA but does include data on world production.
Time factor: the 1978 edition, published in 1978, has data from 1966 to 1977.
§   En.

1349   Statistical bulletin   (Department of Agriculture)
Agricultural Marketing Service, Department of Agriculture, Washington DC 20250.
1923-   irreg.   not priced.
Includes such subjects as production, movement from farms, receipts at principal markets, farm and market prices, imports and exports, etc.   Titles of sub-series include:
Annual report on tobacco statistics   1936-
Dairy market statistics   1965-
Commodity futures statistics   1942/43-
Federal milk order market statistics   1947/56-
Poultry market statistics   1965-
Fresh fruit and vegetable prices   1945-
Farm income statistics.
§   En.

1350   Census of commercial fisheries   (Bureau of the Census)
Government Printing Office, Washington DC 20402.
1967-   1967.   not priced.
Contains data on the number of operators, employment, payroll, operating costs, receipts, by major type of catch and selected states.
§   En.

1351   Fishery statistics of the United States   (Department of the Interior: Bureau of Commercial Fisheries)
Government Printing Office, Washington DC 20402.
1939-   1968.   US$5.   578 p.
A general review of landings; processing, canning and packaging of fishery products; the frozen fishery trade; and the foreign fishing trade.   There are chapters on regional fisheries, including Puerto Rico.
Time factor: the 1968 issue, published in 1971, has data for 1968.
§   En.

1352   Current fishery statistics   (National Marine Fisheries Service, Department of Commerce)
National Marine Fisheries Service, Department of Commerce, Washington DC 20230.
1970-   monthly and/or annual.   not priced.
Contains a number of sub-series, including:
Fishery statistics of the United States (annual preliminary figures)
Canned fishery products (annual preliminary summary)

[continued next page]

¶   B.ii,   continued

1352,   continued

Fish meal and oil (monthly)
Fish sticks, fish portions, and breaded shrimp (quarterly)
Frozen fishery products (monthly)
Gulf coast shrimp data (monthly)
Imports and exports of fishery products (annual summary)
Industrial fishery products (annual summary)
Packaged fishery products (annual summary)
Processed fishery products (annual summary)
Shrimp landings (monthly)
There are also sectional bulletins on Alaska, Chesapeake, Great Lakes, Gulf, Middle Atlantic, New
England, Pacific Coast states, and South Atlantic fisheries; and annual state landing bulletins.
§   En.

1353   National food review (Economics, Statistics and Co-operative Service: Department of Agriculture)
Economics, Statistics and Co-operative Service, Department of Agriculture, Washington DC 20250.
1978-   quarterly.   not priced.
Includes a statistical appendix with data on consumer price index; livestock products – per capita
consumption; major food products – per capita consumption; producer price indices; market basket
of farm foods; personal consumption expenditure; and per capita food consumption indexes.
§   En.

Note: supersedes 'National food situation'.

Refer also to 1324, 1325, 1326.

iii.   Industry

1354   Census of manufactures   (Bureau of the Census)
Government Printing Office, Washington DC 20402.
1809-   1972.
Contents:
Vol I   Subject and special statistics (US$20)
Vol II   Industry statistics
Part 1   SIC major groups 20-26 (US$19)
Part 2   SIC major groups 27-34 (US$19)
Part 3   SIC major groups 35-39 (US$17)
Vol III   Area statistics
Part 1   Alabama to Montana (US$15)
Part 2   Nebraska to Wyoming (US$14)
Vol IV   Location of manufacturing plants
Part 1   Industry statistics by state and county
Part 2   County statistics by industries
Vol V   Production indexes
Advance and preliminary reports were also published.
Time factor: the results of the census were published from 1977.   A census is taken every five years.
§   En.

1355   Annual survey of manufactures   (Bureau of the Census)
Government Printing Office, Washington DC 20402.
1949/50-   1976.
Content:
Vol 1   General statistics for industry groups and industries (US$0.70)

[continued next page]

¶ B.iii,   continued

1355,   continued

      Vol 2   Value of product shipments (US$0.70)
      Vol 3   Value of manufacturers' inventories (US$0.35)
      Vol 4   Fuels and electric energy consumed
             4.1   Industry group and industries (US$0.50)
             4.2   States, by industry group (US$1.65)
             4.3   Standard metropolitan statistical areas, by major industry groups (US$1.30)
             4.4   Manufacturers' alternative energy capabilities, (1977-78 heating season) (US$0.75)
             4.P   Preliminary statistics for the US (US$0.25)
      Vol 5   Expenditure on new plant and equipment; book value of fixed assets; rental payments for
           buildings and equipment (US$0.65)
      Vol 6   Statistics for states, standard metropolitan statistical areas, large industrial counties and
           selected cities (US$4.20)
      Vol 8   Origin of exports of manufacturing establishments (US$1.60)
    Time factor: the reports were published from December 1977 onwards.
   §   En.

1356   Current industrial reports (Bureau of the Census)
      Subscriber Service Section (Publications), Bureau of the Census, Department of Commerce, Suitland,
        Maryland 20233.
                        prices vary - usually $0.25 or $0.30 each issue.
    The reports contain up-to-date information for particular industries on production, employment, sales, etc,
      and are issued monthly or quarterly with annual summaries.
      Titles are:
        Aluminium ingot and mill products   (m)
        Asphalt and tar roofing and siding products   (m)
        Backing of orders for aerospace companies   (q)
        Broadwoven fabric (gray)   (q)
        Canned food, stocks, pack, shipments   (q)
        Carpets and rugs (q)
        Clay construction products   (m)
        Closures for containers   (m)
        Complete aircraft and aircraft engines   (m)
        Confectionery, including chocolate products   (m)
        Construction machinery   (q)
        Consumption on the cotton system   (m)
        Consumption on the woolen and worsted systems   (m)
        Converted flexible packaging products   (q)
        Copper base mill and foundry products   (q)
        Electric lamps   (m & q)
        Farm machines and equipment   (q)
        Fats and oils, production, consumption and stocks   (m)
        Fats and oils, oilseed crushing   (m)
        Flat glass   (q)
        Flour milling products   (m)
        Fluorescent lamp ballasts   (q)
        Glass containers   (m)
        Heating and cooking equipment   (m)
        Industrial gases   (m)
        Inorganic chemicals   (m)
        Inorganic fertilizer materials and related products   (m)
        Inventories of brass and copper wire mill shapes   (m)
        Inventories of steel mill shapes   (m)
        Iron and steel castings   (m)
        Knit fabric production   (q)
        Manufacturers' export sales and orders of durable goods   (m)

[continued next page]

¶   B.iii,   continued

1356,   continued

        Manufacturers' shipments, inventories and orders   (m)
        Mattresses, foundations, and sleep furniture   (m)
        Mattresses, foundations and convertable sofas   (q)
        Men's apparel   (m)
        Metal cans   (m)
        Metal working machinery   (q)
        Non-ferrous castings   (m)
        Paint, varnish and lacquer   (m)
        Plastic bottles   (m)
        Plumbing fixtures   (q)
        Pulp, paper and board   (m)
        Refractories   (q)
        Rubber, supply and distribution for US   (m)
        Sheets, pillow cases and towels   (q)
        Shipments of knit cloth, including interplant transfers   (q)
        Shipments of thermoplastic pipe, tubes and fittings   (m)
        Shoes and slippers   (m)
        Steel shipping drums and pails   (m)
        Titanium ingot, mill products and castings   (m)
        Tractors, except garden tractors   (m)
        Truck trailers   (m)
        Typewriters   (m)
        Women's, misses' and juniors' apparel   (m)
        Woven fabrics, production, inventories and unfilled orders   (m)
§   En.

1357   Production prices and price indexes   (Bureau of Labor Statistics)
    Government Printing Office, Washington DC 20402.
    1956-   monthly.   US$1.80 or US$16 yr (US$20 yr abroad); supplement US$2.70.
    A comprehensive monthly report on price movements of both farm and industrial commodities, by industry
        and stage of processing.
    Time factor: each monthly issue has data for that month and is published about two or three months later.
§   En.

    Note: formerly 'Wholesale prices and price indices'.

1358   Fairchild fact files   (Fairchild Books)
    Fairchild Books, 7 East 12th Street, New York, NY 10003.
        1978.   US$7.50 each issue, payment with order.
    A series of market research reports, each on a different industry, but mainly in the textile field, which
        include data on production, shipments, price trends, foreign trade, retail trade, consumer
        expenditure and buying habits, etc.   Titles available for 1978 are on consumer market develop-
        ments; department store sales; fashion accessories; floor coverings; home electronics; home
        textiles; household furniture and bedding; infants', girls', and boys' wear; major appliances and
        electric housewares; men's clothing, tailored sportswear, rainwear; men's furnishings, career/work
        wear; men's sportswear and casual wear; men's and women's hosiery and leg wear; men's, women's
        and children's footwear; textile/apparel industries; toiletries, beauty aids and cosmetics; women's
        coats, suits, rainwear, furs; women's dresses; women's inner fashions: lingerie, loungewear,
        foundations; women's sportswear and casual wear.
§   En.

    Note: Fairchild Books also issue directories which include statistical summaries such as 'Fairchild's
        financial manual of retail stores' (49th ed, 1976 US$40) and 'Fairchild's textile and apparel
        financial directory' (1976 issue: US$40).

¶   B.iii,   continued

1359   Distilled spirits industry: annual statistical review   (Distilled Spirits Council of the United States)
        Distilled Spirits Council of the United States, 1300 Pennsylvania Building, Washington DC 20004.
            1977.   not priced.   54 p.
        Contains statistics of operations of the beverage distilling industry, including production, taxes, stocks,
            bottled output, trade, foreign trade, consumption, retail licenses, etc.
        Time factor: the 1977 issue, published in 1978, has data for 1976 and 1977.
        §   En.

1360   Monthly statistical release...   (Alcohol, Tobacco and Firearms Bureau; Treasury Department)
        Alcohol, Tobacco and Firearms Bureau, Treasury Department, Washington DC 20224.
                        not priced.
        Monthly statistical releases are issued on cigarettes and tobacco, distilled spirits, beer, and wines.
            Each contains statistics on manufacture and trade.
        §   En.

1361   Alcohol and tobacco and firearms summary statistics   (Alcohol, Tobacco & Firearms Bureau, Treasury
            Department)
        Government Printing Office, Washington DC 20402.
        1953-   1976.   US$2.50.
        Contains data on establishments and permits; comparative statistics on materials, production, stocks,
            withdrawals, losses, etc, for all types of alcohol, wines and spirits, vinegar, tobacco, and firearms.
        Time factor: the 1976 issue, with data for 1976, was published in 1978.
        §   En.

1362   Green coffee: inventories, imports and roastings   (Bureau of the Census)
        Subscriber Services Section (Publications), Bureau of the Census, Department of Commerce, Suitland,
            Maryland 20233.
        1964-   quarterly.   US$0.25 or US$1 yr.
        §   En.

1363   Canned food: stocks, pack, shipments   (Bureau of the Census)
        Subscriber Services Section (Publications), Bureau of the Census, Department of Commerce, Suitland,
            Maryland 20233.
                5 issues a season   US$0.35 or US$1.25 yr.
        Contains estimates of wholesale distributors' and canners' stocks of selected canned food items.
        Time factor: published in January, April, June, July and November.
        §   En.

1364   Textile organon: featuring man-made fibers: monthly review   (Textile Economic Bureau Inc)
        Textile Economic Bureau Inc, 489 Fifth Avenue, New York, NY 10017.
        1979-   US$100 yr (US$150 yr abroad)   Single issues for June and November US$10 (US$15
                        abroad); other months US$8 (US$12 abroad) each.
        Contains data on imports, exports and balance of man-made fibre and manufactures, cotton manufactures
            and wool manufactures, etc.
        Time factor: each issue has data for several years and months up to one month prior to the date of
            publication.
        §   En.

¶   B.iii,   continued

1365   Textile hilights   (American Textile Manufacturers' Institute)
          American Textile Manufacturers' Institute, 400 South Tyron Street, Charlotte, NC 28285.
                    quarterly.   not priced.
          Contains statistics on consumption by US mills of fibres, spindle activity, loom hours operated, production
                    of fabrics, price indices, employment, plant, etc.
          Time factor: each issue has long runs of figures to the quarter prior to the date of publication.
          §   En.

          Note: there is also a monthly supplement.

1366   Cotton and wool situation   (Department of Agriculture: Economic Research Service)
          Department of Agriculture, Economic Research Service, Washington DC 20250.
          1962-   quarterly.   not priced.
          Includes statistical data on cotton, man-made fibres, wool and mohair.
          Time factor: each issue has long runs of figures to the latest available.
          §   En.

1367   Hosiery statistics (National Association of Hosiery Manufacturers)
          National Association of Hosiery Manufacturers, 516 Charlottetown Mall, Box 4314, Charlotte,
                    NC 28204.
          1934- 1977   US$35.   58 p.
          Covers all aspects of the industry - production, stocks, exports, imports, manpower and plants.
          Time factor: the 1977 issue, published in 1978, has data for several years to 1977.
          §   En.

1368   Wool statistics and related data   (Department of Agriculture: Economic Research Service)
          Department of Agriculture, Washington DC 20250.
          1959-   3rd, 1930-1969.   US$2.25.,   294 p.
          Contains data on production, consumption, foreign trade and prices of wool, mohair and similar hair
                    fibres; and selected data on cotton and man-made fibres.
          Time factor: the 1930-1969 edition was published in 1970.
          §   En.

1369   The Carpet and Rug Institute Industry Review
          The Carpet and Rug Institute, Dalton, Georgia.
          1970- 1976-77.   US$2.   29 p.
          Contains data on carpet and rug shipments, average prices, contract market, imports and exports, yarn
                    consumed, primary and secondary backing consumed, etc.
          Time factor: the 1976-77 edition, published in 1977, has long runs of figures to 1976.
          §   En.

1370   Synthetic organic chemicals, United States production and sales   (Tariff Commission)
          Government Printing Office, Washington DC 20402.
          1917- 1976.   US$5.25.   c 300 p.
          Contains data on production and sale of tars, tar crudes and crudes derived from petroleum and natural
                    gas; production and sales of intermediates and finished synthetic organic chemicals by groups; and
                    an alphabetical list of products, etc.
          Time factor: the 1976 issue, published in 1978, has data for 1976.
          §   En.

          Note: there is also a monthly preliminary report on US production of selected synthetic organic chemicals
                    available from the Tariff Commission, Washington DC 20436.

¶   B.iii,   continued

1373   Facts and figures: the US chemical industry   (American Chemical Society)
      Chemical & Engineering News, 1155 16th Street NW, Washington DC 20036.
      Published annually in a June issue of 'Chemical & Engineering news' it includes statistical data on
          production, prices, sales, company performance, employment, wages, foreign trade for the United
          States.   Also chemical production, trends, company data, foreign trade and prices in Canada,
          Europe and Japan.
      Time factor: the 1978 issue has data for several years to 1977.
      §   En.

1374   Facts and figures of the plastics industry   (Society of the Plastics Industry Inc)
      Society of the Plastics Industry Inc, 355 Lexington Avenue, New York, NY 10017.
          1976.   US$7.50 to S P I members; US$15 to non-members.   98 p.
      Contains statistical data on manufacturing, production, sales and use, major domestic markets, balance
          of trade for plastics.
      Time factor: the 1976 issue, published in 1976, has data for several years to 1975.
      §   En.

1375   Statistics of paper and paperboard   (American Paper Institute Inc)
      American Paper Institute Inc, 260 Madison Avenue, New York, NY 10016.
      1934-   1978.   US$45 in North America; US$50 overseas.   76 p.
      Contains data on shipments, production, capacity, finances, etc.
      Time factor: the 1978 issue, published late 1978, has long runs of data to 1977.
      §   En.

1376   Pulp, paper and board: quarterly industry report   (Bureau of Domestic Commerce)
      Government Printing Office, Washington DC 20402.
      1944-   not priced.
      Contains data on current trends, raw materials, production, stocks, shipments, imports and exports, etc.
      Time factor: each issue has data for the quarter and cumulative data for the year to date and the previous
          year.
      §   En.

1377   Containers and packaging: quarterly industry report   (Bureau of Domestic Commerce)
      Government Printing Office, Washington DC 20402.
      1948-   not priced.
      Contains data on current trends, wholesale price index of selected containers and container materials,
          exports and imports of selected containers and container materials, aluminium shipments by domestic
          markets, tinplate produced by country, commodity trends.   There is also a section titled 'Statistical
          series' on economic trends, and shipments, production and stocks or glass containers, metal cans,
          closures for containers, paper, and plastic bottles.
      Time factor: each issue has cumulated quarterly data to three months prior to the date of the issue and for
          the previous year.
      §   En.

1378   Annual statistical report   (American Iron and Steel Institute)
      American Iron and Steel Institute, 1000 16th Street NW, Washington DC 20036.
      1856-   1977.   not priced.   98 p.
      Contains data on selected highlights, financial and economic statistics, employment and wages data,
          shipments and steel production, exports and imports, raw steel production, pigiron and ferroalloys,
          basic materials, Canadian statistics, and world statistics – production.
      Time factor: the 1977 issue, published in 1978, has data for 1977 and 1976 and some earlier figures.
      §   En.

¶   B.iii,   continued

1379   Copper: quarterly report   (Bureau of Domestic Commerce)
        Government Printing Office, Washington DC 20402.
        1954-   US$3 each issue (US$3.75 abroad)
        Contains data on production, shipments, stocks, etc.
        Time factor: each issue has quarterly data and cumulated data for the year to the date of the issue.
        §   En.

1380   Automotive trade statistics: series B...1964-76   (International Trade Commission)
        International Trade Commission, Washington DC 20436.
                            not priced.   93 p.
        Contains data on new passenger automobiles; statistical data relating to factory sales, retail sales,
            imports, exports, apparent consumption, suggested retail prices and US bilateral trade balance
            with the eight major producing countries.
        Time factor: published in 1977.
        §   En.

1381   Motor vehicle facts and figures   (Motor Vehicle Manufacturers' Association of the United States Inc)
        Motor Vehicle Manufacturers' Association of the United States, Inc, 300 New Center Building, Detroit,
            Michigan 48202.
        1972-   1977.   not priced.   96 p.
        Contains data on production and registration, use and owners, and the economic impact.   Related to
            all types of cars and trucks.
        Time factor: the 1977 issue, published in 1977, has data for 1976, 1975 and some earlier years.
        §   En.

1382   American trucking trends   (American Trucking Association Inc)
        American Trucking Association Inc, 1616 P Street NW, Washington DC 20036.
        1974-   1975.   not priced.   36 p.
        Includes statistical data on ton-miles, carrier size and location, motor freight tonnage, products, revenue,
            taxes, manpower, equipment, etc.
        Time factor: the 1975 edition has data for 1973 and there is a 1976 supplement with data for 1974 and
            1975.
        §   En.

1383   The production figure book for US cars   (Jerry Heasley)
        Motorbooks International, Osceola, Wisconsin 54020.
        1949-   1977.   US$6.95   180 p.
        Intended for the enthusiast, the book has very detailed information on production by makes and models.
        Time factor: the 1977 issue was published mid-1977.
        §   En.

1384   Aerospace facts and figures   (Aerospace Industries Association of America Inc)
        Aviation Week and Space Technology, 1221 Avenue of the Americas, New York, NY 10020.
        1953/54-   1978/79.   US$6.95.   152 p.
        Contains an aerospace summary and data on aircraft production, missile programme, space programme,
            air transportation, research and development, foreign trade, employment, and finance.
        Time factor: the 1978/79 issue, published mid-1978, has data for several years to 1977 and some estimates
            for 1978 and 1979.
        §   En.

1385   Electronic market databook   (Electronic Industries Association)
        Electronic Industries Association, 2001 Eye Street NW, Washington DC 20006.
        1970- 1978.   US$25.   126 p.
        Contains statistical data on consumer electronics, communication and industrial products, government
            products, electronic components, and world trade.
        Time factor: the 1978 issue, published in 1978, has long runs of statistics to 1977.

        Note: the Association also issues a monthly 'Electronic market trends'.

        Refer also to 1324, 1325, 1326.

    iv.   Construction

1386   Census of construction industries   (Bureau of the Census)
        Government Printing Office, Washington DC 20402.
        1935- 1972.   2 vols.
        Final report is in two volumes:
                Vol I   Industry and special statistics   (US$10)
                Vol II   Area statistics   (US$12)
        Vol I has summary data for the construction establishment with and without payroll, by total receipts,
            size of establishments, for industry groups and industries, number of employees by type, etc.
            Vol II has data for the US geographical divisions, and States.
        Time factor: the report of the 1972 census was published in 1976.
        §   En.

        Note: a quinquennial cumulation of census of construction industries reports was published in 1978.

1387   Current construction reports   (Bureau of the Census)
        Subscriber Services Section (Publications), Bureau of the Census, Department of Commerce, Suitland,
            Maryland 20233 for C21, C22, C25, C27, C41 and C50.   Government Printing Office,
            Washington DC 20402 for C20, C30 and C40.
        C20   Housing starts.   monthly.   (US$0.55 or US$6.50 yr domestic; US$0.70 or US$8.15 yr
            foreign).
        C21   New residential construction in selected standard metropolitan statistical areas.   quarterly.
            (US$0.50 or US$2 yr)
        C22   Housing completions.   monthly.   (US$0.30 or US$3 yr)
        C25   New one-family houses sold and for sale.   monthly and annual.   (US$0.25 or US$5.25 yr
            including annual issue; annual issue only US$2.25)
        C27   Price index of new family houses sold.   quarterly.   (US$0.50 or US$2.50 yr)
        C30   Value of new construction put in place.   monthly.   (US$0.80 or US$9.40 yr; US$1 or
            US$11.75 yr abroad)
        C40   Housing authorized by building permits and public contracts.   monthly and annual summary.
            (US$2 (annual issue US$5.25) or US$31.05 yr including annual; US$3 or US$41.25 foreign)
        C41   Authorised construction - Washington DC area.   monthly.   (US$0.25 or US$3 yr)
        C50   Residential alterations and repairs.   quarterly and annual.   (US$0.30 or US$1.90 yr)
        §   En.

1388   Construction in Hawaii   (Bank of Hawaii)
        Bank of Hawaii, PO Box 2900, Honolulu, Hawaii.
        1967- 1977.   not priced.   40 p.
        Includes statistical tables on summary of construction, residential construction, commercial and industrial
            construction, neighbour island construction, mortgage activity and land transactions, government
            construction.
        Time factor: the 1977 issue, published mid-1977, has data to 1976.
        §   En.

¶   B.iv,   continued

1389   Construction review: monthly industry report   (Bureau of Domestic Commerce)
          Government Printing Office, Washington DC 20402.
          1955-   monthly.   not priced.
          Includes statistics on construction generally, housing building permits, contracts, costs and prices,
                construction materials, and contract construction employment.
          Time factor: each issue has long runs of figures to about three months prior to the month of the issue.
          §   En.

          Refer also to 1324, 1325, 1326.

     v.   Energy

1390   Monthly energy review   (National Energy Information Center)
          National Energy Information Center, Springfield Va 22161.
          1975-   US$6.25 (US$12.50 abroad); US$50 yr (US$100 yr abroad)
          Includes statistics on petroleum and petroleum products, natural gas, coal, electric utilities and nuclear
                power, prices, international petroleum consumption, and crude oil production.
          Time factor: each issue has data to about three months prior to the date of the issue.
          §   En.

          Note: formed by the merger of 'PIMS monthly petroleum report' and 'Monthly energy indicators'.

1391   Energy perspectives: 2   (Department of the Interior)
          Government Printing Office, Washington DC 20402.
          1975-   No 2. $5.40.   c 230 p.
          Contains data on world energy reserves, consumption, capital requirements and environmental effects of
                energy use.
          Time factor: No 2 was published in 1977.
          §   En.

1392   Statistical yearbook of the electric utility industry   (Edison Electric Institute)
          Edison Electric Institute, 90 Park Avenue, New York, NY 10016.
          1933-   1976.   US$10 to member companies; US$15 to others.   68 p.
          Contains data on generating capacity, electric power supply, generation, energy sales, customers,
                revenues, operating data and ratios, finance, and economic data (price indices, etc).
          Time factor: the 1976 issue, published late 1977, has data for several years to 1976.
          §   En.

          Note: also issued is 'Historical statistics of the electric utility industry through 1970'.

1393   Statistics of publicly owned electric utilities in the United States   (Federal Power Commission)
          Government Printing Office, Washington DC 20402.
          1946-   1975.   US$3.75.   c 100 p.
          Contains financial and operating statistics of large publicly owned electric utilities.
          Time factor: the 1975 issue, published in 1977, has data for 1975.
          §   En.

1394   Statistics of privately owned electric utilities in the United States   (Federal Power Commission)
          Government Printing Office, Washington DC 20402.
          1940-   1975.   US$6.20.   c 700 p.
          Contains financial and operating statistics of large privately owned electric utilities.
          Time factor: the 1975 issue, published in 1977, has data for 1975.
          §   En.

¶   B.v,   continued

1395   Report on equipment availability for the ten year period 1964-1973   (Edison Electric Institute)
            Edison Electric Institute, 90 Park Avenue, New York,   NY 10016.
                                            not priced.   44 p.
            Time factor: published in 1974.
            §   En.

1396   Biennial survey of power equipment requirements of the US electric utility industry   (National Electrical
                    Manufacturers' Association)
            National Electrical Manufacturers' Association, 2101 L Street NW, Suite 300, Washington DC 20037.
            1968-   1977-1986.   US$10.   27 p.
            Time factor: the 1977-1986 issue, published early 1978, has long runs of figures to 1976 and forecasts to
                    1986.
            §   En.

1397   Steam-electric plant construction cost and annual production expenses   (Federal Power Commission)
            Government Printing Office, Washington DC 20402.
            1938/47-   1974.   US$3.
            Contains for each plant, installed generating capacity, net generation, peak demand, net continuous
                    plant capability, cost of plant, production expenses, types and quality and cost of fuels, and
                    average numbers of employees.
            Time factor: the 1938/47 issue is a basic volume and the publication has been issued annually since 1948.
                    The 1974 issue, published in 1978, has data for 1974.
            §   En.

1398   Hydroelectric plant construction cost and annual production expenses   (Federal Power Commission)
            Government Printing Office, Washington DC 20402.
            1953/56-   1974.   US$2.15.
            Contains for each plant, installed generating capacity, net generation, peak demand, net continuous
                    plant capability, cost of plant, production expenses, types and quality and cost of fuels, and
                    average numbers of employees.
            Time factor: the 1953/56 issue is a basic volume and the publication has been issued annually since 1957.
                    The 1974 issue, published in 1978, has data for 1974.
            §   En.

1399   Electric power statistics   (Federal Power Commission)
            Government Printing Office, Washington DC 20402.
            1961-   monthly.   US$9.85 (US$12.35 abroad) yr.
            Contains summaries of statistics taken from reports filed by electric utilities with the Commission.
            Time factor: each issue has data for that month and is published about ten months later.
            §   En.

1400   Retail prices and price indexes of fuels and utilities   (Bureau of Labor Statistics)
            Bureau of Labor Statistics, Washington DC 20210.
            1972-   monthly.   not priced.
            Time factor: each issue has data for that month and is published the following month.
            §   En.

            Note: earlier title was 'Retail prices and price indexes of fuels and electricity'.

1401   Gas facts: a statistical record of the gas utility industry   (American Gas Association)
            American Gas Association, 1515 Wilson Boulevard, Arlington Va 22209.
            1918-   1976.   US$8.   203 p.

[continued next page]

¶   B.v,   continued

1401,   continued

    Provides statistics on energy reserves, natural gas production, energy consumption, natural gas sales, prices, and finances of the leading companies, etc.
    Time factor: the 1976 issue, published in 1977, has data for several years to 1976.
    §   En.

    Note: also issued by the association is 'Historical statistics of the gas industry' published in 1961.

1402   Basic petroleum data book: petroleum industry statistics   (American Petroleum Institute)
    American Petroleum Institute, 2101 L Street NW, Washington DC 20037.
    1975-   1975.   US$30 in USA, Canada & Mexico; US$35 overseas.   looseleaf.
    Contains current statistical information on energy production, investment, refining, consumption, employment, reserves of crude oil, finances, prices, demand, imports and exports, offshore, transport, natural gas, and OPEC.
    Time factor: the 1975 issue, has data for several years to 1974, 1975 or 1976.
    §   En.

1403   Statistics of interstate natural gas pipeline companies   (Federal Power Commission)
    Government Printing Office, Washington DC 20402.
    1942-   1976.   US$4.50.   c 700 p.
    Contains financial and operating statistics of 80 natural gas pipeline companies under the Commission's jurisdiction.   Includes balance sheets, R & D costs by company, gas prepayments, sources of funds, etc.
    Time factor: the 1976 issue, with data for that year, was published in 1978.
    §   En.

1404   The oil producing industry in your state   (Independent Petroleum Producing Association of America)
    Independent Oil Producing Association of America, 1101 16th Street NW, Washington DC 20036.
    1971-   1978.   not priced.   119 p.
    Contains data on productive and non-productive acreage, rigs, wells drilled, production, employment, consumption, costs, etc.
    Time factor: the 1978 issue, published in 1978, has data for 1974 to 1977.
    §   En.

1405   Annual statistical review   (American Petroleum Institute)
    American Petroleum Institute, 1801 K Street NW, Washington DC 20006.
    1940-   1956-70.   US$2.50.   60 p.
    Contains statistics on fuel reserves, number of oil wells drilled, production of oil, oil imports and exports, refinery capacity, energy consumption, gasoline prices, etc.
    Time factor: the 1956-70 issue was published in 1971.
    §   En.

    Note: the institute also issues a weekly 'Statistical bulletin'.

1406   Monthly petroleum statistics report   (Federal Energy Administration)
    National Technical Information Service, Springfield, Va 22161.
    1975-   US$6.25 or US$50 yr (US$12.50 or US$100 yr abroad)
    §   En.

    Note: there is also a 'Monthly petroleum product price report', prices on application to NTIS.

    Refer also to 1324, 1325, 1326.

¶ C - External trade

1407 Foreign commerce and navigation of the United States (Bureau of the Census)
        Government Printing Office, Washington DC 20402.
        1821- 1965.   Vol I US$7; Vol II US$8.25; Vol III US$9.
        Volume I contains detailed statistics of foreign trade arranged by the SITC and subdivided by countries of
            origin and destination; vol II has data arranged by area and country subdivided by the SITC; and
            vol III has data arranged by Schedule A and Schedule B commodity classifications subdivided by
            countries of origin and destination.
        Time factor: data was prepared and published annually from 1821 to 1946; then a summary volume was
            produced to bridge the gap between 1946 and 1963; then annual volumes were published for 1964
            and 1965.   Publication ceased with the 1965 edition, being superseded by the various FT reports
            mentioned below.
        §   En.

        Note: Schedule A is the commodity classification used for imports, and Schedule B the commodity
            classification used for exports of the US foreign trade.

1408 FT 410. US exports - schedule B - commodity by country (Bureau of the Census)
        Government Printing Office, Washington DC 20402.
                monthly.   US$10.20 (US$12.50 abroad) or US$122.20 yr (US$152.55 yr abroad.)
        Detailed statistics of exports arranged by the US Schedule B commodity classification and subdivided by
            countries of destination.
        Time factor: each issue has data for the month and cumulated figures for the year to date and is published
            about four or five months later.   The December issue has the annual figures.
        §   En.

1409 FT 135. US general imports - schedule A - commodity by country (Bureau of the Census)
        Government Printing Office, Washington DC 20402.
        1967- monthly.   US$6 (US$7.50 abroad) or US$71.85 yr (US$89.85 yr abroad)
        Detailed statistics of imports arranged by the US Schedule A commodity classification and subdivided by
            countries of origin.
        Time factor: each issue has data for the month and cumulated figures for the year to date and is published
            about six months later.   The December issue has the annual figures.
        §   En.

1410 FT 150.   US general imports, Schedule A commodity groupings by world areas (Bureau of the Census)
        Government Printing Office, Washington DC 20402.
        1967- 1977.   US$5.25   378 p.
        Time factor: the 1977 issue, published in 1978, has data for 1977.
        §   En.

1411 FT 450. US exports, commodity groupings by world area (Bureau of the Census)
        Government Printing Office, Washington DC 20402.
        1967- 1976.   US$5.25.   c 450 p.
        Time factor: the 1976 issue, published in 1977, has data for 1976.

1412 FT 155. US foreign trade: general imports, world area, country, Schedule A commodity groupings, and method
            of transportation (Bureau of the Census)
        Government Printing Office, Washington DC 20402.
        1967- 1976.   US$6.25.   c 450 p.
        Time factor: the 1976 issue, published in 1977, has data for 1976.
        §   En.

¶   C,   continued

1413   FT 975. United States foreign trade: vessel entrances and clearances   (Bureau of the Census)
            Subscriber Service Section (Publications), Bureau of the Census, Suitland, Maryland 20233.
            1945- 1977.   US$0.25 (US$14.90 yr for FT 900, 975, 985 and 986 combined – see 1414, 1415,
                1417).
            Contains data on the number and net registered tonnage of US and foreign flag vessels entered and
                cleared with cargo and in ballast by customs district, by port, total vessels, US vessels, and foreign
                vessels.   Includes data for Puerto Rico and the Virgin Islands.
            Time factor: the 1977 issue, published mid-1978, has data for 1977.
            §   En.

1414   FT 985. United States foreign trade: US waterborne exports and general imports   (Bureau of the Census)
            Subscriber Services Section (Publications), Bureau of the Census, Suitland, Maryland 20233.
                    monthly and annual.   US$0.50 (US$14.90 yr for FT 900, 975, 985 and 986 combined – see
                        1414, 1415, 1417).
            Contains data by trade area, district, port, type of service, and US flag.
            Time factor: each issue has data for that period, the monthlies being published about four months later
                and the annuals about eight months later.
            §   En.

            Note: the Department of the Army has issued since 1953 an annual 'Waterborne commerce of the United
                States', with data by regions of the US.

1415   FT 986. US airborne exports and general imports   (Bureau of the Census)
            Subscriber Services Section (Publications), Bureau of the Census, Suitland, Maryland 20233.
                    monthly and annual summary.   US$0.35 (US$14.90 yr for FT 900, 975, 985 and 986 combined
                        – see 1413, 1414, 1417).
            Contains data on shipping weight and value, customs district and continent.
            Time factor: each issue has data for that period, the monthlies being published about three months later
                and the annual summaries about five months later.
            §   En.

1416   US foreign trade. FT 246: imports, TSUSA commodity and country   (Bureau of the Census)
            Government Printing Office, Washington DC 20402.
            (annual)   1976.   US$5.75.   442 p.
            Time factor: the 1976 issue, published in 1977, has data for 1976.
            §   En.

1417   FT 900. Summary of US export and import merchandise trade   (Bureau of the Census)
            Subscriber Service Section (Publications), Bureau of the Census, Department of Commerce, Suitland,
                Maryland 20233.
            1968- monthly.   US$0.30 (US$14.90 yr for FT 900, 975, 985 and 986 combined – see 1413, 1414,
                1415).
            Summary statistics of seasonally adjusted and unadjusted data on trade in merchandise, including unadjusted
                data on imports of petroleum and petroleum products.
            Time factor: each issue has data for the month of the issue and is published three or four weeks later.
            §   En.

1418   FT 990. Highlights of US export and import trade   (Bureau of the Census)
            Government Printing Office, Washington DC 20402.
            1967- monthly.   US$3.15 (US$3.95 abroad) or US$37 yr (US$46.80 yr abroad)
            Seasonally adjusted and unadjusted data by commodity, country, customs district, and method of
                transportation.
            Time factor: each issue has data for that month and the corresponding month of the previous year and is
                published about three months later.
            §   En.

¶ C,   continued

1419   FT 210. US imports – consumption and general, SIC based products by world areas   (Bureau of the Census)
            Subscriber Service Section (Publications), Bureau of the Census, Department of Commerce, Suitland,
                Maryland 20233.
            1964–   1975.   US$3.85.   320 p.
            Time factor: the 1975 issue, published in 1977, has data for 1975.
            §   En.

1420   FT 610. US exports – domestic merchandise, SIC-based products by world areas   (Bureau of the Census)
            Government Printing Office, Washington DC 20402.
            1965–   1976.   US$6.50.   612 p.
            Time factor: the 1976 issue, published in 1977, has data for 1976.
            §   En.

1421   FT 800. US trade with Puerto Rico and United States possessions   (Bureau of the Census)
            1956–   monthly.   US$1.35 (US$1.75 abroad) or US$16.30 yr (US$20.40 yr abroad)
            Imports and exports, arranged by commodity subdivided by method of transport, between the US and
                Puerto Rico, Virgin Islands of the US, Guam and American Samoa.
            Time factor: publication ceased with the 1975 cumulation.
            §   En.

1422   FT 810. Bunker fuels: oil and coal laden in the United States on vessels engaged in foreign trade   (Bureau of
                the Census)
            Subscriber Service Section (Publications), Bureau of the Census, Department of Commerce, Suitland,
                Maryland 20233.
                monthly with an annual issue.   US$0.25 or US$3.25 yr.
            §   En.

1423   Agricultural trade in the Western Hemisphere: a statistical review   (Department of Agriculture: Economic
                Research Service)
            Department of Agriculture, Washington DC 20250.
                            not priced.   124 p.
            Contains historical series showing USA agricultural trade with countries and regions of the Western
                Hemisphere.
            Time factor: published in 1972, the review covers the years 1962 to 1970.
            §   En.

1424   FT 130. General imports of cotton manufactures: country of origin and Geneva agreement category   (Bureau
                of the Census)
            Subscriber Service Section (Publications), Bureau of the Census, Department of Commerce, Suitland,
                Maryland 20233.
                monthly.   US$0.30 or US$3.60 yr.
            Time factor: each issue has data for that month and is published about two months later.
            §   En.

1425   Foreign agricultural trade of the United States   (Department of Agriculture: Economic Research Service)
            Economic Research Service, Department of Agriculture, Washington DC 20250.
            1962–   monthly.   not priced.
            Contains detailed statistics of imports and exports of agricultural products.
            §   En.

            Note: this publication is supplemented by the annual publications 'US foreign agricultural trade
                statistical report', 'US foreign trade by countries', 'US foreign agricultural trade by commodities
                (fiscal year)', and 'US foreign agricultural trade by commodities (calendar year)'.

¶   C,   continued

1426   NAABI annual statistical report   (National Association of Alcoholic Beverage Importers Inc)
          NAABI, 1025 Vermont Avenue NW, Washington DC 20005.
                 1977.   not priced.   36 p.
          Contains data on imports of distilled spirits, wines and beers from the principal countries of export to the
               US and shipments to the US from Puerto Rico and the Virgin Islands.
          Time factor: the 1977 issue, published in 1978, has long runs of figures to 1977.
          §   En.

1427   FT 2402. US exports and imports of gold   (Bureau of the Census)
          Government Printing Office, Washington DC 20402.
                 monthly and annual.   US$0.10 or US$1 yr.
          Time factor: ceased publication in 1975.
          §   En.

1428   Imports of benzenoid chemicals and products   (Tariff Commission)
          Tariff Commission, Washington DC 20436.
          1964-   1976.   not priced.   105 p.
          Contains data on intermediates, dyes, medicinals, flavour and perfume materials, and other finished
               benzenoid products.
          Time factor: the 1976 issue, published in 1977, has data for 1976.
          §   En.

          Refer also to 1324, 1325, 1326.

     ¶   D   -   Internal distribution and service trades

1429   Census of wholesale trade   (Bureau of the Census)
          Government Printing Office, Washington DC 20402.
          1929-   1972.   2 vols.
          Contents:
               Vol I   Summary and subject statistics   (US$17)
               Vol II   Area statistics   (US$20).
          Summary statistics on number of establishments, sales, inventories and payrolls are given by type of
               operation and kind of business for the United States, states, counties, etc.   Subject statistics
               include reports on establishment size and firm size, value produced, capital expenditures, fixed
               assets, labour costs, sales, etc.   Area statistics have the above information arranged first by
               areas.
          Time factor: a census is taken every five years and the final reports of the 1972 census were published in
               1976.
          §   En.

          Note: included as part of the Census of Business prior to 1972.

1430   Monthly wholesale trade, sales and inventories   (Bureau of the Census)
          Government Printing Office, Washington DC 20402.
          1968-   US$0.60 (US$0.75 abroad) or US$7.20 yr (US$9 yr abroad)
          Time factor: each issue has data for the month of the issue and is published about two months later.
          §   En.

¶   D,   continued

1431   Census of retail trade   (Bureau of the Census)
          Government Printing Office, Washington DC 20402.
          1929-   1972.   3 vols in 6.
          Contents:
                    Vol I   Summary and subject statistics   (US$8.50)
                    Vol II   Retail trade - area statistics
                              Part 1   US summary, Alabama-Indiana   (US$16)
                              Part 2   Iowa-North Carolina   (US$19)
                              Part 3   North Dakota-Wyoming   (US$18)
                    Vol III   Retail trade - major retail center statistics
                              Part 1   Alabama-Indiana   (US$15)
                              Part 2   Iowa-North Carolina   (US$15)
                              Part 3   North Dakota-Wisconsin   (US$15)
          Summary statistics on number of establishments, sales, number of businesses operated by sole proprietorship
              or partnership, and payrolls, by kind of business for the United States as a whole, regions, divisions
              and states.   Subject statistics include reports on establishment and firm size, capital expenditures,
              fixed assets, merchandise line sales, etc.   Area statistics Vols II & III have the above information
              arranged first by areas and states.
          Time factor: a census is taken every five years and the final reports of the 1972 census were published in
              1976.
          §   En.

          Note: included as part of the Census of Business prior to 1972.

1432   Monthly retail trade, sales and accounts receivable   (Bureau of the Census)
          Government Printing Office, Washington DC 20402.
          1970-   US$30.10 yr (US$37.65 yr abroad) including 'Weekly retail sales' and 'Advance
                              monthly retail sales'.
          Time factor: each issue has data to the month of the issue and is published about two months later.
          §   En.

          Note: 'Monthly department store sales in selected areas' (US$3.60 yr) has the more limited subject
              coverage.

1433   Estimated retail food prices in cities   (Bureau of Labor Statistics)
          Bureau of Labor Statistics, Washington DC 20210.
          1964-   monthly and annual.   not priced.
          Contains data for the US and seven large cities.   Also includes the Virgin Islands.
          Time factor: each issue contains data for that month or year and is published a month later.
          §   En.

1434   Retail prices on food   (Bureau of Labor Statistics)
          Government Printing Office, Washington DC 20402.
          1941-
          Contains price indexes by commodity group, average price indexes of principal foods in the United States,
              and also in 23 cities.
          Time factor: issued at 5-yearly intervals.
          §   En.

1435   Distribution study of grocery store sales in 289 cities   (Supermarket News)
          Supermarket News, PO Box 714, Cooper Station, 7E 12th Street, New York, NY 10003.
          1975-   1978.   US$25.   204 p.
          Includes ranking of metropolitan areas by supermarket sales, grocery store statistical profile, etc.
          Time factor: the 1978 edition, published in 1978, has data to 1977.
          §   En.

¶   D,   continued

1436   NPN fact book   (National Petroleum News)
                National Petroleum News, PO Box 430, Hightstown, NJ 08520.
                        1978.   US$11 or free with 'National Petroleum News'.   210 p.
                Contains data on market trends, capital spending for marketing, retail outlets, retail market share, etc.
                Time factor: the 1978 issue, published mid-1978, has data for 1977 or 1978, and some earlier years.
                §   En.

1437   The sporting goods market: a statistical study of retail sales for representative categories of sporting goods and
                recreational equipment.   (National Sporting Goods Association)
                Irwin Broh & Associates Inc, 1001 East Touhy Avenue, Des Plaines, Illinois 60018.
                        1977.   US$35.   47 p.
                Time factor: the report relates to 1977 and was published in 1977.
                §   En.

1438   Census of the industry   (Vend)
                Vend, 165 West 46th Street, New York, NY 10036.
                1946-   1971.   US$0.50.   32 p.
                Published in the periodical 'Vend' and also available as a reprint, the census shows the market for vending
                        machines for drinks, tobacco, confectionery, foods, etc.
                Time factor: the 1971 results were published in the May 1971 issue of 'Vend' and contain data for 1969
                        and 1970.
                §   En.

1439   Census of selected service industries   (Bureau of the Census)
                Government Printing Office, Washington DC 20402.
                1929-   1972.   2 vols.
                Contents:
                        Vol I   Selected service industries - summary and subject statistics   (US$12)
                        Vol II   Selected service indusrries - area statistics
                                Part 1   US summary, Alabama-Indiana   (US$18)
                                Part 2   Iowa-North Carolina   (US$19)
                                Part 3   North Dakota-Wyoming   (US$18)
                Vol I has data on size of establishments and firms, by kind of firm and business for the United States as a
                        whole and for states, etc.   Vol II has the data arranged first by states.
                Time factor: the census is taken every five years and the final results of the 1972 census were published
                        in 1976.
                §   En.

                Note: included as part of the Census of Business prior to 1972.

                Note: also issued are a series of 8 final reports on specific topics:
                        1.   Establishment and firm size (including legal form of organisation)   (US$3.25)
                        2.   Hotels, motels, trailering parks, and camps   (US$1.80)
                        3.   Motion picture industry   (US$1.50)
                        4.   Legal services   (US$1.60)
                        5.   Architectural, engineering and land-surveying services   (US$1.30)
                        6.   Arrangement of passenger transport   (US$0.85)
                        7.   Nonregulated motor carriers and public warehousing   (US$1.50)
                        8.   Miscellaneous subjects   (US$2.50)

¶   D,   continued

1440   Monthly selected services receipts   (Bureau of the Census)
       Subscriber Service Section (Publications), Bureau of the Census, Department of Commerce, Suitland,
          Maryland 20233.
                   US$0.30 or US$3.60 yr.
     Time factor: each issue has data for that month and cumulated figures for the year to date, and is issued
        about two months later.
     §   En.

1441   Summary and analysis of international travel to the US   (United States Travel Service)
       United States Travel Service, Department of Commerce, Washington DC 20230.
       1962-   monthly.   80 p.
       Contains statistics on visitors arrivals and market analysis of international travel by residents of foreign
         countries.
       Time factor: the 1975 issue, published late 1976, has data for 1975.
     §   En.

       Note: there is also a monthly publication with the same title, which up-dates the annual.

       Refer also to 1324, 1325, 1326.

¶   E - Population

1442   Census of population   (Bureau of the Census)
       Government Printing Office, Washington DC 20402.
       1790-   1970.   prices vary.
       Contents:
           Vol I   Characteristics of the population
                Part A   Number of inhabitants
                  Section 1:   US, Alabama to Missouri
                  Section 2:   Mississippi to Wyoming, Puerto Rico and outlying areas
                Part B   General geographic characteristics
                Part C   General, social and economic characteristics
                Part D   Detailed characteristics
           Vol II   Subject reports [containing detailed information on cross-relationships for the US, regions
         and some states, etc, on such subjects as national origin and race, fertility, families, marital
         status, migration, education, employment, occupation, industry, and income]
     Time factor: the results of the 1970 census were published between 1971 and 1974.
     §   En.

1443   Current population reports   (Bureau of the Census)
       Government Printing Office, Washington DC 20402.
       1947-   irregular.   US$56 yr for all titles, plus US$14 for foreign mailings; prices of single issues
                 vary.
       Titles are:
          P 20   Population characteristics (1947-)
          P 23   Special studies (1949-)
          P 25   Population estimates and projections
          P 26   Federal-state co-operation program for population estimates (1969-)
          P 27   Farm population (1945-)
          P 28   Special censuses (1943-)
          P 60   Consumer income (1948-)
          P 65   Consumer buying indicators (1963-1977)
     §   En.

¶   E,   continued

1444   Vital statistics of the United States   (National Center for Health Statistics)
        Government Printing Office, Washington DC 20402.
        1937-   1975.   3 vols in 4.
        Contents:
            Vol. I   Natality   (1973 issue cost US$7.70)
            Vol II   Mortality   (1975 issue of Part A cost US$10.75 and Part B US$12)
            Vol III   Marriage and divorce   (1973 issue cost US$6)
        Time factor: the 1973 issue of vols I & III were published in 1977 and contain data for 1973; the 1975
            issue of vol II was published in 1978 and contains data for 1975.
        §   En.

1445   Monthly vital statistics report: provisional statistics   (National Center for Health Statistics)
        National Center for Health Statistics, 3700 East West Highway, Hyattsville, Maryland.
        1953-   free.
        Up-dates the above (1444).
        §   En.

        Note: also available is 'Monthly vital statistics: advance report'.

1446   US decennial life tables   (National Center for Health Statistics)
        Government Printing Office, Washington DC 20402.
                     1969-71.   2 vols in 6.
        Contents:
            Vol I   No 1   United States life tables, 1969-71
                    No 2   Actuarial tables based on United States life tables, 1969-71
                    No 3   Methodology of the national and state life tables for the US
                    No 4   Some trends and comparisons of the United States life tables data 1900-1971
                    No 5   United States life tables by causes of death, 1969-71
            Vol II   consists of 51 state reports.
        Time factor: the 1969-71 life tables were published in 1975.
        §   En.

1447   Annual report   (Immigration and Naturalization Service)
        Immigration and Naturalization Service, Justice Department, Washington DC 20536.
        1892-   1976.   US$3.75.   c 125 p.
        Includes a statistical appendix on immigration, aliens and citizens admitted and departed, temporary
            visitors, detentions and deportations, passenger traffic between the US and foreign countries, etc.
        Time factor: the 1976 issue, published in 1978, has data for 1976 and some earlier years.
        §   En.

1448   The status of children   (Herner & Co, for Department of Health, Education and Welfare)
        Department of Health, Education and Welfare, Baltimore, Maryland 21235.
        1975-   2nd, 1977.   US$4.   203 p.
        Some statistical tables in the text, which deals with the changing demographic profile, changes in the
            family, special conditions of children in the family, health status, and education.
        Time factor: issued biennially, the 1977 report was published in 1978.
        §   En.

1449   Handbook of labor statistics   (Bureau of Labor Statistics)
        Government Printing Office, Washington DC 20402.
        1947-   1976.   US$4.30.   373 p.
        Incorporates the major series produced by the Bureau, and related series produced by other US government
            departments and foreign countries.   Contains tables dealing with the labour force, employment,

[continued next page]

¶   E,   continued

1449,   continued

        unemployment, labour productivity, compensation, consumer price index, living conditions, etc.
Time factor: the 1976 issue, issued as the Bureau's Bulletin No 1905, has data for several years to 1975
        and was published in December 1976.
§   En.

1450   Monthly labor review   (Bureau of Labor Statistics)
        Government Printing Office, Washington DC 20402.
        1940-   US$1.40 (US$1.80 abroad) or US$16 yr (US$18.20 yr abroad)
        Includes a detailed breakdown of the consumer price index and also important statistics on wholesale
          prices, earnings of workers, employment and unemployment.
§   En.

1451   Regional employment by industry, 1940-1970 (Bureau of Economic Analysis)
        Government Printing Office, Washington DC 20402.
               US$9.05.   542 p.
        Contains data on employment in various industries for states, regions and counties.
        Time factor: published in 1975.
§   En.

1452   Employment and earnings (Bureau of Labor Statistics)
        Government Printing Office, Washington DC 20402.
        1966-   monthly.   US$1.50 (US$1.90 abroad) or US$18 yr (US$22.50 yr abroad)
        Contains household data and establishment data, including employment, hours and earnings, and labour
          turnover.   Seasonally adjusted and figures not seasonally adjusted are given.
        Time factor: each issue has data to one or two months prior to the date of the issue.
§   En.

        Note: Historical volumes are 'Employment and earnings, states and areas, 1939-1975' (US$8.25) and
          'Employment and earnings, United States, 1909-72' (US$5.75).

1453   Chartbook on prices, wages and productivity (Bureau of Labor Statistics)
        Government Printing Office, Washington DC 20402.
        1974-   monthly.   US$0.95 or US$11 yr.
        Contains 19 analytical charts and detailed supporting tables on price, wage and productivity movements.
        Time factor: each issue has long runs of figures to the previous month.
§   En.

1454   Manpower report of the President... (Department of Labor)
        Government Printing Office, Washington DC 20402.
        1963-   1976.   US$2.75.   c 350 p.
        Includes a statistical appendix with data on labour force, employment, unemployment, manpower
          programme, etc.
        Time factor: the 1976 report, published in 1977, relates to 1976.
§   En.

        Note: the 1976 issue was titled 'Employment and training report...'

1455   Work stoppages (Department of Labor)
        Department of Labor, Washington DC 20210.
        1941-   monthly.   not priced.
        Contains data on strikes and lockouts.
        Time factor: each issue has long runs of figures to the date of the issue.
§   En.

¶   E,   continued

1456   Current wage developments   (Bureau of Labor Statistics)
Government Printing Office, Washington DC 20402.
1948-   monthly.   US$1.35 or US$12 yr (US$1.70 or US$16 yr abroad)
Contains statistical summaries on wage changes negotiated or effective during the preceding month.
Time factor: each issue has long runs of monthly and annual figures to the month prior to the date of the
        publication.
§   En.

1457   Census of housing   (Bureau of the Census)
Government Printing Office, Washington DC 20402.
1940-   1970.   prices vary.
Contents:
        Vol   I   Housing characteristics for states, cities and counties
                    Series HC(1)-A   General housing characteristics
                              B   Detailed housing characteristics
        Vol   II   Metropolitan housing characteristics
        Vol III   Block statistics
        Vol IV   Components of inventory change
        Vol   V   Residential finance
        Vol VI   Estimates of 'substandard' housing
        Vol VII   Subject reports
Vol I is in 58 parts, vol II in 58 parts, vol III in 278 parts, vols IV to VI in one volume each.
Time factor: the results of the 1970 census were published between 1971 and 1974.
§   En.

1458   HUD statistical yearbook   (Department of Housing and Urban Development)
Government Printing Office, Washington DC 20402.
1966-   1976.   US$5.   307 p.
Brings together comprehensive and detailed data on the programme and financial operations of the
        Department, and related statistical information on housing and urban development activity.
Time factor: the 1976 issue, published in December 1977, has data for several years to 1976.
§   En.

1459   Annual housing survey   (Bureau of the Census)
Government Printing Office, Washington DC 20402.
1973-   1975.   6 vols.
Contents:
        Part A   General housing characteristics   (US$4.75)
        Part B   Indicators of housing and neighbourhood quality   (US$3.75)
        Part C   Financial characteristics of the housing inventory   (US$4.50)
        Part D   Housing characteristics of recent movers   (US$3.25)
        Part E   Urban and rural housing characteristics   (US$4)
        Part F   Financial characteristics - by indicators of housing and neighbourhood quality   (US$6.25)
Issued as series H-150 in 'Current housing reports'.
Time factor: the 1975 survey reports were published in 1976.   Advance reports were also published.
§   En.

1460   Annual housing survey: housing characteristics for selected metropolitan areas   (Bureau of the Census)
Government Printing Office, Washington DC 20402.
            1974.   19 vols.   prices vary.
Time factor: the 1974 reports were published in 1978.
§   En.

Note: also available in the 'Current housing reports' series are 'Housing vacancies' and 'Housing
        characteristics', issued quarterly and annually (US$1 or US$5 yr).

¶   E,   continued

1461   Housing and urban development trends   (Department of Housing and Urban Development)
            Department of Housing and Urban Development, Washington DC 20410.
            1948-   quarterly.   not priced.
            Contains data on housing production; the housing market; prices, costs and employment; mortgage
                financing; etc.
            Time factor: each issue has data to the date of the issue and is published about four months later.
            §   En.

            Note: continues 'Housing statistics' (Current construction reports C20).

            Refer also to 1324, 1325, 1326.

¶   F   -   Social

1462   Social indicators   (Office of Management and Budget)
            Government Printing Office, Washington DC 20402.
            1973-   2nd,   1976.   US$7.   647 p.
            Sub-titled 'Selected data on social conditions and trends in the US' the volume contains data on
                population; family; housing; social security and welfare; health and nutrition; public safety;
                education and training; work; income, wealth and expenditure; culture, leisure and use of time;
                social mobility and participation.
            Time factor: the 1976 edition, published late 1977, has data mainly to 1970.
            §   En.

1463   A statistical portrait of women in the United States   (Bureau of the Census)
            Government Printing Office, Washington DC 20402.
                              US$2.10.   90 p.
            Contains historical data on the demographic and economic status of US women, with comparative data for
                blacks, whites and Spanish-surnamed.
            Time factor: published in 1976, the volume has data from 1900 to 1975.
            §   En.

      i.   Standard of living

1464   CPI detailed report   (Bureau of Labor Statistics)
            Government Printing Office, Washington DC 20402.
            1940-   monthly.   US$1 or US$12 yr.
            Contains the consumer price index, US and city average and selected areas.
            Time factor: each issue has data to the month of the issue and is published about two months later.
            §   En.

1465   Consumer expenditure survey   (Bureau of Labor Statistics)
            Government Printing Office, Washington DC 20402.
            The results of the interview survey, 1972-73 were published in three volumes:
                Annual expenditures and sources of income cross-classified by family characteristics (1972 and 1973
                    combined)
                Average annual income and expenditure for commodity and service groups classified by family
                    characteristics
                Inventories of vehicles and selected household equipment, 1973
            The results of the diary survey, July 1972 - June 1974 were published in one volume.   (US$5.50)
            Time factor: surveys are conducted every 10 or 12 years and the results of the 1972 to 1974 survey were
                published in 1977 and 1978.
            §   En.

¶   F.i,   continued

1466   Household food consumption survey   (Agricultural Research Service: Department of Agriculture)
            Government Printing Office, Washington DC 20402.
            1936-   1965.   US$1 each report.   10 volumes.
            A series of reports on food consumption of households in the United States as a whole, the north east,
                north central, south and west regions; and on dietary levels in the same areas.
            Time factor: published in 1970 and 1971.
            §   En.

1467   Statistics of income. Individual income tax returns   (Internal Revenue Service: Department of the Treasury)
            Government Printing Office, Washington DC 20402.
            1954-   1975.   US$4.50.   237 p.
            Time factor: the 1975 issue, published early 1978, has data for 1975.   Preliminary figures are issued
                about a year earlier.
            §   En.

1468   Local area personal income, 1960-1974   (National Technical Information Service)
            NTIS, Springfield, Va 22161.
                                four volumes priced at US$10, $13.75, $16.25, and $16.25 each; microfiche versions
                                    of each volume US$2.25.
            Contains total and per capita personal income by place of residence, personal income by type of payment
                and labour, and proprietors' income by major industry and place of work.
            Time factor: published in 1976.
            §   En.

            Refer also to 1351, 1324, 1325, 1326.

    ii.   Health and welfare

1469   Health: United States   (National Center for Health Statistics)
            Government Printing Office, Washington DC 20402.
            1975-   1976-77.   US$5.25.   c 600 p.
            Covers areas such as health care expenditures and revenues, facilities and services, manpower and health
                statistics by age group, and trends in the health care field.
            Time factor: the 1976-77 issue, published in 1978, has data for 1976 and 1977.
            §   En.

1470   Vital and health statistics   (National Center for Health Statistics)
            National Center for Health Statistics, 3700 East West Highway, Hyattsville, Maryland.
            1963-   irregular.   not priced.
            General series
                series 1   Programs, definitions and procedures
                series 2   Research in statistical methodology
                series 3   Analytical studies
                series 4   Committee reports and documents
            Health survey series
                series 10 Health interview survey statistics
                series 11 Health examination survey statistics
                series 12 Institutional population survey statistics
                series 13 Hospital discharge survey statistics
                series 14 Health resources data: manpower and facilities
            Vital statistics series
                series 20 Mortality data
                series 21 Natality data, marriage and divorce
                series 22 National natality and mortality surveys data
            Note: also available is 'Advance data from vital and health statistics of the NCHS'.

¶   F.ii,   continued

1471   Health resources statistics: health manpower and health facilities   (National Center for Health Statistics)
       Government Printing Office, Washington DC 20402.
       1968-   1976/77.   US$6.20.   c 350 p.
       Provides current data on a wide range of health areas as baseline data for the planning, administration
            and evaluation of health programmes.
       Time factor: the 1976/77 issue, with data to 1976, was published in 1979.
       §   En.

1472   Decennial census data for selected health occupations: United States, 1970   (Health Service: Department of
            Health, Education and Welfare)
       Government Printing Office, Washington DC 20402.
                      US$1.70.   93 p.
       Time factor: published in 1975.
       §   En.

1473   Annual report   (National Reporting System for Family Planning Services: Department of Health, Education
            and Welfare)
       Government Printing Office, Washington DC 20402.
       1969-   1975.   not priced.   245 p.
       Time factor: the 1975 report, published late 1977, has data for 1975.
       §   En.

1474   Health manpower: a county and metropolitan area data book, 1972-75   (National Center for Health Statistics)
       Government Printing Office, Washington DC 20402.
                      not priced.   74 p.
       Numbers of professional persons actively employed in nine health occupations in counties and metropolitan
            areas.
       Time factor: published in 1976.
       §   En.

1475   Hospitals: a county and metropolitan area databook, 1972   (National Center for Health Statistics)
       Government Printing Office, Washington DC 20402.
                      US$4.15.   360 p.
       Numbers of hospitals by type (General, special, personnel, ownership, number of beds, admissions,
            occupancy rates, etc).
       Time factor: published in 1975.
       §   En.

1476   Hospital statistics...   (American Hospital Association)
       American Hospital Association, 840 Lake Shore Drive, Chicago III 60611.
       1945-   1976.   US$7.50.
       Contains data on trends in hospital utilisation, personnel, finances, facilities and services, unit beds and
            visits, accreditation, admissions, assets, average stays, Blue Cross participation, dental services,
            interns, emergency services, extended care facilities, gross revenues, and total number of nurses,
            pharmacists, inpatients and outpatients.
       Time factor: the 1976 issue was published in 1976 and contains the latest data available.
       §   En.

¶   F.ii,   continued

1477   Mental health statistics series   (National Institute of Mental Health: Department of Health, Education and
                Welfare)
            Government Printing Office, Washington DC 20402.
            1968-   irregular.   not priced.
            A series of statistical reports on mental hospitals, patients, staff, etc.
            §   En.

1478   Mental health: statistical notes   (National Institute of Mental Health: Department of Health, Education and
                Welfare)
            Alcohol, Drug Abuse and Mental Health Administration, 5600 Fishers Lane, (Rm 6-105), Rockville,
                Maryland 20857.
            1970-   monthly.   free.
            Various subjects are covered and statistical tables included in the text, but there are no regular tables.
            §   En.

1479   Statistics on consumption of alcohol and on alcoholism, 1974   (Rutgers Center for Alcohol Studies)
            Rutgers Center for Alcohol Studies, New Brunswick, NJ.
                            US$2.   18 p.
            Time factor: published in 1974, the data is for 1972-1973.
            §   En.

1480   National Institute on Drug Abuse statistical series, quarterly report, series D
            National Institute on Drug Abuse, Department of Health, Education and Welfare, Rockville,
                Maryland 20852.
            1975-   not priced.
            §   En.

1481   Social security bulletin   (Social Security Administration)
            Government Printing Office, Washington DC 20402.
            1938-   monthly.   US$1.35 or US$14 yr including supplement (US$1.70 or US$17.50 yr abroad)
            The monthly issues include statistical tables in articles and features, and have a section on current operating
                statistics.   The annual statistical supplement (issued from 1955) contains data relating to trends in
                social welfare and its components.
            §   En.

1482   Public assistance statistics   (Social Security Administration)
            Social Security Administration, Department of Health, Education and Welfare, Baltimore, Maryland 21235.
            1977-   monthly.   not priced.
            Data is primarily on welfare payments, but also includes medical assistance.
            Time factor: each issue has data for that month and is published the following month.
            §   En.

1483   Social services USA   (National Center for Social Statistics)
            National Center for Social Statistics, 330 C Street SW, Washington DC 20201.
            1975-   quarterly.   not priced.
            Contains statistical tables, summaries and analyses of services under the Social Security Act, Title XX,
                IV-B and IV-C for fifty states and DC.
            §   En.

¶   F.ii,   continued

1484   Monthly benefit statistics...   (Social Security Administration)
         Department of Health, Education and Welfare, Social Security Administration, Baltimore, Maryland 21235.
                  not priced.
         Sub-titled 'Old-age, survivors, disability, and health insurance, and supplemental security income'.
         §   En.

         Refer also to 1324, 1325, 1326.

   iii.   Education and leisure

1485   Digest of education statistics   (National Center for Education Statistics)
         National Center for Education Statistics, Washington DC 20202.
         1962-   16th, 1977-78.   US$4.   206 p.
         An abstract of statistical information covering the entire field of American education from kindergarten
                  through graduate school, the digest deals with elementary and secondary education, college and
                  university education, adult and vocational education, federal programmes for education and
                  related activities, and special studies and statistics relating to American education.
         Time factor: the 1977-78 issue, published in 1978, has data for several years to 1976 or the academic year
                  1975/76.
         §   En.

1486   Projections: education statistics   (National Center for Education Statistics)
         National Center for Education Statistics, Washington DC 20202.
         1983/84-   1984/85.   US$3.
         A companion volume to the above publication, it contains forecasts on enrolment, graduates, teachers,
                  expenditures, elementary/secondary schools and institutes of higher education.
         Time factor: the 1984/85 issue, with projections to that academic year, was published in 1977.
         §   En.

1487   Statistics of state school systems   (Office of Education)
         Government Printing Office, Washington DC 20402.
         1869/70-   1973/74.   US$1.85.
         Contains data on organisation, staffing, enrolment, financing of public, elementary and secondary day
                  schools.
         Time factor: published biennially, the report for 1973/74 academic year was issued in 1977.
         §   En.

1488   Statistical tables on greyhound racing in the US   (National Association of State Racing Commissioners)
         National Association of State Racing Commissioners, PO Box 4216, Lexington, Ky 40504.
         (annual)
         §   En.

1489   Statistical tables on horse racing in the US   (National Association of State Racing Commissioners)
         National Association of State Racing Commissioners, PO Box 4216, Lexington, Ky 40504.
         (annual)
         §   En.

         Refer also to 1324, 1325, 1326.

¶ F,   continued

iv.   Justice

1490   Uniform crime reports   (Federal Bureau of Investigation: Department of Justice)
         FBI, 9th Street and Pennsylvania Avenue NW, Washington DC 20535.
         1930-   ·quarterly.   not priced.
         Titles of individual issues vary and supplements are also issued.   Data is published on crime trends,
               crime rates, offences in individual cities, police employees, offences cleared, and persons arrested.
         §   En.

1491   Crime in the United States   (Federal Bureau of Investigation: Department of Justice)
         Government Printing Office, Washington DC 20402.
         (annual)   1977.   US$5.   308 p.
         Includes data on crime index, crimes cleared, persons arrested, persons charged, law enforcement
               personnel.   Includes figures for the nation, states, towns, and the Panama Canal Zone and Guam.
         Time factor: the 1977 issue, with data to 1977, was published late 1978.
         §   En.

         Note: published in the quarterly series 'Uniform crime reporting'.

1492   Juvenile court statistics   (National Center for Juvenile Justice and Delinquency Prevention)
         National Center for Juvenile Justice and Delinquency Prevention, Department of Justice, Washington
               DC 20534.
         1936-   1974.   not priced.
         §   En.

         Note: also published, at irregular intervals, is 'Statistics on public institutions for delinquent children'.

1493   Statistical report   (Federal Prison System)
         Federal Prison System, Department of Justice, Washington DC 20534.
         1965/66-   1974/75   not priced.
         Contains data on prison population, committals, discharges, Parole Board actions, and medical activities.
         Time factor: the 1974/75 issue, published in 1977, has data for 1974/75.
         §   En.

         Note: published in the series 'National prisoner statistics'.   Other titles in the series include 'Capital
               punishment', 'Prisoners in state and federal institutions for adult felons', 'State prisoners:
               admissions and releases', and 'Characteristics of state prisoners'.

         Refer also to 1324, 1326.

¶   G   - Finance

1494   Federal Reserve bulletin   (Federal Reserve System)
         Federal Reserve System, Division of Administrative Services, Washington DC 20551.
         1915-   monthly.   US$2 or US$20 yr on the American continent (US$2.50 or US$24 yr elsewhere)
         Includes articles of general and special interest, official statements of the Board, and statistical tables
               relating to domestic financial and economic developments and to international financial develop-
               ments.
         Time factor: each issue has the latest data available.
         §   En.

         Note: Also issued are a number of Federal Reserve statistical releases, the titles including 'Deposits,
               reserves and borrowings of member banks' (weekly), 'Finance companies' (monthly), 'Selected
               interest rates and bond prices' (monthly and weekly), 'Consumer instalment credit' (monthly),
               and 'Index numbers of wholesale prices'.

¶   G,   continued

1495   Federal Reserve chart book on financial and business statistics   (Federal Reserve System)
            Federal Reserve System, Division of Administrative Services, Washington DC 20551.
            1947-   monthly.   US$1.50 or US$12 yr, including annual 'Historical chart book'
            Graphic presentation of economic and financial data, with the charts up-dated monthly.
            §   En.

1496   Annual statistical digest   (Federal Reserve System)
            Federal Reserve System, Division of Administrative Services, Washington DC 20551.
            1972/76-   1977.   US$5.   c 350 p.
            Contains historical data for many of the tables published in the 'Federal Reserve bulletin' (1494).
            Time factor: the 1977 edition, published in 1977, has data for 1970 to 1975.
            §   En.

            Note: earlier data is in the two issues of 'Banking and monetary statistics' for 1914-1941 and 1941-1970.

            Refer also to 1324, 1325, 1326.

      i.   Banking

1497   Banking operation statistics   (Federal Deposit Insurance Corporation)
            FDIC, 550 17th Street NW, Washington DC 20429.
            1967-   1977.   not priced.   not paged (reduced computer print-out).
            Contains data on assets, liabilities and equity capital of insured commercial banks; income and expenses
                  of those banks; and reports on condition analysis and income analysis of those banks.   Data is
                  given on a national basis, for the 20 largest banks, individual states, Puerto Rico and Guam.
            Time factor: the 1977 issue, published late 1978, has data for 1977.
            §   En.

1498   Finance facts yearbook   (National Consumer Finance Association)
            National Consumer Finance Association, 1000 16th Street NW, Washington DC 20035.
            (annual)   1975.   not priced.   79 p.
            Includes general statistics and statistics on consumer credit, bankruptcies, etc.
            Time factor: the 1975 issue, published in 1975, has data to 1973.
            §   En.

1499   FHA trends of home mortgage characteristics   (Department of Housing)
            Department of Housing, Washington DC 20410.
            1964-   quarterly.   not priced.
            §   En.

            Note: there are also supplements titled 'State trends' and 'Area trends'.

            Refer also to 1324.

      ii.   Public finance

1500   Treasury bulletin   (Treasury Department)
            Government Printing Office, Washington DC 20402.
            1939-   monthly.   US$4.25 or US$50 yr (US$5.35 or US$62 yr abroad)
            Includes data on federal fiscal operations, federal obligations, accounts of the US Treasury, monetary
                  statistics, federal debt, public debt operations, United States savings bonds and notes, ownership
                  of federal securities, Treasury survey of ownership and of commercial bank ownership, market
                  quotations on Treasury securities, average yield on long term bonds, international financial statistics,
                  capital movements, foreign currency position, & financial operations of government agencies & funds.
            Time factor: each issue contains the latest data available.
            §   En.

¶   G.ii,   continued

1501   Annual report of the Secretary of the Treasury on the state of the finances
            Government Printing Office, Washington DC 20402.
                    1975.   US$5.15.   628 p.
            Statistical tables include a summary of fiscal operations, receipts and expenditures, public debt, savings,
                securities, trust funds, money circulation, customs statistics, federal aid, etc.
            §   En.

1502   National income and product accounts of the United States: statistical tables, 1929-1974   (Bureau of
                    Economic Analysis)
            Government Printing Office, Washington DC 20402.
                    US$4.95.   372 p.
            Contains statistical data on a quarterly basis on national income and product accounts, personal income
                and outlay, government receipts and expenditures, export and import of goods and services
                including transfer payments and foreign investments, gross savings and investment and implicit price
                deflations, etc.
            Time factor: published in 1976.
            §   En.

1503   Facts and figures in government finance   (Tax Foundation)
            Tax Foundation, 50 Rockefeller Plaza, New York, NY 10020.
            1941-   1977.   US$10.   c 250 p.
            Contains data on federal, state and local government organisation, expenditure, income, debt,
                employment, etc.
            Time factor: the 1977 issue, published in 1978, has data to 1977.   The title is issued biennially.
            §   En.

1504   Statistics of income. Business income tax returns; sole proprietorships, partnerships   (Internal Revenue Service)
            Government Printing Office, Washington DC 20402.
            1965-   1974.   US$4.
            Contains summary tables on financial information obtained from tax returns.
            Time factor: the 1974 issue, published in 1978, has data for 1974.   A preliminary report is published
                about a year earlier.
            §   En.

1505   Statistics of income. Corporation income tax returns   (Internal Revenue Service)
            Government Printing Office, Washington DC 20402.
            1916-   1974.   US$0.90.
            Contains summary tables on financial information obtained from tax returns.
            Time factor: the 1974 issue, published in 1978, has data for 1974.   A preliminary report is published
                about a year earlier.
            §   En.

            Note: Other publications in the series 'Statistics of income' include 'Estate tax returns', 'Farmers'
                co-operative income tax returns' and 'Fiduciary gift and estate tax returns', all published at
                irregular intervals, and 'Fiduciary income tax returns', published biennially.

¶   G.ii,   continued

1506   Quarterly summary of state and local tax revenue   (Bureau of the Census)
        Subscriber Services Section (Publications), Bureau of the Census, Department of Commerce, Suitland,
           Maryland 20233.
        1963-   US$0.30 or US$1.20 yr.
        §   En.

1507   An analysis of federal R & D funding by function   (National Science Foundation)
        Government Printing Office, Washington DC 20402.
        1960/72-   1969/78.   US$2.75.   74 p.
        Time factor: the issue covering the years 1969 to 1978 was published late 1978.
        §   En.

1508   National patterns of R & D resources: funds and manpower in the United States   (National Science
          Foundation)
        Government Printing Office, Washington DC 20402.
        1953/73-   1953-1977.   US$1.50.   c 30 p.
        Time factor: the issue covering the years 1953 to 1977 was published late 1977.
        §   En.

        Refer also to 1467, 1324, 1325, 1326.

    iii.   Company finance

1509   Quarterly financial report for manufacturing, mining and trade operations   (Federal Trade Commission)
        Government Printing Office, Washington DC 20402.
        1947-   US$10 yr (US$12.50 yr abroad)
        Contains income statement and balance sheet for all manufacturing corporations, classed by both industry
          and size.
        Time factor: each issue has data for about five quarters to the date of the issue and is published about
          four months later.
        §   En.

1510   Statistical report on mergers and acquisitions (Bureau of Economics: Federal Trade Commission)
        Federal Trade Commission, Washington DC 20580.
        1973-   1977.   US$4.25.   c 250 p.
        Time factor: the 1977 issue, published late 1978, has data for several years to 1976.
        §   En.

1511   Tables of bankruptcy statistics (Administration Office of the United States Courts)
        Administration Office of the United States Courts, US Supreme Court Building, Washington DC 20544.
        1941-   annual.   not priced.
        Contains data on bankruptcy cases commenced and terminated in the US district courts.
        §   En.

    iv.   Investment

1512   Statistical bulletin (Securities and Exchange Commission)
        Government Printing Office, Washington DC 20402.
        1942-   monthly.   US$1.25 or US$15 yr (US$1.60 or US$18.75 yr abroad)
        Contains data on new security offerings, registrations, underwriters, trading in exchanges, stock price
          indexes, and other financial series.
        Time factor: each issue has the latest data available for each table.
        §   En.

¶   G,   continued

v.   Insurance

1513   Insurance facts: property, liability, marine, surety   (Insurance Information Institute)
         Insurance Information Institute, 110 William Street, New York, NY 10038.
         1976- '1978.   not priced.   80 p.
         Contains chapters on the dimensions of insurance, insurance statistics for all types of insurance, facts
             about losses, and background information.
         Time factor: the 1978 issue, published in 1978, has data for 1977 and also for earlier years in some
             tables.
         §   En.

1514   Summary of mortgage insurance operations and contract authority   (Department of Housing)
         Department of Housing, Washington DC 20410.
         1935-   monthly.   not priced.
         §   En.

         Refer also to 1324.

¶   H   -   Transport and communications

1515   Census of transportation   (Bureau of the Census)
         Government Printing Office, Washington DC 20402.
         1963-   1972.   various prices.
         Contents:
             Vol I   National travel survey   (3 reports)
             Vol II   Truck inventory and use survey   (52 reports for the US states and DC)
             Vol III   Commodity transportation survey
                     Part 1   commodity and special studies
                     Part 2   area statistics, northeast and north central regions
                     Part 3   area statistics, south and west regions and US summary
         Time factor: the census is taken every five years, and the results of the 1972 census were published in
             1974.
         §   En.

1516   Transport statistics of the United States   (Interstate Commerce Commission)
         Government Printing Office, Washington DC 20402.
         1954-   1976.   6 vols.
         Contents:
             1   Railroads, their lessors and proprietory companies, The Pullman Company, the Railway Express
                     Agency Inc (US$2.60)
             2   Motor carriers (US$1.50)
             3   Freight forwarding (US$1)
             4   Private car lines (US$0.80)
             5   Carriers by water (US$2.40)
             6   Pipe lines (US$1.40)
         Time factor: the issues for 1976 were published in 1978.
         §   En.

         Note: supersedes the 'Annual report on the state of the railways in the United States', published from
             1888 to 1953, and other publications.

         Refer also to 1324, 1325, 1326.

¶   H,   continued

i.   Ships and shipping

1517   Merchant vessels of the United States   (Coast Guard)
      Government Printing Office, Washington DC 20402.
      1924-   1977.   US$32 for 2 vols.   2 vols.
      Contains data on numbers of vessels for the US (excluding yachts); steam, motor and sailing vessels by
          customs district; vessels by major rigs, land of document, material of build, age, services,
          tonnage groupings, horsepower groupings, vessels removed from documentation.
      Time factor: the 1977 issue, published in 1978, has data for 1977.
      §   En.

1518   Boating statistics   (Coast Guard)
      US Coast Guard, Department of Transportation, Washington DC 20590.
      1966-   1977.   not priced.   39 p.
      Contains data on numbers of motor boats, boating facilities, boating accidents (nationally and by state),
          etc.
      Time factor: the 1977 issue, published mid-1978, has data for 1977.
      §   En.

  ii.   Road

1519   Highway statistics   (Federal Highway Administration: Department of Transportation)
      Government Printing Office, Washington DC 20402.
      1945-   1975.   US$4.75.   313 p.
      Contains data on motor fuel, motor vehicles and driver licencing; highway usage characteristics; federal
          fuel and automotive taxes, and the Highway Trust Fund; highway finance summaries; federal and
          state highway finance and programmes; local road and street finance; roadways; and data by US
          territories (including Puerto Rico).
      Time factor: the 1975 issue, published in 1978, has data for 1975.
      §   En.

1520   Transit fact book   (American Public Transit Association)
      American Public Transit Association, 1100 17th Street NW, Suite 1200, Washington DC 20036.
      1974/75-   1976-1977.   not priced.   47 p.
      Contains data on the number of operating systems, passenger vehicles owned and leased, passenger revenue,
          total operating revenue, revenue passenger rides, total passenger rides, vehicle miles operated, and
          energy consumed.
      Time factor: the 1976-77 edition, published mid-1977, has data for 1976 and earlier figures.
      §   En.

  iii.   Rail

1521   Transport economics   (Interstate Commerce Commission)
      Interstate Commerce Commission, Washington DC 20423.
      1941-   monthly.   not priced.
      Includes an appendix with condensed statistics of Class I railroads, including net railway operating income,
          net income, working capital, employees, service hours and compensation.
      §   En.

1522   Yearbook of railroad facts   (Association of American Railroads)
      Association of American Railroads, 1920 L Street NW, Washington DC 20036.
      1967-   1978.   not priced.   64 p.
      A pocketbook with data on revenues, expenses, passengers, freight, line, tracks, etc.
      Time factor: the 1978 edition, published in 1978, has data for 1977 and some earlier years.
      §   En.

¶   H.iii,   continued

1523   Statistics of railroads of Class I in the United States: statistical summary   (Association of American Railroads)
           Association of American Railroads, 1920 L Street NW, Washington DC 20036.
           1917-   1967 to 1977.   not priced.   16 p.
           Contains data on finance, employment, freight traffic, passenger traffic, locomotives, mileage,
                distribution of operating revenues, fuel consumed, selected statistics of AMTRAK, etc.
           Time factor: the 1967 to 1977 edition, with data for those years, was published in 1978.
           §   En.

1524   Summary of accidents/incidents reported by all line-haul and switching and terminal railroad companies
                (Federal Railroad Administration: Department of Transportation)
           Federal Railroad Administration, 400 7th Street SW, Washington DC 20590.
           1924-   monthly.   not priced.
           §   En.

     iv.   Air

1525   Census of civil aircraft   (Federal Aviation Administration)
           Government Printing Office, Washington DC 20402.
           1964-   1973.   US$3.50.   292 p.
           Summarizes and analyses all civil aircraft registered with the FAA.
           Time factor: the results of the 1973 census were published in 1975.
           §   En.

           Note: a further census was taken in 1977 and the results are being published by the National Technical
           Information Service.

1526   FAA statistical handbook of aviation   (Federal Aviation Agency)
           Government Printing Office, Washington DC 20402.
           1944-   1977.   not priced.   c 250 p.
           A general handbook of statistics on airports, airways, production and expenditure in aeronautics, airport
                and air carrier statistics, and accidents.
           Time factor: the 1977 issue, published in 1978, has data for 1977.
           §   En.

1527   FAA air traffic activity   (Federal Aviation Agency)
           Government Printing Office, Washington DC 20402.
           1966/67-   1977.   not priced.   c 250 p.
           Contains data on air traffic activity of the FAA system as measured by fix postings, departures and overs,
                aircraft operations, instrument approaches, aircraft contacted and flight plans originated, and
                intermediate field landings.
           Time factor: the 1977 issue, with data for 1977, was published in 1978.   There are also issues for fiscal
                years.
           §   En.

1528   Air carrier traffic statistics   (Civil Aeronautics Board)
           (Civil Aeronautics Board) 1825 Connecticut Avenue NW, Washington DC 20428.
                     monthly.   not priced.
           Contains data on changes in revenue load-factors, and capacity operated, ton-miles, passengers and
                passenger miles, etc.
           §   En.

¶   H.iv,   continued

1529   Air traffic financial statistics   (Civil Aeronautics Board)
            Civil Aeronautics Board, 1825 Connecticut Avenue NW, Washington DC 20428.
                    quarterly.   not priced.
            Contains income statement data, earning position and average investment, and balance sheet data.
            §   En.

1530   US international air travel statistics   (Transportation Systems Center)
            Transportation Systems Center, Kendall Square, Cambridge, Mass 02142.
                    monthly, with quarterly cumulations to calendar year.   not priced.
            Contains data on arrivals and departures by scheduled and charter flights, by US and foreign flag carriers,
                by ports and foreign countries, etc.
            Time factor: each issue has data for the month and cumulative figures for the quarter and year to date,
                and is published one or two months later.   There are also issues for fiscal years.
            §   En.

            Note: supersedes the Immigration and Naturalization Service's 'Passenger travel between the United
                States and foreign countries'.

1531   Profiles of scheduled air carrier passenger traffic: top 100 US airports for May 2, 1975   (Aviation Forecast
                Branch: Department of Transportation)
            Aviation Forecast Branch, Department of Transportation, 800 Independence Avenue SW,
                Washington DC 20591.
            Time factor: published in 1976.

1532   Annual review of US air carrier accidents occurring in calendar year... (National Transportation Safety
                Board)
            National Technical Information Service, Springfield, Va 22161.
            1964-   1978.   not priced.   'loose-leaf for up-dating'
            Contains statistical data of accidents, including conditions, circumstances, probable cause, aircraft hours
                and miles flown, passengers carried, etc.
            Time factor: the 1978 issue, published late 1977, will have data for 1978.
            §   En.

            Note: the Board also issues 'Annual review of aircraft accident data: US air carrier operations' and
                'Annual review of aircraft accident data: US general aviation'.

1533   Handbook of airline statistics   (Civil Aeronautics Board)
            Government Printing Office, Washington DC 20402.
            1944-   1973 with supplements for 1973/74 and 1975/76.   US$18.10 for basic volume; supplements
                                                                    not priced.
            Contains statistics for each airline, showing trends in passenger, freight, express, and mail revenues and
                traffic; flying operation expenses; aircraft maintenance expense; aircraft depreciation; promotion
                and sales expenses; administration expenses; income tax, capital gains, dividends, investment,
                debts, etc.
            Time factor: the basic 1973 volume has data for individual carriers from 1964 to 1972 and for carrier
                groups for 1926 to 1972; the supplements up-date the basic information.
            §   En.

¶   H,   continued

v.   Communications

1534   Statistics of the communications industry   (Federal Communications Commission)
        Government Printing Office, Washington DC 20402.
        1939- .1976.   US$4.
        Contains financial and operating information on all common carriers engaged in interstate or foreign
            communications service, covering telephone carriers, domestic and international telegraph carriers.
        Time factor: the 1976 issue, published in 1978, has data for 1976.
        §   En.

1535   Quarterly operating data of 70 telephone carriers   (Federal Communications Commission)
        Federal Communications Commission, Washington DC 20554.
                        not priced.
        Contains selected data on operating revenues, expenses and taxes, and other income items, etc.
        §   En.

        Note: the Commission also publishes an annual 'Statistics of Class A telephone carriers reporting annually
            to the Commission'.

1536   Quarterly operating data of telegraph carriers   (Federal Communications Commission)
        Federal Communications Commission, Washington DC 20554.
                        not priced.
        Contains data on revenues and expenses and other items.
        §   En.

        Note: the Commission also publishes an annual 'Statistics of principal domestic and international
            telegraph carriers reporting to the Commission'.

1537   Independent telephone statistics   (United States Independent Telephone Association)
        United States Independent Telephone Association, 1801 K Street NW, Suite 1201, Washington DC 20006.
        1897- 1977.   Vol I   US$2
                        Vol II   US$6 to members, US$25 to others.   2 vols.
        Vol I contains summary data on finance, construction, telephones and telephone companies, employees,
            plant, revenue and expenses, etc.
        Time factor: the 1977 issue, published mid-1977, has data for 1976 and some earlier years.

        Note: the Association also publishes an annual booklet for general consumption titled 'Independent
            phone facts'.

1538   Statistical trends in broadcasting   (Blair Television and Blair Radio)
        Blair Television and Blair Radio, 717 Fifth Avenue, New York, NY 10022.
        1965- 1978.   US$10.   48 p.
        Contains data on advertising trends, television trends, and radio trends, and includes statistical data on
            the numbers of stations, station revenues, markets, advertising expenses, etc.
        Time factor: the 1978 issue, published in 1978, has long runs of figures to 1978 estimates.
        §   En.

URUGUAY

Central statistical office

1539   Dirección General de Estadísticas y Censos   [General Office of Statistics and Censuses] ,
Cuareim 2052,
Montevideo.
† 290734 & 201105.

The Office is responsible for the collection, analysis and publication of the official statistics of Uruguay, other than foreign trade statistics.   Unpublished statistical information may be supplied on request when available.

Another organisation publishing statistics

1540   Centro de Estadísticas Nacionales y Comercio Internacional del Uruguay (CENCI)   [Centre for Uruguayan National Statistics and International Trade],
Misiones 1361, Montevideo.
† 91-53-56.   Cables: CENCIURU

The Centre has been responsible for the compilation of the official foreign trade statistics of Uruguay since 1957.

Libraries

The Dirección General de Estadística y Censos (see above) has a library which is open to the public for reference to statistical publications.   The Headquarters of the Banco Central in Montevideo also has a library.

Libraries and information services abroad

The Uruguayan embassies abroad receive the official statistical publications of the country; embassies include:
United Kingdom   Uruguayan Embassy, 48 Lennox Gardens, London SW1   † 01-589 8835
USA   Uruguayan Embassy, 1918 F Street NW, Washington DC   † (202) 331 1314

Statistical publications

¶   A - General

1541   Anuario estadístico   [Statistical yearbook]   (Dirección General de Estadística y Censos)
Dirección General de Estadística y Censos, Cuareim 2052, Montevideo.
1884-   1967-69.   not priced.   10 vols.
Contents:
Vol   I   Area and climate
Vol   II   Demography
Vol   III   Agriculture and livestock
Vol   IV   Industry
Vol   V   Trade, transport, communications, and tourism
Vol   VI   National income and product, banking and finance, and national accounts
Vol   VII Prices, wages and consumption
Vol VIII   Social situation
Vol   IX   Education and culture
Vol   X   Public administration and justice
Time factor: the 1967-69 edition, published in 1971, has data for the years 1967 to 1969 and also earlier years in some tables.   Publication ceased with this edition.
§   Es.

¶   A,   continued

1542   Boletín estadístico mensual   [Monthly statistical bulletin]   (Banco Central del Uruguay)
        Banco Central del Uruguay, Montevideo.
        1942/44-   not priced.
        Contains data on money and credit, balance of payments, foreign trade, public finance, prices and
            wages, and production.
        Time factor: each issue has data to the month of the issue or the latest data available, and is published
            five or six months later.
        §   Es.

1543   Indicadores de la actividad económico-financiera   [Indicators of economic-financial activity]   (Banco Central
            del Uruguay)
        Banco Central del Uruguay, Montevideo.
        1976-   quarterly.   not priced.
        Contains data on money and banking, balance of payments, foreign trade, public finance, prices, wages,
            production, etc.
        Time factor: each issue has long runs of annual, quarterly and monthly figures to about two months prior
            to the date of the publication.
        §   Es.

        Note: the bank also issues an annual 'Uruguay: reseña de la actividad económico-financiera' [Review
            of economic-financial activity].

¶   B - Production

ii. Agriculture, fisheries, forestry, etc.

1544   Censo general agropecuario   [General census of agriculture and livestock]   (Ministerio de Ganaderia y
            Agricultura)
        Ministerio de Ganaderia y Agricultura, Montevideo.
        1961-   1961.   not priced.   55 p.
        Contains data on the utilisation of the land, crops, livestock, employment, etc.
        §   Es.

        Refer also to 1539.

iii. Industry

1545   Censo económico nacional...industrias   [National economic census...Industry]   (Dirección General de
            Estadística y Censos)
        Dirección General de Estadística y Censos, Cuareim 2052, Montevideo.
        1968-   1968.   not priced.   71 p.
        Contains the principal statistics of the manufacturing and mining industries, including number of establish-
            ments, production and wages for each industry.
        Time factor: the report of the 1968 census was published in 1972.
        §   Es.

1546   Encuesta anual de producción: sector industrial   [Annual survey of production: industrial sector]   (Dirección
            General de Estadística y Censos)
        Dirección General de Estadística y Censos, Cuareim 2052, Montevideo.
        1970/71-   1976.   not priced.   12 p.
        Contains data on the value of production, employment, hours of work, and wages.
        Time factor: the report of the 1976 survey was published mid-1978.
        §   Es.

        Refer also to 1539, 1540, 1541.

¶   B iv.   Construction

1547   Indice del costo de la construcción   [Index of the cost of construction]   (Dirección General de Estadística
y Censos)
Dirección General de Estadística y Censos, Cuareim 2052, Montevideo.
1977-   monthly.   not priced.
Time factor: each issue has data to the month of issue and is published about two months later.
§   Es.

¶   C   -   External trade

1548   Analisis estadística: Uruguay: importación - exportación: intercambio comercial por secciones, items,
procedencia y dentano - zonas geograficas - económicas - paises - indices comparativos -
porcentajes - volumenes y valores - graficas   [Statistical analysis - Uruguay: imports -
exports:...]   (Centro de Estadísticas Nacionales y Comercio Internacional del Uruguay)
CENCI, Misiones 1361, Montevideo.
1957-   1977.   not priced.   379 p.
Contains data on imports and exports by geographical and economic zones and by countries of origin and
destination, subdivided by commodities; and imports and exports by commodity groups subdivided
by country, and also by a detailed commodity breakdown.
Time factor: the 1977 issue, published mid-1977, has data for 1976 and 1975.
§   Es.

1549   Importación - exportación del Uruguay   [Imports and exports of Uruguay]   (Centro de Estadísticas Nacionales
y Comercio Internacional del Uruguay)
CENCI, Misiones 1361, Montevideo.
1970-   quarterly.   not priced.
Contains statistics of imports and exports arranged by geographic regions and economic zones, and by
broad commodity groups.
Time factor: each issue has cumulated figures for the year to the end of the quarter of the issue and
corresponding data for the previous year, and is published about two months later.
§   Es.

1550   Exportación: volumen estadístico mensual   [Exports]   (Importación)
Importación, Colon 1580, esc 7, Montevideo.
monthly.   not priced.
Contains detailed statistics of exports arranged by commodities and subdivided by port of exit and country
and/or port of destination.
Time factor: each issue has data for the date of the issue and is published one or two months later.
§   Es.

1551   Importación: volumen estadístico mensual   [Imports]   (Importación)
Importación, Colon 1580, esc 7, Montevideo.
monthly.   not priced.
Contains detailed statistics of imports arranged by commodities and subdivided by port of entry and country
of origin.
Time factor: each issue has data for the date of the issue and is published one or two months later.
§   Es.

1552   Indice de precios al por mayor de productos importados   [Index of wholesale prices of imported products]
(Dirección General de Estadísticas y Censos)
1972-   1977.   not priced.   12 p.
Time factor: the 1977 issue, with data for 1977, was published in April, 1978.
§   Es.

Refer also to 1539, 1540, 1541.

URUGUAY, continued

¶ D - Internal distribution and service trades

Refer to 1539.

¶ E - Population

1553   Censo general de...población y...vivienda   [General census of population and housing]   (Dirección
              General de Estadística y Censos)
         Dirección General de Estadística y Censos, Cuareim 2052, Montevideo.
         1860-   1975.   not priced.
         Volumes published so far are:
              Datos preliminares   [Preliminary results (by departments)]
              Muestra de anticipación de resultados censales   [Advance sample of census results (population,
                 housing and households)]
         Time factor: the results are being published from 1976 onwards.
         §   Es.

1554   Estadísticas vitales   [Vital statistics]   (Dirección General de Estadística y Censos)
         Dirección General de Estadística y Censos, Cuareim 2052, Montevideo.
         1961/74-   1975.   not priced.   62 p.
         Time factor: the 1975 issue, published in 1978, has data for 1975 and for 1961 to 1975 in some tables.
         §   Es.

1555   Encuesta de emigración internacional, 1976   [Survey of international emigration, 1976]   (Dirección General
              de Estadística y Censos)
         Dirección General de Estadística y Censos, Cuareim 2052, Montevideo.
                            not priced.   50 p.
         Contains data by periods of emigration; countries of destination; characteristics of emigrants - age, sex,
              civil state, place of birth; educational characteristics; and occupational characteristics.
         Time factor: the report of the survey was published in 1976.
         §   Es.

1556   Encuesta de hogares   [Survey of homes]   (Dirección General de Estadística y Censos)
         Dirección General de Estadística y Censos, Cuareim 2052, Montevideo.
         1969-   half-yearly.   not priced.
         Contains data on occupied and unoccupied homes in Montevideo.
         Time factor: each report has data for the six months and is published about three months later.
         §   Es.

         Refer also to 1539.

¶ F - Social

1557   Costa de la vida   [Cost of living]   (Centro de Estadísticas Nacionales y Comercio Internacional del Uruguay)
         CENCI, Misiones 1361, Montevideo.
                            monthly.   not priced.
         Time factor: each issue has data for several months to about three months prior to the date of the issue.
         §   Es.

1558   Indice de los precios del consumo   [Index of consumer prices]   (Dirección General de Estadística y Censos)
         Dirección General de Estadística y Censos, Cuareim 2052, Montevideo.
         1968-   quarterly.   not priced.
         Time factor: each issue has data for the three months of the issue and earlier figures and is published
              about three months later.
         §   Es.

¶   F,   continued

1559   Indice medio de salarios   [Index of wages]   (Dirección General de Estadística y Censos)
        Dirección General de Estadística y Censos, Cuareim 2052, Montevideo.
        1976-   quarterly.   not priced.
        Time factor: each issue has annual and monthly data to the month of the issue and is published several
            months later.
        §   Es.

        Refer also to 1539.

¶   G   -   Finance

1560   Producto e ingreso nacionales: actualización de las principales variables, 1977   [National product and
            income: up-dating the main variables]   (Banco Central del Uruguay)
        Banco Central del Uruguay, Montevideo.
                            not priced.   18 p.
        Contains indices - estimates at current prices, at constant (1961) prices, and implicit prices.
        Time factor: published in 1978, the volume includes data from 1955 to 1976 (estimated).
        §   Es.

1561   Formación bruto de capital, 1977   [Gross capital formation]   (Banco Central del Uruguay)
        Banco Central del Uruguay, Montevideo.
                            not priced.   102 p.
        Contains estimates at current prices, estimates at constant prices, and implicit prices.
        Time factor: published in December 1977, the volume has data for 1960 to 1975 or 1976.
        §   Es.

        Refer also to 1539, 1540, 1541.

¶   H   -   Transport and communications

        Refer to 1539.

VENEZUELA

Central statistical office

1562   Oficina Central de Estadística Información   [Central Office of Statistical Information],
Edificio Fundación La Salle,
Avenida Boyaca,
Cota Mil,
Caracas 105.
† 74 61 11.

The Office is responsible for the collection, analysis and publication of official statistics of Venezuela.

Libraries

The Office Central de Estadistica Información (see above) has a library which is open to the public for reference to statistical publications.

Libraries and information services abroad

Venezuelan embassies abroad have copies of Venezuelan statistical publications, including:

United Kingdom	Venezuelan Embassy, 1 Cromwell Road, London SW7 † 01-581 2776
USA	Venezuelan Embassy, 2445 Massachusetts Avenue NW, Washington DC † (202) 797 3800
Canada	Venezuelan Embassy, 2000-320 Queen Street, Ottawa † 235 5151

Bibliography

1563   Catalogo de series estadísticas   [Catalogue of statistical series] (Dirección General de Estadísticas y Censos Nacionales)
Published in 1965, the catalogue is arranged by subject, geographical coverage, source, periodicity, title of publication, and first year of publication.

Statistical publications

¶   A - General

1564   Anuario estadístico   [Statistical yearbook] (Oficina Central de Estadística Información)
Oficina Central de Estadística Información, Edificio Fundación La Salle, Avenida Boyaca, Cota Mil, Caracas 105.
1887- 1975. not priced.   579 p.
Main sections:

Area and climate	National accounts
Employment and remunerations	Population
Electric energy	Public health
Mines and mining	Education and sciences
Transport and communications	Justice
Hotels and tourism	Industrial manufacture
Banking, finance and insurance	Public finance
Prices and cost of living	Agriculture

Time factor: the 1975 edition, published in 1978, has data for 1975 and also some earlier years.
§   Es.

¶   A,   continued

1565   Boletin mensual   [Monthly bulletin]   (Dirección General de Estadística y Censos Nacionales)
     Oficina Central de Estadística Información, Edificio Fundación La Salle, Avenida Boyaca, Cota Mil,
       Caracas 105.
     1941-   not priced.
     Contains data on demography, culture and social, construction, etc.
     Time factor: each issue has runs of figures to about four months prior to the date of the issue.
     §   Es.

1566   Informe económico   [Economic report]   (Banco Central de Venezuela)
     Banco Central de Venezuela, Caracus.
     1950-   1976.   not priced.   358 p.
     Includes a statistical appendix dealing with aspects of international economy, aspects of finance, price
       movements, public finance, foreign economic relations, industrial production, commercial sales,
       petrol and oil, construction, etc.
     Time factor: the 1976 issue, published late 1977, has data for the years 1972 to 1976 and monthly figures
       for 1976.
     §   Es.

1567   Boletin mensual   [Monthly bulletin]   (Banco Central de Venezuela)
     Banco Central de Venezuela, Caracus.
     1944-   not priced.
     Includes a statistical section on financial aspects, prices (indices), public finance, and production
       (petrol and oil, construction, industry, commercial sales, foreign trade).
     Time factor: each issue has data for several years and months to the date of the issue, and is published
       about four months later.
     §   Es.

1568   Indicadores socioeconómicos y de coyuntura   [Socio-economic indicators]   (Dirección General de Estadística
       y Censos Nacionales)
     Oficina Central de Estadística Información, Edificio Fundación La Salle, Avenida Boyaca, Cota Mil,
       Caracas 105.
     1974-   irreg.   not priced.
     Contains current statistical data and projections to 2000 for socio-demography (for Venezuela and most
       Latin American countries), industrial production, foreign trade, finance and money, etc.
     Time factor: No 5 was dated December 1977.
     §   Es.

1569   Anuario estadístico municipal   [Municipal statistical yearbook]   (Oficina de Planificación e Presupuesto,
       Gobernación del Distrito Federal)
     Oficina de Planificación y Presupuesto, Gobernación del Distrito Federal, Caracas.
     1970-   8th ed, 1977.   not priced.   553 p.
     Contains data on municipal finance, demography, culture and education, health and social assistance,
       security and public order, employment and wages, etc, for the Federal District.
     Time factor: the 8th edition was published in 1977.
     §   Es.

¶   B   -   Production

i.   Mines and mining

1570   Monthly bulletin   (Ministry of Mines and Hydrocarbons)
     Ministerio de Minas e Hidrocarburos, Caracas.
     1966-   not priced.
     Includes production, sales, export statistics of iron ore, and also some information on oil production.

¶   B.i,   continued

1570,   continued

> Time factor: each issue has runs of annual and monthly figures to about three months prior to the date of the issue.
> §   En & Es eds.
>
> Note: the Ministry also issues 'Memoria y cuenta' [Report and accounts] which includes a few statistics of production, etc, as well as financial ones.
>
> Refer also to 1562.

ii.   Agriculture, fisheries, forestry, etc.

1571   Anuario estadístico agropecuario   [Statistical yearbook of agriculture]   (Ministerio de Agricultura y Cría, Dirección de Planificación y Estadística)
> Ministerio de Agricultura y Cria, Caracas.
> 1961-   1975.   not priced.   732 p.
> Contains data on crops, fisheries, agricultural reform, credit, foreign trade, livestock, value of production, prices, etc.
> Time factor: the 1975 issue, published in 1976, has data for 1975, 1974 and 1973 and some earlier years in some tables.
> §   Es.

1572   Censo agropecuario   [Census of agriculture and livestock]   (Dirección General de Estadística y Censos Nacionales)
> Oficina Central de Estadística Información, Edificio Fundación La Salle, Avenida Boyaca, Cota Mil, Caracas 105.
> 1937-   4th, 1971.   not priced.   2 vols.
> Volume 1 is in 21 parts, one for each state and district; volume 2 has data for the country as a whole.
> Time factor: the reports of the 1971 census were published in 1972.
> §   Es.

iii.   Industry

1573   Encuesta industrial   [Industrial survey]   (Oficina Central de Coordinación y Planificación, Dirección de Planificación Económica)
> Oficina Central de Coordinación y Planificación, Dirección de Planificación Económica, Caracas.
> 1961-   5th 1975.   not priced.   2 vols.
> Contains data on number of establishments, employment, finance, raw materials used, energy consumed, investment, etc.   One volume contains national results and the other volume has regional results.
> Time factor: the volumes were published in 1976.
> §   Es.

1574   Estadística industrial   [Industrial statistics]   (Dirección General de Estadística y Censos Nacionales)
> Oficina Central de Estadística Información, Edificio Fundación La Salle, Avenida Boyaca, Cota Mil, Caracas 105.
> 1941-   quarterly.   not priced.
> Contains data on number of establishments, production, employment, finances, etc.
> §   Es.
>
> Refer also to 1562, 1564, 1565.

¶   B,   continued

iv.   Construction

Refer to 1563, 1564, 1565.

v.   Energy

1575   Petroleo y otros datos estadísticos   [Statistical data on petroleum, etc]   (Ministerio de Minas e Hidrocarburos)
Ministerio de Minas y Hidrocarburos, Caracas.
1952- 1976.   not priced.   199 p.
Contains data on the economy and oil; oil in Venezuela (general activities, concessions and exploration, drilling, reserves and production, refining, consumption, exports, sales and transport, gas, social aspects of the oil industry, finance); petrol in the world (general activities, prices, transport), production and consumption of energy in the world, and petrochemical products.
Time factor: the 1976 issue, published in 1978, has data for 10 years to 1976.
§   Es.

Refer also to 1562, 1564, 1565.

¶   C - External trade

1576   Estadísticas del comercio exterior de Venezuela   [Statistics of the foreign trade of Venezuela]   (Dirección General de Estadística y Censos Nacionales)
Oficina Central de Estadística Información, Edificio Fundación La Salle, Avenida Boyaca, Cota Mil, Caracas 105.
1975- 1975.   not priced.   951 p.
Main tables show detailed statistics of imports and exports arranged by commodities and subdivided by countries of origin and destination.
Time factor: the 1975 issue, published in 1977, has data for 1975.
§   Es.

1577   Boletín de comercio exterior   [Bulletin of foreign trade]   (Dirección General de Estadística y Censos Nacionales)
Oficina Central de Estadística Información, Edificio Fundación La Salle, Avenida Boyaca, Cota Mil, Caracas 105.
1959- quarterly.   not priced.
Main tables show exports, imports and re-exports arranged by commodity and subdivided by countries of origin and destination.
Time factor: no recent issues have been traced.
§   Es.

Refer also to 1565.

¶   D - Internal distribution and service trades

Refer to 1562, 1564, 1565.

¶ E - Population

1578   Censo general de población y vivienda   [General census of population and housing]   (Dirección General de
           Estadística y Censos Nacionales)
       Oficina Central de Estadística Información, Edificio Fundación La Salle, Avenida Boyaca, Cota Mil,
           Caracas 105.
       1873-   10th, 1971.   not priced.
       Main volumes are:
           Resumen nacional   [National summary]
               Vol   I   General characteristics
               Vol   II   General characteristics
               Vol   III   Characteristics of large centres of population
               Vol   IV   By residence and place of birth
               Vol   V   Educational characteristics
               Vol   VI   Work force
               Vol   VII Results of federal entities (parts A, B, C, D, and E)
           Resumen nacional: caracteristica general de la viviendas   [National summary: general character-
               istics of housing]
       Time factor: the reports of the census were published between 1974 and 1976.
       §   Es.

1579   Boletín de estadísticos demograficas sociales   [Bulletin of demographic and social statistics]   (Dirección
           General de Estadística y Censos Nacionales)
       Oficina Central de Estadística Información, Edificio Fundación La Salle, Avenida Boyaca, Cota Mil,
           Caracus 105.
       1941-   quarterly.   not priced.
       Time factor: each issue has data for that period and is published some months later.
       §   Es.

1580   Anuário de estadísticas del trabajos   [Statistical yearbook of employment]   (Ministerio del Trabajo: Dirección
           de Estadística Laboral)
       Ministerio del Trabajo, Caracas.
       1968-   1975.   not priced.   145 p.
       Contains data on employment, hours of work, contracting, and accidents at work.
       Time factor: the 1975 issue, published in 1976, has data for 1975 and also nine earlier years in some
           tables.
       §   Es.

1581   Anuário de epidemiologia y estadística vital   [Yearbook of epidemiological and vital statistics]   (Ministerio
           de Sanidad y Asistencia Social)
       Ministerio de Sanidad y Asistencia Social, Caracas.
       1938-   1976.   not priced.   3 vols.
       Time factor: the 1976 issue, published in 1977, has data for 1976.
       §   Es.

1582   Encuesta de hogares por muestreo: resumen nacional   [Sample survey of households: national summary]
           (Oficina Central de Estadística Información)
       Oficina Central de Estadística Información, Edificio Fundación La Salle, Avenida Boyaca, Cota Mil,
           Caracas 105.
       1955-   1977 (1st half-year)
       Time factor: the 1977 issue was published in 1978.
       §   Es.

       Refer also to 1562, 1563.

¶   F   -   Social

i.   Standard of living

Refer to 1562.

ii.   Health and welfare

Refer to 1562, 1563.

iii.   Education and leisure

1583   Memoria y cuenta del Ministerio de Educación...   [Report and accounts of the Minister of Education]
Ministerio de Educación, Caracas.
1967-   1976.   not priced.   c 570 p.
Contains data on free schools and primary day schools; medium day schools; art, music and artistic
schools; adult education; and university education.
Time factor: the 1976 issue, published in 1977, has data for several years to the academic year 1975/76.
§   Es.

Refer also to 1562, 1563.

iv.   Justice

Refer to 1562.

¶   G   -   Finance

1584   Informe anual   [Annual report]   (Superintendencia de Bancos)
Superintendencia de Bancos, Caracas.
1960-   1976.   not priced.   215 p.
Contains data on commercial banks, mortgage banks, financial institutions, etc.
Time factor: the 1976 issue, published in 1977, has data for 1976.
§   Es.

1585   Boletín estadistico   [Statistical bulletin]   (Ministerio de Hacienda: Dirección de Investigaciones Económicas)
Ministerio de Hacienda, Caracas.
monthly, with annual supplement.   not priced.
Contains statistics of public finance.
Time factor: each issue has data to the date of the issue and is published some months later.
§   Es.

Refer also to 1562, 1564, 1565.

¶   H   -   Transport and communications

Refer to 1562.

Central statistical office

1586   Bureau of the Census,
        Department of Commerce,
        Suitland, Maryland 20233, USA.
        † (202) 655 4000.

        The Bureau is responsible for the collection, analysis and publication of economic statistics for the
        islands.

Statistical publications

1587   Annual report: Virgin Islands   (Government of the Virgin Islands)
        Department of Commerce, St Thomas, Virgin Islands.
        1926- 1973/74.   not priced.
        Mainly textual with one or two statistical tables on tourism and foreign trade, etc.
        Time factor: the 1973/74 report, published in 1975, has data for the fiscal year 1973/74.
        §   En.

1588   Economic census of outlying areas: vol 5; Virgin Islands of the US   (US Bureau of the Census)
        Government Printing Office, Washington DC 20402.
        1957- 1972.   US$0.95.
        Contains data by kind of business for manufactures, construction industries, retail trade, wholesale trade,
            and selected service industries.
        Time factor: the results of the 1972 census were published in 1975.
        §   En.

¶   B - Production

        Refer to 1342, 1588.

¶   C - External trade

1589   External trade statistics with foreign countries   (Virgin Islands Department of Commerce; Division of Trade
            and Industry)
        Department of Commerce, PO Box 1692, St Thomas, VI 00801.
        (annual) 1972.   not priced.   90 p.
        Contains data on imports and exports arranged by commodities and subdivided by countries of origin and
            destination.
        Time factor: the 1972 issue has data for 1972.
        §   En.

        Refer also to 1413, 1421, 1587.

¶   D - Internal distribution and service trades

        Refer to 1433, 1587, 1588.

¶   E - Population

1590   Census of population   (US Bureau of the Census)
           Government Printing Office, Washington DC 20402.
           1960-   1970.   various prices.
           Vol I Characteristics of the population, part 55 has data for the Virgin Islands of the United States.   It
               is in four parts, which were initially available separately
                   PC(1)-A: number of inhabitants;
                   PC(1)-B: general population characteristics;
                   PC(1)-C: general, social and economic characteristics; and
                   PC(1)-D: detailed characteristics.
           Time factor: the results of the census were published between 1971 and 1974.
           §   En.

1591   Vital statistics   (Virgin Islands Department of Health)
           Department of Health, St Thomas, Virgin Islands.
           (annual)   1972.   not priced.
           Time factor: the 1972 issue, published in 1974, has data for 1972.
           §   En.

1592   Census of housing   (US Bureau of the Census)
           Government Printing Office, Washington DC 20402.
           1940-   1970.   prices vary.
           Vol 1 Housing characteristics for states, cities and counties, part 55 has data for the Virgin Islands of the
               United States.   It is in two parts-
                   HC(1)-A: General housing characteristics;
                   HC(1)-B: Detailed housing characteristics.
           Time factor: the results of the census were published between 1971 and 1974.
           §   En.

INDEX OF TITLES - INDEX DES TITRES - TITELREGISTER

References are to serial numbers used in the text

INDEX OF TITLES

INDEX OF TITLES

INDEX OF TITLES

INDEX OF TITLES

References are to the serial numbers used in the text

SUBJECT INDEX

Whilst this index refers to the main subjects covered by
the publications listed in the guide, it does not refer to
all the detailed headings included in those publications.

Accidents
  Brazil   487
  British Virgin Islands   550
  Canada   697
  Costa Rica   801, 821
  Guatemala   938
  Haiti   957, 958
  Panama   1110, 1144
  Paraguay   1149
  Puerto Rico   1189
  El Salvador   1233, 1234
  Turks & Caicos Islands   1308
  USA   1524, 1532
Advertising   253, 254
Agriculture   21, 22, 23, 38, 46, 47, 49, 50, 52,
              53, 56, 57, 59, 60, 88, 89, 90, 91,
              92, 93, 97, 113, 236
  Antigua   336
  Argentina   346, 347, 354, 356, 384
  Bahamas   394, 395, 397
  Barbados   428, 431
  Belize   446, 447, 448, 449
  Bermuda   454, 455, 456
  Bolivia   463, 470, 471, 472
  Brazil   487, 492, 496, 497, 498, 499, 501
  British Virgin Islands   549
  Canada   570, 572, 573, 574, 585, 588
  Cayman Islands   719, 720
  Chile   727, 728, 729, 732, 736-738
  Colombia   776-778
  Costa Rica   801, 803-805
  Cuba   824, 825, 827-829
  Dominica   840
  Dominican Republic   844-846
  Ecuador   859, 860, 862, 864, 865
  Greenland   895
  Guadeloupe   906, 908, 909
  Guatemala   914, 916, 920-922
  Guyana   940
  Haiti   958, 960, 961
  Honduras   967, 968, 971, 972
  Jamaica   987, 992, 996, 997
  Martinique   1024, 1027
  Mexico   1034-1036, 1039, 1042, 1044, 1048,
           1049
  Montserrat   1075, 1077
  Netherlands Antilles   1085, 1086
  Nicaragua   1097, 1099-1101
  Panama   1110, 1113-1115, 1117-1119
  Paraguay   1149, 1152, 1153-1155
  Peru   1162, 1165, 1168, 1169
  Puerto Rico   1187, 1188, 1192-1194
  St Lucia   1218
  El Salvador   1233, 1235, 1236, 1238, 1240-1242

Agriculture,   continued
  Surinam   1252, 1254-1256
  Trinidad & Tobago   1266-1268, 1274-1277
  USA   1324-1327, 1342-1349, 1423
  Uruguay   1541, 1544
  Venezuela   1564, 1571, 1572
Aid   21, 22, 32, 35, 61
  USA   1324
Air transport   34, 330-332
  Argentina   390
  Bahamas   423
  Bolivia   483, 484
  Canada   706-713
  Cayman Islands   720
  Haiti   958
  USA   1525-1533
Aircraft production
  USA   1384
    see also Production
Alcohol
  USA   1359-1361, 1426, 1479
    see also Food; Production
Aluminium   80
  USA   1343
    see also Minerals
Animal health   114
    see also Agriculture; Livestock
Area   see Geographical area
Arts   see Culture;
Assistance   see Social assistance; Social welfare
Assistance to developing countries   see Aid
Assurance   see Insurance
Aviculture
  Chile   728
    see also Agriculture
Balance of payments   21, 22, 26-28, 30, 36, 41, 42,
                       53, 56-59, 61-64, 310-311,
  Argentina   348, 349
  Bahamas   396
  Barbados   443
  British Virgin Islands   563
  Canada   572, 674, 675
  Chile   769
  Costa Rica   801
  Ecuador   860
  Guatemala   914, 918, 919
  Guyana   940-942, 954
  Haiti   959
  Honduras   969, 970
  Jamaica   992, 993, 1022
  Mexico   1034, 1035, 1037, 1043
  Netherlands Antilles   1085
  Nicaragua   1097-1100
  Panama   1110, 1141

SUBJECT INDEX

Prices and price indices, continued
Brazil 488, 489, 493, 536, 537
British Virgin Islands 549
Canada 572-574, 604, 610
Cayman Islands 719
Chile 727, 729, 730, 732-734
Colombia 771-775, 791
Costa Rica 801, 802
Dominican Republic 844, 845
Ecuador 859-862
French Guiana 890
Guadeloupe 906, 908, 909
Guatemala 914, 915, 917
Guyana 942
Haiti 957, 958
Honduras 969
Jamaica 987, 990
Martinique 1024, 1027
Mexico 1035-1039
Montserrat 1075
Netherlands Antilles 1085, 1086
Nicaragua 1097, 1100
Panama 1110
Paraguay 1153
Peru 1165
Puerto Rico 1187
St Lucia 1218
St Pierre et Miquelon 1224
El Salvador 1233-1235, 1237, 1238
Surinam 1252, 1253, 1263
Trinidad & Tobago 1266, 1267, 1269, 1272
USA 1324-1326, 1330, 1357, 1553
Uruguay 1541-1543
Venezuela 1564, 1566, 1567
see also Consumer prices and price indices; Cost
of living; Retail prices and price indices;
Wholesale prices and price indices
Productivity
USA 1330, 1336
Public assistance see Social assistance; Social welfare
Public debt 29, 30, 61, 308
Canada 572
Peru 1162
Public finance 21, 22, 27, 28, 35, 42, 46, 52, 57,
59, 61, 304
Antigua 336
Argentina 346, 348, 349
Bahamas 396, 419
Barbados 428-431
Belize 446, 447, 453
Bolivia 465
Brazil 487, 493, 541
British Virgin Islands 549, 550
Canada 570, 572, 676-678
Chile 728, 733
Colombia 773, 774, 795-797
Costa Rica 801, 802
Dominica 840
Dominican Republic 844

Public finance, continued
Ecuador 860, 861
French Guiana 890
Greenland 895
Guadeloupe 906, 909
Guatemala 914, 917, 918
Guyana 942, 953, 954
Honduras 968, 969, 970
Jamaica 987, 993, 994
Martinique 1024
Mexico 1037
Montserrat 1075
Netherlands Antilles 1085, 1986, 1095
Nicaragua 1098, 1100
Panama 1110, 1140, 1142
Paraguay 1149
Peru 1162, 1164
Puerto Rico 1187, 1190
St Kitts-Nevis-Anguilla 1213
St Pierre et Miquelon 1224
El Salvador 1233, 1234, 1236, 1237
Surinam 1252
Trinidad & Tobago 1266, 1270
Turks & Caicos Islands 1308
USA 1327, 1330, 1500, 1501, 1503
Uruguay 1542, 1543
Venezuela 1564, 1566, 1567, 1585
see also Finance
Public health see Health
Public order see Justice; Police
Public spectacles see Recreation and sport
Public utilities
Antigua 336
Argentina 346
Bahamas 394, 395
Barbados 428
Belize 448
Bermuda 455
Brazil 487
British Virgin Islands 549
Cayman Islands 720
Martinique 1027
Nicaragua 1097, 1099
Panama Canal Zone 1145
Publishing 24, 294
Brazil 487
Canada 608
Cuba 829, 830
El Salvador 1233, 1234
see also Industry
Pulp and paper 160-165
Canada 597
USA 1375-1377
see also Industry; Forestry and forest products
Quarries and quarrying see Mines and mining
R & D (funding)
USA 1507, 1508
Radio and television 23, 24, 32, 34
Brazil 487

380